ERASMUS THE REFORMER

Other books by A. G. Dickens

The English Reformation (2nd Edition)
Reformation Studies
The German Nation and Martin Luther
The Age of Humanism and Reformation
Reformation and Society in Sixteenth-Century Europe
The Counter-Reformation

Other books by W. R. D. Jones

The Tudor Commonwealth 1529–1559
The Mid-Tudor Crisis 1539–1563
Nazi Germany
David Williams: The Anvil and the Hammer
William Turner: Tudor Naturalist, Physician and Divine

ERASMUS THE REFORMER

A. G. Dickens
and
Whitney R. D. Jones

METHUEN LONDON

First published in Great Britain in 1994
by Methuen London
an imprint of Reed Consumer Books Ltd
Michelin House, 81 Fulham Road, London SW3 6RB
and Auckland, Melbourne, Singapore and Toronto

A CIP catalogue record for this book
is available at the British Library
ISBN 0 413 33480 5

Typeset by Deltatype Ltd, Ellesmere Port, Cheshire
Printed and bound in Great Britain by Mackays of Chatham plc, Chatham, Kent

In memoriam

Margaret Mann Phillips

PICTURE CREDITS

1. By permission of the ICCD, Rome, Ripresa – Pezzetta Silvano, E 34720
2. By permission of Smithsonian books. From Johannes Stradanus's *Speculum Diversarum Imaginum Speculativarum*, 1580, in the Smithsonian Institution Libraries. Photo Mark Gulezian/Quicksilver. Published in *The Smithsonian Books of Books* by Michael Olmert, *c.* 1992.
3. By permission of the Bodleian Library. From *Studiosis Omnibus S. D. Accipitio Candide – Lector Erasmi Roterodami* . . . by Joannes Frobenius, 1518. Shelfmark: Vet. D1.*c.* 38.
4. By permission of the Trustees of the British Museum.
5. Portrait of Erasmus by Albrecht Dürer, 1520, Musée du Louvre, Paris. © Photo Réunion des Musées Nationaux.
6. Lutherhalle, Wittenberg.
7. *England in Tudor Times*, L. F. Salzman (Batsford, London, 1926).
8. Lutherhalle, Wittenberg
9. 'Erasmus writing' by Hans Holbein, 1523, Musée du Louvre, Paris. © Photo Réunion des Musées Nationaux
10. Staatliche Kunstsammlung, Dresden
11. From the Department of Prints and Drawings of the Zentralbibliothek Zürich
12. Private Collection. Photograph Courtauld Institute of Art
13. Trustees of the British Museum
14. By courtesy of the National Portrait Gallery, London
15. By permission of the British Library. From *Acts & Monuments* by John Foxe, 1563 (Ref: British Library G. 12101, illustration opposite page 1374)
16. By permission of the Syndics of Cambridge University Library. Engraving from *Acts & Monuments* by John Foxe, 1563 (classmark: Young 198)
17. Bildarchiv Foto Marburg
18. Stadtische Kunstsammlungen Augsburg
19. Öffentliche Bibliothek der Universität Basel
20. By permission of the Bodleian Library. Frontispiece from: *Desiderii Erasmi Roterdami Opera Omnia . . . Volume. 1. 1703.* Shelfmark: T.6.1.Jur.

CONTENTS

Abbreviations and Short-titles ix
List of Illustrations xi
Introductory Preface xiii

Erasmus the Reformer
1 The Inheritance 3
2 The Formation of Erasmus 19
3 The Philosophy of Christ 41
4 The Christian Commonwealth 63
5 The Problem of Theology 93

Reform or Revolution?
6 'This Lutheran Tragedy. . .' 115
7 Protestant Humanism: Lost Leader or Errant Disciples? 148
8 The Radical Reformation 170

The Reception of Erasmus
9 The English Erasmians 193
10 France, Spain and Italy 217
11 Erasmus in Central Europe 243
12 Erasmus: Heretic or Mediator? 267

Conclusion: the Legacy of Erasmus 287
Glossary 299
Notes 301
Time-chart 342
Select Bibliography 345
Index 353

ABBREVIATIONS
and Short-Titles

Adages	M. M. Phillips, *The 'Adages' of Erasmus*
Allen	*Opus Epistolarum Desiderii Erasmi Roterodami*
ARG	*Archiv für Reformationsgeschichte*
Colloquies	*The Colloquies of Erasmus,* trans. and ed. C. R. Thompson
Contemporaries	*The Contemporaries of Erasmus,* ed. P. G. Bietenholz and T.B. Deutscher
CWE	*Collected Works of Erasmus*
DNB	*Dictionary of National Biography*
DeMolen, *Essays*	R. L. DeMolen, ed., *Essays on the Works of Erasmus*
DeMolen, *Spirituality*	R. L. DeMolen, *The Spirituality of Erasmus of Rotterdam*
Dolan	John P. Dolan, *The Essential Erasmus*
LB	*Des. Erasmi Roterodami Opera omnia*
MQR	*Mennonite Quarterly Review*
NCE	*New Catholic Encyclopedia*
ODCC	*Oxford Dictionary of the Christian Church*
Olin	John C. Olin, *Desiderius Erasmus: Selected Writings*
Rummel, *Annotations*	Erika Rummel, *Erasmus' Annotations on the New Testament*
Rummel, *Catholic Critics*	Erika Rummel, *Erasmus and his Catholic Critics*
Williams	G. H. Williams, *The Radical Reformation*
Yearbook	*Erasmus of Rotterdam Society Yearbook*

A number of chapter-specific short-titles will also be indicated, where appropriate, in the Notes.

LIST OF ILLUSTRATIONS

1. Portrait of Erasmus, by Quentin Metsys, 1517
2. Printing in the Sixteenth Century
3. Front page of Froben's edition of the *Adages*, 1518
4. A 'Professional Beggar'
5. Sketch of Erasmus, by Albrecht Dürer, 1520
6. 'Luther and Collaborators'
7. Luther, as seen by the Papacy
8. The Papacy, as seen by Luther
9. Portrait of Erasmus, by Hans Holbein, 1523
10. Philip Melanchthon, by Cranach the Elder, 1523
11. Ulrich Zwingli, by Hans Asper
12. Portrait of Erasmus, by Hans Holbein, 1523
13. Engraved Portrait of Erasmus, by Dürer, 1526;
14. Thomas Cranmer, by Gerhardt Flicke, 1546
15. Martyrdom of Ridley and Latimer, 1555,
16. Burning the Remains and Works of Bucer, at Cambridge
17. Erasmus' Dwelling in Freiburg, 1529–31
18. Sketch of Augsburg, by Georg Seld, *c.* 1530
19. Erasmus dictates to his secretary and friend. Wood engraving, artist unknown *c.* 1530
20. Erasmus inspired by the Truth

INTRODUCTORY PREFACE

The title of this book (adopted with due acknowledgement to Elliott Binns who used it half a century ago) fairly bespeaks our objective: to trace the impact of Erasmus upon the movement for religious reform in early sixteenth-century Europe. We must seek to delineate an arresting personality, but this does not purport to be a detailed biography of Erasmus, nor yet a compendious survey of all aspects of his scholarly works. While due note will certainly be taken of other facets of the writings of this outstanding polymath, our central purpose throughout will be to relate all else to the remarkable contribution to the cause of religious reform which surely became his principal and justified claim to European renown. Considered in this perspective, the inclusion of Chapter Five – the only specifically theological chapter – seems essential to give sufficient depth to this aspect of what is a predominantly historical work.

The shift in balance of its contents as between a biographical, a thematic, and a regional approach, is reflected in the three sections of the book, which are complementary but not repetitive. The first, 'Erasmus the Reformer', traces not only the first fifty years of his life but also the emergence and the nature of his vision of the 'philosophy of Christ'. Next, 'Reform or Revolution' examines in some detail the increasing tensions between Erasmus' concept of reform and what he came to see as the disruptive and revolutionary features of the Protestant Reformation. Finally, 'The Impact of Erasmus' will assess his achievement in communicating 'reforms' of Christianity across the varied societies of western and central Europe, and the responses engendered.

The authors recognise that ideally a lengthier Conclusion could take full account of all the important and revealing critiques of Erasmus written from his own time to the present day. But after much thought we have essayed only a limited survey of the more immediate sequels to his life, realising that presentation of a fuller picture of the changing images of Erasmus after the mid-sixteenth century might well have doubled the length of the book. We commend to the reader wishing to pursue this quest Chapter XV of Preserved Smith's *Erasmus*, and the two capacious and perceptive studies by Bruce Mansfield of *Interpretations of Erasmus* listed in our Select Bibliography. In particular this latter author continues our own story right into the twentieth century.

Moving from content to methodology, we have availed ourselves to the full of authoritative translations of Erasmus' works and correspondence where available. Our debt to the especially admirable Toronto University edition of the *Collected Works* and of *Contemporaries of Erasmus* is particularly notable. Unless otherwise made clear in the references, translations from the Latin, in particular from the massive Allen edition of Erasmus' correspondence, are our own. Such translations are freely rendered and sometimes paraphrased, but in no instance have we altered the meaning of the passage cited. In general, quotations have been put into modern English, with our own occasional interpolations in square brackets.

Inevitably, only a selection of the secondary sources cited in the Notes could possibly be included in our Bibliography. The date and place of publication of works not so included are given where first referred to in the Notes. A Short-titles and Abbreviations List is provided for those sources, primary and secondary, most frequently cited, with the occasional addition of 'chapter-specific' short-titles or references where appropriate at the head of certain Chapter Notes.

The Bibliography and Notes sufficiently attest the extent of our debt to others, without attempting a bibliographical essay. But a special word of thanks for the provision of off-print or as yet unpublished material is rendered to Maria Dowling, David Selwyn, Bob Scribner and Henryk Zins. Our warm thanks are also expressed to the Bodleian Library, the British Library, the Warburg and Courtauld Institutes, Cardiff University Library and Mid Glamorgan County (Mobile) Library. Finally, we record our sincere appreciation of the meticulous editorial assistance rendered by Emma Rhind-Tutt of Methuen.

ERASMUS THE REFORMER

[illegible]

Erasmus of Rotterdam [illegible] leading humanist of Northern Europe [illegible] a sensitive [illegible] dialogues [illegible] and [illegible] These ideas and movements [illegible] century great genius [illegible] understand [illegible] Classical [illegible] public opinion [illegible]

[illegible]

One

THE INHERITANCE

Erasmus of Rotterdam (1467–1536) was a literary polymath: the leading humanist of Northern Europe, a laborious editor of the early Fathers, a sensitive interpreter of the New Testament, a writer of entertaining dialogues, a connoisseur of proverbs, an educationalist, an intelligent critic of state, Church and society. In some other fields he may have been insensitive: for example, he shows little sign of interest in the great art and architecture of his day. For our present purpose he remains most notable as a creative analyst of the major ideas and movements current during the fifteenth and early sixteenth centuries. These ideas and movements he helped to modify but did not initiate. Some had arisen far back in the Ancient World, some during the relatively recent centuries which we call Medieval. Like great ocean-rollers they all surged up from behind him as he swam toward a new age. In order to understand his reactions and to estimate his personal impacts we need first to identify and analyse the most significant of these inherited phenomena. Those we intend to select are five in number, and usually labelled Scholasticism, the Modern Devotion, Neoplatonism, Classical Humanism and Biblical Theology. A sixth influence belonged to a wholly different order, being technological, not ideological. We refer of course to the printing press, which had begun to stimulate both public opinion and literacy by the time Erasmus started to write. It was not an intellect but a megaphone, yet few publicists have ever used it more effectively than Erasmus or than his younger contemporary Martin Luther (1483–1546). For our generation this technological factor is easy to comprehend, but not so the five ideological factors, which we shall discuss in the order given above. By this device we hope to avoid a succession of fragmentary explanations, definitions and interjections, all likely to impair the flow of this present book.

Scholasticism was the factor which Erasmus came to reject, even to hate, as a project dubious from the first, and by his own time collapsing under its inherent faults and its bad management.[1] The term itself refers to the 'schools' of the medieval universities, though the actual exercise antedated these institutions. As a system of thought it has since the late nineteenth century attracted fresh interest, though its abstract character still seems likely to confine its appeal to theologians and to specialist students of medieval culture. It arose in the first place from a remarkably early if somewhat narrow 'Renaissance'. Following the early centuries of patristic theology, Christian churchmen began to reintegrate the philosophical thought of ancient Greece, notably its rival systems emanating from Plato and Aristotle. From these two stockpiles the Christians sought to incorporate into their own doctrines the more acceptable of these hitherto pagan elements, so as to create a comprehensive instrument combining theology and philosophy, revealed truth and rational investigation. By so doing they planned to achieve hitherto unattained certainties and probabilities concerning even the highest realms of thought: the character of God and the nature of his whole creation, even his ultimate intentions toward mankind. To this end they used logical rather than intuitive processes; they brandished aloft verbal definitions, analogies, speculations and dialectical arguments. Some of the scholastic theologians and philosophers were also profoundly religious, but too many appear to have accepted the working assumption that everything in creation could be more or less adequately expressed and analysed in words, even in terminology alien to that of the original sources in the Bible. Certainly they expected to penetrate these mysteries far beyond the reach of their more pedestrian colleagues who merely wrote 'sensible' commentaries on the Scriptures.[2]

Already in his work *On Christian Doctrine*, St Augustine (d. 430) had to some extent adumbrated these ambitions, while Boethius (d.*c.* 524) in his *Consolation of Philosophy* had explained how by such methods the human soul should attain the vision of God. During the Carolingian revival of learning in the eighth and ninth centuries, a syllabus of studies later used by the medieval universities appeared, while John Scotus Erigena (d.*c* 877) impressed on his readers the mandatory character of the task, convinced that God imposed a duty on mankind, not just to receive the Faith passively, but also to understand it better by applying *ratio* (reason) to the *auctoritas* of the Scriptures. Toward this end the monastic and cathedral schools of the eleventh and twelfth centuries began to provide preliminary treatises. Following this gradual approach, the strenuous exercise rose to its climax under the major thinkers whose names adorn this central structure of medieval thought: Anselm, Abelard, Hugh of St Victor and the two Dominican masters, Albertus Magnus and his even greater pupil St Thomas Aquinas (d. 1274). All these achievements received much aid from the humbler scholars who produced improved translations of Aristotle into Latin, and also from the communal studies conducted within each of the two mendicant Orders, the Franciscans and the Dominicans, both having acquired important teaching roles in the developing universities.

Having attained its pinnacle in the *Summa Theologica* of Aquinas, who already encountered some antagonists, scholasticism began to show a more debilitating loss of cohesion during the fourteenth century. Until a few years ago the disruptive force was called Nominalism and associated largely with the influence of William of Ockham (d.*c.* 1349). Since the 1930s an accelerating revolution has occurred in regard to this involved field of late medieval thought. Scholastic theologians hitherto lumped together as Nominalists are now recognised as holding very different positions on important issues. The most striking clash occurred between two groups nowadays called respectively the *Via Moderna* and the *Schola Augustiniana Moderna*. For our purposes these have acquired importance because their rivalry continued into the period of the Reformation and directly concerned Erasmus. One need scarcely add that the older schools also continued to flourish throughout the fifteenth century. Even in 1495, when Erasmus went to Paris in order to study theology, he found hosts of Thomists, Scotists and others wrangling together over what seemed to him obscure, inconclusive, often absurd propositions with little relevance to authentic Christianity.

Nevertheless the conflict between the two 'modern' schools of thought did retain a permanent relevance. They reopened ancient controversies regarding the nature and process of man's salvation, controversies which involved not merely imaginative schoolmen but the interpretation of important passages of the New Testament. The *Via Moderna* in effect followed the teaching of Pelagius (*c.* 354–430), who had maintained that a person could contribute a little toward his own salvation by using his free will and doing his best to deserve God's mercy. This Pelagian interpretation relied upon the notion of a covenant, set up by God between himself and mankind, whereby God should accept these wretched little human contributions and graciously augment their value. On the other hand the *Schola Augustiniana Moderna* followed the teaching of the great antagonist of Pelagius and inspirer of Luther and Calvin. He was of course St

Augustine, who gravely denied this element of self-help, and argued forcibly that, on the high plane of salvation, only God's grace availed. From this authoritative viewpoint, human merits contributed nothing whatever to salvation, which occurred solely through the mediation of Christ upon the Cross. Thus revived by late scholastic disputation, this fundamental if inconclusive issue will become highly significant when we seek to elucidate the complex relationships between Erasmus and Luther. The latter not only accepted but intensified St Augustine's doctrine, while Erasmus, arguably a moderate Pelagian, selected this very same issue in 1524–5 to demonstrate his own independence from Luther.

The numerous attacks made by Erasmus upon all these 'monkish' debates became so indiscriminate as to obscure the positive contributions of scholasticism, which did much to order and refine abstract western thought. Many qualified observers still respect it as a noble ideal, though one beset by several inherent limitations, such as its lack of a well-developed historical and philological criticism of the Bible, and its selection of Aristotle as the supreme master of all secular knowledge. Unfortunately the basic cosmological errors shared by Aristotle with the rest of the Ancient World did not become evident until the times of Copernicus (d. 1543) and Galileo (d. 1642). Moreover anything resembling the true relationship of mankind with the rest of the Creation did not emerge until the discoveries of Darwin. However, as we shall presently show, even medieval thinkers were reviewing the rival system of Plato and the Neoplatonists. It soon occurred to some that Plato, while not replacing the alleged functions of Aristotle, nevertheless constituted a fundamentally more useful ally of Christ and St Paul. Indeed, Aquinas himself had been far from unaware of this other kinship and, while ever a venerator of Aristotle, also sought to retain a Platonist basis for his own scheme.[3] All in all it would seem imprudent to dismiss medieval philosophy in the terms used by Erasmus, though it must be admitted that his contemporaries did include some few silly-clever logicians, who propounded absurd questions irrelevant to either Christianity or serious philosophy, thus attracting not merely the distaste of literary humanists like Erasmus, but also the dismissal of such 'vain', intellectual pursuits by ardent pietists such as Thomas à Kempis (d. 1471), author of *The Imitation of Christ*.

In one passage which he added to his *Adages* in 1526 we find perhaps the clearest expression of the triumphant insight of Erasmus into the basic error of scholasticism. He sees the scholastics, *not* the humanists, as the innovators, who presume to thrust aside the New Testament in favour of Aristotle, the Decretals and the determinations of the schoolmen. He thus inverts the pretensions to authority made by those arrogant Thomists, Scotists and Nominalists who falsely claim by sheer ratiocination to go back to ancient Graeco-Roman thought. More important still, these men perversely fail to grasp the authentic teaching of Christ by their refusal to revert to the literary sources of the New Testament. In their folly

> they call 'new' the things that are the oldest of all, and they call 'old' what is really new . . . It is something new to accept a youth as a student in Philosophy, Law, Medicine or Theology, who can understand nothing in the ancient authors owing to his ignorance of the language they speak. It is something new, to exclude from the Holy of Holies of Theology anyone who has not sweated for years over Averroes or Aristotle. It is something new to stuff young men, who are reading for a degree in Philosophy, with Sophistical nonsense and fabricated problems, mere brain-teasers. . . . It is something new to exclude any arguments which are brought from the sources of Holy Scripture, and only accept those which are taken from Aristotle, from the Decretals, from the determinations of the Schoolmen, from the glosses of the professors of papal law, or from the precedents (inane for the most part) distorted from Roman law. If we are to be offended by what is new, these are the really new things.[4]

The problems set by scholasticism were by no means limited to the academic world. One distinctly practical issue emerged in 1215, when the great pope Innocent III imposed as compulsory on all believers the eucharistic doctrine called transubstantiation, whereby the consecrated elements of bread and wine acquired the 'substance' or reality of Christ's body and blood, while still retaining the 'accidents' or outward appearance of bread and wine.[5] This enthusiastic but (in 1215) modish appeal to Aristotle's categories eventually offered the gravest of threats to questioners and doubters, since henceforth numerous heretics suffered burning alive simply for denying the authenticity of transubstantiation. Such events had become routine when, for example, this offence and its punishment overtook most of the English Protestant martyrs of the sixteenth century, who could perceive no scriptural evidence that Jesus thought or legislated in the Aristotelian terms of 'substance' and 'accidents'. Hence to many honest observers this particular doctrine seemed to depend upon papal authority alone, a situation which in principle scholastic reasoning had sought to obviate.

We pass now to our second movement, the type of pietism originally known as the *Devotio Moderna*, but somewhat rashly rechristened by certain modern historians as 'the Christian Renaissance'.[6] This socio-religious phenomenon certainly existed upon a large scale and over a long period. Its data and historical legacies nevertheless remain torn by controversy, even among learned scholars. The situation should evoke little surprise, since the untidy local evidence often seems to elude confident generalisation. These complexities attended the *Devotio* even within its earliest habitat: the northern Netherlands, mostly in the towns along the River Yssel: Kampen, Zwolle, Windesheim, Deventer, Zutphen. Further variations of background and outlook arose with its steady expansion into northern Germany and the Rhineland. Indeed, the movement awakened more distant echoes and co-existed with comparable phenomena in other parts of Europe.[7] Arising from the mystical traditions of the fourteenth century, it broadened into popular evangelism, pietist literature and a school education, both secular and devotional in character. Its prime foundation, the Brethren of the Common Life, formed a new sort of religious Order, at least in the sense that it avoided autocratic controls and even refrained from imposing perpetual vows upon its members. Its school foundations showed an outward-looking zeal by combining humanist classical studies with Christian instruction. Having raised the young Erasmus in both these traditions, the *Devotio* equipped him – as both scholar and religious reformer – to convey something of this dual inspiration into the age which brought forth both Protestant Reformation and Catholic Counter-Reformation.[8]

In all these areas the historians of our own century have extended factual information while yet leaving some dubious and discordant conclusions. They differ on two vital themes. One of these concerns the degree of influence exerted by the *Devotio* upon Erasmus himself, which we shall discuss in the following chapter. The other theme involves detailed researches into this movement's effects upon religion and culture in northern Europe as the *Devotio* gradually merged into Reformation and Counter-Reformation. Here one may well question the tendency of the erudite R.R. Post of Nijmegen to dismiss the religious and educational achievements of the *Devotio* as not merely conservative but ineffective. Do not its writings, its foundations, the demonstrable duration of its values make this viewpoint untenable? Likewise Professor Post unduly minimised the Brethren as 'completely outside the academic world', since they seldom attended universities or did the classroom teaching, for which they normally employed professional schoolmasters. These harsh verdicts may well seem to be a revisionist exercise which got out of hand through allowing local exceptions to disrupt a broader vision of spirituality. Post nevertheless made some amends by recognising the continuity of the *Devotio* into the days of Luther and St Ignatius Loyola.[9] Writing both before and after Post, the American scholar Albert Hyma adopted a more balanced and sympathetic approach. Following his lead, modern scholarship has tended to view the *Devotio* not merely in Dutch but in European terms. Today we see it as a complex phenomenon, both popular and clerical, but everywhere presenting a joyous, loving Christianity, recalling the Franciscan rather than the Dominican spirit.

On its genesis amid the mystical writers and monastics of the late fourteenth century, a large degree of unanimity has been achieved. Certainly its immediate founder was Gerard Groote (d. 1384), who conceived and motivated the three religious orders at the heart of the *Devotio*: the Brethren and the Sisters of the Common Life, together with the association of strict and traditional religious houses called the Congregation of Windesheim.[10] From this last came by far the most significant literary manifesto of the whole movement, the *Imitation of Christ* by Thomas à Kempis. There can be no doubts concerning the vast influence of this work, which, after being circulated in manuscripts from 1418, has subsequently passed through more than 600 printed editions and – the Bible apart – must have been more widely read than any other manual of Christian devotion.[11] Though Groote, à Kempis and others of the Windesheimers appear to have undergone ecstatic states of mind, the *Imitation* itself deals not with mystical but with ascetical theology: the practical attempt to deserve divine grace by living the Christian life to the utmost of one's powers.[12] This technical distinction should not however be pressed too rigidly, since among the most powerful literary precursors of the *Devotio* was John van Ruysbroeck (d. 1381), a more advanced mystic than Groote.

In some senses the movement might be called 'liberal' in spirit, though its manifestations throughout the fifteenth century must remain broadly speaking Catholic.[13] Despite the important roles of the laity and of the two 'relaxed' Orders, certain traditional religious houses remained at its heart. Nevertheless, while the movement as a whole also promoted an intense reverence toward the Mass and a steady practice of the established Catholic rites and forms of private devotion, its chief manifesto, the *Imitation*, was also destined to become as popular with Luther and his followers as with the Jesuits. Moreover, the omissions from this book remain as significant as its inclusions. It ignores the external and managerial aspects of the Catholic Church, as distinct from the interior life of the Christian. It has no use for scholasticism and does not even discuss the Papacy, the clerical hierarchy, the canon law and Church courts, the world of inquisitors and heretics. Both Groote and that other famous writer of the *Devotio* Wessel Gansfort appear to deny in almost identical terms that the papacy should enjoy the unlimited powers claimed by medieval popes. They write:

> I do not believe that Peter possessed the right either to release whomsoever he pleased from the hand of Satan, or to bind him therewith. For just as there is but One that baptizes in the Holy Spirit, so there is but One that binds and releases . . . with authority. For with what authority can the Pope release, when he does not know whether the person . . . has been released from the bond of Satan or not?[14]

Equally the *Imitatio* ignores the elaborate apparatus of both the priestly and the popular religion: saint-worship, pilgrimages, shrines, relics, liturgies and works of art. In other words the book and the movement as a whole displayed extremely little interest in the terrestrial mechanisms through which the medieval Church did so much of its work. In view of these prophetically negative attitudes, it would seem most unrealistic to exclude the *Devotio* from those many influences which brought about the Reformation, particularly its spiritualising sectarian movements. The aim of à Kempis and his associates was to 'interiorize' the Christian life, even that of lay men and women. Exactly this process was to become the chief religious objective of Erasmus.

Another Erasmian objective, the improvement of classical teaching in boys' schools, had been foreshadowed by the most socially minded wing of the *Devotio*: the Brethren of the Common Life. Their most durable achievement lay in the astonishing number and the quality of the schools they founded throughout the Netherlands, North Germany and along the Rhine. Equally surprising is the fact that they combined literary with religious education, and conducted the former along humanist lines. From this enterprise Erasmus benefited markedly as a boy, as indeed did Luther, another of their pupils. Like St Francis, the Brethren broke away from the claustral spirit of early medieval monasticism and developed wide contacts with society in general, yet especially with those powerful newcomers to feudal society: the hard-headed, orderly, ambitious townsmen of the later Middle Ages. Like à Kempis and the mature Erasmus, these people had no interest in scholasticism. They wanted their sons to become literate, even in Latin, which was still the medium of administration, a living language in public life and the qualification for careers in Church, state and city. Hence came the demand for a secondary, intermediate system of education, distinct from that provided by the still clericalised, theology-dominated universities. At the same period this type of school education was being fostered elsewhere in Europe by founders ranging from bishops to opulent merchants.[15] A parallel combination of piety and business-like literacy was to become a most conspicuous feature of Protestant societies a century later, though it was shared in no small part by the bourgeoisie of the more prosperous Catholic cities. By means of this response to demands as much social as religious, the *Devotio Moderna*, though started by clerical mystics, soon became 'modern' in a literal sense.

From very different origins the cult of Platonism, beginning two thousand years earlier than the *Devotio*, also ended by contributing a great deal to European thought, though mainly to its more imaginative aspects.[16] As we have already noted, Platonism – especially as systematised and expanded by Plato's mystical follower Plotinus (d. 270) – shows a long history of fusion with Christianity, a process deeply appealing to St Augustine and to other patristic observers, both Latin and Greek. Of the Greek Fathers by far the most important was that favourite of Erasmus, Origen (d.*c.* 254). Platonist thought had also dominated a much-read series of treatises written about AD 500 and rashly attributed to St Paul's convert Dionysius the Areopagite. These treatises fascinated numerous medieval and early Renaissance thinkers, who came to realise that visionary Neoplatonism could readily be blended with Christianity. A modern authority, more expert on this process than the present writers, succinctly explains this perennial fascination experienced by Christian scholars.

> They found evidence for the unity of God, pre-existence of the forms of things in the mind of God, creation of the world, Providence, God the true and highest Good, memory as a way to know God, the virtuous life, and the spirituality and immortality of the human soul.[17]

In the twelfth century Platonist ideas attracted St Bernard and the learned canons of St Victor in Paris. In fact at no stage was medieval thought totally swayed by the powerful magnetism of Aristotle. Aided by a good Latin translation of Plato's *Timaeus*, many a medieval scholar acquired a certain buoyancy of the spirit as well as a poetical picture of the universe which time was to prove totally unscientific. The phase of Christian Platonism which eventually affected Erasmus and his English friend Colet arose in 1438–9 with the visit of the learned Byzantine Gemistos Plethon to the Church Council then being held in Florence. Having induced Plethon to remain as a teacher of Greek language and thought, the banker-politician Cosimo de' Medici resolved to erect a Platonic Academy in Florence, selecting his physician's clever son Marsilio Ficino to be purposefully trained to serve as its future leader. By 1480 Ficino had translated into Latin all Plato's dialogues, provided a commentary on the *Symposium* and written his own original treatise, the *Platonic Theology*.[18]

Throughout these labours and the study of Neoplatonist mystical writers, Ficino strove to reconcile the teachings of Plato and Plotinus with those of Christ and St Paul. By such activities he created in Medicean Florence an enthusiastic group of teachers who attracted not only Italians but also foreign humanists, such as the two prominent English scholars William Grocyn and Thomas Linacre.[19] The former of these spent the years 1489–91 in Florence gaining a command of Greek, which subject he then proceeded to implant at Oxford. As for Linacre, he stayed about six years (*c.* 1485–91) in Italy, not only learning Greek but also gaining at Padua the doctorate in medicine which eventually recommended him as physician to Henry VIII and to several other English magnates. After their return to England both these men became lasting friends of Erasmus, Thomas More and John Colet. In his turn Colet paid a long visit to Italy (1493–6) and though he never learned much Greek, he probably helped to draw Erasmus toward Platonist studies. Though Colet is not known to have met Ficino in Italy, he certainly corresponded with the celebrated Florentine after returning to England.[20]

Meanwhile there had appeared a human meteorite within the firmament of the Florentine Academy, then in its most brilliant period under Lorenzo de' Medici (d. 1492). This was the young nobleman Pico della Mirandola (1463–94), who also studied Hebrew, Aramaic and Arabic, not to mention the Jewish theosophy of the Cabbala.[21] He even sought to show that Zoroaster, Moses, Pythagoras and Christ had all said essentially the same things. Not surprisingly, he then left Rome in haste to seek the protection of Lorenzo. Thenceforth Neoplatonism also pervaded the more imaginative literature and art arising from the courts and cities of Renaissance Italy, then gradually overflowing into those of northern Europe. Today one might claim as its most appealing monument a work of art: none other than the *Primavera* of Sandro Botticelli, wherein the lovely central figure combines the attributes of Venus and the Blessed Virgin Mary. Nearby Flora and Primavera herself typify the springtime of human love, while Mercury, symbolising the Intellect, points upwards to a higher world with his winged caduceus. Among the literary equivalents one would readily include the wonderful Platonic oration with which Castiglione closes the *Book of the Courtier* (1527).[22] It is not very deeply Christian, yet at least it is placed in the mouth of a prince of the Church: Cardinal Bembo. More to our present purpose, Ficino conveyed to north Europeans like Colet and Erasmus the sharp division between transient matter and immortal spirit. Platonists saw the human soul as wholly God-given, yet eventually casting off its vile body in order to return to the bosom of its maker,

> . . . when that which drew from out the boundless deep
> Turns again home.

These ideas complemented and adorned Christian doctrine. Independently proclaiming this brief but precious encounter between body and spirit, Plato and St Paul seemed to be thinking together, and we shall presently encounter another aspect of that same dualism in the *Enchiridion* of Erasmus, whose own Christianity became suffused by Neoplatonism and other emanations from the classical world.

On account of its ancient and medieval ancestry, we have discussed the fifteenth-century revival of Neoplatonism as a sequel to medieval thought, yet with equal propriety we might approach it as a part of the general revival of ancient literature known as humanism.[23] This last term derived from the medieval *studia humanitatis*, which comprised grammar, rhetoric, history, poetry and moral philosophy, all based in some degree upon ancient authors. Nevertheless the term *umanista*, meaning a teacher of classical studies, first appears about 1490 as university slang. Long before that date, humanism stood based upon a sophisticated analysis of the philological, historical and aesthetic features of ancient literature. It often involved an emphasis upon Cicero, whose works introduced Stoicism, another tolerable partner for Christian philosophy.

Recognisable groups of humanists have been traced at Padua around 1300, somewhat later at Verona, Vicenza, Venice, Milan, Florence and Naples.[24] From attempting to write Latin like that of Cicero and other approved Roman authors, some of these people went on to locate, transcribe and critically examine old manuscript copies of the classics, preserved for example in cathedral and monastic libraries. Hence there developed an increasingly sensitive appreciation of ancient cultural forms, a fresh range of literary ideals, indeed a whole new way of life. Petrarch (d. 1374), standing at the very centre of early Italian humanism, did much to create the special cult of Cicero, which

Erasmus in later times sought to restrain. On the other hand, even in 'advanced' Italy, the all-important Greek component of classical studies made slow progress owing to the scarcity of Greek teachers any farther north than Calabria. Yet already Robert of Anjou, King of Naples (d. 1343), had begun to employ Greek translators, while Petrarch's friend Boccaccio (d. 1375), managed to acquire a sketchy knowledge of the language from a Calabrian. On this front progress began to accelerate from 1396, when the already distinguished Byzantine scholar Manuel Chrysoloras (d. 1415) first taught Greek in Florence.[25] In later years he continued his work in Venice, Milan, Pavia and Rome, many of his pupils achieving local reputations throughout the first half of the fifteenth century. During this period an ever-increasing band of Greek emigrants – among whom we have already encountered the Platonist Gemistos Plethon – handed on the torch of Hellenistic culture from the doomed Byzantine Empire well before the final disaster of 1453, when the Ottoman Turks sacked Byzantium itself. Thereafter, though but slowly, teachers inspired by Graeco-Roman literary values penetrated even into northern Europe, reaching some of the schools founded by the Brethren of the Common Life.

By these stages the generation of Erasmus, which lived well into the sixteenth century, began to apply to Christian history methods akin to those used by modern historians. They transferred their textual, philological and literary techniques, hitherto used upon the pagan classics, to the New Testament, and not merely to the old, familiar Latin Vulgate, but to such Greek texts as were becoming available in manuscript. From this literary process they began to emerge with a new species of biblical theology. Instead of continuing to rely upon an imperfect text, upon ecclesiastical tradition or upon the philosophising of schoolmen on preconceived dogma, they could seek a more authentic Christianity by re-examining the earliest documents of the Faith. They could even enlist the Greek and Roman historians, not merely as pagan moralists but as providers of backgrounds to the earliest phases of Christianity.[26] The Apostles and their converts became more intelligible when approached also as subjects of the Roman Empire and as members of the Greek-speaking world.

Thence St Paul – and to a lesser degree his follower Augustine – inevitably came to dominate the intellectual ancestry of both Erasmus and Luther. Nevertheless both these latter also acknowledged as a major predecessor Lorenzo Valla (*c.* 1406–57), who died only twelve years before the birth of Erasmus.[27] With Valla the linguistic-philological criteria erupted decisively into biblical studies. In particular he demanded and conducted a close and critical study of the New Testament text in its original Greek. Thus far humanists had done little to expose the Latin Vulgate – compiled *c.* 384–6 by St Jerome – to comparison with the available manuscripts in Greek. When Valla proclaimed the need for such a task, he inevitably encountered opposition from many western Catholics, who resented any subordination of their Latin Bible to sources, however ancient, which emanated from the allegedly heretical Greek Orthodox Church. Valla's own career in the Catholic Church [28] did little to allay their fears, for he was a bold radical with a searching intelligence and a strong grasp of historical and linguistic principles. Born and educated in Rome and ordained to the priesthood in 1431, Valla spent four years as a wandering university teacher before entering the service of Alfonso V, the anti-papal King of Naples and Sicily. In 1439–40 he revealed by intensive research the spurious character of the Donation of Constantine, a forgery long used by the Papacy to authenticate its temporal sovereignty over Central Italy. Though this *tour de force* carried no serious theological implications, it revealed the formidable equipment which Valla was about to use in a greater task: the collation of the Vulgate with its Greek sources.

This crucial work, which Valla entitled *Collatio Novi Testamenti*, is no stylish humanistic oration, but a conscientious chapter-by-chapter commentary.[29] With patient determination and expertise it compares three codices of the Vulgate New Testament with three of the Greek text, at every appropriate point asking the all-important question: what exactly does the Greek mean? In sum he fairly establishes the fact that in a good many places the Vulgate failed to convey the true sense of its Greek original, and in some instances tended to misrepresent doctrines of real importance.[30] He even turns aside to castigate theologians, including Thomas Aquinas, who in Valla's view had lapsed into doctrinal error by using this Latin translation. In one famous case he points out that the Vulgate makes Jesus say (Matthew, 4.17) *paenitentiam agite*, 'do an act of penance', whereas the Greek text has *metanoeite*, 'repent'. Here Valla was undoubtedly correct, since the word patently envisages a mental 'change of heart', not an outward observance: indeed the passage exemplifies the consistent demand of Jesus and St Paul that their followers should replace external formalities by a new interior spirituality. Again, in reference to Luke, 1. 28, Valla pointed out that the Greek has been wrongly translated by the Vulgate as *gratia plena*, 'full of grace', thus suggesting that the Virgin

Mary was an independent source of divine grace. He then proposed *gratificata* or even *gratiosa* – 'accepted into grace', or 'favoured' – as the true sense of the Greek, thus in effect restraining the popular Mariology of the day. In several other passages Valla is not merely indulging in humanist pedantry, but raising genuine theological issues which were destined to acquire significance during the Reformation disputes of the sixteenth century.

Meanwhile the hostile Pope Eugenius IV was succeeded by Nicholas V, who in 1448 recruited Valla's literary talents by appointing him an apostolic secretary. Thus triumphant on paper and ensconced in the Vatican, he died nine years later, though his works could not yet attain print and thus occupy the main focus of European religious controversy. Though his book *The Elegances of the Latin Language* (1442) was soon accepted throughout Europe as a prime arbiter of Latin style, the true climax of Valla's career occurred nearly half a century after his death, when, in the autumn of 1504, Erasmus discovered a manuscript of the *Collatio* in the Abbey of Parc near Louvain, and printed it the following year under the alternative title *Annotationes Novi Testamenti*. At this stage Erasmus greeted Valla as an intrepid victor over stupid and servile theologians and also as one who preferred St Paul and the early Fathers of the Church to the dialectics of Aquinas. This line Erasmus vigorously adopts in a letter sent from Paris about March 1505 to his English friend and former host in Paris Christopher Fisher, to whom he dedicated the *Annotationes*.[31] Here Erasmus analyses with insight the theological role achieved by Valla, whom he first describes as a grammarian (*grammaticus*).

> After all it is from Greek sources that our text undoubtedly comes; and Valla's notes had to do with internal disagreements, or a nodding translator's plainly inadequate renderings of the meaning, or things that are more intelligibly expressed in Greek, or anything that is clearly corrupt in our texts.

Erasmus then maintains that Valla the grammarian should have a status equal to that of a theologian, indeed that many authorities already rank him along with the theologians and philosophers. Moreover the translation of the Scriptures is essentially the function of a grammarian; and though Theology is the queen of the disciplines, she vitally needs the services of her handmaiden Grammar.

> Though Grammar is of less consequence in some men's eyes, no help is more indispensable than hers. She is concerned with small details, but

details such as have always been indispensable for the attainment of greatness. Perhaps she discusses trivial questions, but these have important corollaries.

In other words Valla and Erasmus thought it better to look critically at the Bible text as a historical document of both divine and human history, rather than to venerate its every word as inspired, or to analyse its contents in terms of alien philosophies. Thus fortunate to be so ably preserved, admired and defended by Erasmus, Valla has too often been charged with a contentious vanity. Today might not his departed spirit look down with a legitimate pride, when recalling his own wonderful breakthrough toward what has become 'modern theology'?

As a brief appendix to this bible story, two related episodes should here be recalled. Any enthusiasm we may feel for the 'liberal' values displayed by Valla and Erasmus should not lead us to suppose that conservative Catholic scholars were necessarily and permanently opposed to the study and publication of the Greek New Testament. By a curious irony, the first effective command to print its whole text came from the austere Ximénez de Cisneros, Cardinal Archbishop of Toledo and Inquisitor General of Castile, who in 1514 made it the first volume of his grand Complutensian Polyglot Bible.[32] Though this volume anticipated by two years the appearance of the Greek Testament edited by Erasmus – and is regarded as a better text than his – its actual distribution did not occur until 1522.

Here also one should not overlook the parallel enterprise in regard to the Hebrew text of the Old Testament. Already an established classical humanist, Johannes Reuchlin (1455–1522) had begun in 1485 to co-operate with Jewish scholars with a view to learning Hebrew and to standardising its presentation in print.[33] In 1506 he published his most important work *The Rudiments of Hebrew*, both a grammar and a lexicon, which introduced serious Hebrew studies into the Christian world. Nevertheless while all Christian theologians accepted the Old Testament as a precious heritage, German anti-Semitism remained powerful.[34] Of this Martin Luther himself was typical. Indeed, it is against this background of traditional Christian hostility toward Judaism that Erasmus' own position must be assessed. The anti-Semitism occasionally and sometimes over-harshly attributed to him probably went little farther than the general contemporary readiness to use a handy, if unpleasant, slur against one's adversary if it was available.[35] No admirer of Erasmus now relishes reading the passage, in a letter to Reuchlin himself, in which he describes an opponent as 'that product of the circumcision, who started as a criminal in the ghetto' and who, despite professed conversion 'has done more harm to Christendom than the whole cesspool of Jewry'.[36] Yet his distinction, which we shall later encounter, between the Old and the New Testament should more appropriately be related to theological rather than to racialist issues.

Meanwhile even the humanist establishment failed to back Reuchlin with anything approaching general enthusiasm. The next major advance of his cause came only with Luther. Pending this development, after a direct appeal from Reuchlin, Erasmus himself had kindly written to him and had urged a few influential people to support him.[37] But we shall find that Erasmus finally drew back from involvement in what had then become a sordid squabble between secular partisans.[38] There arose in Germany a ruthless anti-Reuchlin faction led by the convert Johann Pfefferkorn (the target of Erasmus' gibe above), the Dominican friars of Cologne and the inquisitor Jakob van Hoogstraten. The resultant outcry appears grossly unjust to Reuchlin, who to the end of his life remained a loyal Catholic, refusing to join the procession of his humanist associates toward Luther. Moreover in 1520, the Medici Pope Leo X upheld the persecutors, thereby abandoning that liberalism of his Florentine ancestors of which Reuchlin himself took the liberty of reminding him in 1517.[39]

Our retrospective notes upon these five inheritances concluded, we shall now start moving forward to review the career of Erasmus, beginning with his adolescence and early manhood, but for the most part centring our attention on his gradual emergence as a critic and a reformer of European religion and society.

Two

THE FORMATION OF ERASMUS

The personal biography of a major intellectual is often valuable in serving to bridge the gap between two cultural periods: the earlier in which he was educated, the later which he helped to create. One such figure is Erasmus, and before entering upon his most influential writings we must attempt a succinct review of his first thirty years, a period then regarded as carrying on into middle age, though in his case it now appears as a prelude. The man destined above all others to reshape the outlook of sixteenth-century Europe received his basic equipment during the last quarter of the fifteenth. In this long educational process he was beset by that formidable complex of forces we sought to summarise in our previous chapter. The process was by no means serene: it received both stimulants and hindrances from harsh private circumstances and interior crises. We shall observe the sensitive, aspiring adolescent exposed to a series of bereavements, obstacles and psychological tensions exceptional in force and diversity. We shall then become acquainted with the clever but unprivileged student very gradually released from familial and monastic constrictions, and thus eventually enabled to make a resolute bid for intellectual independence within a society still far from liberal or democratic. To him as to other able young men, the later medieval Church offered some ladders, including its most original creation: the University. Yet for many, even this ladder merely led down to a more comfortable prison-cell. In regard to the personal story as distinct from its setting, we shall soon find ourselves deploring the gaps in our extant sources. Though extremely voluminous and often revealing, the correspondence of Erasmus is far from providing a continuous biography, or anything resembling a psychologist's case-book. For the earlier years of Erasmus – as indeed for some later periods of his life – one approaches them with a mixture of distrust and gratitude, caution, curiosity and hope.

The illegitimacy of Erasmus, the early loss of his parents and his enforced entry into a religious house: these events appear to have left permanent scars upon his mind, and possibly upon some of his later judgments. The precise facts themselves depend overmuch upon his own distant recollections, most notably upon three documents: his *Compendium Vitae* of 1524,[1] his so-called letter to Grunnius of August 1516,[2] and the short biography sent to the Emperor in 1540 by his close associate Beatus Rhenanus.[3] In addition, though only a minute proportion of his surviving correspondence relates to these early years, it does furnish us with some reliable dates. Probably in common with most men of his period, Erasmus apparently possessed extremely few records of his own early years. Today opinions vary even regarding his date of birth, and while he gives 1466, this and the rival arguments for 1467 and for 1469 still continue to be debated.[4]

Having achieved public distinction, Erasmus naturally became sensitive concerning his birth out of wedlock. He divulged the blandest information he had received and omitted the more distasteful elements. The prenatal story in his *Compendium* reads like the synopsis of a romantic novel, and did indeed form the plot of a good novel: *The Cloister and the Hearth* (1861) by Charles Reade. Erasmus himself relates how his father Gerard had cohabited with Margaret, the widowed daughter of a physician of Zevenbergen. They expected to marry and 'as some say' they exchanged words of betrothal. Yet Gerard was the youngest but one in a family of ten brothers, the rest of them already married. They placed heavy pressure upon him to remain single, piously urging that in so large a family one son should be 'consecrated to God' by becoming a priest. Erasmus nevertheless believed that their real motive had been to retain as much as possible of the family property for themselves. Seeing himself 'completely barred from marriage', Gerard did 'what desperate people do'. He simply fled abroad and during his journey sent his parents and brothers a letter inscribed with clasped hands and with the sentence, 'Farewell, I shall never see you again.' In due course Margaret had her child, who was brought up at his grandmother's home. Meanwhile Gerard went to Rome, where he supported himself as an accomplished copyist.[5] He also gained a good knowledge of both Greek and Latin, took up legal studies and attended humanist lectures. Yet when his parents learned that he was in Rome, they wrote to him saying that Margaret was dead. 'Believing this, out of grief he became a priest and applied his whole mind to religion.' On his return he discovered the deception, but Margaret 'never afterwards wished to marry, nor did he ever touch her again'.

Instinctively, most readers find some of these allegations unsatisfying. Here Gerard's weakness of character consorts ill with what we know elsewhere of his intelligence and resourcefulness. As a boy Erasmus had opportunities to know his father well, and some modern observers reasonably suggest that Gerard's example as a travelled and cultured humanist may have been taken by Erasmus as a model for his own career.[6] Though most of these sparse details cannot be disproved with certainty, they fail to clarify some significant issues. One might reasonably suppose that a social cover-up caused Erasmus to be born in Rotterdam, a city with which he otherwise developed no significant connections apart from his name. But did Gerard know about Margaret's pregnancy when he so timidly fled abroad? Realising his family's violent opposition, why did he not, before rushing to get ordained, contact his many friends at home to confirm or deny the report of her death? One particular at least occasions little surprise: that Margaret would not continue living with Gerard on his return, despite his undertaking to provide for their children's education. Nevertheless the *Compendium* deliberately conceals some of the facts known from extraneous sources. For example, it is quite certain that Gerard and Margaret had another son called Peter, who was three years older than Erasmus. As will appear, Peter Gerard is a solid historical figure destined to play a part in the melodrama of his brother's adolescent years.[7] Another omission is revealed by a document of 1517, wherein Pope Leo X, already an admirer of Erasmus, granted him permission to continue living outside the house of Augustinian canons which he had entered back in 1486.[8] It appears also to show that Gerard and Margaret had cohabited despite a family kinship proscribed by canon law. Without a measure of papal esteem, such complicated irregularities might well have gravely hampered the whole career and status of any churchman. Doubtless also, Erasmus continued to feel the personal slur and badly wanted to conceal its origins. In 1524, for example, he omitted brother Peter from his *Compendium*, or rather half-concealed him as a 'companion', who had 'betrayed' Erasmus in failing to protect him from enforced entry into a religious order. To this last episode we shall shortly return.

At the age of four Erasmus began to attend a private school at Gouda run by Peter Winckel, a future guardian of the two boys and by chance the recipient of the earliest surviving letter written by Erasmus.[9] Gouda must have been Gerard's home town, since some or all of his numerous brothers lived there around these years. After his return Margaret also ostensibly resided there along with her young sons, while maintaining her personal severance from Gerard. In 1478 Erasmus transferred to the school of St Lebwin at Deventer, where his mother followed him. Long since founded by the Brethren of the Common Life, this prestigious establishment had as headmaster Alexander Hegius, a competent humanist with a knowledge of Greek.[10] Hegius was a friend of the Frisian scholar Rudolf Agricola, also trained in Italy and a bigger fish in the expanding pond of Dutch humanism. When Agricola came to address the boys of St Lebwin's, Erasmus received a deep and lasting impression, perhaps his first strong impulse toward the Latin classics.[11] Beatus relates that at Deventer 'he grasped what was taught him and faithfully retained it, surpassing all his classmates'. The same source notes that at some stage he briefly served as a chorister at Utrecht Cathedral. In the *Compendium* Erasmus writes scornfully concerning his early teachers. He stigmatises the school at Deventer as having been barbarous before the improvements recently introduced by Hegius, yet one cannot doubt that it afforded him a good grounding in Latin and aroused his linguistic enthusiasm.

In 1483 the plague struck many Netherlandish towns including Deventer with great violence, killing his mother Margaret and twenty of his classmates. Gerard then recalled his sons to Gouda, yet soon afterwards he too succumbed to the plague, leaving them alongside his kinsfolk and under the care of guardians headed by Winckel. The latter proceeded to despatch them both to another school of the Brethren, the one situated at s' Hertogenbosch. Erasmus later denounced this school in furious terms, as devoted simply to destroying all the natural gifts of its pupils, and with the objective of packing them off to monastic houses, especially to those of the Brethren.[12] He also recalls that a teacher called Rombolt actually tried to recruit him to the Brethren, and with a touch of irony he adds that he soon had occasion to regret his refusal of Rombolt's advice, because the Brethren, unlike the older Orders, did not demand irrevocable vows. No such liberalism was forthcoming from the Augustinian canons, the Order into which Erasmus and his brother were eventually propelled, and which in its tight discipline resembled not the Brethren, but the Windesheim group of houses, those severer creations of the *Devotio Moderna*.

The process whereby the guardians forced both Erasmus and Peter into Augustinian houses, overriding their wishes to attend a university, is recalled in the lengthy letter of 1516 to Grunnius.[13] In fact Grunnius was a fictitious person, the document being devised for forwarding information to Rome in support of the campaign waged at that time by Erasmus, who wanted Pope Leo to regularise his non-residence in a house of his order. In other words he was seeking permission to become a free and self-supporting scholar, though not a total release from his monastic vows. This retrospective letter calls the boys Florentius (Erasmus) and Antonius (Peter), a device allowing Erasmus to describe his former plight in the third person and to emphasise with tearful pride the pathos of his own case, when, as a boy of quite unusual gifts, he had been brutally sent to s' Hertogenbosch and then forced into a monastery by his guardians. Having at length related this story, the document arrives at a sharply expressed proposition:

> Human felicity consists above all in this, that a man should devote himself to what he is fitted by nature. There are men whom one would compel to adopt celibacy or the monastic life with no more success than one would enter an ass for a race at Olympia or take an ox (as they say) to the wrestling school. Enough by way of introduction! Now listen to the misfortune of this excellent young man and to the abominable wickedness of these body-snatchers . . . There are two brothers, Florentius and Antonius. When quite small, they lost their mother; their father died some time afterwards, leaving a slender estate, but quite sufficient to complete their education, had not the greed of the kinsfolk who attended his deathbed reduced it. Of ready cash there was no trace but what survived in the way of real property or securities, and so was not equally exposed to the harpies' talons, was roughly sufficient to finish their studies in the liberal arts, had not once again a good part perished through the idleness of their trustees . . . The trustees had formed the idea of educating them for a monastery, thinking it showed a wonderful sense of duty to provide them with their daily bread.

With no little eloquence the 'letter' continues to stigmatise Peter Winckel, the chief trustee, as a pious hypocrite who 'lived for himself alone and with no respect for education except the confused and scanty sort he had himself imbibed'. 'Florentius' (Erasmus) had sent Winckel 'a rather ornate letter' along these lines, but Winckel had coldly replied, ordering him to write more plainly in future.

> He [Winckel] seems to be of the same persuasion as many others I have known, thinking that he sacrificed a victim most pleasing to God if he should have consigned one of his pupils to the monastic life, and is wont to recount with pride how many young men every year he had gained for Francis or Augustine or Bridget . . . And so, when the boys were already ripe for the institutions they call universities, for they were adequate grammarians . . . he nevertheless was afraid that there they might breathe in some spirit from the outer world and refuse the yoke.

Winckel had thus sent them to school with the Brethren, whose alleged purpose was to break the spirit of gifted boys by corporal punishment until they were fitted for the monastic life. For this reason, continues Erasmus, the Brethren are popular with the Dominicans and the Franciscans, who say that their Orders would soon come to an end, were it not for the young entry bred up by the Brethren 'for it is out of their yards that [the two Orders] pick up their recruits'. In these somewhat savage terms did Erasmus in 1516 recall the obnoxious events of 1485–7, while the rest of the 'letter' provides a detailed account of the alternate threats and subtle persuasions which the guardians and the family brought to bear upon the two defenceless boys. Nevertheless we are once more entitled to some doubts and reservations. As usual, the heart of Erasmus is with the young, and it cannot be denied that in those days both Church and society often gave the young a raw deal. On the other side the complaints of the ageing Erasmus against his former wrongs may well contain exaggerations, even when, as here, they result in a strong plea for the liberal education which defied monastic claims. He may overstate the role of the Brethren as recruiters for the traditional religious Orders, though some houses openly made the chief purpose of their school to train boys for direct entry into the monastic life.[14] Again, is it certain that the guardians had been so malignant? We have no independent evidence to show that Gerard did in fact leave enough money to put the two boys through a university. Yet again, the impartiality of Erasmus seems tarnished by his eventual vilification of his brother, who 'betrayed' him by submitting. At all events it reads strangely in the light of the letter he sent about 1487 to Peter, which is distinctly affectionate.[15]

Whatever exaggerations may occur in this document, after many months of doubt and uncertainty both boys did join the Augustinian canons, Peter at Sion near Delft, Erasmus at Steyn near Gouda. The latter is now thought to have entered as a postulant in 1486, then being at least sixteen years of age, and to have passed the novitiate by 1487, emerging before the end of that year as a professed religious. As for Peter, his life in religion seems to have remained uneventful until his death in 1527, still a placid canon of Sion. There is evidence to show that he wrote Latin poems and was much esteemed by his colleagues.[16]

Meanwhile during his early years at Steyn Erasmus surmounted his distress on the wings of classical study. The experience he had anticipated as an oppression turned out to be a ripening, whatever resentful thoughts he may sometimes have harboured. In the surviving letters which he wrote during his five years at Steyn there occur few if any signs of the bitter anti-monasticism which marks his later recollections.[17] He shows that the library was capacious and that, besides furthering his already strong classical interests, it led him into a wide range of patristic reading, a highly significant sector of his self-education. Certainly he did not lack a number of congenial colleagues, several of them having interests akin to his own. Again, Steyn appears to have been a relatively relaxed community, in which free conversation among the junior inmates was by no means limited to Sundays and feast days. For this reason alone, we cannot regard the cloying letters to his friend Servatius as either a desperate cry for human affection or a homosexual approach.[18] At Steyn the novices and young canons did not need to communicate with each other on paper. Rather does this florid Latin style represent an exuberant humanist fad of the day. Indeed most of the other pieces written by Erasmus at Steyn, so far from being autobiographical protests, are stylistic exercises for use in modes of debate and controversy.[19] In his biography of Erasmus Roland Bainton demonstrated that in the early work *De Contemptu Mundi* Erasmus is setting forth an eloquent 'case' for the monastic life, which he intended to follow in like manner by the 'case' against it.[20]

Since his entry into Steyn and for a couple of decades later Erasmus had no reason to feel a general resentment against monasticism, still less against his own or any specific religious Order. It seems possible that on the odd occasion he was corrected in regard to the undue time he was devoting to classical studies. By way of contrast his superiors apparently discussed his possible transfer into the service of a bishop before any such prospect emerged.[21] Indeed no evidence suggests that Erasmus left his religious house in any spirit of anger or contempt. In later years he did not hesitate to revisit Steyn or occasionally to support the work of the Augustinian canons.[22] Of course, he is likely enough to have suffered boredom amid the repetitious round of services. Few intelligent young monks throughout the centuries are likely to have avoided such a stage. If this common *ennui* had been the only obstacle, Erasmus would doubtless have overcome it in silence. Yet later evidence proves that his outer affability and sense of humour masked a deeply critical spirit liable to become mordant when confronted by what he saw as irrational conservatism. Once outside the monastery, he was to encounter many examples of clerical reaction against those ideals of spiritual and intellectual renewal which he and others claimed to base upon clear biblical authority. He soon showed impatience and did not hesitate to express it by irony and ridicule. Even so it now seems likely that, before leaving Steyn, his mind was also moving in a different direction. Some scholars familiar with his early writings and correspondence have deduced that in or soon after the year 1489 his dominant interest began already to shift toward specifically evangelical issues.[23] Throughout the succeeding decade this gradual inclination tended to accelerate. He openly expressed it to his friends in 1500–1501 and in the latter year wrote the *Enchiridion*, his first major religious work. One must hasten to add that for him the two great themes, Classical and Christian, were always welded together. At no stage did he lose interest in ancient Graeco-Roman culture. With the works of Augustine and Jerome in mind, he came to realise that the early Christian Church had accepted heavy influences from that culture,[24] while it was also abundantly clear that even the scholastics of the twelfth and thirteenth centuries had vigorously enlisted the support of pagan Greek philosophy. Though with varying emphases, Erasmus remained throughout his career one of the many Christian intellectuals who believed that the great thinkers, poets and statesmen who predated Christ were in fact his forerunners, divinely appointed to supporting roles. Under that ultimate sovereignty the old Graeco-Roman world had been, like the Hebrew world, designed for creative absorption into the new kingdom of Christ.

Shortly after 25 April 1492, the date when Erasmus was ordained to the priesthood, he was permitted by his Order and by the Bishop of Utrecht to become secretary to the Bishop of Cambrai, Hendrik van Bergen (1449–1502).[25] The appointment suggests that by now his unusual proficiency as a Latinist was fully appreciated by his superiors. He now became and remained for well over two decades an Augustinian canon on indefinite leave as opposed to a secular priest, and he continued to wear the distinctive costume of the Order. Nevertheless he retained his ambition to pursue theological studies at a university, an ambition to be gratified much sooner than he can have anticipated in 1492. Yet already Erasmus must have known that Bishop Hendrik aspired to become a cardinal, and that if he succeeded the secretary would attend the bishop on a highly desirable visit to Rome! Hendrik had something more than aristocratic support to recommend such a promotion. A student at Louvain and then at Orleans by 1465–6, he had become a doctor of laws by 1473 and Bishop of Cambrai only four years later. For a non-Italian, the next stage was inevitably more elusive. He presumably failed to influence the right people in Rome, and so continued to live mainly in his family's country residence at Halsteren near Bergen op Zoom. Here Erasmus located his *Antibarbarorum Liber*, giving the dialogue a cast of his local friends, headed by Jacob Batt, in real life a Paris graduate who served briefly (*c.* 1495–6) as town secretary of Bergen.

Multiple evidences prove that Erasmus, while still at Steyn, had conceived and written a considerable part of this work, attacking these clerical 'barbarians' who were denouncing classical studies as anti-Christian. From this early stage of the work there survived a manuscript version, which Erasmus was to revise – in more fiercely anticlerical terms – shortly before publishing it at long last in 1520.[26] Although its commencement dated from the 1480s, Erasmus continued the *Antibarbari* while living with Bishop Hendrik, and probably from time to time while in Paris. Eventually he presented his case as a dialogue or disputation conducted along with four friends in the garden of the Bishop's house at Halsteren near Bergen, the date being the spring of 1495. It constituted an almost one-sided attack upon those benighted monks and other clerical conservatives who persisted in regarding the Greek and Roman classics as an improper basis for a Christian education. By such 'barbarous' critics this great literature had been censured as too often indecent, or at best as a serious dilution of Christian piety. This grim outlook is warmly resisted by three of the five participants: Erasmus himself and his close friends Jacob Batt, town clerk of Bergen, and William Hermans, lately a fellow canon of Erasmus at Steyn and a humanist writer. Lacking this enthusiasm are the burgomaster William Conrad and the town doctor Jodocus, yet these two are mere uneasy doubters, not 'barbarian' reactionaries. Of the humanist trio it has been recently said that, so far from being mere defenders of the classics, they 'represented the conviction of the humanists that they were inaugurating a mighty revolution'. In general the dialogue sets forth the already familiar conviction of Erasmus that classical literature perfects and polishes Christian education, indeed that it had been divinely fore-ordained as the overture to Christ's sacred message. With no little cunning, Erasmus puts by far the greater part of his case not into his own mouth but into that of Jacob Batt.[27]

The complex circumstances of its eventual publication will concern us in Chapter 3. Meanwhile, despite the disappointment about Rome, the move to Halsteren was to prove distinctly broadening for Erasmus. It brought him much closer to the Burgundian court at Brussels and to cities pervaded by French culture, cities more elegant and sophisticated than the northern trading towns in which his early years had passed. He was still given time to continue his own literary activities. Moreover his employer could boast some enviable social connections, being a favourite preacher at the ducal court of the House of Burgundy and chancellor of the ducal order of the Golden Fleece, which included the highest nobility of the Netherlands. In October 1496 Hendrik personally conducted the dynastic marriage of the century: that of Duke Philip 'le Bel', son of the Emperor Maximilian I. This Habsburg had already become heir to the Netherlands and other Burgundian territories through his mother Mary, heiress of the ill-fated Charles the Bold, defeated and slain in 1477 by the Swiss allies of Louis XI of France. Appearing in 1496 as Philip's bride was Joanna, heiress of the Spanish kingdoms, who proved markedly fruitful despite her mental derangement. By Philip's early death in 1506 she had produced two future Emperors in Charles V and his brother Ferdinand I, not to mention four future queens, respectively of France, Denmark, Hungary and Portugal. The Dukes of Burgundy, being also Counts of Holland, were sovereigns of Erasmus. He took rather more interest than is usually acknowledged in these dynasts, whose resources almost rivalled those of the greatest European monarchies. In addition they had patronised a cultural revival at least as brilliant as any of the time, except the one then developing in Italy. Characteristically Erasmus tended to judge the Burgundian dukes by reference to their pacifism and their patronage. He reproved the warlike Charles the Bold, but admired Philip the Good as a patron of the arts of peace.[28] With more realism, he felt a personal devotion toward one of Philip's many bastard sons, David of Burgundy, Bishop of Utrecht, who at the ordination service in 1492 impressed Erasmus by diligently questioning each ordinand and dismissing those whose knowledge he judged inadequate.[29] Such zeal was indeed worthy of notice in an age when bishops normally ordained large groups of miscellaneous applicants after little or no investigation.

From the viewpoint of his new secretary, the affluent Hendrik soon proved a skinflint or, in the more elegant terminology of Erasmus, an *Antimaecenas*. Over the years Erasmus complained to several correspondents that Hendrik was failing to provide him with adequate funds.[30] Conversely, it must have occurred to him that by remaining under direct episcopal patronage he might some day obtain a lucrative office in the Church. Yet at no time did Erasmus want money which would entail responsibility for pastoral functions. He was beginning to acquire a mission, but he wanted to discharge it in print. Consistently he sought to read and write as freely as possible in a hard world where intellectual independence was limited, and where small editions and lack of effective copyright laws often prevented authors from receiving royalties. Quite apart from money, it is hard to believe that, beyond a rather formal amity, there can have been much coincidence of purpose between the bishop and his secretary. Hendrik, the senior by twenty years, was a canon lawyer and a climber who had already won the friendship of great princes. Probably he undervalued the young humanist, who flattered him in graceful Latin verse but had as yet small knowledge of the political world and no influence in the Church. Nevertheless, Hendrik did agree in the autumn of 1495 to send Erasmus – with a promise of financial support – to the queen of all the medieval universities. From any viewpoint the departure of Erasmus for Paris did not constitute a final break from Hendrik, and he is known to have revisited Bergen on some of the vacations he spent in the Netherlands and to have for several years retained connections with the Bergen family.[31]

Some of his biographers have made too little of the initial five years of study spent by Erasmus in the university of Paris, and others too much of the subsequent eight months during which he made his pleasurable first visit to England. Admittedly his life-style in Paris gave him further grounds for grumbling. On Bishop Hendrik's recommendation he entered the Collège de Montaigu, where for many years the rector had been Jean Standonck (*c.* 1450–1504).[32] This austere figure was also by origin a Netherlander, schooled – though long before Erasmus – at Gouda under the Brethren of the Common Life. In France he achieved fame as a church-reformer and became a specialist in disciplining lax French monasteries. At the Montaigu his personal asceticism was matched only by his ingenuity in cutting maintenance costs. Paying students like Erasmus stood dismayed even by Standonck's charity toward penniless students, whom he admitted free of charge, yet with a corresponding reduction in the communal diet. In short, Erasmus met here the Windesheim tradition of the *Devotio Moderna*, transferred belatedly in its severest form to this and other French institutions. The Montaigu was the establishment later ridiculed by Erasmus in one of his most famous colloquies: *A Fish Diet.*[33] His lifelong foes included frequent attacks of dyspepsia arising from the fish imposed by the Church upon the faithful on fast-days. Otherwise he was neither an ascetic nor a gourmand, but – in diet as in matters of religion – the sardonic follower of a *via media*. Meanwhile he admired Standonck but could not greatly love him. After easing his problem by taking several holidays in the Netherlands, he gave up residence at the College and took an apartment of his own, although this meant teaching affluent private pupils, some English and others German.

When Erasmus encountered Paris in the last decade of the fifteenth century the university was still suffering from the effects of war, from national poverty, from the long withdrawals of the royal court to the region of the Loire.[34] Again, kings and popes had successfully conspired to deprive Parisian graduates of that reserve of appointments originally kept for their benefit. Meanwhile the real incomes of the colleges had been much depleted by the general inflation. Too many students starved or lived by their wits in a manner which recalls the criminous world of François Villon.[35] Again, though notorious for their self-esteem and their feuds, the scholastic theologians and philosophers no longer commanded anything like universal respect. Having little fresh to say, the so-called 'Ancients', an alliance between Thomists and Scotists, fought against the 'Moderns', a parallel alliance composed of Occamists and others. In the hard words of modern historians of medieval France, Parisian scholasticism had 'ended in pedantry, in the vain refinement of the syllogism, the ruminations of a language too abstract, too technical and inexact, and ridiculed by all great minds'.[36] Influenced by the spiritual writings of a former Chancellor of the university of Paris, Jean Gerson (d. 1429), and by those of his former pupil Nicolas de Clamanges (d. 1437),[37] many of the theologians had turned to the study of mystical theology, even to the emotional pietism of the popular *Devotio Moderna*. Presently forces still more 'modern' entered the field. In 1470 two of these forces – Italian humanism and the press – were linked together under the leadership of Guillaume Fichet (*c.* 1433–1480). He, having studied in Avignon and Milan both the ancient classics and the works of Petrarch, had located (*c.* 1468) the earliest French printing-press within the university precinct itself.[38]

Soon afterwards there appeared in Paris a new group of humanists from Italy, together with some Greek Platonists.[39] By the arrival of Erasmus the monarch of the French humanist world had become Robert Gaguin (*c.* 1423–1501), a former disciple of Fichet and then from 1473 a most active general of the Trinitarian (Mathurin) order. Latterly he had held important offices in the university.[40] Both for his own order and for the French government, Gaguin had accomplished important diplomatic missions. He had also developed humanist literature along lines hitherto unfamiliar to Erasmus, and had shown that humanism could assume a French flavour. Whereas Erasmus remained a totally convinced cosmopolitan, Gaguin could appeal to a national, patriotic readership, as with his French history, the *Compendium de origine et gestis Francorum*. In order to acquire Gaguin's friendship, Erasmus displayed his usual suave opportunism by offering to fill a page left blank by the printers at the end of the *Compendium*, and then did so with one of his elegant, profuse commendations of the work and its author. Generous with his books and his knowledge, Gaguin must be numbered among the more creative influences upon Erasmus. About this time also, that future pillar of the French Reformation, Jacques Lefèvre d'Étaples, returned from Italy, where he had consorted with Ficino and Pico.[41] Though he and Erasmus had little to do with one another until 1511, by which time Erasmus was paying his seventh visit to Paris, Lefèvre was destined thereafter to figure sometimes as a disciple, sometimes as a controversial opponent. In the long run, the influence of Erasmus did much to steer him into evangelical channels.

The associations of Erasmus with French, Italian and Netherlandish scholars formed by no means the only academic element of his life in Paris. He succeeded in dividing his time between these stimulating contacts and the original purpose of his visit: to gain a qualification in theology. Despite his vociferous contempt for the dialectical gymnastics of the Scotists and other contemporary schoolmen, he presumably acquired some grasp of the scholastic routines, since in 1498 he proceeded to the degree of bachelor in theology. As a mature student he could thence envisage a release from the studies normally required for the master's degree, and so embark upon the doctoral programme either in Paris or at some other university. With this aim in view, he now wanted to move on to Bologna and then to visit Rome in the Jubilee year 1500, but these plans he was compelled to abandon on account of the heavy expenses involved. Meanwhile he co-operated with missionising activities in and around Paris, and especially with those of his fellow canon, Jan Mombaer (*c.* 1460–1501), formerly of Brussels and member of an abbey in the strict Windesheim tradition.[42] Mombaer's devotional treatise the *Rosary of Spiritual Exercises* advocated a method of meditation which in later years probably influenced the famous *Spiritual Exercises* of St Ignatius Loyola, and thus formed one of the several intriguing links between the *Devotio Moderna* and the Counter Reformation. Summoned to Paris in 1496 by Standonck, Mombaer was now waging a campaign to attract the Augustinian houses of the region to the Windesheim discipline. Erasmus can scarcely have been attracted by the ascetical demands of such campaigns, but he was doubtless stirred by the enthusiasm with which Mombaer also called for the production of a corrected text of the Bible. It should be added that Erasmus already admired efforts to deliver monks and nuns from routine observances into more spiritual forms of devotion, and he applauded Mombaer's reforms at the Abbey of Livry, which had this general aim in view. At no stage should Erasmus be dismissed as a cold spectator of such ideals, which he was to embody with such heartfelt eloquence in his *Enchiridion*.

Though the Standonck–Mombaer revivalists were far from hostile toward biblical humanism, their spirit contrasted wholly with that of the more secular Parisian humanists, whether native Italians or Frenchmen educated in Italy. One of the former became a close friend of Erasmus: the philanderer and laureate poet Fausto Andrelini, who lectured to enthusiastic Parisian audiences on the more salacious Roman classics and was apt to ridicule theologians as imbeciles. This man, who seems to have charmed even the grave Gaguin, certainly gave pleasure to Erasmus. The latter had his frivolous moments and describes how they exchanged comic notes even while hearing a lecture, and how on another occasion Andrelini showed him an assortment of love-letters received from various women.[43] This varied and tumultuous life on the famous Left Bank of the Seine undoubtedly helped to develop that 'other Erasmus', the dramatist, the social observer, who came to understand lively, passionate lay people, unmoved and unsedated by the current wave of pietism. Here we refer to his brilliant, varied and highly influential *Colloquies*, published in numerous editions from the year 1518.[44] Though many of them end by drawing a conventional 'moral', they nevertheless underwent attacks from conservative clerics who denounced them as scandalous and even heretical. Eventually in 1526 Erasmus felt compelled to defend his own writings in the essay *De Utilitate Colloquiorum*.[45] Nevertheless in that same year they were formally censured by the Parisian theological faculty, which in 1528 was joined by the other faculties in a second condemnation.

Though the *Colloquies* were dialogues meant to be read and not staged, these outbursts of disapproval may have been aggravated by the notorious licence of the contemporary popular theatre in Paris, which had already shifted beyond the ethos of the medieval drama. The pacifism of Erasmus should not be mistaken for timidity or over-caution concerning issues of public and clerical morality. As Craig Thompson, the translator of the *Colloquies*, has remarked, their 'lively passages on friars, monasticism, pilgrimages, fasting, clerical morality and superstition sometimes troubled even readers whom Erasmus esteemed'.[46] To this anticlerical element one may add that some of the *Colloquies* depict the battle of the sexes with a realism mitigated to a slight extent by their presentation in a learned language. At that time it was still unusual, at all events in northern Europe, for a cleric to write such dialogues as *Suitors and Girls*, *The Young Man and the Harlot* and *The*

Unequal Match. It is no wonder that the *Colloquies* ran into 120 collected editions before 1600, or that a certain Dominican printed a bowdlerised edition. Elsewhere Erasmus remarks that the best way to learn French is from the 'little women of Paris' and serious scholars have conjectured that he did not invariably resist their attentions. Should we connect his experiences in the Paris of the naughty 1490s with the *Colloquies* published from 1518 onwards? Without doubt the answer must be affirmative. Though even until 1533 he kept augmenting the collection, which reached a total number of over sixty dialogues, there remains clear evidence that he was already sketching such pieces from the time of this first visit to Paris. Craig Thompson thought it 'likely that everything in that first edition was written between 1497 and 1501'.[47] Erasmus used dialogues for other purposes during the Parisian years, especially when as a teacher he prepared exercises involving everyday Latin speech (*sermones quotidiani* or *confabulationes domesticae*) in order to help his pupils attain a varied and idiomatic conversational style.[48]

His attitudes toward language were functional as well as aesthetic. He took the starch out of humanism and ridiculed the pompous imitators of Cicero. He and many of his contemporaries wrote and taught Latin as a rich, living language, spoken and written by sophisticated people, yet adaptable to informal, even popular themes. His adult attitudes toward people resembled his attitude toward language. Even when moving toward his most serious, most spiritual writing, he continued to regard human society as a phenomenon to be confronted, examined and satirised, as well as a 'fallen' race, desperately needing to be drawn closer toward the example and imitation of Christ. Erasmus was anything but a 'remote' scholar. He did not begin his missionary phase by sweeping the quirks of real men and women under a carpet of hypocrisy or abstruse theological terms. Despite his strong attraction toward Platonism, he never deserted the human race or sought refuge in the frigid abstractions of the schoolmen.

When in the summer of 1499 his pupil William Blount, fourth Lord Mountjoy,[49] induced Erasmus to accompany him to England, the Dutch humanist found himself moving among wealthy and aristocratic people in country houses and city mansions, not as in Paris with poor intellectuals, monks and students in an overcrowded academic quarter. Though his period with the Bishop of Cambrai must already have habituated him to aristocrats, in England he was treated as a continental *savant*, not as a bishop's underling or a senior doctoral student. Even his physical environment became easier than that of Paris. London was then much smaller than the French capital. Its central streets lay no more than twenty minutes' walk – either northward or southward – from green meadows where cattle grazed, archers shot at targets and weavers pegged out their cloths on natural lawns.[50] Again, both Oxford and Cambridge still resembled country towns where only a few tall buildings towered above the domestic houses. Erasmus also found the daughters of his English hosts less formal than their continental equivalents, and was soon writing – very appropriately to Andrelini – about the new pleasures of a society where the young ladies kissed one upon arrival and departure.[51] While Italianate humanists were less numerous than in Paris, he soon became quite intimate with the ablest of them: William Grocyn, Thomas Linacre, William Latimer and John Colet.[52] At Padua a *collegium engelschi* had existed as early as 1446, while earlier still Humphrey Duke of Gloucester had been bringing Italian scholars to England. In due course humanist Latin qualified numerous English ecclesiastics not only to serve as envoys to the Vatican and to secular rulers, but also to high office in Church and State. The earlier visitors to Italy such as John Free, John Gunthorpe and William Sellyng were clerics who merely absorbed humanist style into their basically scholastic outlook.[53] To learn Greek soon became a major reason for visiting Italy, yet even Greek studies still tended to lead backward into Plato, Aristotle and then to the Greek Fathers rather than into the ancient Greek literary authors. Nevertheless this limited utilitarianism had started to change among those recent visitors to Italy met in England by Erasmus, who still yearned in vain to follow them. Later on he became familiar with other Italian-educated Englishmen such as the diplomats Cuthbert Tunstall and Richard Pace.[54] In addition he was entertained and much attracted by the rising barrister Thomas More (b. 1478), who had not visited Italy but had known Grocyn and Colet in Oxford, where Linacre had taught him Greek. By now these men were associating mainly in London, where Colet had become More's acknowledged spiritual adviser. Not long after the arrival of Erasmus, More took him across the Thames to visit the King's children at Eltham Palace. These were headed by the future Henry VIII, an intelligent boy of nine already well-grounded in Latin, who received a poem from More in that language, and asked Erasmus whether he too had brought one. Though Erasmus had come unprepared, he made haste within three days to write a poem appropriately accompanied by an eloquent letter.[55] On another occasion he met his chief future patron, the diplomat William Warham (*c.* 1450–1532), soon to become Bishop of London and by 1504 Archbishop of Canterbury.

Despite his close relations with More, the most creative English friendship of Erasmus was that with John Colet (?1467–1519), whose influence upon him was exaggerated by Victorian English writers, but now seems to us underestimated by Professor Gleason, Colet's learned but unduly formidable biographer.[56] Though the son of Sir Henry Colet, an immensely rich mercer and twice Lord Mayor of London, John had also received benefices in which he was not required to reside, but which could be farmed out for a profit, thus enabling him to travel and study in Italy from 1493 to 1496. There he became deeply and permanently attracted by Plato and Neoplatonist thought, yet he appears to have remained in Rome without visiting the famous Neoplatonists of Florence: Ficino and Pico della Mirandola.[57] He nevertheless corresponded fruitfully with the former not long after his return. Colet also acquired that humanist approach to the New Testament which enabled him to write the much-admired course of lectures on the Pauline Epistles, delivered at Oxford in the late nineties and in part heard by Erasmus. The latter then sent Colet warm congratulations,[58] and we do not need to assume that these characteristically enthusiastic letters are mere attempts to secure Colet's patronage. Soon thereafter we meet other Erasmian tributes to Colet's academic quality. For example in July 1501, not long after leaving England, Erasmus wrote to an entirely uninvolved Dutch correspondent: 'Sometimes I contemplate returning to England in order to spend a month or two studying divinity with my friend Colet, as I am well aware how profitable this might be for me; but I am terrified of those ill-famed cliffs on which I once was wrecked.'[59] In some respects Colet's 'modernity' exceeded even that of Erasmus. His rejection of scholasticism was more absolute. Whereas Erasmus still respected Aquinas, Colet publicly dismissed even so great a figure. Nevertheless in his correspondence of 1499 with Colet, Erasmus also deprecates scholasticism in general. Such studies, he adds, 'do not impart wisdom, the true breath of life, but rather sap the mind by a certain sterile and thorny subtlety'.[60]

Around 1499–1500, what intellectual influences, if any, had Colet imparted to Erasmus after their frequent contacts over several months? In returning to this difficult question, we join Gleason in dismissing Seebohm's notion of an already advanced Oxford humanist circle led by Thomas More, Colet and Erasmus, people who in fact resided together in England for only a few weeks.[61] Yet going to the opposite extreme, Gleason presents Colet as a *démodé* theologian, disabled by his ignorance of the Greek language and his lack of a historical perspective:

a scholar vastly inferior to Erasmus, and thus unlikely to have influenced him to any significant extent. The present writers believe that this analysis goes too far. We trust that it is neither irrelevant nor unjust if we allude to the personal aversion felt by Gleason toward Colet. With few counterbalancing reservations, he describes Colet as arrogant, miserly, irascible, idiosyncratic, anti-intellectual, opinionated, tactless, an ambitious clerical pluralist 'on the ecclesiastical fast-track', and with an 'alienated' view of the human condition. Few biographers of eminent figures have gone to such lurid extremities, and one must fear lest these emotions may also have overflowed into the author's estimate of Colet's intellect. Whatever the case, one thing remains certain: that Erasmus held a vastly more favourable view of Colet's character and mental capacity. His delightful character-sketch of Colet (1521) was not written in an effort to attract patronage, since the Dean had died two years earlier! While noting his inner tensions, Erasmus here regards him with both affection and reverence, proclaiming him one of the two best Christians he has ever known, and with equal significance he adds: 'I never saw a more highly gifted intellect.' Amid various tributes on hearing of Colet's death, Erasmus exclaimed, 'A true theologian, a wonderful herald of the gospel teaching – how that man had drunk in the philosophy of Christ!'[62]

A major problem regarding their intellectual relationship concerns the effect of Colet's Oxford lectures upon Erasmus, who joined the course near to its end in the autumn of 1499. Unfortunately the five surviving manuscripts containing what remains of the series did not get into print until the later nineteenth century, and even then they appeared without a critical examination of their dates and authentications. How far do they actually reproduce what Colet said at Oxford in 1497–9? With great technical acumen Gleason examines them all, and dates all five manuscripts not to the late 1490s but to various years within the first two decades of the sixteenth century.[63] It is possible, he argues, that toward the end of his life Colet was preparing to rewrite his own works. At all events, he and his scribes are found to have inserted in some of these manuscripts a few short passages relating to developments beyond the year 1499, including a brief reference to a work of Erasmus printed as late as 1516. Nevertheless our quest for the Oxford lectures as actually delivered in 1497–9 would seem far from doomed by Gleason's discoveries. We cannot perceive that in themselves the indubitably late insertions bear significant intellectual weight, or that they impugn the substantial authenticity of these surviving texts. The latter do not show signs of having been reconstituted from more primitive originals. Does not the overwhelming probability remain that we still retain Colet's material very much as he delivered it in 1497–9? Does any proof emerge to the effect that Colet substantially rewrote his lectures in 1516–18 in order to incorporate, for example, what Erasmus and others were saying by that later date? In other words, has Gleason's critique really destroyed the novelty and historical significance of the Oxford Lectures? We think not.

In addition, should not some positive and more generous evaluation of Colet's lively spirit, his approach to religion and scholarship, accompany these cold *post mortem* dissections? Unless one begins with a picture of Colet at Oxford in 1499 as an outdated survivor from the Middle Ages, there emerges nothing in the surviving texts as demonstrably beyond his normal powers. As Sidney Lee pointed out nearly a century ago,[64] Colet throughout abandons here the scholastic and allegorical interpretation of Scripture sentence by sentence or word by word, and supplants it by a free, critical exposition of the text as a whole. He compares Paul's references to Roman policy toward the Jews with those of Suetonius.[65] He rejects verbal inspiration, insists on the need to love rather than to 'know' God, and criticises aspects of the Church itself. He does not cite scholastic authors, but frequently quotes Plotinus and the Neoplatonists, while avoiding their intricacies. Colet also exudes a 'healthy' realism, depicting in human terms Paul the man, his mission, his converts, his backgrounds in the Roman Empire. This historical basis, this plain good sense, this entire freedom from scholastic exegesis, were doubtless the qualities which impressed the Oxford audience and Erasmus himself.[66] These same qualities in Colet's work have been in recent times recognised by historians of Renaissance thought as diverse as Rudolf Pfeiffer and E. H. Harbison.[67] Likewise to theologians and philosophers, Colet's lectures have seemed important contributions toward the achievement of Erasmus. In 1978 Dr Catherine Jarrott demonstrated a whole series of doctrinal correspondences between Colet's writings and Erasmus' *Annotations on the New Testament*.[68] Following Colet's example, she concludes, Erasmus also sought to see Paul's teaching as a whole, 'instead of using bits and pieces to prove extraneous points'. In the end both men proceeded *ad fontes*, thus attaining a Scripture-based vision of Christianity, which 'could have done much to reform the Church of their days, had not the strong factionalism of the Reformation swept it aside'.

Already in 1953 Dr P. A. Duhamel had examined the Oxford lectures and demonstrated the completeness with which Colet, although familar with scholastic methods, deliberately excluded them.[69] 'The lectures', wrote Duhamel, 'are more important in the history of English literary humanism than the *Utopia* of Sir Thomas More, although the latter is sometimes considered as the only work of the English humanists of European significance.' He sees multiple influences behind Colet: Neoplatonism, *Devotio Moderna*, patristic studies, especially the cult of St Jerome. Yet so deep was the contempt of Colet for the scholastics that he discouraged Erasmus from troubling to attack them, 'for what glory could there be in routing and confounding a swarm of flies'. For the view that in 1499 Colet did much to co-ordinate the hitherto somewhat indeterminate thought of Erasmus, Duhamel cites not only Erasmus himself, but the conclusions of scholars such as Albert Hyma and Johan Huizinga.

In 1977 a parallel though different claim for Colet's influence upon Erasmus was advanced by P. I. Kaufman,[70] who argued that his lectures on Romans had anticipated one of the central elements in a book by Erasmus which we shall shortly examine in its entirety: the *Enchiridion militis Christiani*, written in 1501–2 and published in 1503. It lays a particular emphasis for those seeking to imitate Christ: the emphasis upon actual moral behaviour as opposed to mere lip-service and pious outward observances. Yet four years earlier Colet had already stressed this oft-neglected link between God's grace and human conduct.[71] In his view the scrupulous 'Judaic' insistence on outward observances had no relevance to Christian salvation. Christ had demanded not only a new outlook but a new mode of life. Though all virtue sprang from divine grace, a man's spiritual standing could be judged by his life, which should be inspired by his inward faith in the redeeming power of Christ and not by reference to Old Testament legislation. Moreover Colet saw the old legalistic attitudes mirrored in the external formalism which still marked the Christian Church of his own day. In his view, even the sacraments had now become for many people analogous to Hebrew sacrifices. 'Christ is to be eaten by us not only in the sacraments but also by our imitation of him.' Following St Paul,[72] Colet insisted that baptism and the other sacraments become spiritually beneficial in so far as the recipients manifest their efficacy by obeying the Gospel. When we break the Gospel baptism itself becomes unbaptism. Yet when actual performance arises from steady faith, it becomes the strongest argument on behalf of the penitent sinner standing before God. Of course, this practical effort to imitate Christ had also to be judged as incomparably more significant than any vain attempt to meet with Christ through the subtle dialectics and distinctions of scholastic theology. These venturesome emphases became central, first to Colet and then to Erasmus in the *Enchiridion.*[73] We should not, of course, adds Kaufman, expect to find Colet's phraseology followed verbatim in the *Enchiridion*, since, after vainly urging Colet to publish the Oxford lectures, Erasmus had returned to Paris without taking with him any copy of them. Nevertheless, in all likelihood responding to Colet's example, he first began to compose some commentaries on St Paul, which have not survived. Then, urged on by others, he changed his plans and wrote the *Enchiridion*, a practical manual of religion aimed to show people how to live Christian lives. Apart from these issues Gleason, perhaps more arguably, places Colet in a category different from that of Erasmus and ranks him as a homiletic theologian rather than as a fundamental thinker,[74] yet might not the label 'homiletic' adhere also to Erasmus? He too preached to his contemporaries in books and letters, if not from the pulpit.

By way of contrast Colet did not shrink from the personal and public confrontations so disliked and shunned by Erasmus. In particular Colet's notorious sermon to Convocation (1512) never ceases to astonish by its violent and daring denunciation of the shortcomings of the English clergy,[75] even though his charges were almost rivalled by those made by his close friend William Melton, chancellor of York.[76] In London Colet certainly took routine preaching most seriously, planning not merely individual sermons but also integrated courses for his London congregation.[77] By contrast, and perhaps already influenced by the resolute pacifism of Erasmus, Colet preached eloquently concerning the horrors of war and the blessings of peace. Moreover he did so shortly before the young king's departure for France on the campaign of 1513, and had to avert the royal displeasure in a long if ultimately successful interview.[78]

In the light of his later years Colet must be regarded as still a very active associate of Erasmus. In him, it is true, Erasmus did not find a second Lorenzo Valla, a critical mind of the first order. Nevertheless Colet was clearly a great personality, a perfectionist, a devotee of Platonist and mystical ideas;[79] a man as positive in his love of Christ as in his hatred against scholastic theology and hypocritical churchmen. Though careful to placate the King, Colet did not hesitate to defy his own diocesan Bishop Fitzjames, who badly wanted to crush him by a charge of heresy.[80] It was no routine event in the career of Erasmus when, early in life, he joined in a close and enduring friendship with so forceful a crusader, a spirit more forward than he in defying the establishment. Erasmus first met Colet at the 'right' time, even as he began moving toward his own greater and more glorious battle with the entrenched armies of ecclesiastical and cultural conservatism. This association of twenty years was at least as purposefully maintained by Erasmus as any other within his immense circle. In 1504 Colet was appointed Dean of St Paul's and became a national figure by virtue of this commanding office in the metropolitan cathedral. In the following year Sir Henry Colet's death brought the whole of his fortune to John, the survivor from a large but frail family. This money the Dean used throughout the years 1508 to 1512 to found and build his cathedral school. Nourished by a common devotion to the project,[81] the friendship became ever more cordial until, having eagerly welcomed Erasmus' translations of the New Testament, Colet died at the age of fifty-three after a second attack of the virulent sweating-sickness. During the late stages Erasmus wrote textbooks for the school: he took a spontaneous interest in its pupils and it was for them that he composed his attractive *Sermon on the Boy Jesus*.[82] Thus in the light of these many episodes, sealed in 1521 by that moving valedictory memoir, the association with Colet proved his most inspiring inheritance from England. Was its termination one of the reasons why Erasmus, after five previous visits to that country, never returned after the Dean's death?

From this point we shall now revert to the year 1500, when Erasmus returned from England to Paris, having envisaged the preliminary basis of his campaign of scriptural reform and spiritual revival: the need to become a far more proficient scholar in the Greek language, the essential key to the New Testament.[83] Here indeed is the natural starting-point for a chapter comprising not merely the acquisition of convictions and techniques but also the publication of propaganda on a continental scale. In 1500 Erasmus stood on the threshold of a new century, almost prepared to demonstrate in a wider world his immense pertinacity and vast range, not to mention those lesser gifts: a refined showmanship, a zest for book-creation, a love of both languages and printer's ink. During the subsequent two decades the onetime zealous schoolboy, the uneasy monk, the tentative student, undertook a herculean task which in the event became no less than a major liberation of Christian thought.

Three

THE PHILOSOPHY OF CHRIST

This present chapter seeks mainly to analyse the major works written by Erasmus during the years from 1500 to 1518, in particular those which aimed at the revival and reform of European Christianity. Necessarily we also need the biographical background during this middle stage of his life, when amid the dire threat of the plague a man with a mission needed a sense of urgency. Yet during these first two decades of the new century Erasmus also remained physically and intellectually mobile, exploring numerous themes with relish and regarding frequent changes of residence and subjects of study as highly stimulating. Having surmounted the obstacles of his youth, he now moved into the counter-attack, intent to influence public opinion by the stylish exposure of some hard-won convictions.

For some years he tended to gravitate between France and the Netherlands, in particular between Paris and Louvain.[1] In 1500 he published the first edition of his *Adages*, a book destined to make his early reputation and to achieve an ever-growing popularity throughout his lifetime.[2] Its expansion became striking even in its early stages. While the edition of 1505 numbers only 835 adages, the Aldine edition of 1508 has no less than 3,260. By then his growing knowledge of Greek broadened his choice of items from the Ancient World, though not until after 1515 did he start to reinforce the wonderful collection of genuine adages by adding his own mordant essays on contemporary society. Zealously explored, the *Adages* alone almost supply the equivalent of an advanced classical education! In 1501 he composed his *Enchiridion militis Christiani* or *Handbook of the Christian Soldier*, which already outlined his 'philosophy of Christ' and pointed toward his later missionary campaigning. Already its fund of pietism does not conceal some radical criticisms of the Church, and these, as we shall demonstrate, are most relevant to our main theme. There followed that fortuitous but important sequel which we had to anticipate in our first chapter. Having discovered in an old monastery library near Louvain a manuscript of Valla's *Collatio Novi Testamenti*, Erasmus published it in 1505, thus not only making an excellent case for the primacy of the old Greek texts over the Latin Vulgate, but in effect laying the foundations of modern Bible-study.

In that same year Erasmus made a second but brief visit to England,[3] where he gained the favour of his future benefactor Archbishop Warham, and along with Thomas More embarked on a translation of Lucian, the racy Greek satirist whose spirit harmonised so closely with that of his own *Colloquies* and eventually with his *Praise of Folly*.[4] Even as he planned a Christian revival, he never neglected the classics, least of all the Greek classics. From his Latin versions (1506) of the *Hecuba* and the *Iphigenia in Aulis* of Euripides, until those bulky translations of Galen, Ptolemy and Aristotle[5] which he edited during his last years, he did more than any man to maintain this transfusion. In particular, like some earlier scholars, he enlisted Plato as an honorary Christian. He also came to venerate the mystical Origen in preference to the severe Augustine, and longed to reconcile the Roman Church with the Greek Christians, whom Rome had long since thrown overboard as heretics. Indeed, in regard to both religious and cultural history, the ancient Greeks had more than the ancient Romans to tell the contemporaries of Erasmus. Even the Italian Neoplatonists were as yet scarcely transmitting the Greek messages in clear and serviceable terms. Thus alongside those books which we still read with interest, Erasmus also achieved a vast output of routine translating and editing, which collectively demanded great labour from him and from his assistants.

For the man himself, translation, transcription and transport constituted a way of life. Those unsung heroes of his story, the devoted amanuenses, cost him even more than the horses on which he and they moved around Europe.[6] Not even Erasmus could combine scholarship with the simple life-style of the begging friars, and together these unusual overheads required a major share of the income which he managed to beg from his rich friends, from the princes of the Church, and in due course from his eager publishers. In regard to the hotel-accommodation of sixteenth-century Europe, his letters form a sensitive tourist-guide. He vaunts both the food and the comfort of French inns, but detests the smell, confusion and red-hot stoves in those of Germany.[7] We shall shortly add his adverse comments on Italian hospitality. A fastidious traveller, he did not meekly accept the primitive amenities of his period.

In the autumn of 1506 Erasmus seized upon a chance of subsidising his long-awaited Italian journey[8] by accepting charge of two sons of

Giovanni Boerio, the Italian physician of King Henry VII in England. His most immediate objective was utilitarian: the acquisition of a doctoral degree in theology from the University of Turin, a second or third-rate establishment in comparison with the most renowned Italian schools, such as those of Bologna and Padua. A decade later, he recalls that he had also wanted to visit the sacred places and libraries of Rome and to enjoy the company of scholars. These higher objectives he did in large measure attain, yet he irritates modern observers not a little by his seeming lack of interest in the magnificent works of art and architecture then in course of production. He was hardly a 'Man of the Renaissance' as defined by our more glamorous books on the period. Having seen the elaborate Certosa of Pavia, he simply marvelled at the great expense of its construction and at the spiritual pride which made rich people desire to be buried within its walls. In this particular case he was by no means the last observer to entertain such thoughts, yet in Florence and Rome he omitted even Raphael and Michelangelo. At Venice, where he spent over eight months, Bellini, Carpaccio, Giorgione, Palma Vecchio and Titian were all working, but apparently without eliciting a glance from this northern visitor, essentially a man of words and cerebral ideas. In later life he became well acquainted with his portraitists Dürer and Holbein, but without sharing their aesthetic values.[9] In any event, Erasmus strayed into the Italian cast like a wandering actor who had never been auditioned or coached. Even toward the Papacy his initial attitudes seem a trifle naïve. At Bologna he actually saw Julius II entering the city at the head of his troops, having triumphed over the rebellion of the Bentivogli.[10] Lacking intimate biographies of certain recent predecessors of Julius, and in any case detesting all warlike activities, Erasmus was scandalised beyond all measure. In later years his emotions still prompted that 'anonymous' pamphlet, the *Julius Exclusus*, describing how St Peter sternly rejected his arrogant successor at the gates of Paradise.

It seems plain enough that for Erasmus his one solid achievement in Italy occurred during his stay in Venice with the printer-scholar Aldus Manutius. By common consent the maker of the most beautiful books in Renaissance Europe, Aldus began by producing for his visitor the expanded folio edition (1508) of the *Adages*. Erasmus obviously enjoyed working amid the circle of humanists surrounding this Venetian magnate of the press. All the same, he grumbles vociferously against the Italian way of life, even while inhabiting this superior household. Transparently referring to his own hosts, he does so in his colloquy *Sordid Wealth*,[11] deploring the smoky interiors, the fleas, the shellfish collected from the Venetian sewers, above all the flimsy, unsatisfying food and poor wine provided by his affluent but parsimonious friends. He dated his affliction by the kidney-stone from this visit, while stubbornly maintaining that North Europeans needed more food than did the poor southerners.

During the Italian years from 1506 to 1509 Erasmus cannot greatly have advanced his theological knowledge, since his current studies appear to have related almost entirely to the ancient classics. He nevertheless made some generous friendships, as when at Padua he joined the household of Alexander Stuart, Archbishop of St Andrews.[12] This teenage prelate was in fact one of the illegitimate sons of King James IV of Scotland, and had intended to study canon law at Padua. Erasmus taught him logic and rhetoric while they were together. Yet first, anticipating the attack of the formidable league of Cambrai upon Venice, the party moved down to Siena and witnessed the famous carnival and its accompanying bull-fights. Leaving Alexander with a complete programme of study, Erasmus paid his first visit to Rome before returning to Siena and taking his pupil for a brief visit to the papal city, where they spent Holy Week in 1509. Erasmus held the highest opinion of the young man's character, intellect and piety, recalling him several times in subsequent letters. In the tragic sequel Alexander was to die at his father's side in the disastrous battle of Flodden, thus illustrating that favourite maxim of his former tutor, *dulce bellum inexpertis*.

The concluding visit to Rome had its pleasures and its disillusions. The reputation of Erasmus had already reached the papal court, where he was graciously received by the cardinals, including Giovanni de'Medici, the future Leo X.[13] In later years Leo continued to enjoy the satires of Erasmus and in the event took a personal interest in granting him the full dispensation of 1517, to which we shall later return. Indeed the appointment of the Dutch humanist to an office in the Vatican was discussed during his time in Rome, yet such a role Erasmus could only evade, since he sought neither power nor wealth, but simply a handsome stipend on which he could freely travel and write. Again, he was also observing with disapproval the *dolce vita* of the sacred yet undeniably festive city. In particular he remarked on the princely splendour of the prelates' houses, the levity and greed of the lesser Roman clergy, not to mention the host of decorative courtesans quite near the foreground.[14] While planning his next move he received an alluring letter from his faithful English patron Lord Mountjoy.[15] It announced the succession to the throne of the young Henry VIII and confidently predicted the dawn of a golden age for scholars, whom the cultured monarch so deeply admired. Attracted by what he later called 'these mountains of gold', Erasmus scented a new lease of opportunity and he responded without delay. Recrossing the Alps by the Splügen Pass, he came north via Strassburg and the Rhine. Then, after paying some rapid calls at Antwerp and Louvain, he crossed the Channel to reach Thomas More's hospitable home in Bucklersbury, London. Suffering from kidney pains and awaiting the arrival of his books, he then sketched out 'within a week' the book which was to perpetuate his international renown. This was the *Praise of Folly*, the *Moriae Encomium*, a title which, with an unduly obvious pun, he hastened to dedicate to his host.

As first published in both Strassburg and Antwerp during 1511, the texts of the earliest editions of the *Folly* are far from identical with the versions we find in our modern editions, which derive from those of 1514 onwards.[16] As with this and several others of his works, Erasmus liked to improve what he first had written in haste, and, in the case of the *Folly*, a closer study of this gradual process would be worth making. Soon after the first dates relating to the work, the author himself almost disappears from our view, owing to the strange gap in his surviving correspondence from the autumn of 1509 until the April of 1511, at which latter time we meet him again, now preparing to leave England on a short excursion to Paris, where his connections with publishers remained extensive. During most of this eclipse he was probably still living with Thomas More and largely dependent upon wealthy friends. Even so by the summer of 1511 his fortunes began to amend owing to the patronage of John Fisher, Bishop of Rochester and Chancellor of the University of Cambridge since 1504.

For several years Fisher had administered and guided the splendid benefactions made to that university by the Lady Margaret, mother of King Henry VII, whom she survived for a few months in 1509. She and Fisher had in fact begun by founding Chairs of Theology at both Oxford and Cambridge, but then he swayed her affection toward the latter, where her ample estates enabled her to found two colleges, Christ's and St John's. Well educated from childhood, Margaret herself had become a pious translator from the French of some devotional works, including the *Imitatio Christi*. Again, she became fully aware of the importance of printing, as shown by her patronage of both Caxton and Wynkin de Worde, then the leading printers in England. Such activities remind us that humanism prospered in northern Europe not quite solely upon its Italian origins but also upon a preexistent if rather supine aristocratic culture. In England this latter basis continued throughout the reign of Henry VIII, when the King and many of his courtiers could boast a fluent knowledge of the French language, possibly an occasional bond between Erasmus and his aristocratic English hosts.

As for Fisher, though destined along with his friend More to die as a martyr for the unity of the Catholic Church, he had always been an active supporter of humanist education since the start of the century. He fully realised that the employment of Erasmus would contribute to the prestige of both classical and religious studies at his own university. In the summer of 1511, he began by arranging the appointment of the now widely admired scholar as a lecturer in Greek. Then in November Fisher offered him a post which he had formerly occupied himself: a Chair of Theology, which the Lady Margaret had founded back in 1502. Chiefly interested in creating a preaching clergy in England, Fisher also saw in Erasmus the potential author of a standard handbook to preaching. This particular commitment failed to achieve rapid success. As late as 1524 Erasmus sent the bishop an apology for his continuing failure to produce the work, and in the event he did so only in 1535, the year of Fisher's execution.[17] Meanwhile the Cambridge appointment of 1511 provided a stipend of £13 per annum, even then by no means princely, though it was accompanied by free food and rooms in Queen's College. Expressly precluded from charging tuition fees, Erasmus continued to receive private gifts from admirers in London. Already in November 1511 he returned from a visit to the capital with no less than seventy-two nobles in his purse.[18] Meanwhile he sedulously cultivated Archbishop Warham, to whom he produced a letter suggesting that, having been offered an appointment in Brabant, he might well leave England.[19] Not long after this heavy hint, the Archbishop appointed him to the rectory of Aldington in Kent. Subsequently Warham added the proceeds of another benefice, while these bonanzas were supplemented by the continuance of Mountjoy's pension and by lesser grants from Bishops Tunstall and Longland. Erasmus thus amassed and retained for life at least £60 per annum from England, a country he never visited after 1517. In addition the Chancellor of Burgundy assigned him in 1516 a prebend at Courtrai, which he immediately relinquished for an annual payment of 130 florins, equivalent to about £15 of English money. His salary as a councillor to the Duke of Burgundy then occasioned not a little disappointment, since it was irregularly paid and soon discontinued. Nevertheless we should not be too deeply moved by his frequent references to his poverty. Quite apart from the royalties paid him by his publishers – which apparently never became substantial – he was receiving before 1520 at least eight times the stipend of a comfortable vicarage in the English Church and perhaps 15 times the wage of a master mason in England or the Netherlands.

Despite the security which Fisher and Warham had bestowed, his correspondence during the years 1511–14 scarcely depicts a happy man. At no time did he enjoy collegiate life, though too much has been made of his alleged failure to integrate with Cambridge, where indeed he made many cordial friendships. Hereabouts he and others laid the foundations of those critical attitudes toward the Church so prominent in mid-Tudor Cambridge. Certainly poor health dogged his life before and during his Cambridge period. At the same time he probably felt that his career had been badly side-tracked into this relatively provincial situation. After Mountjoy's letter concerning the alleged cultural designs of the young Henry VIII, he must have expected royal patronage and residence in London alongside his distinguished friends. Again, he wanted to teach Europe in books, not through minor scholars in classrooms. He obviously preferred planning and revising proofs along with his publishers to arguing with démodé university theologians. Despite the comfort of his rooms at Queen's – where they are still exhibited by oral tradition – he wrote grudgingly of his lectures in a manner suggesting that his audiences remained small and his services unappreciated. He recalled the gracious days in Italy, hated the cold wind of the Cambridgeshire Fens and wanted to come and keep warm with his friend Ammonius in the latter's cosy London house. From Ammonius he gratefully received consignments of fine wine, which would shield him from the indigestible contents of the Cambridge cellars.[20] The Dutchman and the Italian did not much admire the provincial English. The working people, with whom Erasmus could not converse, he regarded as dirty and uncivil. Among the 'dull and conceited' academic population, Erasmus still discerned too many noxious Thomists and Scotists.[21] When a return of the plague suddenly emptied the university, he feared to retreat to London, where it was proving even more lethal. Therefore he migrated to the even deeper obscurity of Landbeach, a village five miles distant from Cambridge. Yet even had he been able to join the fashionable world of the capital, he could scarcely have enjoyed its spirit in the year 1513, when his pacifism, like that of Colet, was deeply offended by the unnecessary revival of the old war against France. Then unexpectedly came the signal for escape. It took the form of a warm invitation from the eminent printer-publisher Johann Froben[22] to join him at Basel in some important enterprises. Even as he responded favourably to Froben's letter, there began a new phase of his career.

In January 1514 he left Cambridge for London and in April he set off toward the Upper Rhineland, where he entered a more capacious and eventful world. Pausing at Mainz, he observed a great centre of intellectual enterprise and religious reform. At Strassburg, then a wholly German city, he received a triumphal reception from the local association of humanists, one of many such bodies already established in the cities of Alsace and south-western Germany. Under such auspices he began to exhibit a mild but novel teutonic patriotism. Even the cool, almost stateless Netherlander found himself *begeistert* to the point of calling himself 'Germanus', despite his lack of interest in the princes and the politics of the Holy Roman Empire.[23] Unlike some northern humanists, he neither resented supercilious Italians nor gloried in victories over the Ottoman Turks. Nevertheless his reception into a dynamic urban society did entail certain changes of focus, which we shall observe from this point in our eleventh chapter, concerned as it will be with the strong impact of Erasmus upon German scholars, cities and courts in the years around the advent of the German Reformation.

In September 1514 he reached Basel and found in Froben a warm-hearted admirer and an ally who combined commercial enterprise and scholarly enthusiasm. The immediate task assigned to the newcomer was the supervision of a nine-volume edition of the works of St Jerome, conceived and elaborately prepared by Johann Amerbach,[24] Froben's late partner. Of these volumes Erasmus in due course edited the first four, comprising Jerome's letters and based upon texts different from those hitherto printed. To these he prefaced a biography of the saint, denouncing that legend in which an angel accuses Jerome of being a Ciceronian rather than a Christian. Here Erasmus reverts to the spirit of his earlier attacks on the clerical *Barbari* of his own day, who also ignorantly failed to grasp the links between classical and early Christian culture. Amid these labours he recognised the scale upon which Froben could enlarge his own range and productivity. He also began to acquire a special affection for Basel, that pleasant academic and publishing centre which after long hesitation had recently (1501) been admitted to the Swiss Confederation. Nevertheless he did not actually settle there until 1521, but soon returned to work for the time being in the Netherlands, first chiefly at Brussels and Antwerp, then from the summer of 1517 at nearby Louvain. Here his reputation helped to raise the academic status of the Trilingual College, but availed nothing to prevent its relapse into extreme theological conservatism. Meanwhile he maintained close touch with Froben by making several short visits to Basel. In 1515 and again in 1516 he even managed to spend a few weeks in England, during which we have already glimpsed him co-operating with the educational activities of Colet. Yet again in 1517 he paid his last English visit, now mainly in order to receive his dispensation from Leo X, who had deputed none other than Ammonius to act as papal representative. By this document Erasmus at last gained full liberation from residence at Steyn and from wearing the costume of the Augustinian Order, which had so far persistently demanded his return.

Such restless movements matched various literary tasks extending well beyond the work on Jerome. During these years he completed his two chief political manifestos, *The Education of a Christian Prince* and *The Complaint of Peace*, published respectively in 1516 and 1517.[25] These two complemented each other, since rulers educated along humane lines would surely, he hoped, avoid the absurd wars so often waged by their barbarous predecessors in order to snatch land from one another. In addition to these activities Erasmus accepted in January 1516 his appointment to the Council of the new Habsburg lord of the Netherlands, soon to become also Emperor Charles V.

This honour was doubtless intended to mark his status as a leading scholar of his country, but on occasion it could also facilitate political contacts, as when in 1520 Erasmus commended Luther – as an honest critic of ecclesiastical abuses – to Luther's own sovereign, the Elector Frederick the Wise of Saxony.[26] Meanwhile, though the office did not occupy much of his time, neither did it solve his financial anxieties. By Whitsun 1517 the stipend had fallen more than a year in arrears, and by 1522 it appears to have evaporated. By no means unexpectedly, we find him writing to Thomas More: 'Being well clothed, I fear I shall nevertheless die of hunger.'[27] Amid this somewhat histrionic life-style he nevertheless completed his third great Christian-reformist publication, which he at first entitled *Novum Instrumentum*. This task one may regard as a bequest from his august forerunner Lorenzo Valla, being closely related to his former discovery and publication of Valla's *Collatio Novi Testamenti*. His own 'new instrument' sought to base New Testament studies securely upon the Greek language, in which the Apostolic authors had originally written, and not in the Latin Vulgate sanctified in West European eyes by the authority of St Jerome.

At this point, however, we may conclude the biographical narrative of this highly creative middle phase of the career of Erasmus and seek to analyse some of the leading ideas which throughout these years 1500 to 1518 dominated his thinking, and which he called 'The Philosophy of Christ'. To do this we shall need to examine in turn the three leading works already mentioned: the *Enchiridion*, the *Praise of Folly* and the various parts of the *Novum Instrumentum*. We shall discover a marked continuity of thought culminating in a powerful climax.

The *Enchiridion* is a straightforward manual for living the Christian life and it develops an equally straightforward code of basic rules.[28] Believe in God and his Word. Your highroad is the way of virtue, the way of Christ, the highest good. Express your conviction in your morals. Stand firm against temptations and never relax your self-control. Resist sin manfully, and then go over to the attack on Satan. Make use of the Cross, remembering what God has done for you. Compare God with the Devil and then compare the rewards they offer!

This list also reminds one that the treatise was undertaken at the request of a lady whose husband was a habitual adulterer, badly in need of guidance toward a more devout and faithful life. He was Johannes Poppenruyter, by profession a *Waffenmeister*, a maker of arms, who is known to have executed large orders for cannon, entrusted to him by Louis XII of France and Henry VIII of England.[29] In due course (1514) he was to leave his native Nuremberg for Mechelen (Malines), there to serve as a salaried gunsmith to the future Emperor Charles V. Neither of his wives bore him children, but nevertheless seven illegitimate offspring, born between 1511 and 1521, duly occur in his will dated 1533. Erasmus remained a longstanding family friend, who visited the couple at Mechelen in 1514 and who in 1519 mentions Johannes again. The latter bore no resentment against Erasmus or against the book intended to reform him. Knowing however that *Enchiridion* could mean not only a manual but a dagger, the *Waffenmeister* sent a real dagger in friendly acknowledgement to Erasmus, who retorted that 'he no more read the book than I used the dagger'.

During these decades the mind of Erasmus fluctuated constantly between the sacred and the profane. He had first sketched the *Enchiridion* in 1501 while a guest of Anna van Borssele, Lady of Veere, at her castle of Tournehem in the Pas-de-Calais.[30] Yet even during this exercise his mind was not solely in the spiritual world, since he was then vehemently – though in the event vainly – hoping to receive substantial patronage from this opulent lady. Here at least are some external circumstances, yet they throw little light on the origins of this fervent book of devotion, one destined in later years to achieve a just renown throughout Europe. The most obvious and acknowledged masters of Erasmus are St Paul and Plato, both so eloquent on the binary universe and the immense gap between its spiritual and its corporal values. Waging a heroic mission, forever striving to sublimate his human impulses, the militant Paul here looms even larger than the person of Jesus. Though the author's devotion to Christ is obviously deep and sincere, the Paulinism and the Platonism permeate the whole work, thus recalling the values of John Colet, that constant channel of influences upon Erasmus, his recent guest. Here the attitudes of Erasmus seem to approach those of the Manichaeans and the Albigenses more closely than ever they did in his later years. Indeed he seems to override the deepest insight of the Apostle St John, so conscious of Christ as reconciling rather than dividing the two worlds. 'So the Word *became* flesh: he came to dwell among us, and we saw his glory, such glory as befits the Father's only son, full of grace and truth.'[31] Correspondingly the attitudes of Erasmus toward marriage and women seem still most negative, though he is sometimes uncomfortably preoccupied with Eve, both as the mother and the temptress of men. He goes on to deprecate even normal family life as full of obstacles, distractions, even miseries.[32] Closely following upon sexual lust in the procession of sins, comes the greed of the businessman, while not far behind greed there follow the wretched concerns of rulers and worldly officialdom. Thus the Erasmus of 1501 does not seem to have distanced himself altogether from the most rigorous values of the cloister, though he relates also to the Neoplatonists, whom he openly commends as moral guides, useful even to Christian soldiers. Yet the criterion he demands is meditation resulting in moral conduct, not mere aspiration.

On the other hand Erasmus retains little respect for the actual monastic life as commonly lived in his own day. Monks and friars are charged not only with ignorance but with arrogance and sub-Christian living. Whether with them or among the laity, he has no respect whatever for what he calls a 'Judaic' religiosity of outward observances and gestures, mindless repetition, saint-worship, pilgrimages, indulgences, even of fasting.[33] His attack on the fables and superstitions attached to the worship of dubious saints is particularly sharp and satirical. All these external cults, he claims, closely resemble the sacrifices of animals made by the pagan Greeks and Romans. In his view the world of scholasticism remained also unrelated to the ideals of Christ and St Paul, while he clearly longs to spiritualise both the academic and the popular religion of his day.

The Erasmus of the *Enchiridion* is already just as insistent upon the profound necessity of a scriptural religion as the Erasmus of the *Novum Instrumentum*, fifteen years later. In the later pages of the earlier book he outlines the rules applicable to the Christian life, and the first of these demands a total reliance upon the guidance of the Scriptures.

> Be convinced that there is not a single item contained in Holy Writ that does not pertain to your salvation . . . If you believe that God exists, then you must believe that he speaks the truth. Convince yourself that nothing you perceive with your senses is as true as what you read in the Scriptures. The will of heaven, Truth itself, has inspired it; the prophets of old have made it known; the blood of martyrs has proved it, and the constant belief of countless generations has testified to it. Christ himself in his life here below has exemplified its pervading truth.[34]

Even the demons confess the veracity of the Bible and fear it, while the mere beauty of its message should convince every reader. If this is true, would it not be sheer madness to withhold belief? Many incredible things were foretold by the prophets concerning Christ, and not one of them has failed to occur. 'If the prophets did not lie, certainly Christ, the greatest of all prophets, did not deceive us. If, convinced of these truths, you ask God to increase your faith, it will indeed amaze me if you do not recoil from an evil life.'[35]

Personal influences upon the *Enchiridion* are in some cases easy to detect. During recent decades such theologians as Stupperich, Auer and Kohls[36] have devoted lengthy analyses to this aspect of the work. Yet while elements of the *Devotio Moderna* are richly diffused, the literary debt of Erasmus to its greatest figures, including Thomas à Kempis, remains somewhat unclear. Another and better documented influence was that of Jean Vitrier, the Franciscan of St Omer,[37] whom Erasmus first met in 1501–2 and to whom he devoted a brief biography, extolling the Franciscan as a veritable saint. Mystic, scholar, and preacher of distinction, Vitrier also became a fanatical purifier of religious houses, including the nunnery at St Omer, where his severities are said to have driven some of the nuns to attempt his murder. Even so, his influence upon Erasmus and in particular upon the *Enchiridion* became creative. For example, Vitrier did much to endow him with that enduring affection for Origen, to whom Erasmus became almost obsessively attached, even though, along with the rest of the Greek Fathers, Origen was still tarnished by heresy in the official eyes of Catholic Europe. While Erasmus actually names him only three times in the *Enchiridion*, the indirect allusions to his opinions are nevertheless agreed to be numerous and important. However, those few people who knew about the restiveness of Erasmus himself under claustral discipline must have felt somewhat startled when in 1503 they found him denouncing slack monasteries and their unspiritual denizens. So soon had the failed monk transformed himself into the monastic reformer! In this same vein he closely identifies the religious Orders with the *bête noire* of scholasticism. On the other hand the classical studies of Erasmus are related to his moral and religious writings. It has been conjectured with probability that the stern moralism of the *Enchiridion* owes not a little to his almost contemporaneous work on Cicero. Certainly, even as the great Roman's Latin style had made him a Man of the Renaissance, likewise his heavy moralising raised him to the rank of Honorary Christian.

When Erasmus wrote the *Enchiridion* he was not yet marching under the flag of Valla in order to combat the absurd claims made in the West on behalf of the unique authority of the Latin Vulgate, and conversely to exalt the original Greek texts of the New Testament. Yet even so he was powerfully motivated toward intensive biblical study in general by seeing it as the indispensable path of Christians, both clergy and laity, toward true history, spiritual growth and eventual salvation. Despite its severities the *Enchiridion* remained a guide book for a still largely conservative age which for the most part wanted to retain the unity of Christendom. It does not single out for criticism the Papacy, the hierarchy, the canon law of the Roman Church. In contrast with its more entertaining successor, *The Praise of Folly*, the elements of ridicule and anticlericalism are much less oppressive and occur far less frequently. Through the 1520s and 1530s the editions in Latin proliferated while translations into Czech, German, Dutch, English, Spanish and French sold well. By the time of its author's death it had captured the *mens conscia recti* of Europe and later in the century, despite the temporary ban on the works of Erasmus by Paul IV, it went on being read by both Protestants and Catholics.

In the light of these later events, why then through its first decade and more did the book attract scarcely any notice or criticism in the years immediately following the publication of the *Enchiridion* in 1503? True, its dramatic gestures are overlaid by passages of conventional piety. Again, at that date readers were less impressed and less alarmed by intense modes of exposition than they became when controlled by Counter-Reformation pietism some thirty or forty years later. There also remain simpler reasons for the early quietude which at first surrounded this publication. In 1503–5 Erasmus had not yet become a commanding figure throughout Europe, while in its first two editions, then set forth by Thomas Martin of Antwerp, the *Enchiridion* was accompanied by a number of minor items, also written by Erasmus but nevertheless supplying a further coat of camouflage around the main work. These *Lucubratiunculae*, it is true, reappeared also in the third edition of 1515 and in two of the five editions which came in 1515–16.[38] By these years however Erasmus had at least attained international fame on account of his *Praise of Folly*, a far more sensational presentation, despite his resolve to repeat – though in very different forms – the basic principles already enunciated in the modest *Enchiridion*. At all events, between 1511 and 1516 the *Folly* alone had achieved no less than nineteen editions by several publishers. Another twenty had followed by 1525.[39] Meanwhile the *Enchiridion*, which in 1503 had burst upon the world with the squeak of a mouse, also began by 1515–16 to make much more noise. For over half a century its editions outnumbered even those of the *Folly* itself.[40] No less than eighty-five had appeared by 1585, of which twenty-seven were translations into modern languages. Nevertheless it is not difficult to see why throughout the later centuries *The Praise of Folly* brought the author more fame than did any other of his works. It was his most ingenious, most imaginative and most daring production. Even in its early years, it amused sophisticated readers from Pope Leo X down to laymen with little interest in theology. It recruited the Church's critics and angered its conservatives. Having gained a broad readership throughout succeeding decades, the *Folly* introduced Erasmus to a wider public. It must indeed have attracted readers to some of his more conventional books. Somewhat less original than may seem at first sight, its modes of fantasy and ridicule derive much from Lucian, upon whom he had been recently working along with Thomas More. Its hard religious core came from his own *Enchiridion*, as he openly avowed. As usual with Erasmus, the detail often seems to us repetitious. Herself a creature of flickering changes, Folly delivers this lengthy oration on the foibles of mankind with waspish penetration and humour. She seizes upon the weaknesses of each group, whether lay or clerical, most readily observable in contemporary European life. None the less, even the most casual reader cannot have failed to observe that popes, bishops, monks, friars, theologians and clergy in general are here exposed to the most prolonged and painful castigation.

Even so, Erasmus is not satisfied merely to taunt clergymen, much as he apparently enjoyed the exercise: he goes further by exposing the basic shortcomings of the popular religion of the day, in particular its inability to distinguish between the vapid legends and the solid New Testament evidence. A hostile witness, he concentrates on the failures of the medieval Church, without balancing references to its achievements. From chapter 40 to chapter 63 he allows the churchmen and their uninstructed parishioners only a few brief remissions, thus leaving readers with a massive impression of neglect, muddle and ignorance within the contemporary Church. Without a trace of sentimentality for bucolic observances, he feels that such patent ignorance should speedily be overcome as a thing offensive to divine Truth. As in the *Enchiridion*, so also in the *Folly*, he trounces the worship of the saints, especially that of fictitious saints. When you go to hear a parish sermon, you will hear the preacher introduce a trivial theme, just in order to keep his flock awake.

> If he starts to rant on (pardon me, I mean *orate*) with some old wives' tale, the audience sits up and pays attention, open-mouthed. Again, if it concerns some legendary saint – and you can include George or Christopher or Barbara in that class – you will see that they receive far more devout attention than do Peter, or Paul, or even Christ himself.[41]

Many people hasten to devote a candle to the Virgin, even at midday when it is not needed, but few seek to emulate her chastity, her modesty, her love of heavenly things. Meanwhile crazed pilgrims desert their wives and children, making their way to Jerusalem, to Rome or to the shrine of St James at Compostella. From vainglorious prelates down to humble monks and friars, the non-teaching clerics are clearly the villains. With no little venom, Erasmus also makes Folly deride that old enemy, the decadent scholastic logician with his fantastic queries:

> Is it a possible proposition that God the Father could hate his son? Could God have taken on the form of a woman, or a devil, a donkey, a gourd or a flintstone? Shall we be permitted to eat and drink after the Resurrection? Let us cope with hunger and thirst while there is still time! There are many quibbles even more refined, about concepts, formalities, quiddities, which nobody could possibly perceive, unless like Lynceus he can see through the blackest darkness things which don't actually exist. These subtle refinements of subtleties are made still more subtle by all the varied lines of scholastic argument, so that you could extricate yourself more rapidly from a labyrinth than from the tortuous obscurities of Realists, Nominalists, Thomists, Albertists, Ockhamists and Scotists – and I am only listing the chief sects.[42]

Beyond these routine jibes, Erasmus does not fear (chapter 53) to enter more dangerous ground, as when he adds 'St Paul was not a scholastic theologian and even the Apostles knew nothing about Transubstantiation'. It is clear that he felt no personal attraction whatever toward this last monument of scholasticism despite the fact that it had been made obligatory by the Lateran Council of 1215. He then makes Folly attack papal authority in this field, with the acute suggestion that the poor, unintellectual fisherman St Peter cannot have been much of an expert on scholastic philosophy.

> Peter received the keys, and received them from one who would not have entrusted them to an unworthy recipient, yet I doubt whether Peter understood (for nowhere does he show signs of subtle reasoning-power) how a man without knowledge can nevertheless hold the key to it.[43]

Likewise, she adds, the Apostles did not teach our modern subtleties concerning the precise functions of baptism or the different species of divine grace. Yet again, the Apostles refuted both the pagan philosophers and the obstinate Jews, but they did so without using scholastic syllogisms, such as those adduced by Duns Scotus. Thus his rejection of dogma based on scholastic reasoning caused Erasmus to embrace opinions on the fringes of heresy and indeed to hint at them in a far from timid manner.

In chapter 54 Folly begins a long assault on those permanent victims of Erasmus: the monks and mendicant friars.[44] Here she introduces some rather ponderous buffoonery at the expense of the latter. Though called *religiosi*, most of the friars are now far removed from religion, besides being so markedly self-satisfied. Many obtain support by bellowing for bread from door to door and making a nuisance of themselves in every tavern or boat, to the loss of other sorts of beggars. Filthy, ignorant and boorish, they claim to represent the Apostles and do everything according to meticulous rules, as if they are following mathematical calculations which cannot be ignored without committing sin. They fuss about the number of knots in their shoe-strings, the precise measurements of their girdles and their tonsures, the exact number of hours prescribed for sleeping. These absurd trivialities make them feel superior to other men, and yet lead to quarrels among themselves. Some shrink from touching money, as if it were deadly poison, but they are less restrained when it comes to touching wine or women! They are not interested in being like Christ, but rather in being unlike each other, the rival Orders being subdivided into many discordant sects. Yet nobody dares to belittle these, least of all in regard to the mendicant Orders, because they know everybody's secrets from the Confessional. Further blows, largely below the belt, are then directed against their weird notions derived from scholasticism.

At this point Folly turns on the defects of princes and courtiers, though she enumerates these with far more brevity and indulgence. She soon returns to the unfortunate churchmen in chapters 58 and 59, this time attacking the grand life-style of popes and cardinals. After a transparent allusion to the soldier-pope Julius II, she arraigns those other military prelates, the German prince-bishops, who make war on their own wretched subjects in order to extract tithes and taxes. These streams of anticlerical reproach by Erasmus are not intended simply to entertain the reader but also to discredit particular elements within the Church which seemed to him to have forgotten New Testament Christianity. At the same time he strives to retain a light touch, as when he makes Folly refer to himself, though in the mildest terms. 'The second place in this flock belongs to my friend Erasmus, whom I mention from time to time, by way of a compliment.' Yet all in all, having re-read *The Praise of Folly* throughout, we still marvel at those readers who continue to depict Erasmus as an always gentle mediator between the late medieval Church and its enemies. After all, the cat seems a gentle creature until you see it torturing a mouse!

Even so, as the end of the book approaches (chapter 65), he introduces with a sudden change of spirit that sublime paradox, the 'folly' or 'madness' of Christ himself, when he embraced the agony of the Cross in order to rescue the human race. Not content to stage even this unexpected climax, Erasmus proceeds to analyse religious ecstasy itself, another form of 'madness' attained by the highest saints in Christian history. On this issue we leave our readers to consult the fascinating work of Professor Michael Screech, *Ecstasy and the Praise of Folly*. With great erudition he shows that the word *ecstasis* covered a vast effusion of ideas from a host of Greek minds across many centuries: pre-Christian with Plato, apostolic with Paul, endemic among the earlier fathers of the Orthodox Church.[45] Ecstasy is well exemplified in Origen, long dismissed as a heretic by the Roman Church, but then rediscovered by a few intrepid Western explorers, among whom the most courageous and inspired was Erasmus himself. There we shall leave the *Folly*, with Erasmus not exactly analysing medieval mysticism, yet enlarging upon one of its historical foundations with remarkable insight and learning.

Among the sequels to the *Folly* was the controversy between Erasmus and Maarten van Dorp, professor of philosophy at Louvain.[46] Also a humanist and an admirer of Erasmus, Dorp was obviously under pressure from his reactionary colleagues at the Trilingual College. In September 1514 he wrote in still affectionate terms, while reproving Erasmus for the frivolity of the *Folly* and also for his daring intention to correct the text of the Vulgate by reference to surviving Greek texts. In May 1515 Erasmus responded to both points in a 'letter' of great length – and even greater prolixity – which has been reprinted in many editions of the *Folly*.[47] Regarding that book, Erasmus makes the obvious defences. 'As Horace says, what is the matter with saying the truth with a smile?' Again, he pretends that throughout he has tried to preserve good humour and has refrained from traducing anybody or even mentioning his opponents by name. On the more fundamental issue of the Greek texts, he relapses into much bitterness against those scholastics who not only depise Greek and Hebrew, but who stand self-confident in their ignorance, their petty fallacies of logic, their superstitious saint-worship. More attractively he reiterates in magisterial terms the authority of the Greek text as against the Vulgate and denounces the tyranny of the Latin addicts, who have so long despised the whole contribution of the Greek Fathers to Christianity. He reminds Dorp that in support of this claim he, Erasmus, has already published the relevant annotations of Lorenzo Valla. He also takes the opportunity to compare Lefèvre's interpretation of St Paul – unfavourably of course – with his own. In regard to the main dispute, Erasmus has of course all the substantive and enlightened points on his side, while even his prolixity may be pardoned on the ground that, in his time, one's supporters expected and admired an overkill in a dispute over so vital an issue. Following his intervention, the affair gradually subsided. Dorp wrote a second letter, longer but no deeper than his first, and still couched in most amicable terms, while Thomas More wrote to Dorp – also at immense length – in support of Erasmus.[48] Dorp duly secured his promotion to become Rector of Louvain, while Erasmus not only survived him by a decade but had the last word by composing the gracious epitaph on his tomb. By comparison with the normal *odium theologicum* of the age, it was all very civilised!

The *Novum Instrumentum*, a folio volume first published by Froben in February 1516, and dedicated by Erasmus to Leo X, is in subsequent editions entitled *Novum Testamentum*. Both titles were appropriate, but the first can be claimed as the more original, since the book was intended as the operative instrument of the Philosophy of Christ. Throughout the century and beyond, the number of its editions became immense. In its full form the scheme comprised four elements: a Greek text of the New Testament; a new translation into Latin, conservatively revising the Vulgate; the *Annotations* commenting upon the text, and the striking introduction called the *Paraclesis*. The greater part of the later editions omit the Greek text, which the vast majority, even among educated purchasers, could not read. A German version appeared in 1523, a Czech in 1533 and an English version in 1538.[49] Following the expansion of Greek studies, the frequency of Greek-Latin editions again increased from around 1540.

As would be expected, this apparent replacement of the quasi-sacred Latin of the Vulgate gave widespread offence to western conservative opinion, while the printing of any Greek version annoyed those Catholics who still suspected publications in Greek as potentially heretical, even when they realised that Greek had been the language used by St Paul to spread the Gospel. Nevertheless, that such prejudices were now far from universal we have already observed in the case of Cardinal Ximénes de Cisneros and the team of scholars whom he assembled and organised to create the Complutensian Polyglot Bible.[50] The great Castilian statesman was indeed a rigorous ascetic and a figure of unquestioned Catholic orthodoxy. Erasmus may have seen him as one of those offensive military prelates, if only because in his lay capacity he had directed in person a major expedition against the Moors of Oran in Algeria. Yet Erasmus can scarcely have doubted the devotion of Ximénes to Christian learning, if only on account of his foundation of a major university at Alcalá de Henares (*Complutum*). His six-volume Polyglot (1514–17) included not only the New Testament but also the Old Testament in its Hebrew, Greek Septuagint, and Aramaic forms, together with an interlinear translation into Latin. In fact its printing in 1514 of the Greek New Testament preceded by two years that in the *Novum Instrumentum*, even though the death of Ximénes in 1517 and the tardy support of the Papacy delayed its actual publication until 1522.

Had more time been taken to create the *Instrumentum*, its reception in learned circles would doubtless have become warmer, since the zestful enterprise of Erasmus far exceeded his technical competence in Greek philology.[51] His materials nowadays appear grossly inadequate. When first working in England he is said to have collated four Greek texts of the New Testament, their identity being dubious. Then at Basel he usually had five, yet only one of them was genuinely ancient. His impetuosity could sometimes lead him into strange irregularities. Approaching the end of the work, he had only one Greek text of the *Book of Revelation*, and moreover he discovered its last six verses to be missing. He merely took his Latin version of the passage, translated it into Greek, and allowed the result to figure as part of the received text! Yet again, the proof correctors, who included the Hebraist (and future Zwinglian leader) Oecolampadius, allotted only ten months to the production, which Erasmus himself described as 'precipitated rather than edited'. In truth, few epoch-making works can have been so poorly executed in detail as this particular performance of Erasmus, though he afterwards strove gallantly to eradicate its blemishes in four subsequent editions. This did not placate the Victorian scholar Frederick Henry Scrivener, who, having listed no less than 3,000 extant biblical manuscripts – many of course fragmentary – then designated this first effort of Erasmus 'the most faulty book I know'.[52]

Certainly the introductory *Paraclesis* could not possibly be dismissed in such pejorative terms. It is briefly and forcibly expressed, and though in the main it summarises the views of Erasmus already expressed in earlier works, there remains one startling and novel proposition, which we shall examine after briefly paraphrasing the rest.[53] He begins by longing for the eloquence of Cicero, but soon exclaims: 'What trouble we take with the other ancient thinkers, compared with the little we devote to the teaching of Christ!' Indeed, he asks, does it really matter to become expert concerning Aristotle's 'philosophy', to know what he says about the cause of lightning and the nature of the elements? Nobody is any happier for possessing such knowledge, at all events as compared with Christ's doctrines, which came straight from heaven itself. Here indeed is the wisdom which brings felicity and makes the wisdom of the world look stupid. Moreover it is to be found in brief and simple form. True, Stoics and Epicureans, Socrates and Aristotle, have all said things in harmony with the teaching of Jesus, yet his own lessons supply our needs so much better, and conduce so much more effectively toward a peaceful and happy society. Of course, we preserve our friends' letters; we treasure the rules of the religious Orders; we hold in respect even mere outward gestures and observances. We even study the mental gymnastics of the scholastic philosophers! But why not give priority to the creative essentials of both individual and social happiness, to the holy knowledge which all men, however poor and humble, can readily understand?

Suddenly this last thought seems to kindle in the mind of Erasmus a bold and challenging application of Christ's philosophy which goes distinctly beyond the trend of both medieval and Renaissance thought, whether religious, social or political. He seems to have been asking himself what happens to the unprivileged mass of people when, as so often occurs, the clergy give them no helpful teaching or even obstruct their access to the sources of this vital knowledge: the Scriptures. The answer appears to Erasmus altogether obvious, however shocking it may seem to the privileged, the formal, the complacent. Clearly the message of Christ serves all men and women, oblivious of rank, class, even education. It serves them all because the message, as delivered in the New Testament, is perfectly clear and intelligible. The sun itself is not as common and accessible to all as is Christ's teaching. It keeps nobody at a distance, unless a person begrudges himself and keeps aloof.

> Indeed, I disagree very much with those who are unwilling that Holy Scripture, translated into the vulgar tongue, be read by the uneducated, as if Christ taught such intricate doctrines that they could scarcely be understood by very few theologians, or as if the strength of the Christian religion consisted in men's ignorance of it. The mysteries of kings, perhaps, are better concealed, but Christ wishes his mysteries published as openly as possible. I would that even the lowliest women read the Gospels and the Pauline Epistles. And I would that they were translated into all languages, so that they could be read and understood not only by Scots and Irish but also by Turks and Saracens.[54]

Surely, he continues, the first step is to understand in one way or another. Perhaps many people will mock, but some will be captivated.

> Would that, as a result, the farmer should sing some portion of them at his plough, the weaver should hum some parts of them to the movement of his shuttle, the traveller lighten the weariness of the journey with stories of this kind. Let all the conversation of every Christian be drawn from this source.[55]

He seems almost to have fled from scholasticism to something like Methodism! Here was a powerful case, but one bound to prove widely unacceptable to orthodox opinion in this second decade of the sixteenth century. Every traditionalist feared the longstanding menace of the Hussites, flaunting heresies similarly based upon the direct access of the masses to vernacular translations of the Bible. Within a very few years the point would be sharpened not only by the major Protestant Reformers, but also by chaotic, scripture-quoting sectarians throughout the Netherlands and much of central Europe. Nevertheless with no little daring Erasmus already continued the *Paraclesis* itself by returning to his anticlerical attacks from another alarming angle. Here he asks why Christian knowledge, which belongs equally to all, should be reserved to theologians and monks, that very small part of the population. These are styled 'religious'; but too many theologians take far greater interest in earthly matters, while too many monks falsely profess total belief in the poverty of Christ and the contempt of the world. Meanwhile the genuine theologians teach not by intricate syllogisms 'but by a disposition of mind, by the very expression of the eyes'.

> And if anyone under the inspiration of the spirit of Christ preaches this kind of doctrine, inculcates it, exhorts, incites and encourages men to it, he indeed is truly a theologian, even if he should be a common labourer or weaver.[56]

Alongside these works concerning the nature of religion, Erasmus was contemplating a number of short treatises usually labelled 'educational'.[57] Amongst them he reconsidered the publication of the manuscript comprising what he had originally regarded as only the first 'book' of a much longer work in four 'books'. This was the *Antibarbarorum Liber*, described in our previous chapter. Its fate during the early years of the new century had been nothing short of bizarre. In 1506 Erasmus had taken it to Italy along with some unfinished portions. All these were lent out and in effect lost by a person entrusted with their safe keeping. After lengthy enquiries Erasmus succeeded in recovering the completed first book, which he eventually put into print at Cologne in 1520. It scored a rapid success, being not only readable but also still regarded for many years as representing a vital controversy. By 1535 it had achieved twelve editions from several presses before reappearing in the collected edition of Erasmus' works published at Basel in 1540.[58] Indeed, although the parameters of this present book preclude any survey of his educational publications as such, the *Antibarbari* exemplifies the fact that, for Erasmus, education was a key instrument in his evangelism.[59] We may perhaps feel that it belongs more properly to the period during which the young Erasmus first addressed the theme, than to the third and fourth decades of the sixteenth century. Whatever the case, only a year after its first appearance in print, the dominant issues and the whole temper of theological and literary debate entered upon a dramatic change with the advent of a sterner controversialist, a former reader of Erasmus who became a more violent breaker of clerical moulds. His name was Martin Luther.

Four

THE CHRISTIAN COMMONWEALTH

Before we consider the complex relationship between Erasmus and Luther, two aspects of the *philosophia Christi* require more detailed examination: its implication for the Christian Commonwealth, and the problem of theology. Erasmus' own priorities suggest their treatment in that order; for he was concerned above all with the impact of Christianity upon people's lives. Just as his theology emerged from the application of his personal criteria to inherited tradition and scholarship on the one hand and his perception of the needs of the individual Christian on the other, so too did his opinions on political, social and economic issues. While his views on these have sometimes been seen as largely conventional, a closer examination will confirm that in fact they derive directly from the values of his Philosophy of Christ. In many ways he was forward-looking, perhaps most notably in his advocacy of a pacifism based upon unequivocally Christian grounds. His urgent commendation of social reform is seen by some English historians as leading directly into the 'commonwealth' idealism of many mid-century writers, Protestant and Catholic.[1] Indeed, we do well to remind ourselves that the groundswell of much advocacy of social reform was a specifically Christian humanism which ranged across the emergent spectrum of religious opinions and was not geared to narrowly dogmatic issues.

In an age where social and economic relationships were normally evaluated and discussed as moral issues within a religious context, the topic is of quite integral significance. Thus we shall discover that one of the reasons for Erasmus' ultimate, if guarded, condemnation of most Protestants was that their doctrinal and institutional innovations had allegedly failed to produce any improvement in their social conduct. Indeed, for several decades in the present century the debate about the political and sociological implications of the emergence of the Protestant Reformation was intense.[2] Thus two particular caveats must be uttered: first, we shall be concerned with Erasmus' opinions on political and social trends rather than with their examination *per se*; second, the nature of any connection between early and mid-sixteenth-century social and political developments and the emergence of the doctrinal ferment of the Reformation was far from simple. Thus the *De subventione pauperum* of Erasmus' friend and fellow-Catholic, Juan Luis Vives, was criticised by one Franciscan as heretical and Lutheran, while a fellow-Spaniard defended begging as a fundamental human right against any attempt at eradicating it as a social evil;[3] yet despite their personal and doctrinal differences certain of Erasmus' prescriptions within the field of poor relief directly pre-figure the later more detailed approaches of Bucer. Again, in respect of usury or interest, while Erasmus accepted, with some reservations, certain innovatory justifications of the practice of demanding a return for the loan and use of money, Luther remained early medieval in their rejection, lock, stock and barrel.

Thus, while there is no simple relationship between political and social thought and the dogmatic debates of emergent Protestantism, there is an essential connection between Erasmus' teachings in this field and his 'philosophy of Christ'. For this latter was to him the ethos of genuine Christian reform, as reflected in the lives of people, rather than yet another round of sterile theological debate. It remains true that there is perhaps no aspect of his thinking that has been subject to such divergent assessment as his views on social and political issues – ranging between those who find therein little but conventional moralising dressed up with Erasmian wit and polish, and those who would agree with the opinion that there is 'scarcely a single social reform advocated in More's *Utopia* for which a parallel is not to be found in the works of Erasmus',[4] or who would contend that in many of his political implications and in particular in his views on international relationships he was centuries ahead of his time. As always, Erasmus the ambivalent is there for our interpretation! Our own approach to his political, social and economic prescriptions is related to their place within the whole body of his *philosophia Christi*, and particularly to the fact that in regard to man's worldly potential Erasmus was an optimist. In the last analysis, he proffers a sharp contrast with both his friend More, on the one side, and Machiavelli on the other. It could well be argued that, while *Utopia* was indeed an imaginative *jeu d'esprit*, Erasmus' more mundane offerings were directed to a genuine goal of the spirit: what both should and could be if the philosophy of Christ prevailed. Nor is this an anachronistic interpretation, retrospectively imposed. Nothing could be more explicit than Erasmus' own question in his *Paraclesis*: 'What else is the philosophy of Christ, which He himself calls a rebirth, than the restoration of human nature *originally well-formed*?'[5]

It remains true that the concept of the *Respublica Christiana*, best-translated as the Christian Commonwealth, within which Erasmus wrote had deep and respectable medieval antecedents. Even the disreputable papal applicant outside the gates of Heaven in *Julius exclusus* is made to render lip-service.[6] Yet during the late medieval era its nature had been subject to important evolution in ways which proved wholly consonant with Erasmus' ideals. Broadly speaking, it became endowed with more specific content in terms of the social and political responsibilities of the prince alongside its long-term religious and philosophical connotations. In works as widely ranging in date and location as those of Marsilius of Padua and Sir John Fortescue,[7] increasing emphasis upon the powers and the duties of the secular ruler accompanied a growing tendency to regard him not so much as the owner of territory held in trust from God as the custodian of the people who dwelt therein, to whom he owed social and economic as well as political responsibilities.

It is within this framework that Erasmus' opinions and influence on political and social issues must be evaluated. Although the *Education of a Christian Prince* is his only work specifically devoted to these themes, such discussions, embedded within a religious context, are scattered throughout a whole range of writings, from the *Enchiridion*, the *Praise of Folly*, and the *Adages* – works already noticed – to the *Colloquies*, *Querela pacis* and his correspondence. Erasmus' *Colloquies*, first printed in 1518 but written for the most part in the 1520s, were greatly expanded and changed in character from a book of early 'exercises' for students to a highly successful medium for informal, and often provocative, expression of his opinions.[8] Containing much on religious issues, they are also a major source for social and political comment. More specifically related to the political sphere are Erasmus' *Panegyric* to Philip, Archduke of Austria, 1504, and his more general *Querela pacis* or *Complaint of Peace* of 1517. Thus one commentator envisages Erasmus emerging as almost the intellectual arbiter of Europe in a socio-political as well as a biblical sphere;[9] more sceptically, another suggests that Erasmus' optimistic surge of 1516–17 takes his 'moralistic idealism well beyond the realm of practical implementation'.[10] To this charge of *naïveté*, as well as to the question of how much he really knew or understood about political and social problems, we shall recur. Equally often expressed is the criticism that Erasmus, like many of the 'moralising sermonisers' of mid-Tudor England, was long on indignation but very short on positive analysis leading to practicable remedies for social ills. To such charges it would be unrealistic not to concede an element of truth, though not an unqualified acceptance.

Meanwhile Erasmus' own ideal of a 'balanced' commonwealth was well expressed in the 1508 edition of the *Adages*: if only

> the different elements of society could be made so to control and balance each other, as to achieve an eternal truce; thus each part of the body politic would retain its rightful authority, the people would be given their due; the councillors and magistrates would be paid the respect proper to their learning, to law and to justice; the bishops and priests would receive the honour due to them. Nor would the monks be denied what is due to them. The harmonious discord of all these, this variety tending to one and the same end, would serve the commonwealth far better than the present state of affairs, when each tries to grab everything for himself.[11]

Elsewhere in the *Adages* we meet with Erasmus' fundamental optimism, his belief that Nature 'implanted in man a spark of the mind of God', impelling him to disinterested service to all, regardless of reward. For crucially, 'the Lord did not come merely to tell us what was permissible – how far we were allowed to fall below perfection – but to show us the goal we must strive towards with all our might. [For] the end and aim of the faith of the Gospel is conduct worthy of Christ. Why do we insist on those things which have nothing to do with morality, and neglect the things which are like pillars of the structure. . . ?'[12] Such writings evoked a similar optimism in many readers, expressed for example by Jan Becker, Dean of Veere, who welcomed the appearance of the 1518 edition of the *Enchiridion* with a forecast that Erasmus' works 'will contribute to raising the standard of public morality to a truly Christian level'.[13]

Turning in more detail to Erasmus' views on international politics, we observe an idealism which is in stark contrast with the seamy *realpolitik* of Machiavelli. But as to the standpoint from which he made his judgments, the notion that he was essentially cosmopolitan because he was essentially medieval, that he was a citizen of the world with no real home of his own, has recently been modified by James D. Tracy's monograph. This seeks to identify a Dutch–Burgundian base from which many of his criteria derive.[14] Again, the point that, unlike either More or Machiavelli, Erasmus wrote with no practical experience of political affairs, should not be pushed too far. In terms of intelligence he did not dwell in an international backwater, while in terms of balanced political judgment an onlooker sees most of the game. Yet in truth his oft-expressed hopes for a golden age of international peace were blasted, while in retrospect many of his purported expectations from particular monarchs seem almost ludicrously credulous – though hardly more so than the spurious special pleadings for 'just wars', which he so excoriated!

As to the nature of the international comity for which he longed, one must at once insist that he advocated the universal sway of Christ rather than that of any temporal Emperor. The assertion that the vision of a universal Empire lingered longest with scholastics[15] has little validity for Erasmus. 'Is it not enough for every region to have its own master, [lest] the people's slavery is redoubled if the supreme power should fall into the hands of a wicked prince?' The absence of the unattainable ideal of a universally beneficent emperor will not be felt 'if Christian princes are united in concord among themselves. The true and only monarch of the world is Christ.'[16] For Erasmus is at heart concerned far less with political structure, where he is often content to accept the status quo, than with the essential Christian spirit which must quicken it. In short, he envisaged a Christian body rather than an institutional framework. He always wrote in a language appropriate to the unity of late-medieval European culture and religion, *not* to a stable and unitary political framework. The emergence of nation states was no sudden phenomenon. Thus he may be numbered among those humanists who, 'even while professing citizenship in a *Respublica christiana*, were deeply suspicious of the notion of a supra-national empire'.[17]

As for the ideals of conduct which should mould relationships between monarchs, Erasmus had no doubts. His insistence on assessing the exercise of power within a moral framework which Machiavelli had rejected must now itself be evaluated against a longer-term historical perspective. The judgment that 'it is when he writes on war and peace that Erasmus seems nearest to our own time',[18] has even more validity now than when it was written. Pre-eminent among his prescriptions for just rule is the avoidance of war, as 'something so monstrous that it befits wild beasts rather than men'.[19] His *Panegyric* of 1504 contains a diatribe against its horrendous impact as 'the Furies burst out from the underworld'. As for its aftermath, evocatively, 'the fields scarcely ever get rid of the salt deposit if they have ever been flooded by seawater'. If people would remember 'that the Christian world is one country, the Christian Church is one family . . . all members of the same body . . . redeemed at the same price, called on an equal footing to the same inheritance, and that we receive sacraments which are common to all, then they will surely judge that there can be no war which is not a civil war . . . if it is taken up by Christians against Christians.'[20]

A letter written from London in March 1514, in expectation of Henry's VIII's renewal of war with France, repeats such arguments, anticipating Erasmus' famous *Dulce bellum inexpertis* ('War is sweet to those who have not tried it'). Significantly, preparation for war has already brought change; the price of everything is going up while liberality declines. One passage combines his intolerance of cant with a shrewd realism in rebuttal of the argument that the rights of princes must be upheld: 'I only know that often the greater the right, the greater the wrong, and that there exist princes who first make up their minds what they want and afterwards search for a specious reason to cover their action.'[21] Yet briefly, in the early months of 1517, Erasmus was able to convince himself that Francis, Henry, Charles and Maximilian were about to tear out the roots of the nurseries of war, in conjunction with a drive to restore the humanities, and that mankind stood on the threshold of an age of gold, involving the lasting concord of Christendom.[22]

Sadly, by March of 1518 euphoria had been replaced by disgust: 'God help us, what tragic work these princes have in hand! The sense of honour is extinct in public affairs. Despotism has reached its peak.' Rulers think of people not as human beings but – in a phrase which anticipates Zwingli on mercenaries – 'as beasts for the market'. Yet on mercenary soldiers themselves Erasmus deplores the misguided clemency accorded them by princes who show more mercy to godless ruffians and notorious villains such as 'those criminal scum, the Black Band', often the agents of their own oppression, than to their victims, the common people.[23] In *Dulce bellum inexpertis* he asks: 'Who ever heard of a hundred thousand animals rushing together to butcher each other, which men do everywhere? . . . What depths of hell have hatched this monstrosity for us?' Again the Dutchman speaks: 'Vice is like the sea: we have the power to shut it out altogether', but once admitted few can prevent a tidal wave of misfortune. And if princes' bowels may not be moved by compassion, what of the other costs? Who but a lunatic would fish with a golden hook?[24]

Was Erasmus a total pacifist or was he prepared to give qualified approval to a 'just war'? In general, he was grudgingly ready to contemplate a 'just war' in the abstract, provided that he was never asked to define one in a Christian context! He never expresses outright approval of any contemporary conflict, for 'even when it is waged with perfect justification, no man who is truly good approves it'.[25] Any rights which purportedly occasion war smack of an already decadent Christianity. For Erasmus, so often deemed unworldly, is honest enough to face the fact that circumstances sometimes precipitate violent action, professedly in self-defence, without feeling obliged to rationalise in hypocritical fashion or to concede that even a 'just war' is compatible with the Christian ethic. By 1530, in *De bello Turcico,* he has only slightly modified his earlier stance adopted in the *Adages*. Tracing recent events, including the effects of the sad death of Louis II of Hungary and Bohemia, he concedes that the princes of Christendom might feel driven to war against the Turks as an inevitable necessity. But it does not please him, and Christians must beware of becoming like their adversaries.[26]

As Margaret Mann Phillips observes, 'he saw the truth behind the clap-trap'.[27] In a powerful passage in the *Education of a Christian Prince* he deplores the fact that 'bishops are not ashamed to frequent the camp; the cross is there, the body of Christ is there, the heavenly sacraments become mixed up in this worse than hellish business, and the symbols of perfect charity are brought into these bloody conflicts. Still more absurd, Christ is present in both camps, as if fighting against himself . . .'[28] He challenges his critics to find one passage approving war in the teaching of Christ, which always and everywhere condemns it. Most notably, he is also fully aware of the emergent device of recourse to nationalist propaganda in order to whip up war-lust among the ordinary people. Nothing could be more explicit than his *Querela pacis* ('The Complaint of Peace'): The populace is now incited to war by insinuations and propaganda, by claiming that the Englishman is the natural enemy of the Frenchman and the like. What rubbish! The Rhine may separate the French from the German, but not the Christian from the Christian.[29]

Quite often Erasmus derides the very phrase 'just war': ' "Just" indeed – this means any war declared in any way against anybody by any prince.' Or again, the term is used when princes act in collusion to exhaust and oppress the state. A genuine Christian never approves of war – 'perhaps sometimes he may think it permissible, but with reluctance and sorrow'. For in truth a rigorous examination will disclose that almost all wars between Christians originate from stupidity or wickedness. Nor is any lack of realism evident in the modern-sounding comment that

> there are those who go to war for no other reason than because it is a way of confirming their tyranny over their subjects [or that] if there is any advantage to be gained from this worst of all experiences, it is entirely drawn off by a few thieving scoundrels – it goes to pay the mercenaries, the out-and-out profiteers, perhaps a few leaders by whose instigation the war was stirred up . . . and who are never so well off as when the state is on the rocks.[30]

Fundamentally, the charge of lack of realism comes down to this: that in his Christian idealism Erasmus, in contrast with Machiavelli, failed or refused to recognise what really went on in the contemporary world. But this is exactly what he *did* recognise – and what he deplored. What he refused to do was to swallow the specious justifications of aggression and bloodshed which masqueraded as just war – or for that matter, *pace* Machiavelli, as the ineluctable corollaries of political power. A powerful passage in the *Dulce bellum inexpertis* punctures the attempt at scriptural justification of war: 'Since Christ gave the command to put up the sword it is not fitting [in the 1515 edition, unequivocally, 'it is a sin'] for Christians to fight, except in that noblest of all battles, against the most hideous enemies of the Church – against love of money, against anger, against ambition, against the fear of death . . .' As for the much-cited incident of Peter and the sword, 'Christ suffered Peter to err in this, for the purpose of leaving no doubt in anyone's mind that when he was ordered to put up the sword, it meant that war was now forbidden, even though it had seemed to be allowable before.'[31]

In face of all this, it seems difficult to accept Harold Bender's contention that, while fully endorsing a general humanist aversion to war, Erasmus was not prepared to enunciate a condemnation of all conflict on specifically Christian grounds;[32] indeed the many treatments of the issue throughout his writings suggest precisely the reverse. Erasmus clearly advocated Christian pacifism, while recognising that, human nature being what it is, rationalisation of motives would always be forthcoming. Zwingli condemned recruitment of Swiss mercenaries in terms similar to those of Erasmus, yet he himself took up the sword and fell in battle to defend his faith. While Erasmus would not have equated him with *Julius exclusus*, one cannot imagine that he condoned this action. In his attitudes on this subject Erasmus was centuries ahead of his time however indiscriminate his condemnations.

That he was himself aware of this seems to be suggested by the full title of what is described as his most explicit and celebrated plea for general peace, already cited: *A Complaint of Peace Spurned and Rejected by the Whole World.* While often repeating earlier arguments, this is indeed outstanding in its impassioned plea to the truly Christian prince 'to loathe war as the cesspool of every iniquity'. Perhaps of special interest is the lengthy discussion of the roots of conflict and of possible remedies. A sound peace does not rest upon leagues and treaties, which themselves can often lead to war, nor even on marriage alliances and artificial associations. A genuine effort to remove the cause of war involves a change of heart by princes and statesmen, a change of attitude toward it by the Church, and a thought-provoking safeguard that it 'must not be undertaken except by the consent of the whole people'. Most crucially, who better to take the lead in the negotiation and preservation of peace than the representatives of the Christian Church, led by the Pope himself?[33] It is indeed for his persistent commendation of systematic negotiation for peace that Erasmus has caught the imagination of twentieth-century apostles of international organisations. The 'Peace Book Club', in the 1930s, pointed out that while there is no suggestion in his writings of a Council of Princes or an International Court, his advocacy of clerical arbitration had sound roots and a recent precedent in Pope Alexander VI's award of 1493.[34] More recently, Robert Adams observes that the ideal of the *Pax ecclesiae* still seemed practicable to Erasmus.[35]

It is perhaps appropriate in this context to consider the first of the institutions that concerned Erasmus – for it is about the Papacy as an institutional force in international affairs, rather than as a purported leader in regard to faith and doctrine, that Erasmus had at least as much to say. The connection has been bluntly expressed in the assertion that 'it was Julius II who turned Erasmus into a pacifist'[36] – certainly that militant-minded pontiff did much to make his stomach heave at the cant about just wars. In contrast, asserts Erasmus, 'it is the proper function of the Roman pontiff, of the cardinals, bishops, and abbots, to settle disputes between Christian princes; this is where they should wield their authority and reveal the power they possess by virtue of men's regard for their holy office'.[37] The Popes should be fierce warriors against the *real* enemies of the Church: simony, pride, lust, ambition, anger and irreligion. Truly apostolic triumphs are far removed from the bloodthirsty revels of a conscienceless Julius, who has instigated war.[38]

While Tracy has suggested that Erasmus was less than fair in failing fully to grasp the dilemma of the Renaissance papacy, of which, in terms of *realpolitik*, Julius II was possibly the saviour,[39] others might urge that the whole purpose of *Julius exclusus* was to stress the contrast between the contemporary conduct of the papacy and its apostolic origins. Peter, at Heaven's gate, is appalled by what waits outside: 'Not one of the whole mob even looks like a Christian to me. They seem to be the worst dregs of humanity, all stinking of brothels, booze, and gunpowder. I'd say they were a gang of hired thugs . . .' As for the leader of this entourage, 'what monstrous new fashion is this, to wear the dress of a priest on top, while underneath it you're all bristling and clanking with blood-stained armour?' Julius, unabashed, repudiates the charge of being a disaster to the Christian commonwealth with a shameless boast of how his cunning has incited every Christian king to battle, after the wholesale repudiation of treaties. As to the status of the Papacy, 'if we have no worldly possessions, the common people will take no notice of us, whereas now they both hate and fear us. What's more, the whole Christian commonwealth would collapse if it couldn't protect itself against the fury of its enemies.' Peter, aghast at this distorted belief that 'your essential function is to safeguard the regal majesty of the supreme pontiff, rather than the general welfare of the Christian commonwealth', goes on to enunciate some radical-sounding ideas. Julius' smug assertion that, whatever any council or synod may say, nothing can be decided without papal agreement, runs into the counter-blast that 'against such a man it is obviously not a general council that is needed, but a rising of the people, armed with stones, to remove him publicly from their midst'.[40]

Turning to Church possessions, unrepentantly Julius identifies poverty as an abominable disgrace to be avoided at all costs. Surely the scattering of spiritual seed merits a worldly harvest? The Church, once poor and starving, is now enriched with every possible ornament. She is not too greedy, selling dispensations at quite reasonable prices and giving blessings freely; but as for usury, which the Germans condemn, 'for us there is no trade so necessary to the church of Christ' – indeed many a rich money-lender would envy our wealth. In contrast with the golden-chained pontiff of Rome today, Peter, misguidedly, 'must still be dreaming of that ancient church in which, with a few starving bishops, you yourself, a pontiff shivering with cold, were exposed to poverty, sweat, dangers, and a thousand other trials'. Peter, predictably, sees before him a tyrant and an enemy of Christ: 'I was the first to teach Christ to pagan Rome; you have been a teacher of paganism in Christian Rome.'[41]

Erasmus' persistent denial of responsibility for the publication – though never unequivocally for the composition – of this vitriolic work, bespeaks not only his cautious nature but also the fact that, especially in the presence of a new Pope, he harbours no opposition to the Papacy as such. As always, it is the unchristian exercise of power, not its institutional establishment, that evokes his ire. A very different tone is clear in his expression, in 1515, of the hope that 'a far greater, truer glory will accrue to our Leo from the return of peace to the world'.[42] But such hopes were dashed, and by 1518 a less sanguine note is heard in his muted expectation that the beneficent rule of Christian princes 'shall be under the leadership and guidance of the excellent Leo X, unless he is diverted from his endeavours for what is best into another direction by the surge of human affairs'.[43]

When we move to consider Erasmus' opinions of another aspect of human affairs, what would now be called the state, it is tempting, in terms of modern political analysis, to approach this subject in terms of the origins, institutional exercise, limits and responsibilities of power. All of these will indeed occur in Erasmus' writings, but not in ordered exposition. The matrix within which his political and social comments were made was late-medieval and of course fundamentally religious. His approach was morally normative, not institutionally analytical. Despite many modern- and even radical-sounding observations (into which it is both dangerous and unhistorical to read too much), he was primarily interested not in the theoretical origins or the institutional exercise of power but in the enunciation of moral judgments as to the *quality* of its exercise within the Christian ethic. For Erasmus, as for many humanists whom current terminology would call elitist, ordinary people had one fundamental right – the right to be governed well.

Most of what he has to say may be related to his belief that 'what Christ teaches applies to no one more than to the prince'.[44] The relationship between the ideas of sixteenth-century religious reformers and political development is seldom simple but repays investigation, and Erasmus is no exception. First, in regard to the duty ascribed to the temporal prince by some Protestant Reformers, to take over the Church if need be in order to reform it, this he disregards. His emphasis that the prince, though not a priest, has clear religious duties, is not developed, as it is in Lutheranism, into a direct injunction to intervene. Further, in view of his frequent denunciation of Church wealth, it is interesting that the cry of the English Lollards – 'then take their land from them' – is also missing. Second, in respect of the claim that all too often, especially against a German or English background, a sharp increase in the prestige and power of the prince was a corollary of a state take-over, one's impression is that such a trend would have been unwelcome to Erasmus, the drift of whose political criticism was against excessive centralisation of power. Yet when we turn to a third suggested consequence of sixteenth-century religious turmoil, the relationship between religious reform and conflict and the gradual emergence of representative government and democracy, we shall shortly find that there is more to be said.

Meanwhile, if it be true, as it has most cogently been argued,[45] that Erasmus 'is as far as possible from the theory of the divine right of kings', it is equally certain that he was a most fervent advocate of their divine responsibility. True, advice-books for princes, often derivative in character, and stressing the lode-star of 'virtue', were commonplace in the early sixteenth century. Erasmus' friend Budé published along these lines. But the crucial issue in our present context is that Erasmus' guide-lines emerge from the *philosophia Christi*, rather than from neo-classical virtue, and certainly not from the waning myth of chivalry. This much is evident in the themes running through his *Education of a Christian Prince*, published in 1516 and his major work in this field.

First, defining the political entity itself, 'the state is a kind of body composed of different parts, among whose number is the prince himself', and 'what the heart is in the living body the prince is in the state. Since it is the fount of the blood and of the spirits, it imparts life to the whole body, but if it is impaired, it debilitates every part of the body.' Thus we have established at once the corporeal or organic concept of the body politic, the analogy of disease to describe its ills, and the essentially personal nature of responsibility. To the normal contemporary equations of the state with *publica utilitas* or the public weal, free from all private interest, Erasmus adds a third, on which of course his is a special emphasis: 'The model for government is to be taken especially from God himself, and from Christ who is both God and man'. Thus, if it is admittedly true that 'the prince is not a priest', it is still incumbent upon him to follow the rule of Christ himself. For 'what is a king but the father of very many people?' In the discharge of his duties 'he must keep watch so that others are allowed to sleep; he must work so that others may take their leisure. He must show the highest integrity of character.' Underlining this approach Erasmus puts the question: 'What is the prince but a physician to the state? But it is not enough for a physician to have skilful assistants; he must himself be the most skilful and careful of all . . . [For] the parts of the mind are not all equals: some give instructions, others carry them out, while the body does no more than carry out instructions.'[46]

Contingent questions suggest themselves. First, what has Erasmus to say about the origin and form of government? Occasionally we encounter an apparently unequivocal assertion, as in *Sileni Alcibiadis* in the 1515 edition of the *Adages*: 'power, unless it is allied to wisdom and goodness, is tyranny and not power, and *as it has been conferred by popular consent* [our italics], so it can be taken away'. Or again, in *Dulce bellum inexpertis* of the same date, we read that 'no one can have the same rights over men free by nature, as over herds of cattle. This very right which you hold was given by popular consent. Unless I am mistaken, the hand which gave can take it away.'[47] Similarly, *Querela pacis* reminds the Christian prince that, as a ruler of men who are both free and Christian, 'the people in their turn should defer to him only so far as is in the public interest. A good prince should demand no more, and a bad one will in fact have his desires held in check by the combined will of the citizens.'[48] Yet again, in a letter regarding dietary regulations, he counsels that 'the bishops remember that their sheep belong to Christ rather than to themselves. Let them remember that laws rest on the consent of the governed.'[49]

Modern historians rightly concur that despite such repeated assertions Erasmus never attempts to explain how such consent is to be ascertained, and that what is claimed is at best something resembling a tacit contract. Yet the charge of anachronism in reading too much into Erasmus may hardly be levelled against his contemporary Stephen Gardiner who, imprisoned in the Fleet in 1547, found time to read Erasmus and (like others since) was taken aback by what he actually wrote. Writing to the Duke of Somerset, Gardiner is aghast at the contrast between the English *Book of Homilies*, which teaches true obedience of subjects, and Erasmus' *Paraphrases* which is 'able to minister occasion to evil men to subvert, with religion, the policy and order of the realm', by reason of misinterpretation of Scripture on the state of princes. Indeed, 'what so ever might be spoken to defame princes' government is not left unspoken.' In several letters Gardiner develops the theme that 'it is incredible that a king should set forth a book tending to the subversion of his own estate' – a Trojan horse brought into the realm.[50] Ironically, much of what he says repeats what he had written about Bucer in 1541; both attacks may surely be related to conservative fear of the potential implications of those who stressed the *duties* of the prince in a social context.[51]

Reverting to the *form* of government, Erasmus expresses reservations about the fact that, while we choose a skilled steersman or coachman on ability, 'we hand over the state, in which so many thousands of people are in peril, to the first comer' – that is, to the first-born son of an hereditary monarch. 'But there it is, the thing is so established that it is impossible to root it out . . . But if this is a thing we cannot change, the next best plan would be to improve matters by careful education; and if we may not choose a suitable person to be our ruler, it is important to try and make that person suitable whom fate has given us.'[52] Elective monarchy, although desirable, may be impossible; but hereditary monarchy must not be taken to entail incompetent and unbridled despotism. Thus 'monarchy should preferably be checked and diluted with a mixture of aristocracy and democracy to prevent it ever breaking out into tyranny; and just as the elements mutually balance each other, so let the state be stabilized with a similar control.' The good ruler will welcome this help; the bad one needs such a curb.[53]

In this context it is not without interest that Starkey's *Dialogue between Pole and Lupset*, in which the influence of Erasmus has been discerned, was unusual for its age in commendation of reforming the commonwealth by means of limited monarchy, though Pole's concession therein that, in present circumstances, it is wise to stick to hereditary succession,[54] is directly reminiscent of Erasmus' own conclusion. Significantly, the suggestion that Erasmus' assumptions reflected the traditions of the Netherlands, where the notion of consensus had a definite institutional context,[55] receives some confirmation in a letter written from Antwerp in 1519, in which Erasmus is 'sorry for the poor common people, and cannot stomach some persons' more than Turkish tyranny. Behind it all, I see how power is being gathered into few men's hands, while the relics of our traditional democracy are gradually done away with . . . If only princes could be persuaded of this one thing, that the most glorious monarch is he whose subjects are free and happy!'[56]

Embedded amid the conventional flattery of the *Panegyricus* are passages which presage almost exactly the sentiments and the phraseology of his 'set–piece' on princely duties. Thus the ruler is enjoined that 'you do not demand obedience of your people unless you have obeyed the laws yourself', for authority is a public service of which an account must be rendered to God.[57] The *Education of a Christian Prince* asks plainly 'what man thinks highly of himself on the ground that he rules a people kept down by fear like a herd of cattle?'[58] As for the positive characteristics required of the prince, throughout Erasmus his portrait – like that of war – is stripped of the tinsel accretions of chivalrous romance. But Edward Surtz has found at least eight occasions on which the appeal to Plato and the commonplace of the 'philosopher prince' occurs![59] True, *Praise of Folly* derides the notion,[60] but more typical is the assertion in a letter to the young Prince Charles that 'no commonwealth can be happy unless either philosophers are put at the helm, or those to whose lot the rule happens to have fallen embrace philosophy'. For this both 'frees the mind from the false opinions of the multitude' and is conducive to 'the common good, which should be the sole aim both of kings and of their friends and servants'.[61]

Erasmus devotes much space, especially in the *Adages*, to what we might call a picture of the 'anti-prince'. *The Beetle Seeks the Eagle* – which has been dubbed a 'violently antimonarchical essay'[62] – depicts how, beneath the screech of the eagle 'the common people tremble . . . the laws give way, immemorial custom gives way too'. Sometimes, alas, innate rapacity is nurtured by the most corrupt education and thereafter by swarms of flatterers, unprincipled ministers, dishonest counsellors and profligate companions, assisted – in an ingenious variation of the organic analogy – by 'how many ears (of eaves-droppers), eyes (of spies), claws (of officialdom), beaks (of governors), bellies (of judges and lawyers), the latter practically insatiable'.[63] *Sileni Alcibiadis* proffers a vivid contrast between the luxury-glutted tyrant and Erasmus' ideal of a prince as near as possible to the image of God, 'far from all low passions, the diseases of the soul, by which the stupid and common herd is carried away'.[64] Yet Erasmus does not forget the normal caveat that God, displeased by their evil doing, often sends the people the bad ruler they deserve. This becomes doubly dangerous when such a one 'is taught that whatever he wants he can have, he hears that the property of everyone belongs to the prince, that he is above the law, [and] hears the terms *sacred majesty, serene highness, divinity, god on earth* . . .' and so forth.[65]

Thus, since hereditary monarchy is with us for the foreseeable future, it is crucially important to try to make suitable that person whom fate has given us. His preceptor must teach him the difference between Christian administration of the state and mere dominion, for 'he is ruling over free men, and over Christians, that is, people who are twice free'. Again, analogies recur: 'What the eye is to the body, so is a true prince to the body politic. As the sun is to the sky, so is the prince to the people; the sun is the eye of the world, the prince the eye of the multitude. As the mind is to the body, so is the prince to the state . . . Above all, the good ruler is the living portrayal of God, who rules the universe.'[66] Such ideal prescriptions in the *Adages* mirror a significant passage in *Praise of Folly* on the exercise of true sovereignty,[67] and the declaration in *Querela pacis* that 'Christ commands the prince to be the servant of his people'.[68]

Yet Erasmus' alleged lack of realism did not encompass any failure to recognise the realities of the practical exercise of power in early sixteenth-century society. The significance of the court environment, and of delegated administrative and judicial authority, in the quality of governance are stressed almost as often as that of the calibre of the prince himself. Of two chief evils identified at court, malicious accusation and flattery, the second is worse because it vitiates the mind of the king himself by inciting him to set his will above the law.[69] Nothing could be more expressive of contempt than *Praise of Folly*'s sketch of the courtiers' life: 'They sleep till midday, when a wretched little hired priest waiting at their bedside runs quickly through the mass before they're hardly out of bed.' Then breakfast and lunch, with scarcely a break between. 'After that follows dice, draughts, fortune-telling, clowns, fools, idle games, and dirty jokes, interspersed with one or two snacks', and so forth.[70] The Christian prince must avoid not only such an entourage of sycophantic courtiers but also the appointment of idle, vicious and corrupt officers. Yet when the prince himself plainly puts public offices up for sale, civil order is bound to deteriorate and corruption spread through the people like a plague. How can monarchs 'require obedience to the law from their people while they live themselves as if exempt from all law, [or] expect integrity from the magistrates, while they themselves openly sell government posts or make them a matter of favouritism'?[71]

Yet perhaps Erasmus writes most savagely about the prince who abuses his power of peace and war, notably in *Querela pacis* which deplores the creation of widespread chaos to make a tiny territorial gain. He is 'ashamed to recount the disgraceful and frivolous pretexts Christian princes find for calling the whole world to arms': some mouldering, obsolete title, a trivial omission in a lengthy treaty, the interception of an intended spouse, or some trifling slander.

> Most criminally wicked of all, there are rulers who believe that their authority is undermined by harmony amongst their people and strengthened by discord, so they use their despotic power to suborn persons who will set about stirring up war; this gives them an opportunity to divide those who were previously united, and at the same time greater freedom to pillage their unhappy subjects. They are the worst sort of criminals . . .

The wars of the last twelve years have all been started in the interests of princes and conducted with great suffering to the people.[72] An alternative, but hardly more flattering, attribution of their causes is found in the *Adages*, adducing sheer stupidity, whereas the real glory of a prince 'does not lie in extending his sway, in pushing back his frontiers by force of arms; but if he happens to acquire the sovereignty of a region, he must make it flourish by justice, by wise economy, and the other arts of peace'.[73]

Before turning to these, especially in a social context, a few more words may be appropriate on the doubts expressed as to how much Erasmus really knew about courts, politics and international affairs. His travels must surely have widened his international perspective, while his range of correspondents made him well qualified to survey the European scene. Yet the significance of the fact that he was after all 'Roterodamus' both for his political assumptions and for his early international standpoint has rightly been stressed. This is true also in respect of face-to-face contact with men of state. Erasmus was present when Charles met Henry VIII at Calais in July 1520 and Wolsey at Bruges in August 1521; and in respect of such Anglo-Burgundian relations he may well have felt pulled two ways. In 1516 he had been appointed counsellor on the one side, while for long he had been friendly with More, Fisher, and notably with Cuthbert Tunstall during that diplomat's stay in Brussels.[74]

His correspondence contains tantalising hints that at one point his position may not have been entirely honorary. A letter in September 1517 states that 'a piece of business has been entrusted to me as though by authority of the Emperor [Maximilian] . . . of the greatest importance for the prosperity and safety of the state'. Indeed on 25 October Thomas More wrote from Calais invoking 'a blessing on the duties entrusted to you by the Emperor'.[75] But against this tenuous evidence of actual participation is Erasmus' declaration three years later that 'no man on earth refrains from contact with the court more readily than I . . . [For] what a monster is the emperor's court, a beast of uncounted heads' (a similitude more usually applied to the populace!). He goes on to stress that he has no real influence and that his admission to the roll of councillors was 'on the understanding that I do not attend even when summoned, let alone put myself forward'.[76]

Often accused of *naïveté* in assessment of rulers, and of recourse to fulsome flattery of prospective patrons – sometimes to a point where the modern reader is tempted to discern the tongue in the cheek – one must agree with Betty Radice that Erasmus is readier to trace the origins of wars to the unlimited powers of monarchies rather than to the wickedness of individual rulers.[77] There is no lack of realism in his contention that 'there are those who go to war for no other reason than because it is a way of confirming their tyranny over their own subjects'.[78] Nor again at a level of internal political analysis, is any shrewdness missing in his comment (1523) to Adrian VI regarding the suppression of heresy in England, that what may be lawful in that kingdom, where one command is all-powerful, may not be feasible in so large a region divided into so many princedoms as Germany.[79] Yet it is probably fair to say, in the field of political as well as of social criticism, that there are differences between what Erasmus regards as ideally desirable, what he believes to be realistically practicable, and what he deems it wise to say – and to whom!

To Erasmus the internal duties of governance were to be assessed primarily in the context of Christian social obligation rather than in that of constitutional functions. Immediately the organic or corporeal analogy, the equation of *respublica* with the body politic recurs. The Christian prince must so discharge his duties as to avoid the ever-present danger of a populace turned turbulent, remembering always that 'reliable physicians do not take refuge at the outset in their ultimate remedies; . . . they adjust the dose to cure and not to overwhelm'.[80] Far better to let a dormant evil lie than to exacerbate it with unskilful physic; better to leave a wound alone if surgery will harm the whole body.[81] Naturally, in a social context, the *members* of the body attract comment – more in terms of their duties than of their rights.

The duty of obedience, of course, applies to all. In particular, 'the people are bidden to endure worthless magistrates, so as not to disrupt the order of the state, provided that they perform their duties and do not give orders that are opposed to God'.[82] This codicil was to receive full elaboration at the hands of both Protestant and Catholic propagandists in varying circumstances in the mid- and late-sixteenth century. Meanwhile, Erasmus himself explored the nature of obedience in a provocative passage in the famous Colloquy *Concerning the Eating of Fish*. Thus, 'what if a fool or a wicked person gains power over us and makes a foolish and wicked law – must we abide by his judgment and must the people obey, as if having no right to judge?' Not convinced by the reply that this is unlikely to occur, the Butcher in the dialogue goes on to assert that 'a human law is no law at all, unless it is approved by those who use it'. The Fishmonger's rejoinder that it would be better to bear it than to offer seditious resistance evokes only recognition that 'this is a very good way to maintain the authority of persons in power . . . I'd be quite happy to hear anything that aims at the liberty and advantage of the people.' Yet, having ventured so near to the brink we are then pulled up short by the definition of a very limited concept of human liberty.[83]

If the commons possessed, fundamentally, the right only to be governed well, the duty of such governance devolved from the prince not only to the magistrates but also to the upper orders generally, since possession of land was very largely equated with the exercise of power. In this setting the concept – and the obligations – of nobility recurs. Erasmus furnishes a definition of 'three kinds of nobility – the first derived from virtue and good actions, the second from having experienced the best training, and the third as judged by ancestral portraits and family trees or by wealth'. Only the first, strictly speaking, merits the name of nobility, while the third is the lowest variety thereof. Indeed, later in the *Education of a Christian Prince* Erasmus goes on to deride the equation of nobility with ineffective idleness. He would not indeed strip inherited honours from those who attempt to uphold the standards, but the spectacle of idleness and debauchery prompts the question: 'why on earth should this sort of fellow be treated better than a cobbler or a farmer?'[84] Noble birth alone is but an empty name. Yet, discussing profligate expenditure in the *Adages*, he is equally forthright on such as 'fake up their noble birth so as to be able to behave in this way. They bribe people to call them Junkers, they boast about their ancestral castles, they stick a feather in their cap and paint themselves a shield on which a right hand brandishing a sword is cutting up an elephant, and they sign their epistles with three letters, equ.'[85] This condemnation of the upstart, coupled with commendation of sumptuary legislation, is reminiscent of a favourite theme in mid-Tudor England. Thus recent assertions that Erasmus advocated social *mobility* are suspect.[86] For Erasmus, social *change* meant a more Christian fulfilment of one's social obligations – not interference with the social hierarchy.

While it would not be fair to say that nobles were always equated with court parasites, Erasmus expressed his disdain for long-held chivalric myths here as also in the context of warfare. Yet it is important to stress that he cherished no illusions either about the populace. While ever ready to commiserate with those who were oppressed, and in particular with the poor when exploited, his interpretation of the popular saying '*vox populi, vox Dei*' was anything but literal – as in his allusion to 'diseases of the soul, by which the stupid and common vulgar herd is carried away'! *Dulce bellum inexpertis* includes similar references to 'the common people and the naturally fickle mob' and 'the rash impulses of the foolish rabble' as needing restraint by the wisdom and reason of princes.[87]

True, the occasional passage may be found which sounds almost frighteningly radical in its implication. At one point *Querela pacis* declares that 'it is the humble and despised populace which founds noble cities, administers their foundations considerably, and enriches them in doing so. The rulers slip in, and like drones steal the products of other men's industry, so that what was properly amassed by the majority is frittered away by a few, and a sound foundation is brutally destroyed.'[88] But this neo-Marxist-sounding analysis is untypical – although, pursuing the unlikely analogy, a version of the *Lumpenproletariat* is suggested in the well-known letter to Paul Volz, depicting human society as consisting of inner and outer circles: 'In the third circle let us place the common people, as the grossest part of this world, but gross as it is still belonging to the body of Christ.' This last addendum is crucially important, for not only the eyes are members of the body, 'but also the legs, feet and the less honourable parts'.[89] Despite this, their place is clear. In the *Education of a Christian Prince* Erasmus is in no doubt that 'the great mass of people are swayed by false opinions and are no different from those in Plato's cave, who took the empty shadows as the real thing. It is the part of a good prince to admire none of the things that the common people consider of great consequence, but to judge all things on their own merits as "good" or "bad" ' – remaining far removed from the poisonous thinking and degrading opinions and interests of the common folk.[90]

None the less, despite what sounds like an elitist diatribe, when we look in more detail at the *social* duties of the prince, these are related by Erasmus primarily to the *needs* of the ordinary people. Indeed their right to be governed well was interpreted in a social rather than a political context. Among those contemporary values and standards which should determine the thinking and conduct of the prince, and indeed of all those who hold both power and property in trust from God, we may perhaps single out the concepts of liberality, equity, the happy mean and charity. As to the first, Erasmus explains that 'the prince's liberality should by no means be promiscuous. There are those who heartlessly extort from the good citizen what they squander on fools . . . Let merit, not fancy, be the basis for reward.' Within the context of moderation, he heartily approves of sumptuary legislation in order to curb expenditure which is profligate and blurs the genuine and desirable distinctions between degrees within society.[91]

All this is quite conventional, but his views on equity, though by no means exceptional, are perhaps more challengingly expressed. 'Equity does not lie in giving everyone the same rights, the same honour; as a matter of fact, that is sometimes a work of the greatest unfairness.' Then, more strikingly, 'the prince should try to prevent too great an inequality of wealth'. This precept was to become the crucial point of many would-be social reformers: equity did not mean equality, but too great a degree of *inequality* was an affront to equity. His argument goes further, in a more radical direction. Thus, since 'the laws go back to the fundamental principles of equity and honesty, with no other aim than the advancement of the commonwealth', it is surely just that they should 'punish more severely an outrage on a poor man than an offence against a rich one, and provide a heavier penalty for a corrupt official than for a faithless plebian'.[92] Certainly Erasmus was firmly within the progressive trend of thinking which witnessed the expansion of equity jurisdiction in an English context at this time.

The same sense of what would now be called social justice, though a note of expediency also is sounded here, is expressed in discussion of taxation – for 'a great many seditions have arisen from immoderate taxation'.[93] Indeed the *Panegyricus* commends the prince who has, purportedly, 'found a novel way to increase your own and your nobles' revenues: by reducing expenditure rather than by greatly increasing taxes'![94] The *Adages* contain a reminder that not only the prince extorted money, depicting how when the storm-tossed mariner reaches harbour,

> something is extorted from him; there is a bridge to cross, toll must be paid; a river to cross, and you will encounter the rights of the prince. And what is much more cruel, the common people, wretched as they are, are defrauded of their means of existence, and all these tithes and taxes gnaw away the livelihood of the poor. You may not carry the corn from your own fields without paying a tenth. If you grind or mill it, another bit is rubbed off. Wines cannot be imported [a sore point with Erasmus] without being tithed over and over again.

Later in the 1515 edition the question is asked as to how it may be considered an unforgivable sacrilege to take anything from a church, yet be thought a light offence to plunder, defraud and grind down the poor, the living temple of God?[95]

The *Education of a Christian Prince* devotes several pages to revenue and taxation, enunciating the principle that 'as little as possible should be exacted from the people'; abolishing superfluous expenditure and redundant offices, and keeping out of war, will help. But when taxation is inevitable, then directing the rich to austerity is both kinder and less dangerous than reducing the poor to hunger and servitude. Thus the notion of discriminatory taxation is added to that of punishment. The good prince will 'impose as little tax as possible on those things whose use is shared also by the poorest ranks of the people, such as corn, bread, beer, wine, clothes, and all those other things' by which the poorer people are milked dry, placing the burden instead upon 'luxurious and pleasurable refinements and whose use is confined to the rich, such as cotton, silk, dyed cloth, pepper, spices, ointments, jewels . . .' A final paragraph in this section identifies the four ways in which the people are robbed in the process of the coinage of money: through debasement; underweight coins; the clipping of edges; and 'lastly, when it is constantly being devalued and revalued whenever it is seen to be the advantage of the royal treasury'.[96] Edward Surtz has pointed out that this last device – like so much else – is specifically mentioned in *Utopia*,[97] though More may well have had examples other than the writings of Erasmus before his eyes!

The crucial social obligation of charity must be related to the general concepts of the nature and obligations of wealth and property. The rather startling assertion at one point in the *Enchiridion* that the true Christian 'gives credit to God as Author of all his goods and considers them to be the common property of all. Christian charity recognizes no property,' must not be taken too literally or out of context. Clearly contemporary institutions and relationships did accord such recognition, but always ideally in conjuction with certain limitations and Christian obligations. Much safer-sounding is the definition a few pages earlier in the same book that 'he is charitable who . . . lifts up the fallen, who consoles the down-hearted, who supports the needy', with its clear assumption that he possesses the wherewithal to do so![98] A letter written in 1519 contains a remarkably frank, balanced, and modern-sounding exposition of the traditional view that both riches and poverty are of God. For 'if a man has wealth that was left him by his forbears or honourably acquired . . . and expends it only in relieving the poor or some more pious use for riches, if there is one, does not that wealth support him in a process of daily self-improvement?' Indeed perhaps more men are corrupted by poverty than by possession of wealth in moderation. The fact that Christ wished the apostles to be poor does not prove that riches are bad in themselves.[99]

Admittedly, at one point Erasmus quite categorically declares that Christ gave the world only the single command of charity: 'What else does charity exhort than that all possessions of all men should be common?'[100] Moreover, it is suggested that the second book of *Utopia*, depicting the ideal commonwealth where private property does not exist, 'is actually a highly imaginative rendition of the first proverb in all the editions of the *Adages* – *Amicorum omnia communa*: that is, "Among friends all things are shared in common".'[101] But 'among friends' is of course the key. A passage in one of Erasmus' very last works, *On Mending the Peace of the Church* (1533), explains the position, in replying to those who allegedly demand a sharing of all their possessions. This practice of communism was found only in the primitive Church, and even there it was not universally practised. As the gospel spread it became impossible and led only to sedition. Concord will be achieved if we agree that property should remain in the hands of its legal owners and its common use be directed, when occasion arises, out of charity.[102]

As we shall see, this last comment has implications for the contemporary Church. Meanwhile, since riches are clearly not good or bad in themselves any questions for the Christian concern their acquisition and their use. Traditionally, the Church had condemned their pursuit *ad libitum*, and their waste for malignant purposes. Erasmus was fully within this tradition. Property in itself must not be worshipped nor its owners be made the subject of adulation. The reader of More's *Utopia* will recognise the sentiments of two passages from *On the Eating of Fish*: 'Where is a petty theft not punished more severely than adultery?', or again, 'He who steals a little money must be hanged, but those who swindle the public of their money and impoverish thousands, by monopolies, extortion, trickery, and cheating, are held in great esteem.'[103] *On Mending the Peace of the Church* has harsh words for those who wallow in the shame of luxurious expenditure in a good year's harvest, and then when the yield is meagre 'are intent on prices, stingy with the poor'. For 'God has not given a wondrous harvest that the grain might rot in your barns, but that the surplus might be dispensed for the use of the poor'.[104]

The concept of Christian stewardship is the norm. While *Praise of Folly* derides the miser who 'enjoys nothing so much as living like a pauper in order to enrich his heir',[105] equally deplorable is waste on riotous living or pastimes such as the British entertainment of dancing bears: 'Christians are not ashamed of having pets like these when so many poor people are starving.' One cannot but lament 'the ways in which great men spend their money, or how much of it goes on dice, lechery, drinking, unnecessary journeys, pomps, wars for gain, flatterers, jesters, players . . .'[106] But some of Erasmus' most cutting indictments are directed at one property-owner in particular: the Church. A letter of 1519 cites Paul on 'the question of the property and the pay of priests when he plainly lays it down as right that those who are servants of the Gospel should live of the Gospel; but his word is "live" – nothing about growing rich and faring like a prince, and no living either, unless they serve and attend constantly upon the altar'. As to the origins of ecclesiastical riches, men entrusted their wealth to the Church to be spent upon the needs of widows, the aged, and others in need – not to be diverted to the support of selfish personal rule.[107] If one name springs to mind here, we are not disappointed: *Julius exclusus* includes a splendid depiction of 'the mules decked in fine cloth, gold and jewels, some even shod with gold and silver', who accompanied the late pontiff's regal progress.[108]

In one of the *Adages* a clerical spokesman is made to relate how help first spontaneously offered later became exacted as a due. 'Then we received money, but as alms to be distributed among the poor; then for our own use. Why not, since we had learnt that charity begins at home. . . ?'[109] The obligation of alms or charity was of course considered the most crucial duty incumbent on the possession of wealth. Nothing could be more explicit than the declaration that 'to beg one's bread when necessity requires is not shameful, but to refuse to share necessities with the poor or to live on what has been stolen is a contemptible crime'. Again, for the true Christian, not only to restore fraudulent gains but to lavish your possessions on the poor for the love of Christ is a step higher.[110] Such sentiments were indeed in the mainstream of contemporary moralising on wealth, but not many went so far as to contend that 'the man who, impelled by poverty, steals something from a rich man has not committed the same crime as the man who steals the only tattered garment of another when he himself has enough at home'.[111]

One of the clearest statements of Erasmus' all-important belief that the Christian faith should manifest itself in Christian conduct – in social and economic as well as political affairs – is found in his *Contra quosdam, qui se falso iactant Euangelicos* ('Against the Pseudo-Evangelicals'), 1529. Charging his adversary 'Vulturius' (Geldenhauer of Strassburg), that his writing is more likely to excite disorder than conduce to piety, Erasmus proceeds to the issue of Heresy. But of outstanding interest in our present context is his blunt challenge as to whether the convulsions created by the 'pseudo-evangelicals' have in fact produced conduct worthy of the Gospel. Look around at these 'Evangelical' people and ask whether the part played by luxury, lust and money in their lives has in fact diminished? Has the Gospel as preached by them brought forth milder conduct and freedom from avarice and lewdness? No, the position is worse! The images have been thrown out of the churches, but to what effect? For nothing superior in spirit has ensued.[112] It was perhaps the knowledge of a favourite thesis of Erasmus, that Luther had failed because good works were widely absent from the lives of his followers, that emboldened Georg Witzel, a former Lutheran, to write to him on two occasions.[113] In this same context Norman Birnbaum's account of the Reformation in Zurich is of interest. Like Erasmus, Zwingli repudiated the radical and literal biblicism of the Anabaptists. But the usage of confiscated ecclesiastical property for 'welfare purposes' was apparently not free from scandal, while charges that wooden crosses were burnt but the golden stolen away, and that there was some speculation with funds intended for poor relief, were made.[114] This was certainly not limited to Zurich. The sermons and writings of 'commonwealth-minded' divines in mid-Tudor England are full of allusions to those who simply made use of religious changes to fill their pockets.[115]

In approaching more closely the subject of the *relief* of poverty we must state outright that Erasmus – unlike many though not all of his fellow-Catholics – did not advocate indiscriminate charity any more than he had approved of a merely promiscuous liberality. Indeed he represents a vein of realistic diagnosis both of motivations and of efficacy which runs through from his Spanish friend Juan Luis Vives to his Protestant adversary Bucer. In Erasmus, sympathy with poverty is bracketed with contempt for idlenesss. A passage in the *Education of a Christian Prince* reminds its readers that 'Plato thinks that all beggars should be driven from the boundaries of his state. But if there are any persons who are broken through old age or sickness and without any relatives to care for them, they should be cared for in public institutions for the aged and sick.'[116]

Concerning the Immense Mercy of God is traditional in its insistence that 'if you wish to be heard, see that you in turn listen to Him. He cries in the person of the sick and needy.' But it goes on immediately to insist that 'there should be no display in almsgiving, otherwise it loses its name. Those who make a great show of giving alms are not giving alms but making a bid for glory.'[117] Such ideas are in total accord with those to be set forth in great detail by Bucer in a later treatise, and also with the *De subventione pauperum* (1526) of Vives, identified as a landmark in the literature of systematic and effective control of charity, and indeed of poverty, and apparently most influential.[118] Such discussion took place against a background both of a crisis in the growing *need* for organised poor relief and of a questioning of the assumptions and institutions upon which medieval relief had been based. Julius, outside Heaven's gate, is made to condemn poverty as a disgrace in a very different sense.[119] But of whom was Erasmus thinking when he alluded, in *Concerning the Eating of Fish*, to great men who ravage 'almshouses and hospitals, erected through the charity of pious persons for the care of the old, sick, and needy'?[120]

The comment in the *Enchiridion* that 'the kingdom of Heaven does not belong to the lazy'[121] – presumably relevant to those whose poverty was not of God or to those many idlers attached to the families of the rich – may well take us forward to Erasmus and the world of work. Here again, the background to his thinking is traditional. Economic functions and relationships were never considered merely as such by the medieval mind, but were evaluated by standards of social and indeed moral obligation. The absence of any dichotomy between economic and moral issues is encapsulated in an economic historian's definition of scholastic economics as forming an 'integral part of a coherent philosophical system; . . . a consistent body of doctrine according to which economic relations ought to be ruled by the laws of distributive and commutative justice'.[122] Despite his quarrel with scholastic theologians Erasmus never departed from this tradition. Whether in the context of agriculture in the countryside or of the craft gilds in the towns, the idealised picture emphasised the duty of the land-owner or the employer to those in his care, the duty of the worker to his lord or his employer, and the duty of all through a preferably controlled market to the consumer. Erasmus in fact has little to say about agriculture, but is quite conventional in awarding it the highest possible praise, its produce being of course the essential subsistence of all. Trading and financial activities, by contrast, are almost generically suspect, though much depends here upon the particular background and the degree of economic sophistication of the writer.

Thus on finance and trade Erasmus – given the notably mercantile background of the Low Countries, his nodding acquaintance with some North Italian cities and his later personal contact with the great banking house of Fugger – would not have been completely naïve. Late-medieval Catholic theologians had produced a quite sophisticated analysis and justification of interest, a charge made for the *productive* use of money as distinct from grinding usury, as essential for expanding trade and nascent industry. The detailed monograph of J. T. Noonan has suggested that 'the scholastic analysis of usury is the midwife of modern economics', developed to justify the financial practices of the Italian city-states.[123] Yet Erasmus, while recognising contemporary trends, remains cautiously conservative, though without adopting the rigorous stance of Luther. In one of the *Adages* he points to the fact that 'while the tillers of the soil are despised (though no kind of men are more innocuous or more indispensable to the community), usurers, on the other hand, are considered to be among the pillars of the Church. And yet usury was condemned by the earliest of the human race' by Gentiles, Jews and Popes. Yet he concedes that he is not now 'particularly against usurers, whose skill I can see some reasons for defending'. Ironically, the parallel is again with Bucer, whose treatise *On Usury* (1550) was to make a quantitative and qualitative distinction between what would now be termed commercial interest and excessive, exploiting usury. Erasmus himself confesses that, 'especially if one considers the morals of our time, I would sooner approve of an usurer than of this niggardly class of dealers who are on the hunt for profits from every possible source, by trickery, by lies, by fraud, by cheating, buying up here what they sell for more than double there, and robbing the wretched poor with their monopolies'.[124]

In respect of this last issue, it has been pointed out that Erasmus lost favour at the Lisbon court because of his expressing a protest against the royal monopoly of spices and pepper![125] We have noted that he had no illusions about sundry devices designed to fill the royal exchequer. Yet overall Erasmus has most to say – and in nothing more closely resembles early- and mid-Tudor moralisers – about the deceits of trade. Margaret Mann Phillips, who dates his grasp of immediate social problems at the end of the first decade of the sixteenth century, points especially to Erasmus' dual loathing of money-making and despotism.[126] The 1508 edition of the *Adages* contains a contemptuous allusion to 'the merchant class, who have mostly dedicated themselves to the worship of Mammon'. In 1515 he goes a little further: 'The merchant class hold nothing sacred except financial profit, to which they devote themselves entirely as if to God.' Surely they should consider 'that profit no profit at all which is gained by the loss of a good conscience; and nothing useful that is not honest'.[127]

The *Praise of Folly* finds that 'most foolish of all, and the meanest, is the whole tribe of merchants, for they handle the meanest sort of business by the meanest methods, and although their lies, perjury, thefts, frauds, and deceptions are everywhere to be found, they still reckon themselves a cut above everyone else simply because their fingers sport gold rings'.[128] Erasmus is indeed in full accord with the medieval doctrine of the 'Just Price' of any commodity or service, which is taken to include moderate remuneration of all the interests and claims involved.[129] Yet nowadays (in 1524) 'we make a profit of our brother's needs. My brother is starving to death. As his need for food increases, so does our price.'[130] Nor is unwarranted gain made solely by exploiting market forces. Sometimes a trader resolves 'to defraud the customers, to filch parts of the materials you have been supplied with, to offer for sale glass instead of gems, or one wine under the name of another' – again, a sore point! The description of such conduct as 'cheating your neighbour' encapsulates the whole ethos of Erasmus' approach. Sadly, the professions are not exempt – untrustworthy doctors and surgeons, sometimes even rank impostors, may be found.[131]

On social and economic issues we find little or no attempt at suggesting innovatory or corrective measures; it has justly been observed that Erasmus' strictures 'approach the evils of the time from the outside, and have no fundamental solution to offer'.[132] Yet should this be expected? Erasmus wrote as a Christian moralist, concerned to evaluate human behaviour, not as an economist or a sociological analyst. That said, he was at least more advanced than his contemporary Luther in his recognition that the payment of interest for the use of money might be permissible if not welcome, and also more realistic and enlightened in his attitude toward the need for some systematic relief of poverty than many fellow-Catholics. If we look for a common criterion within his approach to such disparate issues, it is surely to be found in a realistic evaluation of Christian attitudes toward one's fellow-men, rather than in any attempt at *a priori* derivation of systematic social and economic teaching from a theological base – in short, the same empiricism which characterised his approach to theology itself. So much has been written about the social and economic implications of the doctrinal innovations of the Protestant Reformation that it is worth reiterating that the crucial contribution of Erasmus lies rather in his powerful advocacy of the need of implementing the real meaning of the Christian faith in the ordinary affairs of life. It might perhaps be suggested that this was a vital ingredient of Christian humanism.

Inevitably, in the field of social thought, comparisons with More have been made. In the widest context, it is worth pondering the judgment of More's own biographer, Richard Marius, that 'Erasmus was much the greater educator'.[133] After all, More's *Utopia*, while far more startling in this context than anything Erasmus wrote, was not to be rendered into its author's native tongue until 1551, while several of Erasmus' works were published in English much earlier. Moreover, while Erasmus' social and economic precepts were at one with the whole of his *philosophia Christi*, the contents of his English friend's *jeu d'esprit*, with its tone of urbane toleration, were poles apart from More's harsh writings against heresy and his actions as Lord Chancellor. While it would be inaccurate to ascribe to Erasmus any more than a general influence for improvement of social conduct among many such voices, his was surely one of the most powerful. Perhaps most important of all in this context is the accuracy of his frequent reiteration of the social duties of the prince as a major road to improvement. Thus one modern edition of Thomas Starkey's *Dialogue between Pole and Lupset* has described it as 'an attempt, based on the teaching of Erasmus, to present a system of secular and ecclesiastical reform'.[134] Undoubtedly, Erasmian reformism is a major thread leading into the Commonwealth idealism of early- and mid-Tudor England.

Direct references to Erasmus in the writings of such as Hooper, Ridley and Becon concern doctrinal issues. Yet his voice may well be echoed in Becon's declaration that 'the gospel of Christ begetteth and bringeth forth new life, and new manners, yea, and those pure, honest, and godly. If such fruits follow not the gospellers' profession, in vain do they brag of the gospel of the grace of God, of the Christian liberty, of the justification of faith.'[135] Hugh Latimer, who likewise derided such card-gospellers, dice-gospellers, and pot-gospellers, who sought not amendment of life, could also cry out 'for God's sake make some promoters . . . men of godly discretion, wisdom and conscience, to promote [that is, report upon] transgressors, as rent-raisers, oppressors of the poor, extortioners, bribers, usurers' for punishment by authority.[136] It is true that Richard Morison, representing a more mundanely-orientated approach to reform in the commonweal, barely referred to Erasmus in his *Remedy for Sedition*, dealing with social problems;[137] but his master, Cromwell, whether or not we believe Foxe's story about memorising the New Testament or accept James McConica's contention that 'Erasmian reform is very clearly the chief inspiration' of his 'Injunctions',[138] most certainly thought of him as a reformist influence. If the social views of Erasmus were often, but *not* always, 'commonplace', there can have been very few who were more widely read or more effective in their expression.

If a combination of truly Christian spirit with official action was increasingly seen by Erasmus' contemporaries as the only way ahead for social justice, as then perceived, we must search for a longer-term perspective to evaluate his political teachings, on which we have had as much to say. While the occasional attempt to make of him an early protagonist of democratic rights (as distinct from a belief in and a respect for established representative institutions) almost certainly ascribes to him more than he really wished to say, we have noted a fair number of shrewd and perceptive pieces of political analysis which came from his pen. But it is in the realm of international relations, as a propagandist for peace and for the method of negotiation by which it might be pursued, that he really stands out. It is particularly interesting that late-twentieth-century commentators have moved away from long-held opinion about unfavourable contrasts with the allegedly much more realistic analysis and precepts of Machiavelli, to a gradual realisation that the way ahead, if mankind is to avoid a final nuclear holocaust, lies in and through Erasmian prescriptions. The Italian people may well have been realists in their own time when, after belated achievement of national unification, 'united *and armed* Italy' rendered homage to Machiavelli. The peoples of the world may gradually become even more belatedly but also realistically disciples of Erasmus in their recognition that in any future world conflict there can be only the vanquished.

Five

THE PROBLEM OF THEOLOGY

To Erasmus, the Christian religion proffered a guide to life in this world, as well as the promise of redemption thereafter. Theology, to be meaningful, must therefore be relevant to both. Like the Church itself, it must encourage, rather than preclude, the active participation of the ordinary man in the pursuit of Christian conduct. Yet these modern-sounding aspects of his thinking must not make us lose sight of the fact that Erasmus always sought to clarify and to promulgate, not to attenuate, the central message of Christ's life and the essential teachings of his Church. His approach to the problem of Christian theology therefore demands inclusion in any balanced survey of his ideas and of their impact. Moreover, if this chapter in one sense marks the completion of our description of the emergence of Erasmus' *philosophia Christi*, it also helps to establish the landmarks for the next part of this book: relationships between Erasmus and, respectively, Martin Luther, the Protestant Humanists, and the Radical Reformation, will inevitably be envisaged very largely in terms of theology.

Erasmus' disenchantment with contemporary scholastic theology derived from his conviction that the clarity and purity of the Christian message had been obscured and even distorted by the super-imposition of a load of hair-splitting and largely irrelevant pseudo-philosophical dialectic. Similarly, the Catholic Church and its clergy had in his view progressively abandoned the real task of nurturing the Christian conduct of its membership in favour of an increasing emphasis upon the supposed achievement of salvation by means of mechanical compliance with its ritual and sacraments. Indeed we have already seen that Erasmus was imbued with a detestation of scholasticism, the normative approach to theology of the era into which he was born. It is tempting to assert that he thought the Christian faith far too important to be left to the theologians! Certainly it seems to be the case that his was an essentially utilitarian theology, related to aspects of the task of saving souls rather than to any canons of scholastic sophistication.

Erasmus had come to see his personal religious objective as being the clearer identification and establishment through scholarship of the original Christian message. This he then proceeded to combine with cogent exposition of its meaning in terms of people's lives. Yet alongside this positive contribution one cannot ignore his sometimes abrasive determination to identify and expose the shortcomings of scholastic theology and of the moral and intellectual calibre of the contemporary clergy. Above all, Erasmus never compromised in what he considered the essential beliefs of Christianity, nor in his conviction of the need for an organised Christian Church as custodian of those beliefs. Accordingly, much as he might deplore its scholastic variety, he could not ignore the relevance of genuine Christian theology as central to his purpose.

It may be as well to define some parameters of our own approach to the problem of Erasmus' theology. An immediate avowal that this approach does not profess to evaluate his linguistic skills may beg some questions, especially in the light of the old adage that every translation is a surreptitious exegesis or interpretation. Yet it may be contended that for Erasmus himself philology, defined as the science of languages, was but a tool, although indeed a crucially important tool, with which to establish the scriptural truth which then served as a basis for his exposition of the Christian faith. Divergent estimates of his own stature as a theologian may well invite a distinction between one who consciously seeks to produce a systematic, coherent and distinctive body of thought, and one whose utterances derive from a consideration of specific issues within a spectrum of religious problems. Without doubt, Erasmus' own theology emerged from his consideration of the reasoned relevance of Christ's teaching to particular human concerns, and not from an *a priori* body of scholastic thought. It is with these aspects of his theology that we shall be concerned, rather than with any attempt at a fundamental critique of Erasmus as a theologian. For his theological views derived from the relevance of the New Testament to man's quest for salvation; they were not a systematic codex imposed upon that quest. Thus it has been suggested that Erasmus' abiding concern was religion, not theological statement, and that by religion he meant Christian faith and practice.[1] Occasionally indeed, in Erasmus' statements of his theological opinions or of his Christian philosophy, one encounters an utterance so striking in its modernity that it is hardly surprising that some contemporaries cried 'Heresy', while certain modern historians project a specifically 'Erasmian' Reformation,[2] conceived of in ethical and philosophical terms and almost denuded of dogmatic content. Yet as against this, Ernst-W. Kohls has rightly insisted that for Erasmus ethics cannot be divorced from theology, in which it is essentially rooted.[3]

Before considering Erasmus' own theology we should perhaps take note of his frequently expressed opinions about the subject and its practitioners. In later life he felt himself increasingly constrained, if only in self-defence, to record his resolute unwillingness to dissent from many aspects of the orthodox theology of the Catholic Church. Yet his earlier years had been marked by expressions of scepticism, sometimes of derision, about the whole tribe of 'theologians'. The dichotomy between the flesh and the spirit which Erasmus often emphasises[4] is reflected in the contrast he makes between the soul-stifling mechanisms of scholastic theology and the realities for the individual of the Christian message. His adage *Illotis manibus* (*With Unwashed Hands*) observes that very many among contemporary scholastic theologians are unqualified, without knowledge of 'the three tongues [Latin, Greek, Hebrew]. He who is ignorant of them is no theologian, but a violator of theology. Truly with hands and feet unwashed, he is taking the most sacred thing of all, not to treat it, but to profane it, pollute it and do it violence.'[5] Years later, in his colloquy *The Sermon, or Medardus* (1531) he deplored the fact 'that many theologians have neglected the cultivation of languages and the study of Latin diction, as well as the ancient doctors of the Church, who cannot be fully understood without these helps . . . You can find some who pay such deference to scholastic opinions that they'd rather distort Scripture than correct human judgments by the rule of Scripture.'[6]

Beyond all doubt such scornfully expressed opinions provoked real anger. A letter from Maarten van Dorp, noted earlier,[7] chides Erasmus with berating his Louvain colleagues for their 'highly confused, and indeed highly foolish, teaching'. Dorp then observes in deflating fashion that 'a beginner finds everything confused the moment he enters the arena of dispute . . . Further, when you set up the hypothesis, Erasmus, that our theologians are interested in nothing but the practice of disputation, you are completely wrong.' Unabashed, Erasmus later alluded to 'those great problems of which our grand theologians with their lordly manner make such heavy weather, whose swelling cheeks bulge until they crack with pride . . .' Moreover, 'even the greatest theologians sometimes make discreditable mistakes and fall into delusions'. Erasmus himself was guilty of no mock-modesty in entering the field, inviting Budé in 1516 to 'take my *Enchiridion*: I have dared to differ widely from this age of ours, undeterred by any man's authority'.

Nor has his own audacity been without success, he claims, for some of his comments on the New Testament 'are welcomed by the most authoritative theologians, and they say they have derived a flood of light from them'.[8]

Yet a few years later Johann von Eck, in a detailed critique, expressed his reservation, albeit in cordial fashion, about Erasmus' New Testament, most notably about his penchant for attributing error to that leading light of the Church, Augustine, and even his tendency to 'set up as the instructor of evangelists'! Erasmus, thin-skinned as ever, replies that in conveying such invidious suggestions his old friend is but recounting other men's malignant attacks. Indeed, in an impassioned letter to Pope Leo himself in August of 1519, he deplores the rubbish vomited by men who 'prepare to attack the new flowering of human letters and the purified theology which bears the imprint of original sources'. He then declares his own purpose 'to release men from those lifeless details which could bring no result but premature old age and to fire them with a zeal for a theology alike more authentic and with higher standards'. He is saddened by those barking curs who distort what contains no error and also often what they do not understand, inflaming sores which Christian gentleness might have healed.[9]

Already, his *Ratio verae theologiae* (1518) had enunciated the requisites of a pure heart, submission to the Holy Spirit, and a knowledge of tongues, for a genuine exegesis of the Scriptures. This integration of philological method into theology, crucially important as it is, must be accompanied by a change in attitude.[10] A letter of 1520 to Campeggio sets out Erasmus' analysis of what has gone wrong: 'In olden days the Christian philosophy was a matter of faith, not of disputation; men's simple piety was satisfied with the oracles of Holy Scripture.' But then, alas, came men who, 'neglecting the study of the ancient tongues and of polite literature and even of Holy Writ, grew old over questions meticulous, needless, and unreasonably minute, as if drawn to the rocks on which some siren sang'. Theology became a form of skill, not wisdom or a means toward true religion; and besides ambition and avarice it was spoilt by other pests, by flattery, strife and superstition. Thus 'the pure image of Christ was almost overlaid by human disputations; the crystal springs of the old gospel teaching were choked with sawdust by the Philistines; and the undeviating rule of Holy Scripture, bent this way and that, became the slave of our appetites rather than the glory of Christ'. At length some men, reverting to the simpler studies of an earlier age, sought to lead it back from pools which are now sullied 'to those pure rills of living water. To achieve this object, they thought a knowledge of the tongues and liberal studies (as they call them) were of the first importance, for it was neglect of them, it seemed, that brought us down to where we are.' Sadly, the result has been great uproar from the very outset, with clenched teeth and faults on both sides.[11]

To this encounter Erasmus himself clearly contributed! Over ten years later a long letter from Agostino Steuco,[12] prior of a convent in Reggio Emilia, amidst a catalogue of reproofs, asks sharply what else but contempt for all theology can be deduced from his repeated assaults upon its practitioners?[13] Again, we shall find that Erasmus' distaste for abstruse theorising by a self-appointed elite at the one extreme was balanced by awareness of the dangers of expecting (or permitting?) all and sundry to debate theological issues at however vulgar a level. All this, as more than one of his contemporary critics pointed out, begs the question of his own authority for the reassessment of theology upon which Erasmus had embarked. In general terms the normal trinity of authoritative sources – the Scriptures, the Fathers and the Church – was accepted by him. But we shall find that each of these, in turn, was subject to qualification. Certainly, to the essential interpretation of these sources, Erasmus made his own distinctive contribution. In his seminal study, *Erasmus. His Theology of the Sacraments*, John B. Payne points to the very personal combination of faith and reason which distinguishes his approach. While faith alone is capable of grasping matters of ultimate mystery, the use of reason is permissible after the establishment of a firm foundation of faith; and in such establishment Erasmus' 'critical tool was not so much logic as philology and historical criticism'.[14] Above all, the *speculative* use of reason is as dangerous as it is time-wasting. Indeed, one plausible suggestion relates Erasmus' 'deep distrust of intellectual subtlety' directly to his background of the Brethren of the Common Life.[15]

In respect of the *sources* of religious truth there can be no doubt that Erasmus accorded Holy Scripture primacy of place. 'What I read in Sacred Scripture and the creed called the Apostles' I believe with complete confidence, nor do I reach further. The rest I leave to theologians to dispute and define if they wish. But if something commonly accepted by Christians is not clearly at variance with Sacred Scripture, I observe it to the extent of not offending anyone.'[16] Yet not only was Erasmus' own interpretation of this primary authority significant,[17] but within the Holy Scriptures themselves all were not equal. Payne suggests Isaiah as favourite in the Old Testament, and Matthew, Romans and Corinthians in the new.[18] Nevertheless, the *vital* distinction, which says much both for Erasmus' intellect and for his courage, lay *between* the Testaments. Nothing could be more explicit than the declaration which he made in a letter to Wolfgang Capito in March, 1518: 'If only the church of Christians did not attach so much importance to the Old Testament! It is a thing of shadows, *given us for a time* [our italics]; and now it is almost preferred to the literature of Christianity. Somehow or other we are all the time turning away from Christ, who was enough for us, all by himself.' Assuredly, for Erasmus, 'the centre of gravity lies in the Gospels, where the *philosophia Christi* is to be found in all its purity and simplicity'.[20]

Yet even at the heart of the Scriptures all is not always clear and simple. To make manifest to the minds and souls of men in words the real meaning of the spirit, elucidation and interpretation are often needed.[21] It has been suggested that sometimes Erasmus passed unperceived from emendation of the different versions to the correction of their contents.[22] And he was not always unperceived! Of course, he does not consign to the dust-bin of history some fifteen hundred years of Christian thought, yet here again the application of reason establishes an order of priority. In general, the more ancient the authority of the Church Fathers the greater the credibility, if only because of proximity to the sources themselves. Among the ancients, Origen, Erasmus' favourite, stood out among the Greeks, and Jerome amidst the Latins.[23]

While Erasmus' opinions about the relative merits of the Fathers aroused disquiet, his openly expressed contempt for much of the work and the apparent objectives of the later scholastics evoked a spluttering rage.[24] Although he conceded that they were not always wrong, he viewed their efforts as being devoted to the construction of a vast inverted pyramid of chop-logic and irrelevance, tottering upon a minimal apex of scriptural knowledge and of Christian faith. In his eyes their barbarous Latin and ignorance of good letters were accompanied not only by an intellectual arrogance as individuals but also by their general over-estimate of the power of the human mind to penetrate divine mysteries, which was as repellent as it was presumptuous.[25]

Predictably, Erasmus' acceptance of the authority of the Church in matters theological was not unqualified. Probably he rated General Councils as superior to the ancient *doctores* and inferior only to the authority of the Scriptures.[26] Yet even here he was at best luke-warm about recent conciliar pronouncements which he did not consider to be grounded upon Holy Writ. Most notable in this respect is Erasmus' concept of the Church itself, which he does *not* equate with the sacerdotal hierarchy alone. In *Sileni Alcibiadis* (1515) he parts company with those who 'call the priests, bishops and popes "the Church", when in reality they are only the servants of the Church. The Church is the whole Christian people, and Christ himself says it is too great to lie down before the bishops who serve it.'[27] Its supreme authority resided therefore not in the decisions of the Roman See but in the consensus of all Christian believers. Indeed some years later, when his position was under constant attack from several directions, he wrote to his old friend Willibald Pirckheimer that he equated the authority of the Church with the 'consensus of all Christian people'.[28] The contention that he thought of the Church primarily not as a hierarchical institution but rather as a community of believers,[29] should perhaps be set alongside the severer assertion that Erasmus 'adhered to the consensus only on theological matters which he considered insoluble or inconsequential'.[30]

Perhaps a cynic would say that Erasmus adhered rigorously only to a position which would give him maximum room for manoeuvre, but this would not be wholly fair. For when we attempt to define the general characteristics of his theology we shall find the notion of consensus combined with an explicit recognition of the concept of *adiaphora*: a belief that some doctrinal issues were *not* crucial for salvation. Indeed one may hardly escape the irony of the contrast between the barbed thrusts of Erasmus' reed quill directed at his theological detractors, and the pattern of gentle tolerance which he outlined in respect of Christian doctrine itself. Thus Albert Rabil has suggested that for Erasmus theology leads not to a systematic intellectual formulation but to a life directed toward religious ends, so that his *Paraphrases* of the New Testament were no academic exercise but an instrument of religious reform by a Christian humanist.[31] Hence the adoption of an allegorical method in order to establish the direct relevance of Scripture to the lives of ordinary Christians. Indeed, Preserved Smith concludes that, as 'a child of the Renaissance, abstract divinity left Erasmus cold'.[32] The notion of relevancy on the one hand, and the concession of *adiaphora* in order to maintain a Christian consensus upon the essential and inner basis of the faith on the other, were distinctive features of Erasmus' whole approach to theology.

The core of his own theology is a belief that the application of reason to the message of the Scriptures will produce a truth which is relatively simple and capable of being grasped by faith alone. And such faith must include reverence for divine majesty and mystery, avoiding impious curiosity or dangerous audacity in a clear recognition that, if the essence of things natural may not fully be comprehended by the human mind, how much farther beyond its grasp must the essence of the divine extend? The concluding sentence of à Kempis' *Imitation of Christ* would seem to apply: 'If the works of God were such that they might be easily comprehended by human reason, they could not be justly called marvellous or unspeakable.'[33] All this emerges very clearly in a letter written (1519) to Jan Slechta[34] in which Erasmus advocates a readiness

> not to define everything over a wide field in the way we should willingly think appropriate for the subject-matter of the faith, but only such things as are clearly laid down in the Holy Writ or without which the system of our salvation cannot stand. For this a few truths are enough, and the multitude are more easily persuaded of their truth if they are few . . . The whole of the Christian philosophy lies in this, our understanding that all our hope is placed in God, who freely gives us all things through Jesus his son, that we were redeemed by his death and engrafted through baptism with his body, that we might be dead to the desires of this world and live by his teaching and example.[35]

To Jean de Carondelet, in 1523, Erasmus asserts that 'the sum and substance of our religion is peace and concord. This can hardly remain the case unless we define as few matters as possible and leave each individual's judgment free on many questions.' Addressing Albert of Brandenburg a few months later, he deplores the havoc wrought by contemporary wrangling. What is our religion worth if it destroys peace? Better to cultivate the joyous fruits of the simple Gospel spirit than to indulge in theological squabbles.[36] Barely eighteen months before his death, Erasmus pleads with Pope Paul III for a tolerant approach as conducive to tranquillity. In particular 'definition of dogma should be reserved for a synod', which itself must pronounce only on those opinions upon which Christianity is indissolubly based. For 'just as variations in ceremony do not tear asunder the concord of the Church, so are there opinions on which it is permitted to disagree, Christian peace remaining unscathed.'[37]

Modern scholars agree in identifying Erasmus' Christocentric piety as the key to his theology. 'Christocentric' in that everything is related not only to personal adoration of Christ but also and more particularly to his teachings in the New Testament and to the precepts and example set for the conduct of life within this world as preparation for the next. Yet one of the principal charges levelled at him by contemporary assailants was that of guilt of the Arian heresy in his alleged denial of the divinity of Christ.[38] One recent study, echoing the verdict of Colet on Erasmus' edition of the New Testament as a crowning achievement, goes on to assert that 'it is Erasmus' picture of Christ that gives content to his notion of the spiritual worship of God'.[39] Yet another, equally emphatic about the New Testament, and especially the Gospels, as providing the basis of Erasmus' philosophy of Christ, rebuts any charge of Arianism but does concede the presence in his Christology of elements which might invite it.[40] Erasmus insisted upon the full humanity of Christ, and upon his role as a model for and a teacher of mankind. At one point in the *Enchiridion* he seems to come close to a simple identification between Christ as such a model and the content of his teaching. Such things opened the door to his opponents' gleeful charge of Arianism. A composition by Erasmus for the boys of Colet's school concluded with the injunction: 'Better to adore than to seek to explain . . . Strive, my dear boys, to sit at the feet of Jesus the teacher.'[41] Another aspect of his insistence upon Christ's humanity emerges in the exchange (1499) between him and Colet when debating the significance of the prayer in the garden of Gethsemane: 'Father, let this cup pass from me . . .' Disappointed that his friend should reproach him for implied agreement with those contemporaries who 'by their stammering, foul, and squalid style of writing . . . render unattractive that great queen of all sciences, theology', he none the less insists that the obvious meaning is correct, and that Christ's human nature was at that moment shrinking from the agony of the Crucifixion.[42]

The reminder of Kohls that Erasmus' oft-cited Christocentricity must always be seen against the background of his Trinitarian view of God[43] points us toward this wider subject. Let it at once be said that to many minds there seems to be a world of difference between Erasmus' God and the Deity envisaged by John Calvin. On the inter-related questions of divine foreknowledge and omnipotence and of human responsibility, predestination, and free will, one has encountered the provocative suggestion that 'Erasmus would rather curtail omnipotence than undercut the religious foundation of the Christian ethic' and that in respect of predestination Erasmus, untrammelled by logic, branded the doctrine as simply monstrous.[44] Certainly his reluctance to accept a rigorous doctrine of justification by faith alone did not reflect any failure to grasp that this must involve predestination![45]

Inevitably questions were posed about Erasmus' opinions on the Trinity. For despite his general endorsement of à Kempis' query, 'what will it avail thee to dispute profoundly of the Trinity, if thou be void of humility?',[46] he was by no means unwilling to question alleged scriptural authority for Trinitarian doctrines. His *bête noire*, Edward Lee, seized upon the omission from the first edition of his New Testament (1516) of the verse (I John, 5:7) traditionally adduced to support the concept of the Trinity as three in one, as clear proof of Arian heresy.[47] This was denied by Erasmus, who declared that pious worship and adoration of the Trinity were more fitting than pseudo-intellectual attempts to pry into its mystery. None the less, even light-hearted sallies fuelled the rage of his opponents. One of his *Colloquies* depicts an urgent Gospeller who, encountering a Franciscan critic of Erasmus, gives him absolution by banging him on the head three times with Erasmus' New Testament, thus 'raising three lumps, in the name of the Father, Son and Holy Ghost'.[48]

Erasmus' opinions on redemption, grace, justification, and free will lie at the heart of our later discussion of his breach with Luther. But, important as these are, Erasmus discusses other theological issues more often. Most notably, these concern his views about the sacraments, ideally those instituted by Christ himself or at least with a basis in the Scriptures and the Early Fathers rather than in later and questionable accretions. The distinction noted earlier between the letter and the spirit influenced his views on the Eucharist, Confession, and Baptism. There is no mistaking Erasmus' distaste for a formalistic and pseudo-mechanical sacramentalism. Indeed it has been suggested that sometimes his insistence upon the necessity for a spiritual as against a merely physical participation suggests a tendency toward complete spiritualism, totally discounting things physical.[49] But Erasmus always avoided this, and disavowed any imputation of wishing to strip the priesthood of its sacramental role. He accepted all the seven sacraments, but as efficacious only within the context of the *philosophia Christi*.[50]

The Godly Feast (1522) puts his case against 'Judaic ritualism' with a typically light but most effective touch. 'If you observe the great majority of Christians, isn't it true that their main reliance in life is on ceremonies?' How scrupulously are the ancient rites of the Church performed in baptism? Thereafter,

> the child is called a Christian – and is one after a fashion. Soon he's anointed again, finally he learns to confess, takes Communion, becomes accustomed to keeping quiet on holy days, to hearing divine service, to fasting at times, to abstaining from meat. And if he does these things, he's considered a Christian beyond question. He marries – and receives another sacrament. He takes orders – and is once more anointed and consecrated; his clothes are changed, prayers are said. All this I approve of, but their doing it from custom rather than from conviction I don't approve of. The notion that

> nothing else is needed for Christianity I reject absolutely, since a large part of mankind, while trusting to these things, loses no time in making money by hook or crook and becoming enslaved to anger, lust, gluttony, ambition, until at last they come to death's door. Here again ceremonics are ready. Confession is made over and over; extreme unction added; the Eucharist administered; sacred candles, a crucifix, holy water are at hand; indulgences produced . . .

Such ceremonies, sanctioned by ecclesiastical usage, are acceptable; 'yet there are also other, more interior means of helping us to depart from this life with cheerfulness and Christian trust'.[51]

Yet always Erasmus retained a careful balance. Thus, while never losing sight of his belief that real Christianity should shine through in the everyday lives of ordinary men – and in this sense he has been discerned as a champion of lay Christianity – he would have nothing to do with any purported concept of a 'priesthood of all believers'. On at least one occasion he characterised as plain insanity the notion that the laity should administer, as distinct from participating fully in, the sacraments. In so far as the sacraments were conducive to the Christian life, they must be administered by those holding holy orders within the Church.

In respect of Baptism, the first of the sacraments administered to Christians, Erasmus accepted and indeed emphasised its normally indispensable character. One authority places this sacrament at the very centre of Erasmus' theological beliefs, not only in the *Enchiridion* but as a crucial theme throughout all his theological writings.[52] In one sense this denotes his undeviating adherence to the framework of the Catholic Church, within which the ordinary mortal may hope to be led to salvation. But here again he eschews any merely external or automatic and physical operation of its power. Grace is received not through but *along with* the water in the ceremony. At the same time we shall find that (while always ready to accord a charitable recognition that they possessed certain good qualities) Erasmus was to oppose the teaching of the Anabaptists on this and on several other issues. His occasional reference to the possibility of an understanding is perhaps explained by his proposal, in the preface to his paraphrase of Matthew, that the rite of Baptism should be *re-enacted* at the age of puberty, when participants understood its significance. Thus it has been ingeniously suggested that Erasmus was the only genuinely professing *Ana*baptist in the sixteenth century![53]

As for Confirmation, or for that matter Extreme Unction, while not hostile toward either, he accords them little emphasis. On

Confession,[54] Erasmus' comments in his *Annotations* (1516) on Acts, 19:18, angered Lee, Zúñiga and the authors of the Valladolid Articles.[55] Nor were the orthodox reassured by his later references, including a passage (dated 1524) in which Erasmus remains unconvinced that Scripture establishes that the *rite* of Confession was instituted by Christ, and also by his balancing of nine advantages of Confession by nine disadvantages![56] He *was* quite certain that effective Confession required sincere contrition. He recognised that despite the need for a genuine moral transformation, in order to give real meaning to a Christian's life, even the sacrament of Baptism cannot quite eradicate the old Adam. This led him to concede the virtue of Penance, but this recognition most certainly did not extend to any endorsement of its perversion into a justification of Indulgences. Thus his translation, in his *New Testament* of 1516, of Jesus' injunction (Matthew, 4:17) to 'be penitent', rather than 'do penance', pleased Luther by its removal of any philological basis for the sacrament of Penance. Again in the *Annotations* of 1519 he introduced a scathing reference to the way in which genuine confession and penance were effectively ruined by the introduction of absolutions and dispensations.[57]

On the sacrament of Marriage, as perhaps might be expected against the background of his personal struggle for a number of years to be released from the restrictive orders of his early monastic years, Erasmus aired his own very challenging opinions. At one point he observed that Marriage, instituted by God himself, and sanctioned by Christ, could be honoured pre-eminently as first among the sacraments. Indeed, while some other sacraments were ordained as a remedy for fallen nature, this one was established as a fellowship in felicity within nature itself, as divinely constituted![58] One authority has gone so far as to describe Erasmus as 'a proponent of marriage over against sacerdotal and monastic celibacy'.[59] Certainly the colloquy *The Godly Feast* contains the even-handed verdict that 'some find the priesthood to their liking, some celibacy, some marriage . . . And in fact it often happens that . . . this man's marriage is more acceptable in the sight of God than the celibacy of many others.'[60] Yet despite (or arguably because of) this high estimate of the sacrament of Marriage, Erasmus argued for a liberalising of attitudes toward divorce. It may be fair to suggest that this was quite logical. If other sacraments were efficacious only if permeated by the right spirit within the participants, then surely this should apply to marriage? Hence the suggested paradox that the spiritualising of marriage could lead to its readier dissolution. At this point Erasmus might well argue that the admission of divorce in a relatively few exceptional cases would not harm the retention of marriage as a sacrament – any more than the occasional departure from monastic orders would impair their general validity. Finally in this context, it is not surprising that for numerous reasons Erasmus avoided potentially dangerous embroilment in perhaps the most notorious marital debate of his time, that of Henry VIII and Catherine.

There remains the question of the Eucharist, for most of Erasmus' contemporaries the most controversial sacrament of all. More than one biographer has observed that he himself wrote very little on this subject in his more formal works. Indeed, in August 1527 one George Thomas, a parish priest, regretted that, while all and sundry are publishing their views, 'you alone are silent'.[61] Yet, just as his correspondence of the early and middle 1520s is awash with the Lutheran tragedy, so that of the following decade is bespattered with discussions, at varying lengths, on the Eucharist. This became a crucial test-case of Catholic orthodoxy, entailing martyrdom, and it is not difficult to discern, alongside his innate and genuine wish for free debate, an increasing note of anxiety, sometimes of near-desperation, in Erasmus' attempts to establish and to defend his position as the years passed by and darkened.

One of his earliest dicta on the topic appears in a playful passage in a letter to Thomas More. Here the note of badinage, revealing much about their early relationship, stands in ironic contrast with the final tragedy. Apparently Erasmus failed to return, at least with sufficient promptitude, a horse which he had borrowed. In reply to a reminder of this he launched into Latin verse, which may loosely but not unfairly be rendered thus:

As you once said to me
About 'Corpus Christi',
'If you believe that you eat it,
You will do';
So I write back to you
About your palfrey too,
'If you think that you have it,
It's with you!'[62]

In his *Praise of Folly* Erasmus observes that 'the apostles consecrated the Eucharist with due piety, but had they been questioned about . . . transubstantiation, and how the same body can be in different places, about the difference between the body of Christ in heaven, on the cross, and at the sacrament of the Eucharist, about the exact moment when transubstantiation takes place . . . they wouldn't, in my opinion, have shown the same subtlety in their reply as the Scotists do'.[63] On this issue one may suggest a significant distinction between what Erasmus believed to be certain, what he considered a fitting subject for debate, and what he deemed it expedient to say – and to whom! One very full treatment of the subject deals in turn with his views on the institution and spiritual meaning of the Eucharist, on the issue of symbolism and the Real Presence, and finally on the authority of the Church.[64] But before relating these, and several other issues, to the evidence of Erasmus' own words, it is perhaps of crucial importance to emphasise straight away that his objections to a merely mechanical concept of the Mass derive not from his holding it in low esteem but from the precise reverse – a most exalted estimate.[65]

Discussing Christ's institution of the Eucharist in a letter to Hermann Busch[66] (1520) Erasmus recounts how one critic has taken him to task for coming dangerously near to heresy in his Scriptural Annotations of 1519. Specifically, he has expressed some doubt not on the judgment of the Church but on the precise wording and implication of Christ's own consecration of the bread and wine.[67] Almost a decade later, against a much more dangerous background, a letter to Justus Decius, secretary to King Sigismund of Poland, went further. Erasmus here asserts that 'nowhere can I find in Holy Scripture certain confirmation that the Apostles consecrated bread and wine into the body and blood of the Lord'. But he is careful to add: 'If you can do this, I greatly approve.'[68] Clearly these questions about the initial institution of the rite and any consequently transmitted power of consecration during the Mass, lead into the whole problem of its nature and meaning. By contemporary standards Erasmus' position here was anything but conventionally orthodox.[69] His approach has been related to his general emphasis on the flesh–spirit concept, and historians agree that a major focus of the Reformation in his native Holland concerned the spiritualising of the sacrament of the Lord's Table.

From at latest 1519 Erasmus' known leanings attracted not only critics but also those who wished to read into his words far more than he would ever openly concede, and who essayed to drag him into their camp. Writing to Melanchthon (1524) he mentions Carlstadt's teaching that only a 'sign' of the Lord's body and blood is present in the Eucharist.[70] In later correspondence he also cites Zwingli and

Oecolampadius on this question, comparing the way in which this error so speedily captivates men's minds with the pouring of naphtha upon flames.[71] Yet ironically Melanchthon himself declared that Erasmus' own opinions 'with respect to the sacrament of the altar would have given rise to much graver tumults had not Luther arisen to channel the zeal of men in another direction'.[72] By October 1525 Erasmus feels forced to react to a report that Conrad Pellican is stating openly that the interpretation of the Eucharist advanced by Carlstadt and adopted by Oecolampadius is now accepted by Erasmus himself. A lengthy disclaimer addressed to Pellican ends in Erasmus' dramatic and impassioned assertion that, sooner than concur that there is present in the Eucharist 'nothing but bread and wine, I would tear my limbs apart rather than profess what you avow'.[73] A further exchange of denials and counter-denials attests Erasmus' near-desperate attempt to distance himself from the Carlstadt-Oecolampadius-Zwingli camp.[74]

We now reach the point at which the reader may feel entitled to ask precisely what Erasmus *did* believe; but in so doing we also arrive at what the seeker for definition may well regard as a 'grey area'. For Erasmus now declares to his trusted friend Pirckheimer[75] that Oecolampadius' views on the Eucharist would not displease him were they not opposed to what is accepted by the Church. And while concurring that the body without the spirit can accomplish nothing, 'from the agreement of the Church I can not deviate, nor have ever deviated'.[76] Thus some questions must now be asked about Erasmus' views concerning, first, the definition of the Real Presence, and second, its effects upon the lay participants both individually and collectively. Writing (March 1529) to Ludwig Baer,[77] Erasmus appears to be unequivocal about Christ's presence in the Sacrament. For nothing will persuade him that for centuries the Church could have erred so abominably as to teach a mistaken adoration of what is merely a cake of flour. He therefore accepts the age-old judgment of the Church.[78] Yet such unquestioning compliance is not evident in a letter to Justus Decius a few months later. Rejecting any total abrogation of the Mass, Erasmus goes on to urge that, whether the body or the spirit of Christ is taken to be present, it is the divinity itself which is adored. Yet what is the populace to make of this? It would be easy to teach the people that nothing is present to be adored; for is it quite certain that the host becomes consecrated, if not sacrificed, by the rite?[79]

Our doubts are not assuaged by what is almost certainly Erasmus' fullest treatment of the question, in a letter of 1530 to Balthasar

Mercklin, Bishop of Hildesheim.[80] This was in effect the preface to a much older publication on the Mass. Among the points discussed are the problems of how and in what sense the body and blood of Christ become present during the Communion Service. While some deny anything to be present other than symbols of the Lord's body and blood, others believe that Christ is really present, but in the substance of bread and wine. Yet others assert that by the words of consecration the substance of the bread and wine perishes, to be replaced by the body and blood of the Lord. Clearly then, the Sacrament is surrounded by innumerable questions: in what way transubstantiation occurs, at what moment Christ's body and blood are created, and so forth. Erasmus goes on to maintain that 'it is enough *for the vulgar* [our italics] to believe that after consecration there is present the true body and blood of the Lord'. But what did he think? As for any sordid and criminal speculation about the physical implications and consequences involved, he insists that the Sacrament must be treated with reverence. For in short, over and against all human thoughts and scruples there stands the enormous power of God, a power to which nothing is impossible or difficult.[81]

Even in replying to so close a personal friend as Boniface Amerbach[82] – who complained bitterly in March 1532 of Oecolampadius' attempt to enforce attendance at his own version of the 'Last Supper' – Erasmus does not abandon his circumspection. Thus, 'of the truth of the Body of the Lord nothing is uncertain. Of the method of its presence it is permitted in a certain way to be uncertain', for on this the Church itself seems readier to debate than to pronounce, and it is assuredly wiser to follow the Church's guidance rather than that of laymen.[83] Confronted by this posture of resolute and reverent ambivalence, we may well conclude our attempt to define 'Erasmus on the Real Presence'. Yet another question is raised in the letter to the Bishop of Hildesheim cited above. If the Mass is indeed to be celebrated in the proper spirit, then any unseemly conduct by the participant is just as reprehensible as any by the celebrant.[84] Anxious as he was to avoid excessive definition on some issues, Erasmus was determined to enunciate quite specifically the role of the participant in the Eucharist. Just as he was content to rest upon his belief (expressed in a letter of 1530 to Andrew Cricius in Poland) in 'the true presence of the body and blood of Christ in the Eucharist', so he was at pains to demand the true presence thereat of the spirit of the Christian participant. To Erasmus this latter presence seems almost indeed to be the more important to establish.[85]

While Erasmus was notably cool toward any concept of the Mass as sacrificial, since the sacrifice of Christ upon the Cross was unique, he was eager to emphasise that in the mind of the participant that sacrifice was renewed. Together with this memorial aspect of the rite, which required that it be approached in the correct spirit, went the idea of communion between like-minded souls one with another. Alongside the suggestion that for Erasmus grace *accompanies*, but is not conveyed through, the act of physical participation in the Sacrament, and also – more provocatively – that he sees Eucharistic Grace as operating not so much sacramentally as psychologically, we meet what has been described as the 'synaxis conception' of the Lord's Supper as a coming together, a communion in love of fellow-Christians.[86]

Certainly, in Erasmus' general approach to the Sacrament of the Eucharist his vision of its potential spiritual importance far transcended any question of the mechanics of the ritual. However elaborate these might be, and whatever the degree of scholastic sophistication employed to explain and justify them, the participant who approached and ate 'unworthily' gained nothing for his soul's health. For this reason the pacifist Erasmus viewed with horror the spectacle of pre-combat Eucharist for those who were about to shed the blood of fellow-Christians. In this sense he may be credited with a genuinely exalted estimate of the function of the Mass, as demanding much of its participant instead of purveying mechanical magic.

In exploring Erasmus' views on this, the most crucial of the sacraments to contemporary eyes, we have identified 'grey areas'. A cynic might wonder whether the ostensibly submissive appeals of Erasmus to the age-old authority of the Church – to which, when dangerously pressed, he always withdrew – was in fact a decision to retreat to what was for him the safest grey area of all! Before dismissing this as too outrageous a paradox we should do well to recall that the doctrine of transubstantiation dated only from the thirteenth century.[87] Thus the 'age-old consensus of the Church' left some room for manoeuvre. Too much should not be made of this, and certainly as the years went by the sixteenth-century Catholic Church became progressively less and less of a refuge for any agile-minded adiaphorist. Within Erasmus' own era the execution of Berquin in Paris would have produced a tremor of apprehension even in a less timid soul, while by the mid-century he himself – or rather his books – found a place on the Index. Yet a persistent reading of his correspondence cannot fail to yield the impression that the 'judgment of the Church' was for him a refuge rather than a strait-jacket. It has been suggested that although the authority of the Church informs Erasmus' understanding of the Real Presence, it does not entail his acquiescence in that dogma.[88] It might perhaps with equal validity be contended that his general acquiescence in the dogma does not determine his *precise* understanding of any agreed meaning. In this context, Book IV of Thomas à Kempis conveys a spirit closely related to that of Erasmus, most notably in its emphasis upon reverence in preparation and participation and in its injunction 'That a Man should not be a Curious Searcher in the Holy Sacrament'.[89]

Few historians would ascribe to Erasmus a coherent and integrated theology, and as yet we shall not take final leave of this subject. Thus far we have tried to sketch his own positive expression of his opinions up to the mid-1520s but with occasional excursions into the following decade. Throughout that decade Erasmus was to find himself under siege from several directions. In the course of the following chapters we shall inevitably need to consider the grounds of contention, theological and otherwise, between Erasmus and Luther, Zwingli, Bucer and his Strassburg allies, the Radicals, and last but by no means least with his 'orthodox' Catholic critics. Although discussion of the Eucharist has unavoidably drawn us into this later period, in general we have as yet related his theology to the basic features of his scriptural studies and his 'philosophy of Christ'.

The touchstone applied by Erasmus in determining that philosophy seems to have been the application of right reason, impelled and directed by faith, to the scriptural evidence as accurately established by the scholarship of theology.[90] Thus, given his insistence upon the simple acceptance of the plain truths of Scripture, he did not scruple to question certain recently established dogmas which were not demonstrably grounded therein, notably transubstantiation, as distinct from the Real Presence more generally defined. Far more important to him was the relationship of theology to the moral life of the Christian. Finally, we should not leave this subject without reverting to the significance for Erasmus, and for many modern commentators' assessment of his distinctive contribution to religious history, of *adiaphora*. The concept plays an almost dominant role in his approach to doctrine, seeking to restrict rigorous definition as far as possible, leaving considerable freedom for each to follow his own judgment. Indeed, among the 'non-essentials', issues as important as any degree of precision about the theory of the Trinity, the omnipotence of God and the extent of papal authority, have been listed. Certainly, Erasmus was among the first to use the notion of *adiaphora* extensively in the interests of what would now be called religious liberty. Nor was this in any way opposed to Erasmus' emphasis upon the significance of *Mysterium* – defined as that realm which lies behind and beyond what is accessible to perceptive cognition by the mind of Man.[91]

REFORM OR REVOLUTION?

Six

'THIS LUTHERAN TRAGEDY . . .'

Essentially, this chapter will take up some of the fundamental issues encountered in our examination of Erasmus' theology. For in tracing the emergence of divergences between Erasmus' *philosophia Christi* and the Protestant Reformation, his clash with Luther is the first overt disagreement we shall encounter. Moreover, the purported subject of that clash has sometimes also been taken to symbolise a fundamental difference between the theology of 'Renaissance religion' or 'Christian humanism' on the one hand and that of Protestantism on the other. Yet any such identification or indeed dichotomy *tout court* must be questioned. First, because certain aspects of the Protestant Reformation, most specifically of the Radical Reformation, which went much further than Luther himself ever intended and which were disowned by him, may plausibly be traced directly back to Erasmus. Secondly, because many would apportion the reasons for the ultimate breach between the two men as much to mode of approach, to personality, and to the contingent influences upon them as to theology, while perhaps some sceptical modernists might discern a difference in *philosophy* as of really long-term significance.

Undoubtedly, in the context of any study of Erasmus, the clash with Luther must assume major importance. Our earlier chapters might be described as depicting the evolution and establishment of the religious philosophy and influence of 'Erasmus the Reformer'. Those which follow will outline the ever-widening consequences of the emergence of Lutheranism and of Erasmus' disavowal thereof, and might be characterised as portraying 'Erasmus under Siege' – and under siege indeed from several sides. Erasmus himself alludes to sustaining 'a threefold struggle – with those pagans of Rome, who wretchedly envy me; with certain theologians and monks, who leave no stone unturned to ruin me; with certain rabid Lutherans, who rage at me as alone, so they say, delaying their triumph'.[1] A cynic might suggest that ambivalence became a necessary condition of survival. Yet Erasmus maintains his position and his principles with total consistency in seeking at once to protect the *reformer* Luther from persecution by obscurantists, and the Christian Church itself from schism recklessly precipitated. Admittedly we shall find Erasmus under pressure to take action which is not always to his taste, and sometimes driven to understandable equivocation in the face of those who would over-state or distort his opinions. Nor is the pressure upon him to enter the arena the product of his own considerable vanity. For all too much evidence attests the appeals made to him to exercise leadership, but again in different directions! Perhaps supremely ironical is the appeal which was made to Erasmus at the time of the false rumour of Luther's death, in its clear assumption that the torch of Protestantism has in effect now fallen back into his hands.

The general agreement as to the debt owed by Luther to Erasmus for what have been succinctly termed 'the latest expository and exegetical tools',[2] is equalled by the consensus as to the genuine nature of their ultimate quarrel. Yet although open conflict was delayed until 1524–25 the first recorded contact between the two men, in December 1516, demonstrates a crucial realisation (at least by Luther) of a major theological disagreement. A letter to Erasmus from Spalatin, secretary to Luther's protector Duke Frederick, in effect hands on the views of Luther. Spalatin's 'Augustinian priest' conveys thus indirectly his reservations as to Erasmus' interpretation of St Paul in respect of 'justification by works', and indeed his advice that 'he should read Augustine in his treatise against the Pelagians'.[3] Erasmus did not reply. Already, points out Gordon Rupp, Luther had avowed that his own priority as between Jerome and Augustine was precisely the reverse of that of Erasmus.[4] By March of 1517 he had become ready to state that 'I am reading our Erasmus but daily I dislike him more and more . . . [fearing] that he does not advance the cause of Christ and the grace of God sufficiently . . . Human things weigh more with him than the divine . . . The discernment of one who attributes weight to man's will is different from that of him who knows of nothing else but grace.' Yet Luther will keep secret this opinion, lest he should strengthen the conspiracy of Erasmus' enemies, and also in the hope that God will give him true understanding.[5]

For his part, Erasmus seems determined to avoid acknowledgement of any doctrinal difference, although when forced at last to do so he will choose this very topic. For many years, when he skirts what one suspects he himself had long identified as a minefield, he seems content to erect warning notices as to the danger of blundering into a search for heresy. Consistently he deplores those who seek to lump together Luther and the humanities amid 'cries of Heresy! and Anti-Christ!' For 'all error is not heresy without more ado, nor does something instantly become heretical if this man or that disapproves of it'.[6] As late as August 1521, in a letter probably intended for the eyes of the future Pope Adrian, he expresses his resolve to 'refrain from laying down the law, for I would rather purvey good advice than dogma'. Yet he also confides that 'Luther's party sometimes attack me in their public lectures, and call me a Pelagian'.[7] This suspicion finds support from one or two more references in Luther's letters to the fact that, speaking as a theologian rather than a philologist, 'there are many things in Erasmus which seem to me to be completely incongruous with a knowledge of Christ', and to his perception 'that Erasmus was far from the knowledge of grace, since in all his writings he is not concerned for the cross but for peace'.[8]

Despite his alleged ambivalence, Erasmus seems always to have been clear as to the limits of his conditional approval of Luther – which he never withdrew. A friendly, even effusive letter from Luther himself, in March 1519, citing the remark of their mutual friend Capito 'that my name is known to you through the slight piece I wrote about indulgences', goes too far in adducing from Erasmus' recent preface to his *Enchiridion* 'that you have not only seen but approved the stuff I have written'.[9] Yet Erasmus' 'Letter to Paul Volz' indeed included a condemnatory reference to 'the profit of those who traffic in indulgences', and he later confided that Luther 'is approved by all the leading people . . . I imagine that his Conclusion satisfied everyone, except for a few of them on purgatory', who may lose income![10]

A long letter to Albert, Cardinal Archbishop of Brandenburg, Elector of Mainz – rightly described as 'a fundamental statement of Erasmus' views on the conflict' – points to the tyranny of the mendicant friars and to the overburdening of the world with man-made ordinances so that 'the spark of Christian piety, from which alone the spent fire of charity could be rekindled, would be finally put out', smothered by a more than Jewish ceremonial. Thus 'Luther has written much which is not so much irreligious as ill advised.'[11] Luther commended this 'magnificent letter' as protection by Erasmus 'in his usual skilful way, which is to defend me strongly while seeming not to defend me at all'![12] Elsewhere, Erasmus declares of Luther that 'I wish well to the good things in him, not the bad; more accurately, I wish well to Christ not to Luther. If I do answer him, it is to correct him', for Erasmus is neither prosecutor, counsel for the defence, nor judge.

Again, in May 1520, claiming to have stopped a projected burning of Lutheran books in England, he asserts that 'I am not the man to pass judgment on what Luther writes, but I cannot swallow this dictatorial procedure'.[13]

At this point the letter Erasmus sent to Luther himself on 30 May 1519 is worth more detailed treatment, as expressing most of his concerns. 'No words of mine could describe the storm raised here by your books, [including] the most groundless suspicions that your work is written with assistance from me [as] a standard-bearer of this new movement.' His enemies seize the chance to attack both him and humane studies, which they hate as detracting from Queen Theology, and a great part of Louvain University is afflicted by epidemic paranoia. While well aware that highly placed people in Germany think well of Luther's writings, Erasmus is resolved to keep himself uncommitted, 'in hopes of being able to do more for the revival of good literature. And I think we get further by courtesy and moderation than by clamour. That was how Christ brought the world under his sway. . . Things which are of such wide acceptance that they cannot be torn out of men's minds all at once should be met with argument, close-reasoned forcible argument, rather than bare assertion. Some people's poisonous propaganda is better ignored than refuted', though here Erasmus proved better at precept than example![14]

A year or so later a note of exasperation may be detected in the wish, expressed to Spalatin, 'that Christ Almighty may moderate Luther's pen and his mind in such a way that he may be the greatest benefit to the religion of the Gospel'. Yet soon afterwards, reiterating this sentiment, he still insists that it would be wrong now 'to leave him quite without support, or in the future no one will dare to speak the truth'.[15] Indeed, writing at length to no less a person than Lorenzo Campeggio, he avows that he has 'perceived that the higher a person's character and the nearer he came to the simplicity of the Gospel, the less opposed he was to Luther'. Admittedly, 'in his writings it was not long before I stumbled on something rude and harsh, which did not properly reflect the gentle spirit of the Gospel; and I warned him to take example by Christ and the Apostles', and not to attack the Roman pontiff and the majesty of princes. Yet still he has supported Luther up to the point of not wishing to see him handed over to the tender mercies of those who seize any pretext to undermine the humanities, for 'it must at least be more civilized to cure him than to snuff him out'.[16]

At this stage Erasmus certainly did not lack the courage of such convictions. Immediately after an interview with Frederick, Luther's protector, at Cologne on 5 November 1520, he produced for his guidance what has been described as one of the last expressions of a truly pro-Lutheran stance. These *Axiomata* 'in behalf of the cause of Martin Luther, theologian', deplore the plots of men imbued with bitter hatred of letters, who mislead the Pope and procure a bull unworthy of the most gentle vicar of Christ, who lack credible academic or theological support, and whose hate-filled measures should be resisted. Since the world thirsts for the Gospel truth, and Luther seeks public debate, 'it seems to the advantage of the pope that this affair be settled by the mature deliberation of serious and impartial men'.[17] Alas, the cause of moderation was already as good as lost. Luther had already published *De Captivitate Babylonica* in October, and proceeded in December to a public burning of the papal bull *Exsurge Domine*.

Thus Erasmus expresses with equal frequency his reservations as to the expediency of Luther's approach, deriving largely from his dislike of 'uproar' which follows such a head-on assault. Despite his early criticism of Luther's attacks and his 'wish they had been as happily expressed as they were outspoken'[18] the clamour on either side increased. In February 1520 Erasmus warned that 'this witch-hunt they are starting is both foolish and dangerous; they will realize later that what I am supporting is not Luther but the peace of Christendom. No matter what Luther has written, no intelligent person can be happy with the present uproar.' To a variety of correspondents throughout 1520 he confides the wish that Luther's views had been 'more courteously and moderately expressed. But it is too late to tell him so now. I can see that they are heading towards civil strife.'[19] Erasmus is 'filled with forebodings about that wretched Luther . . . If only he had followed my advice and refrained from that offensive and seditious stuff!' But sadly, 'even if every word Luther wrote was true, he has written in such a way as to prevent the truth from doing any good', and by now he 'writes more ferociously, they tell me, every day'. Despite an admixture in his books of much that is worth reading with some things that would have been better left out, 'the whole is too bitter in tone, not to say revolutionary'.[20] This vein persists in 1521: 'Luther is piling on both liberal studies and myself a massive load of unpopularity. . . Oh, if that man had either left things alone, or made his attempt more cautiously and in moderation!' In particular his *De Captivitate Babylonica* has alienated many: this is doubly regrettable, for if he exercised restraint he would owe a great deal to the stupidity of his enemies. Again writing to Spalatin, Erasmus claims that he had always foreseen this outcome 'when I saw Luther taking on so many things at once, and with such ferocity. It was better to put up with what was wrong than try to mend it so clumsily.'[21]

Such disapproval becomes increasingly shot through with apprehension. Writing to an English friend, Erasmus declares plainly that 'mine was never the spirit to risk my life for the truth. Not everyone has the strength needed for martyrdom.'[22] Yet in fairness his fears of the consequences of Luther's approach and of the equally violent overreaction of his opponents were not merely personal but directed also to liberal studies and, more importantly, to the cause of the Church and of Christianity itself. Early on, he identifies 'an extraordinary conspiracy of those who hate more liberal studies'. This conviction that a plot exists to associate Luther, Reuchlin, himself and the humanities in one vast purge becomes a major theme in his correspondence. Genuine concern had at first been awakened by the very painful example of successive attempts to prosecute 'the supreme glory and shining light and ornament of the whole of Germany', the eminent linguist Reuchlin.[23] Erasmus' letters amply attest not only reciprocated esteem but also his dread of 'virulent personal attacks': 'I am no "Reuchlinist". I belong to no man's party and detest these factious labels.'[24] To Reuchlin himself he declared plainly in November 1520 that 'it has always been my aim to separate the question of Luther from your cause, which is also the cause of the humanities, because the confusion exposed us equally to the risk of sharing his unpopularity and did not assist him in the least.'[25] But in the same month the much more combative Ulrich von Hutten, also at one stage an admirer of Erasmus, asserted roundly that 'they have burnt Luther's books; do you think you can stay in peace where you are – as though his condemnation were not a precedent in your own case? . . . Escape, man, escape!'[26] Hutten had already started to discern in Erasmus' efforts to remain outside the arena nothing but time-serving hypocrisy, and after Reuchlin's death in 1522 was to publish against Erasmus his *Expostulatio*.

Not surprisingly, Erasmus was increasingly concerned to define and defend his own position, and to fend off charges of at best complicity in heresy from the one side and of timid or even cowardly equivocation from the other. One loses count of the number of times he takes refuge in the pretence that he has not read Luther's books – except to leaf through them or sample snatches![27] Wolsey may well have recognised an Erasmian variant of Morton's Fork in the letter which protested that 'if what he has written is right, none of the credit is mine; if not, I deserve no blame, for in all his work not a jot anywhere belongs to me'.[28] To Albert of Mainz, Erasmus is indignant that, after trying to prevent publication of some of Luther's work and urging its author to proceed with all mildness, 'these words have been read by some blockheads to mean that I supported Luther'.[29] His letters contain some striking vignettes of a couple of these blockheads. Pre-eminent perhaps is the Louvain theologian Egmond (Nicolaas Baechem), whose heart is as black as his garb is white, who insulted him to his face in a public address, but equally engaging is the picture of the opponent 'blear-eyed with drink, who ranted before the public whole hours at a time against Luther and myself, calling us beasts, donkeys, storks, and blockheads', not having read Erasmus but identifying his lofty Latin as a certain camouflage for heresy![30]

Much more dangerous of course were such people as Aleander, who is described as a good scholar 'but made, it is clear, for troubles of this kind. He has burnt several of Luther's books . . . They are as indignant with me as they are with Luther himself, supposing me the only obstacle which prevents Luther's complete and universal destruction.'[31] Despite Aleander's denials of any enmity, he is indeed on record as asserting that 'I have long known that Erasmus is the source of all this evil . . . He is the corner-stone of this heresy.'[32] Understandably, we find Erasmus assuring Rosemondt, Moderator of Louvain University, that his arguments against Luther have always received his support.[33] Likewise to Lorenzo Campeggio he claims that he had been the very first to look at Luther's work with suspicion, lest it breed discord, and again cites his opposition to its printing in Basel. For above all, he tells Campeggio, 'I have no intention to be a captain or coadjutor in civil strife. Let others court martyrdom; it is an honour of which I find myself unworthy.'[34] By March 1521 the name of Cardinal Cajetan – who was later to show respect for Erasmus – is linked with that of Aleander, 'obviously a maniac, a wicked, stupid man', as malignant influences on papal policy. Erasmus even repeats the canard that in Paris several outspoken Lutherans 'have been put out of the way' by poison![35]

The approach of the Diet of Worms, attendance at which he deemed it prudent to avoid, made him eager to secure his position by protestations to Gattinara,[36] Aleander and others at the Imperial Court. To Bishop Luigi Marliano he explains that Luther's supporters have done all they can to lure him into their camp, and his persecutors to drive him there by raving more offensively than they do against Luther himself. But none of these tricks will shift Erasmus: 'Christ I recognize, Luther I know not; the church of Rome I recognize, and think it does not disagree with the Catholic church. From that church death shall not tear me asunder, unless the church is sundered openly from Christ.' The charge that Luther has drawn heavily on his books Erasmus considers a shameless invention.[37] Back from Worms came cordial reassurance from Gattinara to the chief luminary of liberal studies in Germany, who has 'employed all your labours and life itself in the glory and elucidation of the orthodox faith', but Marliano replied in cooler terms.[38] Meanwhile Erasmus had heard that a sermon before the French King had identified him as one of the forerunners of Anti-Christ.[39] By the summer of 1521, really worried that the campaign against him might reach a new crescendo, he despatched yet another apologia to the theologians of Louvain and invited them to scrutinise every word he has written or uttered, even 'light-heartedly over the wine'. He believed his enemies there to be engaged in a private vendetta against him, using as their tool Aleander, who was mad enough by nature, needing no encouragement.[40]

By March 1522, writing to his good friend Willibald Pirckheimer, he depicts how he was threatened by Luther's party with scandalous pamphlets, whereas 'the Emperor was nearly convinced that I was the fountain-head of all the trouble over Luther'. He thus finds himself 'in the splendid position of danger from both sides'. Yet, in a touch of wry humour, he wishes that 'Luther's people had published an attack on me two years ago: they would have delivered me from a load of ill-will'.[41] In March there came a special blast of such ill-will from the Spaniard Diego Lopez Zúñiga, then in Rome, describing him as 'openly siding with Arius, Apollinaris, and Jovinian, and also with the Wycliffites and the Hussites and indeed with Luther himself; for it was Erasmus and Erasmus alone who armed and equipped and trained Luther with these blasphemous notions of his . . .' Contemptuously, Zúñiga wished the northerners joy of their *Panerasmius*.[42]

The first real inkling of attacks from the Lutherans had come ironically enough from his friend Wolfgang Capito, already struggling to forge an alliance as early as April 1519. In a brief but unmistakable warning he advises Erasmus not to let the Louvain theologians deter him from supporting Luther: 'Better make enemies of all the theologians than of his supporters' – who include several princes and leading churchmen in Germany, where Erasmus is still revered.[43] But by 1521 Erasmus' chagrin at the erosion of old and valued friendships, as several humanists depart for the Lutheran camp, is increasingly mingled with anxiety at the virulence of attacks now coming from that quarter. A long appeal to Justus Jonas, deploring just such a defection, recalls his fear that all might end in uproar and split the world openly in two. Why has it been necessary for Luther 'to pile one cause of hatred on another? . . . Why need they so often mention my name in a tendentious way, when this was quite uncalled-for?' Most interestingly, he asks Jonas to put these points to Melanchthon and others like him, not wishing to see him carried off by this tempest, like Hutten. To avoid ruinous discord 'we need a sort of holy cunning; we must be time-servers, but without betraying the treasure of gospel truth from which our lost standards of public morality can be restored'.[44]

In October 1521 Capito writes again, increasing adhesion to Luther's doctrines not inhibiting his clear apprehension of the fact that his party are now 'crazier and more insolent and more self-assertive in everything . . . such is their public contempt for all brains except their own . . . I hope that in future they will be more respectful in their references to you. There is no declaration in which they do not criticize you when they are by themselves, and in public they set you up as the leader of their party in the most preposterous fashion!'[45] Thus, to Pirckheimer Erasmus laments that he is now a heretic to both sides: some still try to persuade the Emperor that he is leader of the rebels, for no better reason than his failure to publish against Luther, whose party in turn 'tear me to pieces as a Pelagian, because they think I give more weight than they do to free will'. After his friend writes back from Nuremberg to confirm this disapproval, Erasmus again protests that expert theologians can find nothing wrong in what he has said – unless it be incorrect to attribute anything, however slight, to free will.[46] To Jerome Glapion, a confessor to Charles V, he confides that no true Lutheran now wishes him well, but instead utters 'clamorous abuse, calling me a Pelagian and time-server instead of a herald of the gospel teaching'.[47]

In an exceptionally long letter of February 1523 sent to Marcus Laurinus, a close friend for some years, he again regrets the loss of many friendships, and then reverts to his own interpretation of 9 Romans, in which his allotment of a very small share of freedom of the will, following Origen and Jerome, had happened 'before Luther put out his opinion, or rather Wycliffe's, that whatever we do, whether good or bad, is a matter of absolute necessity'. He explains that his own interpretation derived from 'fear of opening a window for such a mortal form of sloth, which consists in everybody abandoning all efforts towards an improvement of life and doing just anything he takes a fancy to', having as yet no inkling that anyone had 'entirely abolished all the force of free will'. The lay reader may well feel that he is perhaps listening to a plain man's guide to theology, taken further by what follows concerning

> these insoluble problems about foreknowledge, about predestination by God, about human free will, about contingency of future events, in which I think it the best course not to spend too much anxious time, since this is an abyss no man can get to the bottom of. I would rather teach the doctrines that encourage us to try for the best in every way we can, while yet at the same time claiming no credit for ourselves, but leaving the judgment of everything to God, having developed perfect confidence in his goodness above all else.[48]

We are now on the verge of the crucial debate of 1524–25, yet first we must take note of what Erasmus rightly discerned as the wider issues of the 'Lutheran tragedy': its potential damage to the Church, including the Papacy, to the cause of truth, and to Christianity itself. His not entirely consistent amalgam of hopes and fears had in May 1519 been set forth for Johann Lang, Vicar of the Augustinians:

> The best men all support Luther's idea of liberty; his wisdom, I do not doubt, will ensure that the affair does not issue in discord and rupture. I believe our objective should be to implant Christ in the hearts of men, rather than to fight in the arena with men who wear the mask of Christians, from whom glory or victory will never be won until the tyranny of the Roman See has been abolished, and its hangers-on, Preachers, Carmelites, Minorites – I mean of course the bad ones. I do not see how such an attempt is to be made without grave disorders.[49]

Certainly Erasmus was to modify his views about the Papacy on the one hand and about Luther's wisdom on the other, but he never wavered in his basic objective. Occasionally he expressed more mundane forebodings: while some indeed had no ulterior motive, others saw only a chance to covet the worldly wealth of churchmen: 'and it would be a pretty service to mankind to rob priests impiously of their property in order that military men may put it to worse uses'. Uncharacteristically, another aspect is also regretted: 'Luther in this torrent of pamphlets has poured it all out at once, making everything public and giving even cobblers a share in what is normally handled by scholars as mysteries.'[50] This sentiment seems uncomfortably reminiscent of Henry VIII.

More fundamentally, he confides to Warham his fear that 'we shall escape this Scylla only to fall into some more disastrous Charybdis. If those who will stick at nothing to be bullies with full bellies win the day, nothing remains but to write R.I.P for Christ, who dies to rise no more. Farewell to the last spark of gospel charity, farewell to the twinkling light of the gospel star . . .' To Pirckheimer he alike confides that Luther's mistaken tactics and increased asperity 'have opened a great rift which divides the world everywhere, which will last maybe for many years and get steadily worse. In return for a clumsy attempt at liberty slavery is redoubled.'[51] As late as March 1523, writing to Spalatin, he deplores Luther's arrogance and the venom of his followers, yet insists that 'if Luther were to be overthrown, no god or man would ever again be able to deal with the monks'.[52]

Erasmus' claim to have enjoined prudence almost from the outset is justified. As early as July 1519, writing to Albert of Mainz, he employed the image of the smoking flax and bruised reed in expressing the wish to see Luther's heart, 'which does appear to have some glowing sparks of the gospel teaching, not overwhelmed but set right'.[53] To Luther himself, in August 1520, he sent a long letter which disclaimed any intent to oppose his teaching, lest it is inspired by the spirit of Christ, yet he also expressed the desire, on behalf of all who wished Luther well, that he had written some things with more prudence and moderation.[54] What is quite clear is that purblind repression is counter-productive. Erasmus' 'only object is to have Luther dealt with on moderate principles rather than with violence and cruelty . . . The burning of his books will perhaps banish Luther from our libraries; whether he can be plucked out of men's hearts, I am not so sure.' Luther may well show crass folly in much of what he writes, but the tactics of his opponents are sometimes so stupid that one might suspect them of collusion with him! Little has done more to endear him to the people than the savagery and uproar of those who rant against him, thus persuading more people to read his books.[55]

Amid the deteriorating atmosphere of 1523 Erasmus still declares that 'I dismiss no one from my friendship if he is a little over-inclined towards Luther, nor will I renounce the friendship of anyone if he is more than normally hostile to Luther, since each acts as he does from honest conviction'.[56] Two years earlier he had rightly claimed, to Ludwig Baer, that 'I did my best, when I was in Cologne, to arrange that Luther should earn credit for obedience and the pope for clemency, and there were certain monarchs who thought well of the idea'. But alas, Luther had burnt the decretals, put forth his *De Captivitate Babylonica*, and made the evil appear incurable. None the less, if we pursue the medical image, Erasmus remains convinced that 'reliable physicians do not take refuge at the outset in their ultimate remedies [but] adjust the dose to cure and not to overwhelm'.[57]

In so far as Erasmus has any positive proposals to make for dealing with what he once called 'this evil monster in such a way that it does not grow afresh hydra-headed', they centred upon his favourite notion of arbitration and negotiation. As early as November 1520 he expressed support for Faber's plan 'to commit the whole question to arbitration by some learned and upright men'. This, with more optimism than realism, he hoped Pope Leo might perceive as the road to peace.[58] He was later to repeat the idea that 'if learned men had once pooled their ideas and submitted sealed opinions to the leaders of both church and state on the things they judged to pertain to the gospel-teaching in its purity, I might perhaps have been one of them'. Better this than scandalous pamphlets and lunatic uproar.[59] In default of such an opportunity, in March 1523 he despatched to Pope Adrian VI all that is extant of any such plan which he evolved. Risking papal wrath by pointing to the range and depth of penetration of support of Luther and hatred of the Papacy, and by demurring at invitations to come to Rome 'or write some really savage attacks on Luther', he goes on to state that in his opinion severity 'has long been a mistake. For I see more danger than I could wish that this business will end in appalling bloodshed. I am not discussing now what they deserve, but what is best for the public peace. This cancer has gone too far to be curable by the knife or cautery.' In former times, admittedly, the Wycliffite party had been suppressed in England; but it was suppressed, not extinguished, while what was then practicable in a realm subject to one man may hardly now be feasible in a vast area divided among so many princes. After repeating the idea of calling together influential and humanely minded men, the copy of this epistle breaks off.[60]

This is indeed symbolic, for by now the breach between Rome and Luther was quite irreparable. It only remained for Erasmus to face, with increasing desperation, what had now become peremptory demands that he should declare his allegiance in public. In January 1521 Sadoleto, conveying on behalf of Pope Leo a restoration of his affectionate regard, does not miss the chance to observe that 'never was the time more opportune or the cause more just for setting your erudition and your powers of mind against the impious'.[61] Paolo Bombace spoke more bluntly: if Erasmus enjoys the Pope's goodwill while saying 'nothing in defence of his just and holy cause, what result might you not expect if you were to take up arms and do battle vigorously?' This was only what most people expected, 'as though those monsters had been provided by some destiny for you alone as a road to greatness and immortality'.[62] Replying to a plea from his long-time patron Lord Mountjoy, Erasmus disclaims that 'it was in my power to bring all this discord to an end', but promises that, his other work permitting, he may attempt something conciliatory.[63] He later repeats this partial resolve upon a healing publication. But alas by March 1522, although now safely domiciled in Basel, he confides to Pirckheimer that 'I had decided to write something not against Luther but about steps towards peace', but that both sides are now so angry that it is better to keep quiet![64] To Jean Glapion, confessor to Charles V, he gives a somewhat different account: 'I had already made a fair start with a short treatise on how to end this business of Luther; but ill health has interrupted all my work.'[65] Perhaps the best of his repertoire of evasions is the promise to Warham that, as an essential preliminary to satisfying all these urgent requests, 'I shall devote myself to reading all the works of Luther and his opponents. It is a task not to be lightly undertaken.'[66]

The number of princes and potentates who, as he claimed, tried to compel him to write against Luther grew longer, including Duke George of Saxony and Pope Adrian, who repeated his concern for Erasmus' reputation with an indication of a task reserved especially by God.[67] Erasmus' reluctance infuriated Duke George, who on 23 January 1523 rebuked him: 'that you should be so anxious to evade the task of writing against Luther and should decline to do so does not at all surprise us, now that we have learned that you find so many good things in what he writes'.[68] But in a letter to Laurinus, written in February, Erasmus refers to an even more persuasive turn of the screw. He explains his failure to attend the Diet of Worms, to which he was invited, by his reluctance to become closely involved and by his fear 'that the task of doing battle with Luther's party might be entrusted to me by a personage to whom it would have been unlawful to say no . . .' For the Emperor Charles 'had been persuaded by men in high places, but wrongly, that I was above all the ideal person to undertake the task'.[69]

Amidst a train of events which begins to suggest a remorseless inevitability, it was apparently the knowledge of the letter to Laurinus that later triggered off Hutten's *Expostulatio*, with its consequences. Meanwhile the welter of correspondence attesting pressures for an unequivocal declaration against Luther includes a batch to and from England. P. S. Allen remarked on the firmness with which Erasmus maintained his mediating attitude against the suasion of his patrons across the Channel. But now Tunstall, Bishop of London, speaks plainly of Erasmus clearing his own reputation[70] – indeed one scholar attributes to Tunstall the suggestion of the theme of Free Will[71] – while the shorter of two letters sent to Henry VIII by Erasmus (September 1523) contains a specific allusion to 'attempting something against the new dogmas', and a later reference appears to link that monarch with the title *De libero arbitrio.*[72] During the summer of 1523 Erasmus was disturbed by news of Lutheran martyrdoms in Paris and by the appearance of Hutten's *Expostulatio*, which accused him unequivocally of selling out on his principles. Perhaps he was cheered by the fact that Charles V gave orders to resume payment of his imperial pension, which had ceased when he left Louvain.[73] On 19 July he complained to Pirckheimer of Hutten's attack[74] and within a month was writing a reply, his *Spongia* ('Sponge against Hutten's Aspersions'), which first appeared in September.

This has been seen as directed not merely at Hutten but to the whole Lutheran party one printing is specifically addressed to Ulrich Zwingli, and indeed some passages present a general apologia for Erasmus' position. The first pages are mainly devoted to a review of recent events – including the vexed point that when 'Hutten came to Basel, he was not admitted to our company'.[75] The Basel October edition makes it clear that his adversary's death must not deflect Erasmus from the need to wipe away the charges made.[76] Oh that Hutten had conducted himself in a different way! His opponents' strictures, and Erasmus' attitude to Reuchlin, are rehearsed, while he even feels constrained to explain his former friendship in Venice with Aleander, an admirably erudite man, long before Luther was heard of![77] Yet more generally significant are the later passages in which Erasmus justifies his stance toward Luther in the context of contemporary religious problems. Above all, he declares, 'I love liberty. I will not and cannot be devoted to any faction . . .' He has never condemned Luther, but would wish to find in his writings a modest and gentle Gospel spirit. Most significantly, Lutheran doctrine cannot be totally opposed – for when Luther teaches aright it is not he but Christ who speaks. Erasmus challenges his critics to cite from his writing one harsh word against Luther: 'I mention no heresies nor heretics: I speak of tragedy, of discord and tumult . . .'[78]

As for Rome, whilst deploring tyranny and rapacity, Erasmus has not condemned indulgences *in toto*, although he detests their impudent peddling. On ceremonies in general, his books attest his views: where has he excoriated Canon Law and the Pontificate? Despite a multitude of wrongs, without the Papacy we have no Church. What boots it then to write of an 'Impious Antichrist, destroyer of the Gospels, oppressor of public liberty, fawner on Princes', and so forth?[79] Accordingly, 'for Luther and for Luther's paradoxes I am not disposed to perish. It concerns not articles of faith, but whether the pre-eminence of the Roman Pontiff is of Christ . . . whether Christ instituted Confession . . . whether free will contributes to salvation: whether any work of man can be called good: whether the Mass for any reason may be called a sacrifice.' These should be themes for scholastic debate, not matters of life and death. Thus, once more, 'to be a martyr for Christ is desirable if one is equal to it, a martyr for Luther I do not wish to be'.[80]

By 21 November 1523 Erasmus is able to write to John Faber, informing him not only of the issue of 3000 copies of his *Spongia*, which angers Luther, but also of the fact that, given strength, the book *De libero arbitrio* will be added to it – though the work is not finished and Faber's prudence is appealed to.[81] During the many months of 1524 before that work's appearance – reflecting, surely, indecision and anxiety rather than any difficulty with content – Erasmus continues his fending off of criticism from both sides, while letting others know of the task now in hand. To Bombace at Bologna he complains that while in Rome there are still those who label him Lutheran, in Germany itself he is now 'Antilutheranissimus', while letters to Campeggio liken his campaign against Luther to tackling a hydra with many heads, while a crab (Stunica?) creeps up and bites one's foot. They also cite the King of England as pre-eminent in encouraging his work.[82] In February he informs Pope Clement himself of the 'book now in hand, *De libero arbitrio*, against Luther', and in the following month he despatched a first draft of the work, 'not yet finished', to Henry VIII, together with the caveat that finding a printer in Basel may not be easy.[83]

Against such a background, what are we to make of the appearance in print of one of Erasmus' most famous Colloquies, the *Inquisitio de fide* ('Examination Concerning Faith'), in March 1524? Here, under the guise of an amiable combination of inquisition and exposition of the Apostles' Creed, Aulus the Catholic (Erasmus) and Barbatius (a Lutheran who speaks with a rather Erasmian voice) discover that on many basic essentials of the Christian faith there is very little if any difference between them. Yet the whole approach is adiaphoristic, and such crucial issues as the freedom of the will, justification by faith alone, papal authority and indulgences are virtually ignored, or at best circumvented. True, Aulus catechises Barbatius and finds him guilty of no fundamental error, but there is surely little doubt that both a papist and a rabid Lutheran would argue that what is acquitted can only be described as a very Erasmian version of Lutheranism. Given Erasmus' knowledge, first, that Luther's challenge to papal authority had made the breach irreparable, and second, that the complex issue of free will and grace, which Luther had long perceived as crucial, had already become the subject of a well-advanced draft of his *De libero arbitrio*, one wonders what was now to be achieved by publishing a colloquy which avoided such problems.

Unless its publication was unduly delayed, its actual composition would appear to have taken place alongside that of *De libero arbitrio*. Thus Craig Thompson suggests that the *Inquisitio de fide* should be regarded 'as a sort of final, regretful statement of what might have been' had his counsels of irenic moderation been listened to. Yet again, should we interpret it as a declaration by Erasmus, before he entered the lists, that agreement between Catholics and Lutherans on so many of the fundamental articles of Christianity was so broad that the issue on which he was soon to joust in the Catholic cause was really a matter of indifference? Alternatively it could be argued that the publication of the *Inquisitio* makes most sense when viewed not in the context of the steadily worsening relations between Erasmus and Luther, and certainly not in that of the fairly imminent printing of *De libero arbitrio*, but rather in that of Erasmus' attempting to justify his earlier restraint toward and even conditional approval of many aspects of Luther's teachings in the eyes of his increasingly hostile Catholic critics. Aulus' remark therein that 'I am afraid lest I should seem to favour heretics' may be near the mark![84]

In mid-April Luther himself, very possibly aware of developments, broke the silence of nearly four years in a letter to Erasmus of crucial importance. He attributes the overt and covert criticisms brought against him to Erasmus' concern to win the favour or at least mitigate the fury of the papist enemies, since God has not yet granted him the courage needed to oppose these monsters. Yet while paying unstinted tribute to Erasmus' contribution to biblical scholarship, Luther is now afraid that 'induced by our enemies, you might publicly attack our teachings'. In this context, having held back his own pen, the appearance of the *Expostulatio* and the *Spongia* is regrettable; would that Erasmus' enemies would desist so that he, in old age, 'could peacefully fall asleep in the Lord'. But above all, 'if you absolutely cannot and dare not join our cause, then leave it alone and stay with your own things. . . . I ask you, if you can do nothing else, in the meantime to be only a spectator of our tragedy.' Was Luther thinking of Erasmus' own words?

'Only do not give comfort to my enemies . . . and do not publish booklets against me, as I shall publish nothing against you.'[85] A few weeks later Erasmus, stung (as he tells Pirckheimer) by Luther's manner in 'professing to pardon my cowardice, if only I would not write against his teaching',[86] replied and, after conceding mutual concern for the Gospel, burst forth in an impassioned forecast: 'I see from this emerging much that is ruinous and seditious. I see the destruction of good letters and learning. I see the severing of friendships, and fear the outbreak of cruel tumult.' His expression of unconcern as to whether Luther writes against him, and the challenge in his penultimate paragraph – 'Is it this way, forsooth, that portends the restoration of the Gospel?' – are hardly conciliatory; yet again there seems to be no outright condemnation of Luther's teaching as heretical.[87]

In May another prod arrived from Duke George, perhaps the most persistent and sharply pointed of his many goads, but the die was now cast. In June Erasmus wrote to Casper Hedio that he had undertaken to produce something '*de libero arbitrio*, before Luther writes *de libero arbitrio*' – a very interesting forecast.[88] Other letters express his anxiety as to reactions to his book, however moderately written, his specific disavowal of any intent to attack Luther as an undoubted heretic, and his conclusion, perhaps as much in desperation as exasperation, that he has been left with no choice but to write 'either by those who favour Luther, or those who little favour him'. Then in September the despatch of copies of the book itself, to friends, patrons, and a few others, accompanied a clutch of very revealing correspondence. Several recipients – including Aleander, Duke George, and Warham – are told that this should suffice to close the mouths of those who have taken his moderation to imply complicity with Luther. To Tunstall – one of a number of English recipients, including Henry VIII and Fisher – he confides his fear that his book, although most moderately written, will excite grave uproar. The long letter to Melanchthon will concern us in another context.[90]

In the prefatory observations to his *Diatribe* or 'Discourse' on the freedom of the will, which indeed has fairly been seen as reiterating many themes from his correspondence,[91] Erasmus sets out his limitations and makes it clear that he will confine controversy strictly to this one doctrine. Anxious to record his dislike of *assertions*, he uses a phrase which was to be torn out of context by Luther: 'I would readily take refuge in the opinion of the Skeptics, wherever this is allowed by the inviolable authority of the Holy Scripture and by the decrees of the Church, to which I everywhere willingly submit my personal feelings, whether I grasp what it prescribes or not.' He would sooner play the debater than the judge, and warns indeed that we should not 'through irreverent inquisitiveness rush to those things which are hidden, not to say superfluous: whether God foreknows anything contingently; whether our will accomplishes anything in things pertaining to eternal salvation; whether it simply suffers the act of grace . . .' He goes on to question the wisdom even of such investigation before common ears, pointing to Paul's perception that what is lawful is not always expedient. Even if there is some truth 'in the doctrine which Wyclif taught and Luther asserted, that whatever is done by us is done not by free choice but by sheer necessity', what could be more useless than the publication of this paradox? 'What a window to impiety would the public avowal of such an opinion open' to the slothful, the weakling, the evil doer? The crucial issue regarding such teachings is how most people will interpret them.[92]

Thus far, to the lay reader, the whole drift seems to maximise the notions of *adiaphora* and of scriptural piety rather than of doctrinal precision, to urge expediency in the context of taking the Christian faith to the minds and lives of ordinary people. Thus, in his Introduction proper, observing that no one yet 'save only Manichaeus and John Wyclif' has sought to eliminate freedom of choice, leaving no room either for our prayers or our endeavours, he delivers a favourite thrust at the Lutherans: 'if you seek of them a life worthy of the Spirit, they reply that they are just by faith, not by works'. After conceding that scripture passages that support free choice may be countered by others, he goes on to explain, in another passage seized upon by contemporary and modern critics, that 'by free choice in this place we mean a power of the human will by which a man can apply himself to the things which lead to eternal salvation, or turn away from them'. Significantly, in discussing the issues of sin, grace and free will he urges that 'the forgiveness of sins *restores* freedom of choice through grace'. The range of opinions from Pelagius across the spectrum is briefly surveyed, as are the types and stages of grace. Undoubtedly, 'faith, which is the doorway to salvation, is the free gift of God', but Erasmus seems to welcome the idea that 'we may apply our wills to grace, or turn away from it, just as we can open our eyes to the light that is borne in upon them or close them again'. Much more hard-line is the opinion of those 'who contend that free choice is of no avail save to sin, and that grace accomplishes good works in us, not by or with free choice but in free choice, so that our will does nothing more than wax in the hand of the craftsman when it receives the particular shape that pleases him', those indeed 'who say that free choice is a mere empty name'.[93]

Both Erasmus' specific declaration that 'I write as a plain man to plain men'[94] and Gerrish's contention that 'the message of the book concerns the relation of theology to piety at least as much as the relation of grace to freedom'[95] are borne out in the citation of scriptural evidence which comes next. Thus, 'what does the parable of the labourers in the vineyard mean? What kind of labourers are they who do nothing?' And as for the many exhortations in the Gospels and the Epistles, 'are they not intended to incite us to striving, to endeavouring, to industry, lest we perish by neglecting the grace of God?' Without the reality of free will, why should Christ pray upon the Cross: 'Father forgive them; for they know not what they do'? Indeed 'how does God invite to penitence, if he is the author of impenitence'? Luther's own words are thrown back at him: 'free choice is in reality a fiction, or a name without reality'. Moving on to scriptural passages that seem to oppose free choice, Erasmus finally arrives at the rather facile conclusion that 'these passages, which seem to be in conflict with one another, are easily brought into harmony if we join the striving of our will with the assistance of divine grace'.[96]

Part III, examining Luther's arguments in his *Assertio*, cites the Fathers as saying 'that there are certain seeds of virtue implanted in the minds of men by which they in some way see and seek after virtue, but mingled with grosser affections which incite them to other things. It is this flexible will which is called free choice'; without it, what merit can there be in anything? Erasmus concedes that some passages in Paul appear entirely to destroy any power of free choice, but then, in a crucially important passage, proceeds to argue that grace confers the gift that our will might be *synergos* (a fellow-worker) with grace, which would be meaningless if our will is to God as a vase to a potter. Ironically, 'synergism' was later to establish itself in one *Lutheran* school of thought. Thus, repeating an argument encountered in his correspondence, these Pauline admonitions 'are not intended to take away free choice, but to deter us from presumption, which is hateful to God'.[97]

An Epilogue commends a reasonable approach, reiterating 'how destructive it is of true godliness to trust in one's own powers and merits and how intolerable is the arrogance of some who boast their works and sell them by measure and weight'. Yet what can one make of those who 'so diminish free choice that it avails nothing whatever toward a good work, or even cut its throat entirely by bringing in the absolute necessity of all things'? 'For when I hear that the merit of man is so utterly worthless that all things, even the works of godly men, are sins, when I hear that our will does nothing more than clay in the hands of the potter, when I hear all that we do or will referred to absolute necessity', how is it then 'that we hear so much about reward if there is no such thing as merit'? And as to our very concept of the Godhead, how can it be 'a mark of his justice (for I will not speak of mercy) to hand over others to eternal torments in whom he has not deigned to work good works, when they themselves are incapable of doing good, since they have no free choice or, if they have, it can do nothing but sin'?[98]

Having underlined the dilemma, Erasmus characteristically seeks what he calls a mediating view. Disclaiming the opinions of both Manichaeus and Pelagius, he rests content that the very small contribution of free choice is itself 'part of the divine gift, that we can turn our souls to those things pertaining to salvation, or work together with grace', remembering always that 'this very thing which it can do is a work of the grace of God who first created free choice and then freed and healed it'. Then, posing the question, 'if God works in us as the potter in clay, what can be imputed to us, for good or ill?', he claims that 'these people seem to me in one place to restrict the divine mercy that in another they may widen it'. For 'when they say that even those who are justified by faith do nothing but sin, nay, that in loving and trusting God we earn God's hatred, do they not here make extremely niggardly the grace of God, who so justifies man by faith that he still does nothing but sin?' Thus he devises for the Lutherans a paradox of his own: 'Having cut the throat of free choice, they teach that a man is now led by the Spirit of Christ, whose nature will not suffer any association with sin. And yet these same people assert that even when he has received grace, a man does nothing but sin.'[99]

Predictably, reactions to this *Diatribe* were very mixed. Huizinga[100] has pointed out that not only Vives but also more orthodox Catholics such as Sadoleto applauded Erasmus, while among German humanists some such as Zasius and Pirckheimer were reinforced in their stance against Lutheranism, while others like Capito (once a firm ally) were confirmed in their desertion of their former patron. In terms of its doctrinal significance, while clearly it did not resolve the issues raised, one should not discount its impact even in the Lutheran ranks. Thus it has recently been urged that in the Augsburg Confession and its Apology, the whole issue of freedom of the will is discussed in a much more careful and moderate way.[101] Beyond any doubt is the fact that

Melanchthon was brought to modify his views towards what became known as synergism, while Erasmus, as if to illustrate a mind open to persuasion, also came to adjust his views. Meanwhile, the very fact that Melanchthon could compliment Erasmus on the restraint and urbanity of his approach would hardly placate those Catholics who had looked for a virulently expressed anti-Lutheran blast which would smite the Amalekites hip and thigh. Yet the more rabid Lutherans were of course infuriated.

It has been suggested that the faint praise accorded both by some contemporaries and by many modern critiques – including one very notable Catholic study[102] – to Erasmus' presentation of his case suffices to strip it of any high theological pretensions; but its author made no such claim. One modern assessment identifies a basic preoccupation with the problem of man's freedom alongside God's omnipotence. But in respect of the assertion that Erasmus did not perceive the logical involvement of predestination in the doctrine of justification by faith alone, one might assuredly suggest that this is precisely what he *did* perceive, and was concerned above all to avoid.[103] Indeed, the negation of free will, with its logical outcome of predestination, has been identified as the crucial point of separation between Christian humanist and Protestant Reformer.[104] Erasmus would surely have approved the sentiment if not the inelegance of a modern derisory jingle about a doctrine which would make of man 'but a creature that moves in predestinate grooves: I'm not even a bus, I'm a tram!' The description of *De libero arbitrio* as less a theological essay than an attempt to find scriptural justification for a belief in the dignity of man seems to be in full accord with a more recent contention that Erasmus' unquenchable optimism stands apart both from the conservatism of Rome and from the pessimism of Luther.[105]

Indeed, the lay reader might well conclude, in view of Erasmus' explicit declaration, that some theological criticisms resemble condemning a man for failing to demonstrate the finer skills of cricket after his avowed intent to play an innings at baseball. It is true that Erasmus' writing of this work was undertaken in response to pressure and also that the choice of subject was at least in part made for him by his opponents' long-term identification of the issue between them; yet that identification was accurate and the issue indeed crucial.[106] Thus all of Erasmus' utterances in the *Diatribe* are in full accord with his *philosophia Christi*.[107] He writes as a plain man for plain men, concerned above all with the import of religious doctrine for the understanding and the life of the ordinary Christian. His oft-cited allusion to 'Skeptics', taken in context, surely points not to irreligious cynicism but to *adiaphora*: Erasmus would 'not permit any scepticism about the clear meaning of the Holy Scriptures or the clear decisions of the Church'.[108] Nor is his claim to strive for a mediating approach lightly to be dismissed. It might be argued that he writes primarily as a moralist and a philosopher rather than as a reconditely rigorous theologian, yet his morality was that of the *philosophia Christi*. If it is rightly urged that he never solves the dilemma[109] of attributing the gift of saving grace wholly to God, while seeking to retain the idea that man's free will can make *any* contribution, it is equally true that when it comes to reconciling double predestination and the lot of the reprobate with the universal justice and mercy of God, his opponents ask the ordinary man to take every bit as much on trust.

Despite Luther's first reaction of purported nausea and his complaint to Spalatin that 'it is irksome for me to have to reply to such an educated man about such an uneducated book',[110] he paid grudging tribute to Erasmus: 'You alone have gone to the heart of the problem instead of debating the papacy, indulgences, purgatory, and similar trifles. You alone have gone to the core, and I thank you for it.' His *De servo arbitrio* ('Of the bond will'), published in December 1525, exposes what many, then and since, would regard as the over-simplifications of Erasmus' case, and in particular its alleged misunderstanding of Luther's limited but real recognition of the part played by reason and free will in strictly mundane affairs.[111] For Luther, the very notion that man can do anything to achieve or merit saving grace by freely doing what in him lies is simply blasphemous, though admittedly he has a species of freedom amid the circumstances of his temporal life.[112] Yet it was precisely this dichotomy, with its potential implications, which so affronted Erasmus, enabling him in turn to accuse Luther of paradox and inconsistency, of introducing the language of determinism and of sacrificing human moral responsibility to his concept of divine sovereignty – an issue which indeed has concerned more than one Lutheran specialist.[113]

One such scholar concedes that on more than a few occasions Erasmus' exegesis was more accurate than Luther's, while his recognition that the former's doctrine of grace was firmly based in scholastic teaching[114] points us toward a necessarily brief consideration of the 'Pelagian' issue. Late-fifteenth-century scholastic theology was indeed semi-Pelagian in allowing man to contribute *something* toward his salvation through 'works' – though ironically the extension of this to include benefiting from the works of others led to the 'indulgence industry' – by performing morally good acts that might fittingly be conducive toward divine grace.[115] As to Erasmus' own position, his tract in truth was clearer on what it attacked than in its positive prescriptions. Not all assessments would acquit Erasmus of Pelagianism.[116] Outlining alternative formulations of grace which range from the Augustinian position to ideas deriving from Origen and Ockham, Erasmus asserts his preference for that which attributes but a minor part to man's free choice but is, as ever, reluctant to get off the fence, and some discern a 'Semi-Pelagian' leaning.[117] Nor must we forget Erasmus' resolute recognition of 'pagan virtues'[118] in antiquity, which would enrage his new adversary at least as much as his Catholic detractors. Perhaps a non-specialist modern mind may be pardoned for identifying, in this grey area between theology and philosophy, an unresolved tension within Erasmus between Augustinian theology and an optimistic philosophy which veers toward what has been termed the principle of intrinsic perfectibility.

De servo arbitrio, nearly four times as long as Erasmus' *Diatribe*, was written in no irenic spirit: 'I . . . *have not discoursed, but have asserted and do assert*.' Nor is its content solely cogently argued theology: thus Erasmus, who disgusts Luther by using elegance of style to purvey trash, 'like refuse or ordure being carried in gold or silver vases', surely fosters in his heart 'a Lucian, or some other pig from Epicurus' sty'! Doctrinally, what would Erasmus, with his declared priorities, have made of Luther's rejoinder to his contention that a window to impiety was opened by his dogmas: 'let it be so; such people belong to the above-mentioned leprosy of evil that must be endured'? Or again, if indeed Erasmus believed that divine justice and mercy were in a sense superadded to natural justice, how could he have accepted the assertion that, since 'God moves and actuates in all, he necessarily moves and acts also in Satan and ungodly man . . . as they are and as he finds them' – the instruments remaining guilty of the evil things they do.[119] One may suspect that Erasmus might perhaps subconsciously have felt that God's *exercise* of his omnipotence was limited by his moral rectitude and was itself almost made subject to natural justice – which Luther would reject as supremely presumptuous blasphemy.[120]

Many theologians would urge that, since Christianity is a supernatural religion, Erasmus had the worst of the argument.[121] Yet some would accord him partial victory in that his views came close to those adopted later on this issue both by Melanchthon and in the decrees of Trent.[122] Of course, then as now, many verdicts were delivered by people who were not highly skilled theologians but who were very considerably *parti pris*. In due course some reassuring reactions to the *De libero arbitrio* arrived: Henry VIII's approval came quite speedily albeit via Juan Luis Vives, while in mid-December 1524 Paul Volz conveyed his pleasure at seeing how temperately and scrupulously Erasmus had distanced himself from Lutheran doctrine.[123] Yet to Vives, towards the year-end, while relating with pride how his book has been accorded a friendly reception by Melanchthon, Erasmus repeats his fears as to the course of events in Germany. A few days earlier he had felt constrained to write again to Duke George, whose letter commending his confutation of the abominable and seditious Lutheran tumult had alas been delayed. Here he rounds once more on those who would upbraid him for not entering the arena sooner, 'as if, had this been done, the affair would not have progressed thus far'. When so many had actually applauded Luther's first efforts against corruption whereas Erasmus had warned of disorder and tumult, what injustice now to blame him for the outcome! By now, alas, such vulgar remedies as imprisonment and fire can do little but exacerbate the malady; if its spread had been restricted to a few, amputation might have served, but of late it has infected even kings.[124] One of his last letters of the year includes Erasmus' famous citation of the utterance attributed to the Franciscans of Cologne: ' "I laid the egg, Luther hatched it," ' at which he demurs, for 'I laid a poultry egg, Luther hatched a very different bird'.[125]

Of particular interest also concerning the impact of his *Diatribe* is Erasmus' claim to Jacopo Sadoleto, Bishop of Carpentras and Papal Secretary, who favoured attempts at reconciliation, that some have been persuaded thereby to abandon Lutheran dogma. He would have been gratified to learn that Albert Pighius, Papal Chamberlain, had instructed the theologians of Louvain to desist from their insane clamour against a man, admired by the Pope himself, who has recently opposed Luther on behalf of the Catholic faith. Erasmus would also have been pleased to receive a commendation from Gattinara, in brief but cordial terms, not only of his efforts but also of the fact that his attack on this 'pestiferous dogma' had already made no small impression.[126]

Meanwhile, doctrinal differences were perhaps now sharpened by an undercurrent of personal dislike. Several of Erasmus' letters cite the rumour, which he later acknowledges to be false, that Luther's marriage with a former nun, 'a young woman of elegant form . . . but without dowry', had been followed within a scandalously short time by the birth of a child.[127] Moreover Erasmus considered Luther's reaction to his modestly written *Diatribe* 'so virulent, so scurrilous and equally malicious' as to verge upon insanity. Predictably, a letter from Luther apparently designed to mitigate Erasmus' expected indignation about *De servo arbitrio* and to forestall any reply, failed to produce any such effect. Erasmus' furious rejoinder, in April 1526, asks why Luther had felt impelled to load upon him so much scurrilous abuse and so many slanderous lies, depicting him as an Epicurean, a sceptic and a blasphemer? In any case, the letter has arrived too late! For already in February, expecting from his adversary nothing but malicious calumny henceforth, he had speedily produced Part I of his *Hyperaspistes* ('Protective Shield') *Diatribae adversus Servum Arbitrium Martini Lutheri* – a copy of which had, apparently, only reached him quite shortly before.[128]

Part I, not in fact published until June, was approximately thrice as long as Erasmus' *Diatribe*, and Part II (September 1527) twice as long as Part I. Both achieved a very considerable circulation and several reprintings. Modern assessments consider the second part superior to the first – described as something of an injured epilogue.[129] Two passages are especially significant as cogent statements of Erasmus' position on two crucial issues. First, on free will, he alludes to a law which is 'deeply ingrafted in the mind of man, to such an extent that the Ethnics also conclude: God is supremely just and good. If he is just, he does not punish for eternity those who sin, not through their guilt but from inevitable necessity, nor ordains punishment by reason of the wickedness which he himself operates in man.' Secondly, on a different but equally fundamental question:

> I have never been an apostate from the Catholic Church. I know that in this Church, which you call the Papist Church, there are many who displease me, but such I see also in your Church. One bears more easily the evils to which one is accustomed. I therefore bear with this Church, until I shall see a better, and it cannot help bearing with me, until I shall myself be better. And he does not sail badly who steers between two evils.[130]

The whole tone of this bespeaks Erasmus under siege, albeit still in resolute adherence to a considered and completely logical position.

This impression is confirmed by his continual compulsion to write in several directions to complain of Luther's raving lies and attacks upon him, so that no vestige of friendship remains, while also reflecting with some bitterness to his good friend Pirckheimer that 'even while I strive against Luther, I know that there are those who would rather wish me dead than that same Luther'.[131] In August 1526, more happily,

Charles V himself wrote from Granada to express his gratitude and joy at Erasmus' efforts, including Part I of *Hyperaspistes*, against the impious Lutheran faction.[132] A month later, Erasmus wrote again to Duke George, acquainting him with progress on Part II but also wondering sadly what effect his earlier *Diatribe* has had upon Luther other than to harden him in his beliefs.[133] Writing from England a few months later his old friend Thomas More commended a continuation of this task as most fruitful, as highly welcome for his friends, and – in what sounds almost like a note of warning – as most specially necessary *for himself*.[134]

Luther forbore to compose a formal reply either to Part I or to Part II (when it appeared) of the *Hyperaspistes*. But his silence was not that of capitulation or consent, and the fact that he did publish another attack upon Erasmus within a year or so before the latter's death attests the severance of all near-cordial relations, despite the continued efforts of Melanchthon to prevent further open conflict. On Erasmus' side his persistent declarations that he would neither condemn Luther for heresy nor restrict his right to speak, though would that this were exercised more diplomatically, were to be yoked with bitter reproaches for his adversary's vituperation. As for Luther, his *Table Talk* conveys his contempt for what he sees as the cowardice and hypocrisy of the dilettante reformer, voiced in such gibes as: 'I consider Erasmus to be the greatest enemy Christ has had these thousand years past.'[135] With due allowance for hyperbole, this would clearly imply that Luther is concerned to register not only his personal but also his doctrinal aversion. Erasmus' attitude seems to have been somewhat more generous, and we shall find that on the infrequent occasions when his correspondence mentions the basic issue of the great debate, it is in relatively open-minded terms. Indeed for the years between 1527 and 1532 his principal concerns within a 'Lutheran' context were to combine continued efforts to enjoin a moderate approach with persistent attempts to clear his own name from the charge of being the originator of Lutheran error. Again, Erasmus sought to draw attention to the mounting danger of religious and doctrinal anarchy brought about by what some discerned as Lutheran offshoots.

As for his own position, he confides to More that his own efforts have but stirred up a hornet's nest, so that 'the greater part of the Lutheran faction is persuaded that I am the sole obstacle to the spread of the Gospel through all Germany'. In a letter to Spain he seems to imply that the Emperor has entrusted him with the lead in fighting the Lutheran evil, though alas there are now not one but four identifiable threats.[136] Vives' assurance of a favourable response from Spain appears to be reinforced when Pope Clement VII writes to Alonso Manrique, Archbishop and Inquisitor General, in glowing terms about Erasmus' having written '*summa cum laude*' against the heresiarch Luther.[137] Meanwhile the second part of *Hyperaspistes* is duly despatched in September 1527 to Duke George and also to Gattinara. He assures them that this reply to Luther's *Servum arbitrium* makes plain 'how cruel is the conflict between us'.[138] For Erasmus' increasingly grave anxiety in face of the condemnatory Valladolid Articles levelled against him by hostile Spanish monks is attested in a clutch of letters, including one to Charles V himself, sent off to Spain.[139]

In Germany, Erasmus continued to disappoint Duke George and his like by his counsels of moderation; a letter to that ruler in January 1528 must surely have displeased him by what would be taken as implied criticism of princes. For Erasmus once more suggests that use of the scalpel and the cautery is too harsh when a major part of the body is diseased: 'pernicious is the medicine which rather kills than cures'.[140] And again, in another brave plea for restraint: 'neither in this matter do I argue for the heretics, but for the princes and the orthodox'. For the pestilence has spread so widely that resort to arms will harm many who are good and pious, while its actual outcome is surely uncertain. The Lutherans may have merited severity, but 'what must be borne in mind is not always what impious heretics deserve, but what is expedient for the *Respublica Christiana*'.[141] Reverting to the impact of *Hyperaspistes* Part II, Melanchthon expressed the uncomplimentary but perhaps realistic opinion that 'This work will not be understood by the public. It is both confused and prolix.'[142] Yet understandably Erasmus writes to Clement to stress that its appearance should serve finally to eliminate all suspicion of collusion with Luther.[143] Another brief letter to Gattinara in July 1528 couples the hopeful assertion that 'these days the Lutheran fever is abating' with the ironical comment that Luther himself has now written what are almost recantations, in his disavowal of attempts to associate him with crazy heresies.[144]

Indeed Erasmus becomes increasingly concerned with what he sees not so much as a proliferation but as the near-disintegration of the 'Lutheran' cause. A long letter to the Spanish Primate in March 1529, while reiterating his own stance vis-à-vis Luther, appears to be equally concerned to present his own assessment of religious trends. He is desperately afraid lest pharisaism will be followed by paganism. In some 'Lutheran' cities the Eucharist is still celebrated in a form not far removed from that of the Church; but elsewhere the sacerdotal as well as the monastic order has been quite uprooted.[145] Soon afterwards Erasmus felt himself compelled by the victory of the Reformers to quit Basel, and it was from Freiburg that he sent an interesting and open-minded analysis to Justus Decius, secretary to King Sigismund of Poland. Therein, despite his distaste for Luther's approach, Erasmus avows that the questions 'of free will, of good works and merits, and such-like, are themes which with the benefit of piety can be dicussed between erudite men'. Indeed, what Luther urges, if moderately handled, comes close to the Gospels.[146] His Catholic adversaries remained unplacated. In June 1530, recovering from three months' illness, his letters complain of those who still comb his work for agreement with Luther's teaching (which they discern in the mere absence of calumny!) and bemoans the appearance of a book by Alberto Pio which seeks 'to make me the seed-bed of the whole Lutheran tragedy'.[147]

His concern for the prospects at Augsburg is reflected in an exchange of letters with Melanchthon (below, p. 153), and his fair-minded assessment in his comment on 29 October, to Erasmus Schets, who became his agent, that, despite agreement on many articles between the Lutherans and the Catholics, 'at least two assertions of the Emperor were displeasing, first the term sect, and secondly the aspersion that in the Lutheran basis is much that is subversive of the writings of the Gospels and of the Apostles'.[148] Should conflict ensue, he later forecasts, while the princes may indeed fight, kill and pillage, the piously titled war upon which they embark may prove as deadly to the Church as it will be ruinous to the Germans. As late as this he still protests that if his first advice had been followed, then this evil would not have gone thus far.[149] While one correspondent appeals to him to exercise the authority which God has given him to mediate amidst this turmoil, another writes from Italy to warn against those who still berate him as the author of the 'Saxon Heresies'.[150] Replying at some length to Julius Pflug, Erasmus disclaims any real power to influence an age in which it seems six hundred Furies have been loosed, but he proffers the wistful thought that had Pope Adrian lived for ten years things *might* have changed.[151]

In general, during the years after 1527, Erasmus' focus shifts from Luther to Lutheranism, and from the chosen battle-ground of free will to other aspects of dogma which characterise the emergent Zwinglians, Strassburgers and Radicals. Yet if Erasmus' own perspective is widening, the range of references to him in a sample of Luther's *Table Talk* for 1532–33 remains depressingly narrow. Although fewer in number than one would expect, they are almost uniformly derisory. By now he is no longer even a worthwhile adversary but only one of a number of 'croaking toads', whose levity of approach is matched only by the folly and scurrility with which he assails the Lutheran cause. If his heart were opened nothing would be found therein about the Trinity or the Sacrament, while Luther hates him profoundly 'because he calls into question what ought to be our joy': the Virgin Birth. His very countenance betrays his craftiness; having irritated the papacy, Erasmus now draws his own head out of the noose. 'He never has anything to say about the article of justification. He mentions Christ for the sake of his stipends, but he doesn't care.'[152]

The catalyst which precipitated this continued doctrinal and personal enmity into one last outburst of published ill-will was apparently Georg Witzel, who wrote to Erasmus from Frankfurt on 5 September 1532. An early supporter of Luther, Witzel had fallen foul of him, was at one time suspected of anti-trinitarian views, and had been driven from pillar to post by Lutheran influences. Most probably, he had remained at heart an Erasmian, now retreating from the Lutheran camp in search of ecumenical concord. He shared Erasmus' opinion that Luther was a failure because good works were absent from his followers' lives, and his letters urged him to continue fending off schismatics on the one side and sophists on the other in his fight for orthodoxy and the defence of the old theology. Writing again in March 1533, Witzel suggested that 'best of all would be an Oecumenical Synod', before making another impassioned plea to Erasmus to make his presence felt: were Witzel Emperor, *he* would not accept the excuse that 'I cannot come'. For it is not the voice of Luther, nor that of the Sophists, which will be heard, but that of Erasmus.[153]

Alas, his hero replied to neither letter, but Amsdorf, reporting to Luther on Witzel's activities, identified Erasmus as the real nuisance. His leader had apparently already taken offence at Erasmus' *De Symbolo*, alluding to its 'Satanic' composition and sneering that 'our king Amphibolus sits securely on his amphibolous throne',[154] and his reply to Amsdorf was so vitriolic as to shock Erasmus into producing his *Adversus calumniosissimam epistolam Martini Lutheri* (alternatively, and engagingly known as *Purgatio adversus epistolam non sobriam Martini Lutheri*). This was reprinted five times, attesting at once the enduring magic of Erasmus' name and also a quickening of interest in what must have seemed a 'return contest'.[155] Margaret Phillips describes its tone as almost playful alongside Luther's violence, and indeed a note of badinage persists in his treatment throughout of 'Martin'. Yet this only sharpens some telling points, while the work is also of interest as a comparatively late 'statement of faith'.

At the very outset Erasmus is at pains to state that, had he written to Witzel, he would have admonished him not to wound Luther – whose doctrines he has nowhere called heretical. Soon after, Erasmus declares his fundamental belief that it has pleased God 'that the World, through the sin of Adam and Eve fallen from its original state, be through his Son Jesus Christ mercifully restored. To this grace moreover equal access is *for all* [our italics] through sincere faith in Christ. Furthermore faith is the gift of God, which no one gives to himself, but is to be entreated of God.'[156] In more combative vein, when Luther terms him a 'suspect author' Erasmus can hardly restrain his laughter: to whom is he suspect but to some monks by whom Martin himself is not suspected but condemned as the most pestilential heresiarch on earth! Allusions to the attacks of Pio of Carpi and the Spanish monks evoke similar scorn. Very lengthy sections are devoted to repeated rebuttal of charges to which Erasmus is very sensitive: the related issues of Arianism, of questioning the Divinity of the Holy Spirit, and of insufficient reverence for the Virgin Mary.[157] Labels such as 'Democritus and Epicurus' are ascribed to a mind lacking in temperate and Christian modesty, and a few final pages deride the notion that such sectaries as Arians, Anabaptists and Epicures derive 'from four ambiguous words of Erasmus', alongside the gibe that his works 'furnished the seed-bed for Luther'. Predictably, he concludes with his customary declaration that, while conceding the need for some ceremonial adjustment, through a Synod, the Church alone can sanction doctrinal change.[158]

Three long letters to Erasmus from John Choler in Augsburg, in May and June 1534, complain most bitterly of this latest Lutheran attack: is it not enough for him to call Erasmus double-tongued, Satan's artificer, King Amphibolus, Sacramentarian, Arian, and goodness knows what else? How on earth can Erasmus say in his *Purgatio* that he has never abandoned all regard for a man who will assuredly never keep quiet – for not even Melanchthon can make him.[159] Revealingly, Allen and Garrod cite Melanchthon's comment to Bucer: 'I regret that Luther has renewed strife with Erasmus'. Well might Erasmus claim that Luther's writing against him in such furious and lying fashion has displeased even the Lutherans.[160] Perhaps we may close this depressing scenario with two contemporary comments which may have made Erasmus smile wryly. First, a book by the Franciscan Herborn (apparently in favour at Rome), updates an old saw in urging that it was 'Luther *and others* [our italics] who hatched the chicks', but prefaces this – *pace* the notion of a 'Third Church'? – by asserting that 'Luther drew to himself a large part of the Church; so too, Zwingli and Oecolampadius; [but] the greatest part, Erasmus': better he had never been born. Second, on 16 March 1535 an infrequent correspondent, John Rinck, makes use of a device so often directed against Erasmus himself in asking whether it was not the *Lutheran* seed-bed which had sprouted Zwinglians, Anabaptists, Melchiorites and other heretical pests?[161]

Pursuit of such wider problems will clearly concern us in the next two chapters. Meanwhile, can we proffer a few concluding generalisations about Erasmus and what he so often called 'the Lutheran tragedy'? The phrase itself repays a moment's thought, for one need not turn to Erasmus' wounded *amour propre*, which perhaps proved rather less than that of Luther, to explain the mingled chagrin, fear, and sheer exasperation which were his successive reactions. For Luther, who must at first have seemed a welcome ally in his fight to restore the spirit of true Christianity within the Church, proceeded by rash and choleric over-assertion not to amend but to rend the very fabric of the Church itself. Whatever one's assessment of the relative importance of a clash of temperament, a difference over tactics, and a genuine disagreement about specific doctrines, Wallace Ferguson's perceptive amendment of the well-known dictum – 'Erasmus laid the egg that Luther *broke*' – surely brings us close to the heart of the matter.

Yet while Erasmus basically sought to purify and correct medieval Catholic theology, while Luther rejected it, in many ways it was Erasmus not Luther whose ideas proved more congenial both to the 'Radicals' of the sixteenth and the liberals of the eighteenth century. Although he remained Catholic in considering predestination to be something not wholly attainable by human intelligence or logic, we may also suspect that Erasmus stopped short of any explicit resolution of this mystery because he foresaw its inevitable implications for his own optimistic assessment of man's innate capabilities when working together with Christ's spirit and teaching, implications which appalled him on moral and philosophical grounds. For while Luther conceded and relegated free will in man to mundane affairs, as much less important than issues of salvation and his relationship with the Godhead where it vanished in the face of omnipotence and predestination, Erasmus envisaged the whole exemplification of the *philosophia Christi* precisely within man's exercise of practical Christianity in his everyday activities. Luther's distinction between free will in the theological sense and free choice in mundane affairs was surely exactly the sort of dichotomy which Erasmus strove to avoid. In what to the lay mind is a grey area between theology and philosophy, for Erasmus 'cheerfulness kept breaking through'. Yet further, citing Erasmus' avowal to Luther in his *Hyperaspistes* that 'what you affirm, I hope; what you state you know, I try to learn', Marjorie Boyle suggests that underlying the theological issue in dispute was a wider difference in philosophical attitudes as to the mode of discovery of truth.[162]

In the more limited context of sixteenth-century religious problems, a revealing contrast may be suggested between Erasmus and his friend More on the one hand, and Erasmus and Luther on the other. More remained committed to the sacramental character of the Catholic Church, with salvation available to all but only in and through the sacerdotally administered sacraments. Luther rejected papal supremacy and several of what he considered to be distortions of the sacramental doctrines of the Church. But he also went on to enshrine in place of salvation via allegedly mechanical observances an equally total reliance upon a narrowly Pauline interpretation of justification by faith alone, with its ineluctable corollary of predestination. Erasmus was fundamentally more optimistic in regard to human potential than either More or Luther. He rejected as equally mechanical both any picture of sacerdotally dispensed access to salvation regardless of real spiritual striving, and also the affront to his own 'philosophy of Christ' implied by a totally arbitrary selection for redemption. This he saw as the outcome of a solifideism which permitted no effective freedom to the human will. Thus the choice of topic on which he took issue with Luther bespeaks not any retraction of his earlier attack upon an over-mechanical concept of religion, but rather a revulsion against what he saw as an attempt to impose a doctrinal strait-jacket, which in its own way would be just as restrictive of any innate capacity of the human mind or soul to seek God.[163] Logically, this suggests not fence-sitting or wavering indecision but rather a completely consistent rejection of both extreme positions for the same basic reason.

Reverting finally to the historical, as distinct from the doctrinal, significance of Erasmus' breach with Luther, to the Catholics it was a rather meagre propaganda victory and to the Lutherans a grievous disappointment. Yet in the context of the emergence of the Magisterial Reformation its influence was surely in no way determinative. It is perhaps in the wider context of the Reformation defined to include the Radicals that its full significance may be seen – and this at least as much in the debate between the Magisterial Reformers and the Radicals as between 'Catholicism' and 'Protestantism'. For if Erasmus' biblicism and Christocentricity were basic ingredients of the Reformation as represented by Luther, Zwingli and Calvin, then his emphasis upon free will, upon the spirituality as distinct from the sacramental aspect of real Christianity, and upon the tolerance implied by *adiaphora*, leads directly into several aspects of the Radical Reformation – and in a longer time-scale perhaps into a less dogmatic approach toward religion and morality in general. If the Erasmus–Luther debate is indeed of real historical import, it is perhaps in the context of a continuing debate between Christian humanism and narrowly doctrinal ecclesiasticism.

Seven

PROTESTANT HUMANISM: LOST LEADER OR ERRANT DISCIPLES?

The question of 'Reform or Revolution' becomes yet more complicated when we turn to the relationships of Erasmus with those widening manifestations of Protestantism represented by such figures as Zwingli and Bucer. But before we do so, his position with regard to Melanchthon, considered now in his own right, must be examined more fully, if only as demonstrating the importance not solely of doctrinal issues but also of personal empathy. Moreover, the doctrinal picture itself is by no means simply a case of developments out of and beyond Lutheranism; for on at least one issue, that of the Eucharist, some Protestant theologians professed that their rejection, or at best modification, of Wittenberg's interpretation derived at least in part from *Erasmian* writings preceding the entry of Luther himself into the debate. Indeed there were those who maintained that the positions they adopted were basically Erasmian – which alas he lacked the nerve precisely to enunciate and from which he sometimes retreated as they advanced further. When we add all this to the continued carping of his dissatisfied Catholic critics, the description of 'Erasmus under siege' is surely apposite. Moreover, in his correspondence from the mid-1520s onward his growing preoccupation with other Protestant reformers bulks progressively larger than continued concern about Luther himself.

It may at the outset be useful to establish a couple of benchmarks. First, personal feelings – which in one case remained constant but in others changed almost violently through the years – seem to have been almost as important as doctrinal differences. Of the three major figures named, relations with Melanchthon remained friendly throughout, though admittedly at the expense of a couple of interludes of prudent silence. But those with Zwingli, despite commencing with a period of near-adulation on the part of the young Swiss, deteriorated to such a point that Erasmus' reaction to the news of his death on the battlefield of Kappel was quite callous. Relations with Bucer gradually descended to bitterness, despite certain temperamental affinities and some close similarities of stance on particular issues.

Personal and doctrinal issues were often inter-related, and in more than one instance the crossing of the 'great divide' between Erasmian humanism and Protestantism was the taking of issue against Erasmus' *De libero arbitrio*, in rebuttal of which Luther was not the first to take up his pen. When a number of far from insignificant figures of the second rank are included, it is tempting to think of this chapter in terms of 'Erasmus and the Lost Disciples' or of 'Protestant Humanists and the Lost Leader'. The defection – as viewed by Erasmus – of Justus Jonas, Conrad Pellican, Johannes Oecolampadius, and Wolfgang Capito, to the Lutheran, Zwinglian and Strassburgers' camps inevitably added personal chagrin to his genuine concern at the course of events. On doctrinal questions it will be fruitful to relate the subsequent debates – and squabbles – to the following themes: the source of authority for the determination of religious dogma, and for its realisation in the lives of ordinary men and women; the inter-related problems of free will, predestination, grace, and justification; and the nature and meaning of the sacraments.

To start with Melanchthon, one relatively recent brief study identifies 'his own philosophico-theological position, taking an intermediary stance between Luther and Erasmus'.[1] Of all the major Protestant leaders, Melanchthon most closely resembled Erasmus because his genuine academic distinction preceded his deep religious commitment and was never wholly superseded thereby. He was Professor of Greek at Wittenberg, refusing to restrict his teaching exclusively to the Faculty of Theology. He never abandoned his humanism; in his case Erasmus' oft-cited gibe that where Lutheranism reigned, learning perished, most certainly did not apply. In the closely meshed world of religious scholarship, Reuchlin was his great-uncle and Oecolampadius his personal friend. As to his temperamental and methodological affinity with Erasmus, the familiar description of Melanchthon as 'the quiet reformer' is indicative.[2]

The more combative Reuchlin, bestowing upon him his Greek name in place of 'Schwartzerd', forecast that only Erasmus would surpass him. He attained professorial rank at the age of twenty-one, and two years earlier had already paid tribute in the form of a poetic eulogy to 'Erasmus Greatest of Men'. The flattered recipient in turn bestowed fulsome praise on the emergent prodigy. At this stage Melanchthon undoubtedly shared the vision of the *philosophia Christi*, and despite later tensions mutual scholarly and personal esteem endured.[3] The first indication of a doctrinal parting of the ways appeared in some critical comments by Melanchthon on Erasmus' Paraphrase of Romans. Yet in a friendly letter of 5 January 1519 Melanchthon disclaimed any real intent to wound, and still felt able to say that 'Martin Luther, who is a keen supporter of your reputation, desires your good opinion at all points'. Replying, Erasmus welcomes honest differences of opinion, temperately expressed,[4] but by the summer of 1520 he confides to Spalatin that in writing to Melanchthon he feels that he is also writing to Luther. Personal goodwill continues, and in December Erasmus remarks that if Melanchthon 'has married a wife, what else can we do except wish him happiness? What's done cannot be undone.'[5] By May 1521, however, a long letter to Justus Jonas expresses alarm at the way things are going. Justus Jonas, an Erfurt humanist whom Erasmus came to regard as a defector from his cause, accompanied Luther to Worms, and in June 1521 became Professor of Theology at Wittenberg. Disappointment, rather than acrimony, is evident in this reasoned attempt to dissuade him from adherence to the increasingly intransigent Lutheran camp. 'Who would not suffer torment,' concludes Erasmus, 'if Philip Melanchthon, a young man of such outstanding gifts, were carried off by this tempest?' He appeals to Jonas to present the points he has put forward to Melanchthon and to others like him, that ruinous discord may yet be averted.[6]

Alas, the contents of Melanchthon's *Loci communes theologici* (December 1521) show that the Erasmian humanist and moralist within him, who had agreed that Christians should be thoroughly transformed, had now become increasingly subordinated to the rigorously biblical Lutheran who denied all meaningful free will in the face of predestination. The primacy of place and of length accorded to his treatment of 'the power of man, especially free will' makes this clear. Melanchthon rebuts the godless doctrine of free will: 'since all things that happen, happen necessarily according to divine predestination, our will has no liberty'. In one sense, he concedes, it possesses a certain freedom in outward works, and would-be philosophers have seized on this contingency. But why boast of freedom in external acts when God requires purity of heart? 'Justification by works is nothing but a Pharisaic tradition.'[7] We may wonder whether Erasmus recognised himself in the charge that 'the new Pelagians of our times . . . do not deny the fact of original sin, they nevertheless deny that its power is such that all deeds of men and all human efforts are sin'. While he would have agreed that 'God judges the heart, and not the external work', could he possibly have countenanced the assertion that all the capacities of human reason are mere shadows and that man by his own natural power can do nothing but sin?[8] In his opinions on the sacraments, in those passages in which he contrasts the spirit with the flesh, and in the scriptural truth with which he ends the *Loci communes* – 'For the kingdom of God does not consist in talk but in power' – Melanchthon's position is often in accord with that of Erasmus.[9] Indeed, in his last letter to Erasmus he was to characterise the second version of the work, printed in 1535, as attempting 'a reliable doctrine and useful for morals and piety'.[10] Yet his contention in 1521 that by nature man pursues nothing divine, so that there is no room for our own merit, conveys an estimate of mankind which is far more pessimistic than that of the great humanist.[11]

Melanchthon now perceived a clear distinction between Luther's supra-rational message of salvation and Erasmus' teaching of civic virtues enjoined by the Christian faith. Despite the diplomatic title of his *De Erasmo et Luther Elogion*, 1522, its publication alongside a piece by Luther did not entirely appease Erasmus, including as it did such declarations as that

> in theological matters we especially seek two different things . . . One is the subject of true, evangelical Christian preaching, to the world and to human reason unknown: that is what Luther teaches, and that is what engenders righteousness of the heart, in which good works then originate. The other is what Erasmus teaches us – good morals, the chaste life. It is also what the heathen philosophers knew about. What, however, has philosophy in common with Christ, blind reason with the revelation of God?

Whether or not this is an *accurate* depiction of Erasmus' position, the drift of Melanchthon's thinking is clear.[12]

He strove to avert open conflict with Erasmus, who in turn came to recognise that Melanchthon and Luther had more extreme 'Evangelicals' with whom to contend. But, perhaps because Erasmus' intention to write against Luther became known, in the summer of 1524, while the friends whom he accompanied rode on to Basel to visit Erasmus and Oecolampadius, Melanchthon himself deemed it wise to halt at his mother's home near Frankfurt.[13] On 6 September Erasmus sent a copy of *De libero arbitrio* to Melanchthon, together with a long and friendly letter conveying his still surviving hope for amicable relations with Wittenberg. This he contrasts with his growing doubts about Oecolampadius and Zwingli, especially in respect of such matters as images, vestments and church offices. Thus, while Melanchthon displays a more tolerant approach toward vestments and bishops, as not in themselves necessarily conducive to idolatry, in Zwingli's eyes all such is apparently impious and unchristian. Melanchthon promptly sent it on to Spalatin, commending Erasmus on abstaining from contumely.[14]

In due course he conveys this sentiment to Erasmus himself, conceding his willingness for temperate debate but pleading that Erasmus should not condemn the Gospel cause because of some people's excesses, nor spoil his own case through any ill will.[15] Indeed, concerning the impact of *De libero arbitrio* itself upon Melanchthon, there is little doubt that, while remaining basically Lutheran in his approach, he *was* influenced toward conceding greater freedom of the will in respect particularly of outward righteousness of conduct. A moderation of his earlier insistence upon predestination has been discerned thereafter, with a greater emphasis not only upon man's duty to behave morally but also upon his capacity to be a fellow-worker in acceptance of God's grace: the concept of Synergism, derived from Erasmus, established itself in one school of Lutheran thought.[16]

Sadly, by the time this letter had reached Erasmus his stance had become more aggressive. On 10 December 1524 he despatched a reply which Melanchthon rightly described as most bitter in its tone, though its content is wholly consistent with Erasmus' declared principles. In particular, he makes a logical distinction between his recognition of the clamant need for reform and the fact that in Luther's teachings much offends him. Alluding to his fruitless appeals for moderation, Erasmus makes plain his longing for the restoration of true religion *while detracting nothing from authority*. Luther has given ample thought to the evils which exist, but not nearly enough to those which might ensue. For how can it be conductive to Christian piety to hear the Pope described as Antichrist; bishops, Confession, and all human institutions denigrated; all works and merits made heretical – free will to be of no account, but everything going forward of necessity, with nothing attributable to the works of men? What impression must this produce upon the vulgar? He goes on to refer to a secret visit to Basel of Carlstadt and to his teaching that only a 'sign' of the Lord's body and blood is present in the Eucharist, and later still to deplore the tumult with which Zwingli has thrown out a few images. Yet amidst all this he is still able to express the hope that, from this bitter and harsh medicine which Luther has proffered mankind, something healthy will emerge for the Church. Nay, 'perchance our conduct has deserved such a harsh physician, who will cure sickness by cutting and burning'. Although Erasmus is careful throughout this epistle not to attack 'most learned

Melanchthon' himself, relations evidently cooled thereafter. Certainly Erasmus went over the top in asserting to Juan Luis Vives later in the month that Melanchthon, while writing that his *Diatribe* has been accorded a friendly reception, does not conceal his fear for the Lutheran cause if he continues.[17]

Thereafter no communication passed either way for some three years. None the less, having declared his own position within the Lutheran camp, Melanchthon was apparently as reluctant to sanction any attacks upon Erasmus as he was to accept the latter's criticisms of his leader. Yet, while remaining loyal to Erasmus' humanistic goals, Melanchthon disapproved of other aspects of his theology and deplored above all the continuance of hostilities in the *Hyperaspistes*. 'Did you ever read', he wrote, 'anything more bitter . . . ? It is almost venomous . . . and yet I think Erasmus has reserved something more offensive for the second part of the work. He does me great wrong in imputing to me a part, and that, too, the most offensive part, of the work. I have decided to bear this injury in silence. Oh that Luther would keep silent!'[18]

When the second part of *Hyperaspistes* duly appeared in 1527, Melanchthon urged Luther not to publish an answer. Indeed, one can hardly refrain from pointing to the irony of the fact that, in the conflict between the two giants, it was Melanchthon who tried to play the humanist irenic role. It is fitting that direct contact was resumed amid the prospects of religious conciliation at the Diet of Augsburg in 1530.[19] During August of that year a minor spate of letters passed between them. Melanchthon reports from Augsburg that no one would credit the ferocity displayed by those who would urge the princes, who are of themselves disposed to moderation, into violence. He has heard that Erasmus has written to dissuade the Emperor from extreme counsels: continued exercise of his wisdom and authority may do much for posterity. Those of Melanchthon's cause have submitted their proposals without invective, and will make concessions on any equitable conditions, lest the Church be ruined. But Erasmus makes it clear forthwith that the report of his having written to the Emperor is false, although he has written to Campeggio and the Bishop of Augsburg that faith should not be settled by warfare. He can do no more to make theologians and princes desist from savagery.[20] In still more sombre vein he sees that all things portend a conflict to which some ecclesiastics seem all too disposed. 'Oh that Luther had thought of this in time!'[21]

This rapprochement in the cause of ecclesiastical peace – alas, abortive – had perhaps been triggered not only by sincere mutual regard but also by the fact that, embedded within two of Erasmus' more combative publications against Bucer and his Strassburg colleagues, which we shall examine later, were explicit and quite glowing tributes to Melanchthon's character and scholarship.[22] None the less, their correspondence thereafter was sporadic.[23] Yet it is perhaps fitting that Erasmus' last exchange of letters, in the year of his death, should have been with Melanchthon – though this had again been preceded by misunderstanding and suspicion. In the introduction to his 1535 edition of *Loci communes theologici* Melanchthon had included some remarks on the difference between Chrstian doctrine and philosophical scepticism – evoking a predictable reaction. His exculpatory and conciliatory letter, dated 12 May 1536, pacified Erasmus, who wrote back to ask pardon for his suspicions and to express his pleasure at the restoration of their friendship.[24]

Undoubtedly, in terms of scholarship and humanist sincerity, and by temperament, the two men were very close. Of all the leading Protestant Reformers, it was with Melanchthon only that Erasmus always managed to avoid open conflict, though sometimes narrowly! It is tempting to ponder the 'if only' of different geographical and contingent influences: a Melanchthon free of Lutheran charisma and an Erasmus not subject to princely and Catholic pressures. But this would be to over-simplify, for there remain genuine doctrinal differences. Yet ironically, although it was the free will controversy which ultimately caused Melanchthon to crystallise his loyalties, the doctrinal impact of the debate was to modify his views in the direction of Synergism, while on the crucial theological issue of the Eucharist he differed from Erasmus largely on the ground that the latter's writings had encouraged speculation in too *radical* a direction. Finally, it is indicative of his repute for an Erasmian moderation of approach, allied with his scholarship, that Melanchthon received overtures from Poland, from France, and from Cardinal Sadoleto. It has been suggested that his influence helped persuade Erasmus to write his last substantial treatise: *On Mending the Peace of the Church*.[25]

While Melanchthon survived Erasmus for many years, Ulrich Zwingli pre-deceased him by half a decade, meeting in 1531 a violent end in conflict with the forces of the Catholic cantons of Switzerland. In this as in several other respects the contrast between the two Protestant leaders is striking. While the rapport between Erasmus and Melanchthon, though sometimes stretched, was never broken, the rupture with Zwingli could not have been more complete: indeed Erasmus apparently destroyed his letters. Yet the young Zwingli had been a most fervent admirer of Erasmus' humanism and efforts for religious reform. Born in 1484 of peasant stock, he attended university before visiting Italy as chaplain to the mercenary troops of his canton – an experience which evoked a revulsion against a system which he described as condoning the sale of flesh for slaughter while condemning the eating of meat during Lent. His appointment as 'people's priest' at Zurich on 1 January 1519 was followed forthwith by his preaching in the form of direct and original scriptural commentaries – though it was not until 1520 that he renounced his papal book grant.[26]

A mutual acquaintance, Henricus Glareanus, regarded by Erasmus as the foremost of Swiss humanists, brought about the first meeting of the two men either in or shortly before April 1516. This unquestionably had a major impact upon the Swiss and upon his own programme of Christian renewal.[27] A surviving letter, in transcript form, records Zwingli's fulsome praise of 'the Great Philosopher and Theologian', who has done so much for both liberal studies and Holy Scripture and who will rescue theology from barbarism and logic-chopping.[28] In his years of near-adulation of Erasmus, not only did Zwingli possess more books from his pen than from that of any other contemporary, but his underlinings attest the close study which he accorded them. In his 'Articles' of 1523, describing how he came to the certitude that Christ is sole mediator, Zwingli relates how, some eight or nine years earlier, he had read a 'most erudite and elegant' poem by Erasmus. This had convinced him that Christ alone is the source of all good, as saviour and benefactor, and as consolation and thesaurus of the soul.[29] The 'Erasmian phase' of Zwingli's evolution, which continued up to and beyond his move to Zurich, established several indelible attributes of his theology: one biographer has identified therein the specific influence of many of Erasmus' major publications. Above all, it was the biblical and Christocentric emphasis which had an enduring impact. Zwingli's debt to Erasmus went far beyond his undoubted reverence for humanist scholarship. Moreover, although it might well be urged that Zwingli's message to the people of Zurich, at least after 1522, became perhaps more evangelical in tone than that of Erasmus, the deeply Erasmian emphasis on Christ as both preceptor and exemplar in the conduct of human affairs was to remain a pre-eminent theme.[30]

Yet almost from the outset Erasmus' response to Zwingli's early reformist writings was one of caution or even inhibition. More fundamentally, Zwingli's own development was influenced not only by the belief that Erasmus was reluctant to face up to certain consequences in regard to papal authority but also by the emergence of a more radical assessment of the scriptural meaning of judgment and of grace, which went further than Erasmus' 'Philosophy of Christ'. It is somewhat surprising to find Gottfried Locher illustrating this with the contention that 'despite some evangelical ideas the Handbook (*Enchiridion*), pious as it is, is not a reformation book; it is a humanist book'. Yet assuredly the issues of revelation as opposed to education and of predestination as against free will were as much involved as any conclusion by Zwingli that Erasmus was but a timid Eli alongside Luther's Elijah.[31] For some years Zwingli clung to the hope of Erasmus' public adhesion to the Protestant cause. Despite suggestions of increasing alienation, Zwingli reputedly visited him in Basel in January 1522, and certainly, though in letters no longer extant, offered him the citizenship of Zurich. It might well be argued that Zwingli's development of his own Christocentric theology based upon Scripture alone derived originally from the Erasmian rather than from the Lutheran example. Yet undoubtedly, between his arrival in Zurich and some time in 1522, he went on to develop doctrines of justification and predestination, as well as a more pessimistic assessment of human nature, which stood at variance with those of his erstwhile mentor.[32]

Certainly Zwingli's petition to the Bishop of Constance in August 1522 forthwith evoked Erasmus' apprehension. His reply to the offer of citizenship had explained his own wish 'to be a citizen of the world'. Relying on the friendly regard of the Emperor, and the support of many cardinals, the only danger is from such as would still rave against him were he in Zurich. This polite but specific rebuff accompanies the injunction: 'Fight on, dear Zwingli, not only with courage but with prudence too.' Alas, such advice had already been ignored, and when Erasmus writes again, having now read what Zwingli has written, his letter bristles with reproof: 'I beseech you by the glory of the gospel . . . if you publish anything in future . . . do not forget the modesty and prudence demanded by the gospel. Consult scholarly friends before you issue anything to the public. I fear that defence of yours may land you in great peril, and even do harm to the church.' Erasmus trusts that this will be taken in good part, for he writes with the warmest affection, and late at night![33] There is little doubt that what so upset him in Zwingli's August declaration was its apparent denial, at least to the present hierarchy, of any right of authoritative judgment either in matters of scriptural interpretation or of Church government. But in December there follows a further expression of Erasmus' horror that 'another piece of nonsense, utter rubbish, has appeared about the pope. If the author had put his name to it, he would have been raving mad.' Apparently

Erasmus had a shrewd idea that the author was Zwingli – who, for his part, would not have relished the observation that 'if all Luther's party are like this, I wash my hands of the whole lot of them. I never saw anything more mad than this foolish stuff.'[34]

This incipient alienation on the side of Erasmus turned to undisguised hostility in the following year, when Hutten was granted asylum in Zurich. The Introduction to his *Spongia* against Hutten, penned in August and published in September 1523, took the form of an address to Zwingli and to Zurich Town Council. The fact that Hutten died before its publication, thus necessitating a new Preface, did nothing to tone down the bitterness with which Erasmus questioned Zwingli's decision to welcome one who had done so much damage to the Gospel cause, as well as that of good letters.[35] A much longer letter sent to Zwingli direct, dated 31 August, is explicit in its criticism of its recipient's own opinions. Erasmus rebuts the charge that he is a temporiser and then accuses Zwingli of dissenting from Luther in nothing. Despite his protestation that he is troubled more by damage to the Gospel and to good letters than by personal injury, and his concluding appeal for a better direction of Zwingli's spirit, this last surviving letter marks the final breach in any real understanding and friendship.[36]

Thereafter Erasmus' letters to others, and his publications, reflect his almost total rejection of Zwingli's works and teachings. We noticed earlier his comments to Melanchthon in 1524 concerning Zwinglian excesses in respect of images and vestments, and on the needlessly engendered tumult. By October 1525 Erasmus deplores a new ingredient added by Zwingli to the tragedy of Carlstadt's teaching that 'in the Eucharist nothing is present save bread and wine'.[37] This alludes to Zwingli's anonymous publication of the *Epistola* ('A Most Christian Letter') composed some years earlier by Cornelisz Hoen, Erasmus' fellow-countryman. This, in its cogent statement of the case against transubstantiation, and in its explicit distinction between 'the bread received by mouth and Christ, who is received by faith', anticipated the teaching on the Eucharist of Zwingli, who now edited the work.[38] In November, Erasmus writes to his friend Conrad Pellican referring to the dog-fight now in progress between his adversaries: Zwingli and Oecolampadius against Luther and Bugenhagen, with Hubmaier joining in.[39]

Erasmus became more and more embittered, at least in part because of what he saw as the desertion of friends, sometimes quite literally, to the Zwinglian camp. Conrad Pellican, a devotee of Erasmus since helping with his edition of Jerome in 1515, since 1523 a professor of theology in Basel, was at one time regarded by him as his 'especially true friend'. But this changed in 1525 when Erasmus accused him of disloyalty in spreading the story that he, Erasmus, held opinions on the Eucharist which in no way differed from those of Oecolampadius. After failing to restore full friendship, Pellican accepted Zwingli's invitation to move to Zurich in 1526. His subsequent attempts at reconciliation bore fruit only shortly before Erasmus' death ten years later, but he always thought of himself as a disciple of Erasmus and may fairly be described as one of those Protestant humanists who looked back in reverence. Johannes Oecolampadius, theologian and preacher, had helped Erasmus with his New Testament in 1515–16, and a period of mutual admiration and friendship ensued. Before returning to Basel as professor of theology in 1523, however, he had already begun to correspond with Zwingli. Although Oecolampadius criticised his *De libero arbitrio*, Erasmus more than once expressed very guarded sympathy with the former's views on the Eucharist. An uneasy friendship remained, although, following his own departure to Freiburg in 1529, Erasmus was to express his sorrow at the course of the Protestant Reformation in Basel under the leadership of Oecolampadius.[40]

Erasmus' criticisms of Zwingli were concerned with his defiance of proper authority, violence of action and extreme measures, together of course with his teaching on the Eucharist. But when Zwingli himself felt impelled to dissent from Erasmus' theology it was free will as against predestination which emerged as the crucial issue. He remained courteous and polite, and continued to hope for a rapprochement. But when *De libero arbitrio* appeared in print it was he who first moved to repudiate its theme. His 'Commentary on True and False Religion', March 1525, has been seen as at least in part a rejoinder to Erasmus, though only in his 'Original Sin' in the following year does the concept of Election clearly emerge. To very many contemporaries this question undoubtedly marked the great divide.[41] Yet Erasmus' correspondence records increasing concern not only at the spread of the various Protestant factions but also at the bitterness of their doctrinal quarrels among themselves, especially about the Eucharist. In 1526 he points specifically to the advance of the Zwinglians, 'who in the matter of the Eucharist dissent from the Lutherans',[42] and in 1527 refers to bitter quarrels between Zwingli, Luther and Osiander, not to mention 'Prophets' and Anabaptists![43] To Lorenzo Campeggio, in July 1530, he laments the fact that Zwinglian influence now seems as widespread as is the Lutheran. Nor is it merely doctrinal matters that distress him. 'I am not so much troubled by dogmas, especially Luther's, as by seeing the emergence under the guise of Gospellers of a type of man who most of all displeases me.'[44]

His reaction at the news of Zwingli's death is hardly surprising. His *Epistola ad fratres Germaniae inferioris*, of the previous year, although primarily directed at Bucer and Strassburg, had found space for several thrusts at Zwingli, a seditious agitator with inflated claims to the inspiration of the Spirit.[45] Perhaps Erasmus discerned poetic justice in what occurred. Writing to one of his closest friends, Boniface Amerbach, on 24 October 1531, he comments starkly that 'Zwingli has his judgment among men: would that he might meet with a kinder from God'. Later, to Campeggio, he recounts how 'there have perished together two principal pillars of the sect of Sacramentaries'. Zwingli is fallen in battle, his body quartered and burned; the news has so distressed Oecolampadius as to cause him to sink into death, in excruciating pain.[46] To be fair, such reactions were not confined to Erasmus, who received letters early in 1532 from Erasmus Schets and Nicholas Olah expressing their unconcealed relief at the news.[47]

In terms of theology, the relationship between Zwingli and Erasmus remains complicated and contentious, not least in the writings of modern scholars. Did the teachings of the Reformation in Zurich emerge from a further development of Erasmus' *philosophia Christi* or from a reaction against its very ethos? That Erasmus feared and condemned what he saw as a pattern of rebellion against inherited and duly constituted ecclesiastical authority, and of over-hasty and sometimes violent action: this is not in dispute. But what of Zwingli's central teachings, especially on the nature of man's salvation? Those principles which have been seen as distinguishing Zwingli from Erasmus may perhaps be subsumed into three basic issues: the Church, authority and discipline; the Eucharist or Last Supper; and the difference between an optimistic and a pessimistic estimate of man's nature and of his hope of salvation.[48] In respect of the first of these, it would be fair to say that Erasmus' position remained fundamentally Catholic while Zwingli's established the basis of the 'Reformed Churches'. But the other two issues are far more controversial.

On the question of the Eucharist, many modern writers accept the assertion that Zwingli thought of the bread and wine as *nuda signa* (bare symbols) in a commemorative service, and that he was thus, as condemned by Erasmus, a 'Sacramentary'. Yet a significant minority opinion believes this to be an over-simplification, and discerns in

Zwingli's interpretation an element of mysticism which at least in part derives directly from the writings of Erasmus himself. We observed in Chapter Five[49] the tendency of Erasmus to cling to a belief in Christ's presence at and in the Sacrament, while simultaneously fighting shy of any clear and meaningful *definition* of such a presence. There is at least a case for arguing that many of the 'Sacramentaries' were entitled to think of Erasmus as their lost leader.

In this context we have already noticed the actual or potential influences of Erasmus, to whom Oecolampadius attributed scepticism on the Real Presence, and also of Carlstadt and of Hoen, although one authority suggests that Zwingli, like Ridley in England, may well have gone directly to the ninth-century Ratramnus for the phrase *hoc figurat corpus meum*.[50] Eventually Zwingli and Oecolampadius reached almost identical positions. The assertion that Erasmus, having advanced in the same direction, then retreated into a cautious profession of Catholic orthodoxy is probably too sweeping, though Leo Jud attempted in 1526 to cite earlier Erasmian writings as pointing the way to a 'spiritual' interpretation by his recourse to the word 'symbol' and his use of John 6 in the *Enchiridion*. Incontestably, both in Erasmus and in Zwingli a contrast is made between the 'outward' and the 'inward', with an emphasis upon spiritual participation. Whatever Erasmus' ultimate conclusions – assuming he ever reached any with total clarity – upon the spiritual and physical significances of the bread and wine, his emphasis upon the spiritual *participation* of the communicants and upon the *corporate* importance of such participation for the congregation, appears an essential contribution to the emergence of the interpretation of the Eucharist which characterised the Swiss Reformed Churches.[51]

We may well move on with some relief to what many would still consider the most fundamental difference between the two men, and some would identify as the crucial difference between 'humanist' and 'reformed' Christianity. This involves the fundamental nature of man and of his hope of salvation. Zwingli's insistence on mankind's utter depravity and total helplessness in the face of sin without divine election to salvation surely stands in total contrast with the allegedly semi-Pelagian position of Erasmus and of the Anabaptists. For Zwingli, it would seem, the gift of grace is no longer freely available in the sense that it is something for which all at least can strive, but a predestined and ineluctable decision and event. Significantly, in our general context, any innate optimism about *humanitas* has disappeared. Whereas Erasmus' *philosophia Christi* surely reflects an optimistic estimate of man's capacity to seek out God and to obey Christ's precepts and example within this world, 'Reformed Christianity' appears to spring largely from despair in contemplation of the great gulf between God's holiness and mankind's state of fathomless sin, with *predestined* salvation the only credible escape. While Erasmus attributed to man enough vestiges of natural good to make it possible at least for him to attempt to search out Christ, for Zwingli everything pertaining to salvation derived from a totally and arbitrarily predestined gift of grace. Well might he and Oecolampadius be seen as pointing the way to Calvin.[52]

Yet despite the stark contrast revealed by this particular perspective, when viewed in more general terms the contention that Zwingli stood at the intersection of humanism and the Reformation still possesses validity. We must reiterate the emphasis of many historians upon Zwingli's debt to Erasmus for the original development of his scriptural and Christocentric principles, and for his stress upon a certain dichotomy of body and of spirit. Important aspects of his theology are demonstrably influenced by Erasmus and are indeed a continuation of and not a revulsion against his 'Philosophy of Christ'. Perhaps most notably, the tendency of what emerged as neo-theocracy in Zurich to attempt to regulate not only religious but also social relations (including a scheme of poor relief) so as to 'objectivize the Word of God' is surely in full accord with the injunction that Christ's precepts should be followed in this life.[53]

The case of a third great leader of this era of the Reformation presents us with similar ironies. Martin Bucer of Schlettstadt (born 1491), a Dominican, was influenced first by the humanism of Beatus Rhenanus and then by reading the works of his friend Erasmus, before experiencing the overwhelming impact of hearing Luther in 1518. He then procured release from his monastic vows and became a preacher before settling in 1523 at Strassburg, where he became the leader of religious reform. His own doctrinal evolution reflected divergent influences, but in his early years he looked chiefly to Erasmus, on whom at one time he aspired to model himself. Like Zwingli an avid collector of the great humanist's works, as late as 1520 he confided that he had recourse to discreet economies in order to procure them.[54] Despite Bucer's contention that 'Luther is wholly in agreement with Erasmus, except that he proclaims openly what Erasmus has restricted himself to insinuating', the influence of Wittenberg altered things. This influence, in turn, was to be countered by that of Zwingli. Yet in some respects Bucer and his Strassburg colleagues continued to follow Erasmus, notably in their continued efforts to display ecumenical principles. A fair number of Anabaptist leaders, including Hubmaier, Denck, Sattler, and Hoffmann, found the city not uncongenial, until their expulsion in 1527 – a year in which Bucer made one more unsuccessful attempt to win Erasmus over to what he perceived as the true cause of the Reformation.[55]

Yet by then relations between Erasmus and Strassburg had long deteriorated, although the former's hostility may well have derived initially not so much from Bucer as from Wolfgang Capito, who settled there in mid-1523 and became the co-architect of reform in that city. Capito (born *c.* 1478), sometime professor of theology at Basel and friend of Oecolampadius and Pellican, had been described at one time as Erasmus' *alter ego*.[56] But from 1519 onward[57] he expressed concern lest Erasmus take issue against Luther, and voiced the justified fear that the former would end up hated by both sides.[58] In 1523, while deploring Hutten's publication, he made clear his discontent with Erasmus' attitude.[59] The decisive juncture in their increasing estrangement was, once again, the writing of *De libero arbitrio*. Capito's critical remarks about an early draft of the *Diatribe* led Erasmus to express his regret at having nourished 'this monster', and his comments on this 'bishop of the new Gospel' were henceforth unflattering. His bitterness became so deep that, while he continued to write to other Protestants such as Melanchthon and Bucer himself, a curt letter in 1524, in which he repeats his suspicion that his former friend had instigated attacks upon him, was his last to Capito.[60] The impact on Erasmus of this defection may well have resembled that of Oecolampadius to neo-Zwinglianism and of Pellican to Zurich itself.

Meanwhile, Bucer also openly declared himself for Luther. In November 1524 he urged Luther to reply to the pestiferous pamphlet of Erasmus, 'that unhappy slave of glory, who pushes forward to prefer the spittle of his own opinion to Scripture'. Better that 'that miracle of erudition' (that is, Erasmus) should perish rather than be permitted to obscure the glory of Christ.[61] Ironically, the specific doctrine at issue was Luther's teaching on the Eucharist, on which Bucer himself was to veer towards Zwingli. Despite such harsh words, as late as 1527 he wrote Erasmus a letter now lost requesting an interview when, with friends, he proposed to pass through Basel. In Erasmus' substantial reply, a couple of scathing allusions to Capito stand in stark contrast with his avowal to Bucer that 'I have never disliked you as far as concerns private feelings'. But the heart of the epistle is devoted to serious issues of principle.

In reply to Bucer's conjectures as to why he has not 'joined your church', Erasmus lists three basic reasons. First, 'if my conscience could have been persuaded that this movement proceeded from God, I should have been now long since a soldier in your camp. The second reason is that I see many in your group who are strangers to all Evangelical soundness . . . The third thing which deterred me is the intense discord between the leaders of the movement.' Turning next to specific behaviour which vitiates avowed objectives, Erasmus berates Luther for his betrayal of the cause of the Gospel by his buffoonery against the King of England and by provoking reactions which can only redouble our present slavery – for 'I seem to see a cruel and bloody century ahead, if the provoked section gets its breath again . . .' As for judgment in terms of conduct, were wives more amenable, pupils more obedient, citizens more tractable, workmen more trustworthy, sellers less deceitful, this would have commended the Gospels. But alas, many whose love of piety and abhorrence of pharisaism at first made them favour this movement, together with princes who now see a disorderly host, trailing vagabonds and other questionable categories in its wake, are now unsympathetic. Predictably, Erasmus condemns certain rascals who blame his writings and, more daringly, after sketching how the string of ecclesiastical authority, having been stretched too tightly, has snapped, he goes on to forecast 'that the same will happen one day to the princes, if they too continue to stretch *their* rope too tightly'. Thus the leaders of reform 'should have guarded against all sedition'; proceeding with moderation they would have won support from many of the princes and bishops. Yet alas, 'those who disdain the episcopal regulations do not even obey the commandments of God. Those who disregard the careful choice of foods indulge in greed and gluttony.' After conciliatory comments on Bucer's gift for preaching the Word, and on his courtesy of conduct, the letter ends, understandably, with the hope that 'you will have the good sense not to circulate this letter, lest it cause any disturbance'.[62]

This letter is perhaps more fairly described as a rebuttal of Bucer's cause rather than as an abrupt personal rebuff. Yet contemporaneous accusations from Zwingli, Pellican and Jud of temporising did not improve Erasmus' general temper. What finally brought gathering suspicion and distrust to a head was the decision of Gerard Geldenhauer,[63] a Dutch refugee and former friend of Erasmus now in Strassburg, to print part of the *Apologia adversus . . . monachos* of Erasmus against certain Spanish accusations, together with an added plea for toleration, citing Erasmus as against the persecution of heretics and hence by inference against certain imperial and papal laws. Erasmus, understandably not unmindful of an imperial mandate against Anabaptists issued in January 1528, may well have feared removal of his name from the pension list.[64] Certainly he reacted with considerable speed, and his *Epistola contra quosdam qui se falso iactant evangelicos* ('Against the Pseudoevangelicals') appeared in November of 1529. This work devotes space to several men now seen as adversaries, including Geldenhauer, whom Erasmus labels 'Vulturius', and also to an indignant rebuttal of the atrocious charge of condoning heresy or seeking to take away the princes' sword of justice. Again Erasmus deplores the striking absence of behaviour worthy of the Gospel, despite attacks on the luxury of the clergy, ambition of the bishops, and tyranny of the Roman Pontiff. Look around at this Evangelical people for any less indulgence in luxury, libido and money than exists amongst those so detested! Show me where savagery gives place to gentleness, rapacity to liberality, and so forth. The images have been thrown out of churches, but to what advantage in default of any improvement in spirit? The Mass is abrogated, but what has replaced it?[65]

Bucer's intention to reply becoming known, Erasmus wrote in March 1530 to the Magistrates of Strassburg, attempting to persuade them to forestall any hostile publication, yet in the same month was published an *Epistola Apologetica* in defence of the clergy of that city and issued in their name, but written by Bucer. Despite his contemptuous dismissal of this 'bagatelle' as prolix and fraudulent, Erasmus is rightly described as obsessed with the affair throughout the summer.[66] One letter described two books issued by Strassburg as 'so vain and inept' as to be unreadable;[67] clearly he managed to overcome this quite speedily, for in August there appeared his response to the 'Apology': the *Epistola ad fratres Germaniae inferioris, & Phrysiae Orientalis*. The inclusion of East Frisia in the title is significant, for there Erasmus believes the Sacramentaries and Anabaptists have almost run amok. This is surely one of his most rancorous works.

In rebuttal of what he regards as a tissue of lies and hypocrisy, Erasmus mingles rehearsal of personal injuries, insults and distortions with detailed exposition of the doctrinal errors of the 'pseudo-evangelists', and expressions of horror at the composition of their membership and the shortcomings in their conduct. Indeed, have not their own leaders, including Oecolampadius and Bucer himself, echoed Melanchthon's observation in a letter to Erasmus, that alas many who are lost live under the title of Evangelicals? As for pronouncements on doctrine, if Zwingli and Bucer can claim to be inspired by the Spirit, what inhibits similar pretensions by others?[68] Among their errors in dogma Erasmus includes the reduction of the number of sacraments to two, the questioning of the validity of Infant Baptism, and the assertion that the divine body and blood are not present in the Eucharist.[69] On this last issue, Pellican is followed by Oecolampadius in purveyance of so many lies. Erasmus has clearly testified to the Senate of Basel that his beliefs about the Eucharist accord with those of the Catholic Church. Where in his writings has he referred to the bread and wine therein as mere symbols?[70] Or where again does he teach that the Mass is an abomination, that altars should be torn down, that the Eucharist is idolatrous and Confession neither necessary nor useful, or does he ever counsel rejection of all ceremonies and of the constitution of the Papacy itself as contrary to the Word of God?[71] Later again, sandwiched between glowing tributes to Melanchthon, he sets out his notorious list of the disreputable rag-tag and bobtail, including fugitives, devotees of licence, ignorant women, mercenaries, and so forth, which trails along with the new movements.[72]

While the Strassburgers refrained from yet another rejoinder Erasmus seemed unable to let the sorry squabble rest. Even amidst his concern for the abortive Diet of Augsburg, he found space for a gibe at 'that light-weight Bucer' who, along with his 'Vulturius', has ravingly paraded his wisdom. To Bernard of Cles he complained that 'it rains Gospellers' books'.[73] In a letter to Sebastian Franck, appended to the second edition of his *Epistola contra Pseudevangelicos*, 1531, Erasmus grudgingly admits to some former familiarity with Bucer. But he is pleased to note that the Strassburg Magistrates, apparently in response to his remonstrance, have imprisoned Vulturius' printer.[74] Alas, Franck's own *Chronica*, which we shall encounter in the next chapter, which listed Erasmus among those valiant heretics who opposed papal corruption, was also published in Strassburg, and Erasmus at first charged Bucer with at least encouraging its appearance. Writing to Conrad Goclenius he charges the Strassburgers with stirring up imperial wrath against him by publishing a book in German which cites Erasmus' authority against the Emperor's majesty; doubtless Capito and Bucer are involved, perhaps assisted secretly by Eppendorf.[75]

By far the fullest exposition of Erasmus' assessment of Bucer is found in a long letter sent to him in March 1532, which is also a considered judgment of how and why the Protestant Reformers had gone astray. The nub of his case is that the Church should be moderately handled, not overthrown. Yet his opponents display only sour discord even among themselves. How then can they profess their doctrine to be of

Christ? Unflattering allusions to Zwingli, Capito and Oecolampadius, and Bucer and Geldenhauer, accompany Erasmus' recollections of the tumults in Basel between Catholics and Evangelicals. A declaration that the Lord will judge all hearts precedes Erasmus' citing of Zwingli's death: an armed Evangelical fallen in battle. As for Luther, Erasmus has vainly striven to win him back to moderate counsels.[76] A lengthy rebuttal of Bucer's incorrect imputation to Erasmus of doctrinal agreement with him rehearses many of the points cited earlier. As to ritual innovations, how does demolishing statues and besmearing paintings pertain to the advancement of the Gospel?[77]

Were Erasmus persuaded that it is truly Christ's cause that his opponents profess, he would not require three days to accede to their camp. But even if he found their doctrines less abhorrent, there is one other thing which deters him: 'Once enlisted in your army, I would never be free to secede from you . . . And among you new dogmas are repeatedly brought forth; to which willy-nilly subscription is required, if but once I enlist my name.'[78] What are the fruits of such innovations? Far from producing better Christians, their devotees observe neither laws nor conventions, public or private. 'So much do we hear of "Gospel, Gospel, faith, faith" '; yet Erasmus sees only deterioration into calamity for the Christian domain. In place of waning piety what else can we expect but paganism when 'we have at length as many sects as cities'? Beneath the shelter of the Gospel name there flourish some who are either rascally or stupid, including those who want to change everything. This is not possible 'without either tyranny or a general Synod or a princely and episcopal combination' – and assuredly the medicine of despotism is not the prescription of the Gospel. Only necessary change is justified; the use of images and invocation of saints, if engendering piety, could well be left alone. 'For the rest, what is superstitious may be corrected, and that gradually, and by persuasion rather than force.' As for Erasmus, no fear, and no hope, will induce him to avow a religion of which he is not persuaded.[79]

Quite clearly, both admirers of Erasmus' consistency of attitudes and principles and those who would descry a retreat from previously implied, if not firmly held, positions, might have a field day with much of this material. Predictably, this letter ended direct epistolary relations between Erasmus and Strassburg. Yet all did not end in bitterness and distrust. For when, in the following year, Erasmus published his *De sarcienda ecclesiae concordia* ('On Mending the Concord of the Church') it was Wolfgang Capito who welcomed its sentiments and extended its influence by translating the work into German. Later again, in March of 1536, but a few months before his death, Erasmus was visited by the Strassburg leaders, including Bucer, though friendly conversation did not include vexed points of doctrine. When that death occurred, Capito could not refrain from pointing to its occurrence 'amidst Lutheran heretics' whom Erasmus had always claimed to reject. Nevertheless, time perhaps facilitating a more detached and accurate perspective, Bucer himself, looking back from 1542, was able to declare in his *De vera ecclesiarum* that he identified Erasmus as initiating the Reformation by his condemnation of man's reliance for his salvation upon ceremonies rather than on faith in Christ.[80]

To sum up on Erasmus and Bucer, the tragedy of personal misunderstandings and estrangement between two men who had so much in common need hardly be laboured. But how real and extensive were their doctrinal differences? There is much agreement in discerning a major influence of Erasmus upon Bucer's concept both of Baptism and of its subsequent reaffirmation through Confirmation, in his doctrine of justification and his ideal of the Christian Commonwealth, and yet again in his teaching on the Last Supper or Eucharist. But it is difficult to be precise and dangerous to be dogmatic. Thus, oddly enough, Bucer's own position on the Eucharist had shifted. Ironically, when he wrote declaring his adhesion to Luther in November 1524, after the publication of *De libero arbitrio*, he criticised Erasmus not only for his defence of free will but also for his apparent departure from a near-literal interpretation of the phrase 'This is my body'. But he subsequently moved, whether under the influence of Zwingli – though he did not go as far as the Zurich reformer – or that of Erasmus or even that of the Radicals, to a position which anticipated Calvin's doctrine of 'receptionism'. This drew a parallel between the receiving of the elements and the nourishment of the soul by the body of Christ. Certainly, as we have seen, Bucer claimed to find much precedent for his views in the writings of Erasmus, whom he resembled in his continued insistence that the Sacrament must remain endowed with an element of mystery.[81] It has indeed been suggested that what separated the two men was not so much their eucharistic or any other specific doctrine as their ecclesiology, taken to include not only its institutional aspects but also the crucial issue of the source of authority on religious matters. Yet in spite of Erasmus' scathing comments about 'pseudo-evangelicals', any attempt to discern a difference of position in respect of the implications of faith for conduct begs the question. For many of the precepts of Erasmus are most strikingly reiterated in Bucer's *De Regno Christi*.

This extended exposition of the religious, social and economic responsibilities of the Church and of the Prince was admittedly written as late as 1550, and was dedicated to Edward VI of England. Comment has been made on its relevance to the English background and its occasional resemblance to More's *Utopia*. But Bucer's own version of the *respublica Christiana* is extremely close to that of Erasmus. In respect both of Bucer's general vision of the duties of the Christian prince or magistrate and of many particular aspects of its content, the voice of Erasmus – in his *Education of a Christian Prince* and elsewhere – may clearly be heard alongside the fruits of Bucer's own experiences in Strassburg. In particular, their views on the concept of Christian stewardship (including the duties of the nobility) and of social equity, their whole treatment of the problem of poverty and of its relief, and their combination of a virulent suspicion of merchants with a willingness none the less to concede a distinction between abominable biting usury and moderate interest, display unmistakable resemblances.[82]

How then may we explain the depths of bitterness which Erasmus incontestably displayed at times not only toward Bucer but also to Zwingli, Capito, Oecolampadius, and Pellican – all former Erasmians in a sense in which Luther surely never was – in such marked contrast with the tolerance extended to Melanchthon and a few others despite their resolute adherence to the Wittenberg camp? Perhaps it was because, not content with their defection in siding with Luther over the crucial free-will controversy, they then added insult to injury by moving beyond the Lutheran position. This they did most notably of course on the Eucharist, where they attributed to Erasmus opinions which he denied having held, but which they maintained he lacked only the courage precisely and overtly to avow. It is difficult to dissent from the contention that Erasmus' wounded ego played a far from negligible role in many of his strictures.[83] Yet here again we meet with paradox: for most assessments would characterise such as Capito, described by his biographer[84] as personifying the transition from humanism to Protestant Reformation, or Pellican, Oecolampadius, Zwingli, and Bucer as more humanist than Luther. For their part, their near-unanimous concurrence that it was Erasmus who first pointed them along the road of religious reform was never forgotten amidst their chagrin at what they saw as his failure to face the consequences of much of what he himself had taught. Yet any ambiguity or change of stance were not found only in Erasmus: perhaps we may conclude with the sad irony, given the tragic circumstances of Zwingli's death, that one of the first Erasmian influences discerned in his writings was a tendency toward Christian pacifism.[85]

Eight

THE RADICAL REFORMATION

Unravelling relationships between Erasmus and the Radical Reformation is an intractable and often frustrating task. On the elements of ambivalence in Erasmus enough has been said, while the Radical Reformation – itself a term of relatively recent adoption – has been described as displaying all the tints of the spectrum without their coordination. Less elegantly, the criss-cross interconnections between its leading figures and their ideas may not unfairly be likened to a web woven by a drunken spider. At first sight, even to suggest considerable affinities may beg the question. Erasmus remained, however waveringly, within the fold of the Catholic Church, while this range of lesser figures, against whom almost every man's hand was turned, adopted doctrinal and social teachings which took them well beyond the Magisterial Reformation of Luther, Zwingli and Bucer, which Erasmus always refused to join. Yet relationships both in the realm of ideas and in the shape of personal contact there most certainly were. Of course, distinctions must be made between what the Radicals avowedly owed to Erasmus, what they taught that we may plausibly assign to and sometimes trace quite clearly in his writings, and what they attributed to him that he himself denied. Certainly significant divergences emerged between what they thought about Erasmus and what he in turn believed and wrote about the Radicals.

Construction of too neat and orderly a model would be mistaken, as would also be any retrospective imposition upon the religious ferment of the 1520s and '30s of a pattern derived from the considered doctrinal confessions of later religious denominations. Yet this reflection does much to resolve the apparent paradox of the relationships which certainly existed between the ideas of Erasmus and those of many Radical leaders. For nothing could be more explicit than the declaration by the doyen of historians of the Radical Reformation, a term for which he was indeed responsible, that Erasmus was the unwitting patron of much that was to prove decisive for its whole development.[1]

The adjective unwitting is of course significant, as also is the contention, in respect of the debt of the first Anabaptists to Erasmus, that a dependence can scarcely be conclusively proven.[2]

This admitted, some readers may welcome an effort to indicate the general scope of what was alternatively and earlier described as the Left Wing of the Reformation. Modern research suggests three major divisions: Anabaptists, 'Spiritualists', and 'Evangelical Rationalists' or 'Catholic Evangelicals'. Notable among these last categories were such as Juan de Valdés, Servetus, Castellio, and Bernardino Ochino, who were of Spanish and Italian origin and of sufficient diversity as to meet with persecution from Spanish intolerance on the one hand and Calvinist theocracy on the other. The debts of some of them to Erasmus seem indisputable. The 'Spiritualists' embraced types of what in many contemporary eyes were dreadful heresies, including most notably anti-Trinitarianism, and despite his indignant protests they did sometimes find ammunition in unguarded utterances of Erasmus. But it was the first-named category which served as the almost universal tar-brush for conservative opinion: the Anabaptists. It is perhaps in this area that the largest number of parallels between the teachings of the Radical Reformation and those of Erasmus have been traced. Yet here again it must be stressed that the roots of Anabaptism were diverse and its manifestations far from uniform in respect of such issues as pacifism as opposed to apocalyptic violence, or community of property. Indeed even a general pattern such as this runs risks of over-simplification in terminology. It is worth recollecting that, to contemporaries, second only to 'Anabaptist' as a term to denigrate the Radicals was 'Sacramentary', while 'spiritualising' is used by several modern historians to characterise a general contribution of Erasmus toward the movement as a whole.[3]

Moreover, apropos the reference to apolcalyptic violence, it is worth taking note of a recent, and by no means hostile, survey of Anabaptist historiography. This indeed suggests that attempts to minimise the significance of the 'social-revolutionary' enthusiasts, in the interests of rendering respectable the mainstream of pacific evangelical Anabaptists, may well have been overdone.[4] Much discussion has of course concerned the roots of Anabaptism not in a geographical but in an ideological/doctrinal sense. These roots have been discerned by some historians not only in such medieval heresies as those of the Waldenses and the Bohemian Brethren, or in Netherlandish Sacramentarianism and extremist Zwinglian offshoots, but also in the *Devotio Moderna* which we considered at an earlier stage.[5] Indeed, alongside discussion as to whether Erasmian ideas impinged upon the early Anabaptists directly or indirectly via Zwinglianism, must now be placed the question of whether Erasmus himself is to be seen as the mere agent for transmission of religious ideals which had their latest and perhaps their greatest flowering in the *Devotio Moderna*. By no means novel is the suggestion that this movement anticipated several crucial characteristics of Anabaptism, most notably in regard to the ideal of active discipleship in what has been termed 'Asceticism'. Yet the devotion to this thesis of a long and cogently argued book is comparatively recent.[6]

Thus, in attempting to trace relationships between what unkind critics might describe as the ambivalent and imprecise on the one hand, and the inchoate and disparate on the other, no definitive pattern will emerge. While any overall survey of the geographical incidence of the Radical Reformation is outside our present scope, in so far as concerns the Netherlands, Erasmus was writing of his homeland. Again, at Basel and Freiburg Erasmus lived in cities which, along with Strassburg, were centres of refuge for a surprisingly large number of suspect if not hunted heretics.[7] Here also he could consult an almost unparalleled 'intelligence service' of events in the Lower Rhineland, South Germany, Switzerland, and Bohemia. His correspondence records his reactions to news of the frightening growth of what contemporaries likened to a hydra. The first part of this chapter will therefore examine those aspects of the Radical Reformation which may plausibly, and in many cases conclusively, be related to the known opinions of Erasmus, or at least of Erasmus as understood by Radicals. Thereafter, we shall consider the evolution of his own expressions of opinion concerning ideas and events which, culminating in the tragedy of Münster, led eventually to the virtual submersion of his initial guarded and qualified expressions of sympathy beneath a rising tide of dread.

While it is dangerous to push the evidence for coincidence of beliefs too far, on a fair number of issues the leaders of the Radical Reformation either appealed in their writings to the authority of Erasmus or expressed themselves in terms which are almost conclusively reminiscent of his utterances. Of some ten or twelve distinctive characteristics of the movement which have been identified, not without debate, by its historians, it may be helpful to ask whether some basic principle can be discerned from which very many of them derived? This may in fact be defined with some confidence as a strict and essentially Christocentric biblicism, with all that this entails for theology. Its consequences involve the sacraments, free will, and the Trinity, as well as the nature of the Church itself in the light of a contempt for 'externals' and excessive sacerdotalism. But perhaps most notable of all are the standards now required of the Christian in his relations with his fellow-men, especially in regard to moral behaviour, asceticism, pacifism, social justice and religious toleration.

Admittedly, the concept of a strict biblicism must be both amplified and qualified. For what was itself regarded by conventional opinion as a 'lunatic fringe' of the Reformation possessed its own wilder shores. At the one extreme it comprised those who took literally injunctions to pursue the naked truth or to speak with coals of fire, and, at the other, those zealots whose purported contact with an inner spirit led them to reject the ultimate authority with such contemptuous gibes as 'paper Pope' or 'Bible, bibble, babble'. Yet the mainstream of Radical thinking unquestionably turned to a close study of Christ's recorded teachings and the conduct of the Apostles. If the *Enchiridion* may fairly be taken as the basis of Erasmus' religious precepts, so too does it suggest the key to much Radical thinking. In particular, what has been termed the 'Christian primitivism' of the Anabaptists sought to free the Christian Church from what were seen as the scripturally unauthorised and spiritually debilitating accretions and distortions of the preceding fifteen hundred years. The similarities with Erasmus' approach need hardly be laboured. Significant also is the *Mennonite Encyclopedia*'s identification of the crucial services rendered to the Reformation by Erasmus as being his scholarly work on the Bible and his mockery of certain aspects of clerical conduct.[9]

If we proceed first to explore, as did Erasmus himself and certain of the Radicals, the application of the teachings of Christ and also of the lives of the Apostles to the sacraments of the Church, we meet two supremely important fundamentals: a refusal necessarily to accept non-biblical 'externals', and a determination where they are in fact accepted to spiritualise both their meaning and their celebration. In respect of the Eucharist we have already examined Erasmus' position in some detail. Whether or not one accepts the contention that he tended to replace the celebrant's physical consumption thereat by a spiritual communion therein, there is no doubt that many who were described as 'Sacramentaries' claimed to find in his writings a justification of their interpretations.

In the context of events between 1523 and 1526 it has been urged that it was effectively the influence of Carlstadt, Hoen and Erasmus, by now resident in Basel, which converted the whole of the Swiss Reformation to the sacramentarian position. Yet when, at a celebrated Zurich Disputation in October 1523, Hubmaier concurred with Grebel in declaring that 'the Mass is not a sacrifice', it was to Zwingli and to Leo Jud that he appealed.[10] Nevertheless, Pilgram Marbeck, for some years a leader of one of several Anabaptist groups in Strassburg, apparently cited the authority of Erasmus in describing the practice of the Lord's Supper in the early Christian Church. A word of caution is needed here. We have long taken note of Erasmus' tendency to attenuate any link between spiritual reality and efficacy, and mere physical elements or externals. But whether or not one accepts what has been called a 'mystical/physical' view of the Lord's Supper as appropriate for Erasmus as well as for the Radical Reformation, Erasmus never abandoned his insistence that it must always be celebrated by a priest.[11]

Alongside this ferment of eucharistic debate there looms the issue that gave the best-known aspect of the Radical Reformation its name: consenting and committed *adult* baptism. Here we have already encountered the ingenious suggestion that Erasmus was one of the very few who could fairly be called an Anabaptist, that is, a *re*-baptiser. In fact Erasmus sought to preserve the Catholic rite of infant baptism but also to add to it, rather than substitute for it, the suggestion of adult baptism in full knowledge of the commitment involved. But those who were labelled Anabaptists or re-baptisers by their adversaries believed only in adult baptism as having any real claim to be a sacrament of the religion instituted by Christ, and pointed to the form of his own participation therein.

One of the earliest references to those 'called Anabaptists' – so early indeed that its dating has been questioned – is found in a letter of Erasmus himself, written to Cuthbert Tunstall in June of 1523.[12] But this occurs in the context of ideas thought to be so monstrous that, if they burst forth, they would make Luther look almost orthodox. For the notion that baptism is necessary neither for infants nor for adults, together with the suggestion that nothing is present in the Eucharist but bread and wine, raised the question of what would be left of Church sacraments! Yet although it is hardly permissible to attribute the origins of the Anabaptists' most characteristic or perhaps notorious tenet to Erasmus, it is surely incontestable that they derived support and confirmation therein from a well-known passage in the preface of his paraphrase of Matthew. This quite explicitly proposed a re-enactment of the ceremony of baptism when the age of puberty was reached, after prior instruction of voluntary participants as to the real meaning of the sacrament. As to the Anabaptists' own form of baptism, contemporary Swiss sources quite clearly attest that while in some cases a pan of water was poured over the head (technically, 'affusion'), in others complete immersion was involved.[13] But it is not necessary to trespass into this hotly debated area in order to perceive a near-total agreement as to the objective of adult baptism as advocated both by Erasmus and the Anabaptists. Small wonder that the *Mennonite Encyclopedia* is emboldened to claim that Erasmus was suspected not only of Anabaptist sympathies but also of actual membership of the sect.[14]

Certainly, Erasmus was far removed from the position of George Blaurock, who declared at his trials along with Felix Manz and Conrad Grebel at Zurich in 1525 and 1526 that 'all those who baptize infants are murderers and thieves against God'. Yet he would also have sympathised with the assertion of two other Swiss martyrs in 1528 that 'baptism is for believers, for those who have given themselves over to the Son of God and desist from evil doing'. Perhaps he might have settled for the position of those Strassburg reformers in 1524 who, while conceding that adult baptism was more in conformity with Scripture than infant baptism, would have nothing to do with the Anabaptist contention that the test of voluntary and committed adult baptism set aside a quite separate community of true Christians.[15]

Moving next to the key question of free will in relation to faith and works, an extract from an anonymous Swiss treatment of *Christian Morality and Discipline*, published prior to 1530:

> Blessed is the man who keeps the middle way, not yielding to the work-saints, who promise salvation or the forgiveness of sins through works apart from faith – all their works are like wild plums – nor yet to the scribes who veer to the right and under the name of the Gospel teach a faith without works, taking the poor and obedient Christ as their satisfaction though they do not wish to hear what he says[16]

could surely have leapt straight from the teaching of Erasmus! His influence in this crucial issue has been predicated upon Dutch Anabaptists, but more immediately and particularly on those of South Germany – especially Hans Denck and Balthasar Hubmaier, both of whom actually met him in Basel.[17] In *Whether God is the Cause of Evil*, 1526, Denck concludes that 'God does not wish to have forced anyone and [wishes] to have everyone in his service of one's own free will', while Hubmaier, a year later, scorns the half-truths through which 'unfaithfulness and falsehood sit in their splendid seat [and] Christian work no longer shines with men'. He undertakes to prove by divine writ the freedom of man to choose good or evil, for through Christ man's soul has secured its lost freedom. Thus 'it is clear and evident what rubbish all they have introduced into Christendom who deny the freedom of will in man, saying that this freedom is a vain and empty designation and nothing in itself'. Both men concur, effectively, in Denck's similitude between the Magisterial Reformation and a barren tree which has as yet produced nothing but green leaves and crab apples, and in attributing the absence of any real Christian renewal in the quality of life to Lutheran doctrines of justification and predestination, which effectively did away with man's accountability for his social conduct, while the very title of Hubmaier's work, *On Free Will*, is surely in itself sufficiently indicative.[18]

Hubmaier wrote on this subject in 1527, and there is a certain irony in the fact that, following the *De libero servo/De libero arbitrio* controversy of 1525–26, it was the purportedly more respectable Magisterial Reformation that parted company with Erasmus, and the highly suspect radical wing which rallied to the defence of his ideas. The contemporary Sebastian Franck declared of the Anabaptists that 'they hold free will as self-evident', and indeed one senses a direct correlation between such insistence and the injunction to active Christian discipleship. For without it how can there be any individual moral and Christian responsibility? Thus Denck's assertion that 'it is a fabrication when false Christians say they can do nothing but what God works in them' was later to be echoed in the views of Menno Simons. There is little doubt that Erasmus was a father-figure to those radical Protestants whose insistence upon the ethical implications of genuine Christianity made them no more content with Wittenberg than with the discredited Rome! Finally, the free-will issue must surely be related to the wider context of what may perhaps not inappropriately be termed the religious philosophy of both Erasmus and the Anabaptists, in respect of their general assessment of man's nature and potential. They concur in believing that despite the lusts of the flesh and their influence upon the will, man is not wholly and irretrievably vitiated by the Fall, since the spirit, although a prisoner within the body, retains some consciousness of righteousness and ability to follow reason.[19]

Next, on the question of the Trinity, it has been suggested that Michael Servetus may well have confused Erasmus' expressions of scepticism about a subject upon which mankind was not qualified to pronounce with his own straightforward anti-Trinitarian position.[20] Yet much of what Erasmus wrote may appear at least to have opened the door to radical discussion. To be fair, during the 1520s, in view of its very tenuous scriptural basis, many Protestant leaders have been described as wavering on the question, including Zwingli, Bucer, Oecolampadius, and Melanchthon whose *Loci communes theologici* in 1521 pronounced the doctrine as not essential to salvation. But here again authorities agree that it was Erasmus' scepticism as to the authenticity of I John 5:7 – 'there are three that bear witness in heaven . . . and these three are one' – which led to its omission from the older Anabaptist versions of the Bible and its readmission only in parentheses in the Mennonite Bible of 1560. Erasmus followed this in 1523 by an exposition which cannot but have given further offence to the orthodox and comfort to those who doubted:

> Is he not destined to have fellowship with the Father, Son, and Holy Spirit who cannot disentangle according to the method of philosophy what distinguishes the Father from the Son or the Holy Spirit from both, or what the difference is between the generation of the Son from the Father and the procession of the Spirit? If I believe, as has been handed down, that the three are of one nature, what is the need of laboured disputation? If I do not believe, no human reasons will convince me . . . You will not be damned if you do not know whether the Spirit proceeding from the Father and the Son has a single or a double principle, but you will not escape perdition unless you see to it in the mean time that you have the fruits of the Spirit, which are charity, joy, peace . . .

Yet we have already noted that Erasmus most certainly was not anti-Trinitarian; when we later find Servetus writing to him in search of support for his own explicit position, he will not receive it.[21]

Thus far, we have looked at certain doctrinal aspects of the Radical Reformation which might plausibly be seen not only as rooted in a rigorously biblical approach to theology, but also as finding specific endorsements in Erasmus' teachings. At least as many similarities of approach, if not of derivation, will be found in exploring the perceived implications of a rigorously Christocentric interpretation of the Scriptures both for the conduct of a Christian toward his fellow-men and for the nature of true membership of the Christian Church. The emphasis in Erasmus' *Enchiridion* upon discipleship in life may credibly be seen to imply a concept of the Church as a brotherhood united in love. Yet while this may well have been his own ideal concerning the spirit which should animate the Church, no one would ever contend that he ever considered that concept of a select body of members withdrawn from the world which many Anabaptists were to evolve.[22]

A very early statement of the separatist principle is to be found in an explicit declaration of two Swiss Anabaptists, Grebel and Stumpf, made to Zwingli late in 1523, that 'according to the Acts of the Apostles those who had believed separated from the others [into] a new church. That is just what we must do.' In 1528 the profession of faith by Falk and Reimann, the fifth and sixth of the Swiss Anabaptist martyrs, drew a similar corollary from the tenet that baptism is for believers: 'Those who walk therein are the community of Christ and the body of Christ and the Christian church. Now we hope and are assured that we are in the true church.'[23] The Strassburg Anabaptists likewise evolved a concept of a separate and voluntary church, entered by means of the committal of believers' baptism.[24] Moreover, within the conduct of such churches, abandonment of former liturgical traditions in the interest of simplicity of worship went hand in hand with lay partnership in congregational organisation. Here again, despite the attribution to Erasmus of a certain detachment from the institutional aspects of the existing Church, and even of abstention for some periods from sacramental participation, we may hardly ascribe to him any concurrence with these traits of emergent Anabaptism – especially in the light of his insistence on sacerdotal powers, properly conferred and exercised.[25]

Yet when we restrict ourselves to Christian discipleship in life we are on very solid ground. One historian of Anabaptism goes so far as to say that 'there are formulas for true Christian living in the *Enchiridion* that might have been written by an Anabaptist'.[26] Assertions that all the Radicals shared disappointment with the moral impact of Magisterial Protestantism in its Lutheran and Zwinglian areas, indeed that an ethical imperative lay close to their hearts, suggest a major coincidence of beliefs with those of Erasmus. We have already encountered his repeated and explicit urging that genuine Christianity shines through a man's relations with his fellow-men, and his specific expression of disappointment, as in his 'Epistle against the Pseudo-evangelicals' at Strassburg, that this was not the case with many who termed themselves Gospellers. Now there is little doubt, from a variety of testimony, that – leaving on one side the quite exceptional excesses such as those at Münster – mainstream, pacific Anabaptism was characterised by humility, morality, honesty, sobriety, and charity.[27]

The title of an anonymous work already cited, *On Christian Morality and Discipline*, is crucially indicative in its contention that 'when Paul says in Romans 3 that those who are justified in Christ are justified without any merit or without the works of the Law, he does not mean that a man can be saved without *the works of faith*' [our italics].[28] Denck, again, believed it to be evident that 'none may truly know [Christ] unless he follows after him with his life',[29] and Menno Simons that

1. Portrait of Erasmus, by Quentin Metsys, 1517

2. Printing in the Sixteenth Century

EX TERTIA AVTORIS RECOGNITIONE.

HOMERVS POETA · SALOMON REX · HESIODVS ·

ARISTIDES · DEMOSTH · PLATO · ARISTOT · EVRIPID · ARISTOPHAN

IOANNES
FROBENIVS STVDIOSIS.
OMNIBVS S. D.

Accipito candide lector ERASMI ROTERODAMI, prouerbiorum Chiliadas, iam tertiũ ab ipso non æstimandis sudoribus recognitas, & ex probatissimis autoribus sic locupletatas, ut cui superioris æditionis summæ, fermè quarta pars ab hinc bienniũ accesserat, huic nunc haud multo minus sit adiectũ. Nos neq; sumptui, neq; labori pepercimus, ut tam eruditũ opus, tam copiosum, ut uere flumẽ aureũ uocare possis, q̃ emendatissimũ è nostra officina prodiret in lucẽ, planè nouum, & hactenus à nemine excusũ. Eme, fruere, & Vale.

IN INCLYTA GERMANIAE
BASILEA.

PLVTARCH · LVCIANVS · THEOCRIT · PINDARVS · CICERO · QVINTIL · VERGIL · HORATIVS · PLINIVS · A · GELLIVS · LIVIVS · SALVSTIVS

AN. M. D. XVIII.

3. Front page of Froben's edition of the *Adages*, 1518

4. A 'Professional Beggar'

5. Sketch of Erasmus, by Albrecht Dürer, 1520

6. 'Luther and Collaborators', including Melanchthon (extreme right), Justus Jonas and Erasmus (3rd and 4th from right), by Cranach the Younger

7. Luther, as seen by the Papacy

8. The Papacy, as seen by Luther

9. Portrait of Erasmus writing, by Hans Holbein, 1523

10. Philip Melanchthon, by Cranach the Elder, 1523

11. Ulrich Zwingli

12. Portrait of Erasmus, by Hans Holbein, 1523

13. Engraved Portrait of Erasmus, by Dürer, 1526; note the vase of flowers again in 19

14. Thomas Cranmer, by Gerhardt Flicke, 1546

15. Martyrdom of Ridley and Latimer, 1555, while Cranmer (top right) awaits his turn

16. Burning the Remains and Works of Bucer, at Cambridge

17. Erasmus' Dwelling in Freiburg, 1529–31

18. Sketch of Augsburg, by Georg Seld, *c.* 1530

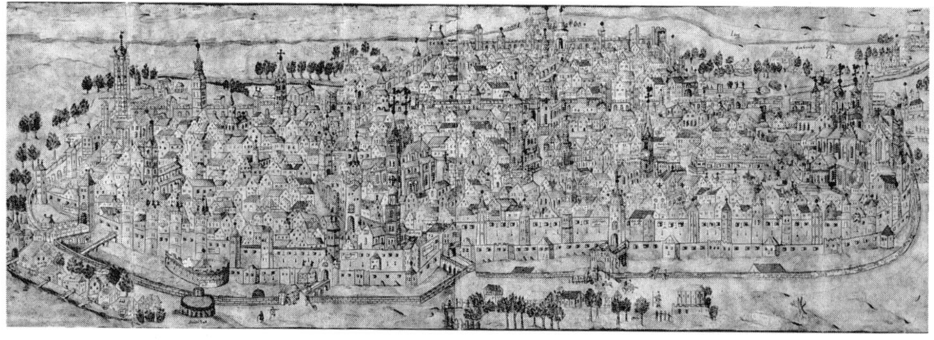

19. Erasmus, dictating, shares a jest with Gilbert Cousin (Cognatus), his secretary and friend. Wood engraving, artist unknown, *c.* 1530

20. Erasmus inspired by the Truth

'whosoever boasts that he is a Christian, the same must walk as Christ walked'.[30] Ironically, a critical assessment by a contemporary of Anabaptism in St Gallen complained that 'they insisted more powerfully on justification by works than the papists', claiming to keep their church pure and unspotted, and punishing transgression by use of the ban and 'daily excommunication among them'.[31] While Erasmus would surely never have accepted the idea of a 'Christian Ban' upon those excluded from a congregation because of moral weaknesses, the groundswell of opinion as to what Christianity must assuredly mean in terms of one's conduct is identical. Indeed, among the complaints that were to be made against him by Stephen Gardiner, writing to the Duke of Somerset in 1547, was his alleged assertion that 'the doctrine of "only faith justifieth" is a very poison', as it is to say we need no satisfactory works – the upshot being that 'by the doctrine of the Paraphrases, every man must come to the high prick of virtue'![32]

Normally included in any list of prescribed Anabaptist virtues – if we exclude the apocalyptically violent fringe – was that of meekness. A basic tenet was refusal to engage in physical violence, whether individually provoked or institutionally organised. Despite certain qualifications, this pacifism seems to be the most frequently cited coincidence of belief between Erasmus and the Radicals. His own views were fully explored in Chapter Four, with chapter-and-verse illustration of their scriptural derivation. It is therefore surprising to find that one notable scholar seeks to confine Erasmus' viewpoint to that of a general humanist aversion to conflict. Although conceding that, apart from Juan Luis Vives, Erasmus was perhaps the only outspoken pacifist of the first quarter of the sixteenth century, he finds that Erasmian pacifism 'was primarily humanitarian in character and not theological and Biblical'[33] – a dichotomy which is difficult to accept. Indeed, a rejoinder in the context of the nature and extent of Conrad Grebel's indebtedness to Erasmus on this issue, points out that both of his best-known anti-war pamphlets, *Dulce bellum inexpertis* and *Querela pacis*, were published in German, the one at Basel in 1519 by a press where Grebel was a proof-reader, the other at Zurich in 1521. Its author proceeds to postulate greater agreement on this issue between Erasmus and the Anabaptists than on any other, precisely because both were scriptural and Christocentric in their approach.[34] In the light of Erasmus' own recorded views this contention seems difficult to resist.

Grebel was also apparently deeply moved by his reading of the unpublished manuscript of the *Philirenus*, Myconius' dialogue 'on not going to war', containing quotations from Erasmus. His own pacifism became unequivocal; in 1524 he declared that 'true believing Christians are sheep among wolves, sheep for the slaughter . . . They use neither worldly sword nor war . . .'[35] Thus it has been contended that both he and Hans Denck, who also preached a doctrine of non-resistance, while indisputably influenced by Erasmus, went beyond the great humanist's general philosophy of peace to enjoin utter personal non-violence in obedience to an innermost spiritual imperative.[36] A plausible distinction suggested is that Erasmus was primarily concerned with pacifism in the context of relations between states, as a social and indeed cosmopolitan issue, whereas the pacific Anabaptists were prepared for a more rigorous version of non-resistance, applying to all the actions of the individual within society.[37] Yet at a later date Menno Simons was, like Erasmus, willing to accept the sword of justice although condemning the sword of war.[38]

When we move on to the matter of Christian social justice, notably in respect of property and charity, the position is perhaps even more complex. We have already recorded Erasmus' explanation that the original presumption among the faithful, that Christian charity entailed the ceding of any claim to private ownership of property in any case of need, could not apply within the wider world lest anarchy and bloodshed ensue. In fairness to most Anabaptist writers it must immediately be added that whenever they preached a Christian and communal ownership of property it was within their own 'gathered' or separated ranks. Thus an account of what has been described as the oldest Anabaptist congregation, that at Zollikon near St Gallen, relates how, because

> they assumed that they were the true Christian church, they also undertook, like the early Christians, to practice community of temporal goods . . . , broke the locks off their doors, chests, and cellars, and ate food and drink in good fellowship without discrimination. But as in the time of the apostles, it did not last long . . . But since it cannot be, we must show our mercy to the poor in other ways and pity their poverty . . .[39]

But alas, it was the sense in which the 'revolutionary theocracy' of the Münsterite Anabaptists established a would-be biblical commonwealth, but one with grotesque contortions, which understandably inflamed the public imagination. Beyond doubt, it was the occasional but undeniable correlation between Anabaptism and social unrest or even revolt which proved the most potent propaganda weapon in their adversaries' hands. A leading historian of millenarian Anabaptism justly observes that, while uneasy about much contemporary use of private property and looking wistfully toward community of goods as an ideal, the majority of adherents had no urge to social revolution.[40] But it was Müntzer's doctrine of revolution and the bloody excesses of the city of Münster, together with the fact that Anabaptism undeniably recruited many of its rank and file from the rural and urban poor, which inflamed European opinion.[41]

The 'Five Articles' of the Hutterian Brethren in Moravia admittedly appeared some eleven years after Erasmus' death, yet came from a sect whose members revered his insight into the ethical implications of the New Testament. They asserted that 'now that God has brought the Christian Church up out of Egypt, as they pass through the wilderness of this world, the rich should not have more than the poor, nor the poor than the rich. One of the chief articles of the creed is to believe in the communion of the saints. This means not only in things spiritual but also in things temporal.' There follows an important concession that, although 'a Christian man may not be a magistrate . . . our will and mind are not, however, to do away with worldly government or not to be obedient to it in goods and sanctions because a government shall and must be in the world, [for] the magistrate is ordained of God'.[42] Yet these careful qualifications were ignored by their opponents. Even with such rubrics, these teachings have clearly passed beyond what Erasmus would have considered practicable, and it will later prove instructive to trace the shift of emphasis in his comments on the Radicals as events unfolded. Certainly the occasional appeal to apocalyptic violence in order to hasten the over-long delayed millennium can occasion from Erasmus nothing but horror.

There remains one other coincidence of belief between Erasmus and the Radical Reformation, in this case more specifically the Anabaptists, which, though but a broad, general attitude, might well be ranked as the most significant of all. Erasmus expected compliance with a relatively strict code of personal conduct from all genuine Christians, whereas the Anabaptists imposed even more rigorous canons only within a segregated body of church members. Yet both he and they were in the forefront of what might fairly be described as advocacy of religious toleration. In marked contrast with the bigotry of such as Beza, Calvin's successor in Geneva, who alluded sourly to religious liberty as freedom for each man to go to Hell in his own way, Erasmus declared that 'the sum and substance of our religion is peace and concord. This can hardly remain the case unless we define as few matters as possible and leave each individual's judgment free on many questions. This is because there is great uncertainty about very many issues . . .'[43] While the Anabaptists were extremely strict about the behaviour of members within their own sects, and adhered most rigorously to several articles of faith, historically they eschewed any appeal to authority to enforce religious dogma, and in this respect were clearly Erasmian in their attitude. As we shall subsequently find, Erasmus never enunciated a doctrine of unqualified toleration, never adopted the position of near indifference to dogma which was to be that of Castellio, and always saw morality as the fruit of Christian beliefs which were genuinely held, rather than as a sole criterion *per se*, yet he none the less believed most fervently that the duty of the Church was to teach and to lead by example, not to coerce. It seems very clear that in this respect it is the Anabaptists – not Lutherans, Zwinglians, Calvinists, or post-Tridentine Catholics – who were the most obvious inheritors of the Erasmian religious ethos.[44]

We shall encounter Erasmus' relationships with other manifestations of the Radical Reformation when we now proceed to look at their emergence through his eyes. The first recorded instance of his receiving an opportunity to display the tolerance which marked his early reactions arose in the context of the alleged Bohemian heresies. Translations into Czech of some of Erasmus' own books had been printed in Bohemia and Moravia from about 1513 onward, while his notorious statement (in a letter to Martin Lips on 7 May 1518) that although Hus was burnt he was not confuted, may well have invited the approaches which followed.[45] Jan Slechta, sometime secretary to the King of Bohemia sent him a long letter in October 1519, giving details of the sects extant in that realm. These include 'those who distribute the Eucharist to the congregation in both kinds', insisting that this was the form of communion instituted by Christ. But most interesting in our present context is the 'sect of those they call the Pyghards', the name apparently a transference from the Beghards of fourteenth-century Flanders. These descendants of *Devotio Moderna* radicalism apparently condemn church dignitaries and property alike. They recognise no authority except that of the Old and New Testaments and have greatly simplified all sacraments, while 'those who adopt their heretical views are compelled to be rebaptized individually in plain water'. Sadly, remarks Slechta, this sect 'has lately made much progress, but especially on account of the dissolute life led by the priests'.[46] Overall, this has been seen as a by no means unfair depiction of the Czech or Bohemian Brethren.

A long and fairly prompt reply expresses Erasmus' concern at the news of such religious divisions, rehearses a list of monstrous errors in past eras, regrets that the sect demanding communion in both kinds is not the only one existing in Bohemia, and then proceeds to review the tenets of the Pyghards. Erasmus is not perturbed by their selection of bishops and priests for themselves, for this does not disagree with the tradition of the Ancients. He sees no harm in their calling each other brothers and sisters. But 'as for their views on the sacraments, they are more fantastic than a religious hearer can easily tolerate'. Infuriatingly, he makes no specific reference to re-baptism, but declares that in regard to the divine nature or the substance of Christ in the sacraments, 'God knows how it happens; enough for me that I believe it does happen'. As for discussion of 'how the same body can exist in so small a form and in different places – all this, in my opinion, has not much to contribute towards progress in religion'. Well might his modern editor discern a noticeable measure of sympathy in this reply, suggesting that to their leaders, if they saw it, Erasmus must have seemed an unprejudiced and open-minded judge of almost unparallelled prestige.[47]

Certainly in June 1520 he was visited in Antwerp by two emissaries of the Czech Brethren. Though he himself makes but a brief reference to this meeting, a fuller account from a Czech source maintains that their presentation of a statement of their faith was followed, a few days later, by Erasmus' avowal that his reading of it had failed to disclose any error. But typically he would refrain from any public endorsement, both in their interest and his own.[48] Then in October of the same year Arkleb of Boskovice, a Moravian nobleman, wrote to seek Erasmus' opinion on the Brethren. But alas for those who would convince themselves of Erasmus' support of their cause, his reply on 20 January 1521 admits that 'the book I had already received six months before by way of two Bohemians, though I have not yet found time to read it through'. We recognise a favourite device for avoiding awkward corners! His tone is cautious but conciliatory: 'who am I to issue pronouncements about other men's beliefs or to make any decisions beyond what has already been decided and is now being followed by the Catholic Church? . . . I have no rules to lay down; I have some wishes.'[49]

Perhaps the first recorded personal contact between Erasmus and a named Anabaptist leader took place in the spring of 1522, when Balthasar Hubmaier visited him in Basel and discussed the concepts of purgatory and regeneration, but was disappointed with a man 'who spoke freely but wrote cautiously'.[50] A projected visit of Conrad Grebel in February of the same year did not materialise.[51] Although there is no doubt as to Erasmus' influence on Hubmaier, we find but sporadic references to him, as in Erasmus' comment that a training in scholastic theology had not in his care precluded heresy, or in the allusion to his Waldshut followers throwing images out through their windows! None the less by November 1525, Erasmus is sufficiently apprised of his notoriety to refer to the irruption of Balthasar Hubmaier into the already contentious debate between Zwingli, Oecolampadius and Luther.[52]

As for Anabaptism in general, after the isolated reference made in the summer of 1523 we have already cited, its first occurrence in Erasmus' correspondence is probably the letter from John Botzheim, dated from Constance on 5 May 1525. This reports on a new element in the widening spectrum of debate, the 'tumult about infant baptism', and relates how he has heard that 'in the countryside around Zurich the rustics openly re-baptise each other in lakes and rivers'.[53] Thereafter, in a long and very frank letter to Juan Maldonado on 30 March 1527, Erasmus himself lists four sects: 'Lutherans, Carlstadtians, Anabaptists and Prophets I know not what'. Writing to Bucer in November he again refers to 'Prophets and Anabaptists' as in conflict with Zwingli and Luther.[54] A brief letter to Thomas More in February 1528 includes a worried reference to the heresy of the Anabaptists which, already more widespread than one would credit, is liable to erupt. Writing to another very good friend, Willibald Pirckheimer, in March, in the context of the problems confronting Archduke Ferdinand he mentions that the Anabaptists excite most alarm, since they are said to be against all princes.[55] Indeed this indication of a fear which would increasingly colour the attitude not only of Erasmus but of most contemporaries had been preceded on 4 January 1528 by an imperial decree of the death penalty against all Anabaptists for their crime of rebellion.

Yet in March and April of 1529 Erasmus penned a couple of kindlier if still very cautious assessments. A long letter to Alonso Fonseca, Primate of Spain, includes a significant reference to the fact that, although the Anabaptists' numbers are large and widely spread, yet in no place have they acquired their own church. Moreover, 'although commended by innocence of life in comparison with others, yet they are oppressed by the other sects also, not solely by the orthodox'.[56] Next, writing to Ludwig Baer on the day of his departure from Basel, expressing his distaste at the burning of a heretic of this ilk, Erasmus explains that the Anabaptist sect is much hated by the princes 'by reason of the anarchy and common ownership which they are said to preach, yet they have no church, nor seek for dominion . . .' Moreover they are said by many to be very sincere in their conduct.[57] In July 1530, writing to no less a person than Lorenzo Campeggio, Erasmus confides that he pities the Anabaptists, 'who could be helped, if baptism alone was at issue; but they lead all things into confusion', though some discern little evil in the sect.[58] In such utterances we may surely discern the tug-of-war within Erasmus between cautious approval of an effort to live according to the injunctions of the Master, tolerance of *adiaphora* and even of honest errors in belief, and horror at obdurate heresy which he seems always to equate with a seditious and violent threat to the established order.

In the early 1530s the problem of the Radicals bulks ever larger in Erasmus' correspondence and becomes more complicated. The very long letter to Bucer considered in the previous chapter was apparently occasioned by the publication of a pantheon of alleged heroes of heresy, written by Sebastian Franck.[59] The author exemplifies the difficulties of any attempt at orderly depiction of the Radical Reformation.[60] A one-time Lutheran pastor, in 1528 he joined the Anabaptist ranks and thereafter embarked on a typical odyssey of harassed wanderings. In Strassburg he encountered Denck, who may well have exerted a formative influence, and perhaps also Servetus; certainly he adopted what has been termed a fully spiritualist position. At Strassburg he published his *Chronica* in German, including a section on Anabaptists, many of them personal acquaintances, but infuriating Erasmus by listing his name also amongst distinguished and unfairly persecuted heretics! The fact that this was not meant in derogation did not placate Erasmus,[61] who identified it in a letter of 14 December 1531 as 'a German book against Imperial majesty, in which from time to time the authority of Erasmus is cited'. His complaint, not only in the letter to Bucer but also directly to the city magistrates led to their suppression of the book as both seditious and personally libellous, to Franck's imprisonment and then expulsion from Strassburg.[62] Ironically, Franck had the utmost respect for Erasmus, whose influence is reflected in his scepticism concerning formal dogma and his pacifism. He translated the *Praise of Folly* into German in 1534, and it seems hardly fanciful to discern an echo of this in a little-known work by Franck, *The Forbidden Fruit*, when it alludes to 'the Knowledge of God that makes us fools and children to ourselves and the world'.[63]

Oddly enough, the very same long letter to Bucer also contains a reference to a book attacking alleged errors in respect of the Trinity, by the physician Michael Servetus[64] – a Spaniard who, after spending more than six months in Oecolampadius' house in Basel, went on to

Strassburg. This book Erasmus wrongly supposes also to have been published in Bucer's city in 1531. Whether or not it was Erasmus' influence which evoked Servetus' first spiritual awakening, it seems fairly obvious – if only from the fact that he submitted his contentious work to the Basel humanist[65] – that he believed his views on this topic to be in accord with those of Erasmus considered earlier. Yet the assertion in Servetus' work *On the Errors of the Trinity* that 'the philosophers have invented besides a third separate being, truly and really distinct from the other two, which they call the third Person, or the Holy Spirit; and thus they have contrived an imaginary Trinity, three beings in one Nature',[66] while occasionally reminiscent in phraseology, quite clearly substitutes for Erasmus' readiness to eschew definition in order to preserve belief a forthright denial of that belief itself. Erasmus, already very sensitive about earlier attempts to represent him as an Arian, would have none of it, and apparently informed Aleander of his receipt of this unwelcome book. The rash but highly intelligent Servetus pursued his campaigns for many years in various cities, before enduring martyrdom in 1553 in Calvin's Geneva.

In terms of Anabaptist references the heavens opened in 1534, though Erasmus would hardly have accepted the provenance, for they were usually devoted to news of violent insurrection. While space precludes quotation, some of the fullest accounts of the origins and course of the Münster episode are found in letters to his Freiburg home. But the first such reference is made by Erasmus himself, in a letter sent to John Sinapius in Ferrara, dated 31 July 1534. Therein he relates briefly how the Anabaptists have inundated lower Germany to an incredible extent, how fifty or sixty ships have been intercepted, and how the chief city of Westphalia, Münster, is led by prophets who include Jan of Leiden and Jan Matthys.[67] Modern historians have identified the allusion to the so-called 'Great Exodus' projected by Anabaptists in Holland in March: about 15,000 assembled for the move to Münster, but it all collapsed when an advance guard of about 3000 on board twenty-seven ships were intercepted by and surrendered to a force of less than one hundred soldiers.[68] While Erasmus' informant is uncertain, on 12 August a long letter was despatched from Viglius Zuichemus, to be followed by several others in which he recounted these events.[69]

Before its receipt, however, Erasmus had already written a substantial missive to Justus Decius in Poland in which he included a paragraph on the Anabaptist threat. By now any sneaking sympathy which he may previously have felt with certain aspects of their case seems to be quite submerged by the universal dread of what they might let loose. They flood into lower Germany in a way which does not differ from the frogs and locusts in Egypt in former times. Unless vigilance is exercised they will overwhelm the whole region. The occupants of the ill-fated invasion fleet, now shrunk in number to forty ships, have been scattered, burned, or drowned in the sea. Münster, capital of Westphalia, is surrounded and besieged; but within, the Anabaptists reign. On the same day, 22 August, Zuichemus writes again, concurring on the urgent need for stern action.[70] At the end of the month Erasmus repeats, to Guy Morillon, his concern with this sect, repeating verbatim his frogs and locusts allusion. 'They enter under a mask of piety, but the outcome will be public brigandage.' Add to this his allusion to absurd teaching, and Erasmian patience is seen to have worn very thin. Indeed by 6 December, writing to Erasmus Schets, he feels impelled to apply the analogy of disease in alluding to the spread of the infection of the sects.[71]

On 3 February of the following year Tielmann Gravius wrote from Cologne to apprise Erasmus of another violent episode. Apparently in response to an appeal by Jan of Leiden to the towns of lower Germany, a force of some thousand Anabaptists rose in combat and suffered defeat near Groningen, while an attempt to enlist the city of Wesel was nipped in the bud.[72] Three days later Erasmus Schets wrote to deplore the blaze of Anabaptist sedition in Holland.[73] At the end of the month Zuichemus wrote again from Dulmen describing how the emissaries of Anabaptist dogma strove daily, especially in Holland and Frisia, and proceeding to give a full account of events at Groningen.[74] Two days later, in a fairly brief 'Polish report' sent to Peter Tomiczki, Erasmus included a reference to the spread of the Anabaptist sect, which occupied a large part of lower Germany – 'especially my Holland'.[75]

A letter from John Rinck in Cologne, dated 16 March 1535, already noted as posing the question as to whether it was the *Lutheran* seed-bed which had nurtured so many heretical pests, is of particular interest here in its specific allusion to the Melchiorites. For although alluded to in this letter only, the strain of Anabaptism which followed Melchior Hoffman was most frightening of all to respectable society: the inclusion of the phrase 'social unrest and apocalyptic visions' in the sub-title of a standard biography is sufficiently indicative! While much of Hoffman's time was spent in Strassburg, with two sojourns in East Frisia, it was apparently in the Netherlands that he secured most active converts. Although a couple of attempts at insurrection within Amsterdam in the February and May of 1535 were pathetic in scale and impact, it has been contended that without the Dutch Melchiorites the Anabaptist 'kingdom' in Westphalia would never have been, that Münster was a symbol of an upheaval which affected a region stretching from Groningen to Maastricht. Assuredly, there can be no attempt to make Erasmus of Rotterdam the inspiration of this variety of Anabaptism, nor yet to relate it to the whole ethos of the *Devotio Moderna* of which it seems to be the antithesis. Only the most peripheral areas of agreement between Hoffman and Erasmus may be traced, as against basic differences of belief in respect of such issues as the nature of the Church and apocalyptic violence. Erasmus could only have identified the Melchiorite movement in the Netherlands and in Westphalia as a mortal sickness.[76]

From Paris, on 29 June 1535, Bartholomew Latomus writes regarding the affair of the 'Placards' in that city but also includes a reference to the insanity of 'your Hollanders'.[77] Whatever the intended reference, Münster had already been re-taken four days earlier, and on 28 July two very long letters from Conrad Heresbach in Düsseldorf – probably Erasmus' informant at an earlier stage – submit an exceptionally full account of these tragic events, followed by Tielmann Gravius again from Cologne in August.[78] Erasmus himself writes to Damien à Goes in Portugal and makes brief reference to the Anabaptists' total loss of lower Germany, the taking by storm of Münster, and the rumour of heavy casualties.[79] His letter to Latomus is fuller in its expression of continued concern. The whole of lower Germany is wondrously infected, while in upper Germany it is merely concealed. The Emperor lays siege to Goletta, the fortress of Tunis, but Erasmus thinks that there is more to be feared from the Anabaptists! Münster has been stormed, but there has been a dangerous insurrection in the city of Amsterdam.[80]

One week later the same news and sentiments are conveyed to Peter Tomiczki, Bishop of Cracow, in what is perhaps the longest and most revealing of Erasmus' comments on this topic. After relating the Emperor's success in North Africa he goes on to say, ambiguously, that 'the pestilence burns in many cities of Germany'. For although Münster has been stormed, with heavy loss of life, the infection has been checked rather than eliminated. Troops of Anabaptists flood out of Holland into these regions, and the Emperor would do better to protect lower Germany from these pests than to assault Goletta. Having taken possession of towns by cunning and deceit, they compel conversion to their sect by violent means, create new kings and queens, and make up new laws for their pleasure.[81]

His death in July of the following year brings to an end our survey of the more notorious aspects of Anabaptism seen through the eyes of Erasmus. Yet it is perhaps worth observing that he saw the worst of this problem. What we may term the violent decade in its history, with Müntzer and the Peasants' Revolt at one end and Münster at the other, often embodied the seditiously egalitarian nightmare which terrified Erasmus and the whole establishment, Catholic and Protestant alike. His own final comments upon Anabaptism were therefore less those of a Christian humanist upon radical religion than those of a worried social conservative upon a threat which seemed to menace all the normal bases of mid-sixteenth-century society. Yet what is now identified as 'mainstream' Anabaptism, evangelical and pacific, survived the excesses both of its apocalyptic wing on the one hand and of the equally violent if understandable revulsion of authority on the other.

Within our context and in a longer-term perspective, it is therefore the judgment of the Anabaptists and other Radicals upon Erasmus which can claim the more lasting importance for the history of ideas. This judgment throughout the following decades proved favourable and indeed grateful. Significantly, those of his teachings which have been identified as leading into the emergence of Anabaptist doctrines considered earlier in this chapter are almost always designated by modern observers as 'pre-1525'.[82] Indeed it is worth reflecting that the years 1524–26 marked a crucial watershed in a double sense. First, after the debate which to contemporary eyes revealed fundamental differences between Erasmus and the major Protestant leaders, it was the Anabaptists and Spiritualists who clung to the Erasmian position in terms of an admittedly limited free will. Yet ironically and almost simultaneously Müntzer and the Peasants' Revolt furnished a permanent stigma of sedition, a tarbrush in the hands of Catholics and Magisterial Reformers alike, in order to discredit every aspect of the Radical Reformation in all professedly moderate eyes, including those of Erasmus.

Oddly enough, it was the Netherlands which not only furnished many of the shock-troops of Melchiorite Anabaptism but also, after the Münster débâcle, witnessed the success of a much more Erasmian version of the sect: that of Menno Simons – a name eventually installed in the annals of American Baptist scholarship. Among several most respectful allusions to Erasmus in Menno's writings, he is particularly concerned to point out that 'the very wise and learned Erasmus of Rotterdam, a man who has read and understood all the worthwhile writers of the world, says that the ancient fathers disputed about infant baptism but never settled it'.[83] Indeed it has been contended that Simons, together with Dirk Philips and Bernard Rothman the seminal leaders of Dutch and North German Anabaptism, considered Erasmus the originator of their new order.[84]

In assessing what now appears as a tripartite cross-relationship between Erasmus, the Magisterial Reformation, and the Radicals, one may suggest that for Luther, Zwingli and Bucer it was Erasmus who provided much of the ammunition for their breakthrough in terms both of biblical scholarship and of scripturally supported criticism against so many aspects of the established Church. But it was the Radical Reformation which best reflected his insistence that Christ's teachings must find conscious and committed actuality in the conduct of the professed believer. Erasmus had criticised the shocking dichotomy within the old order between Christ's message and the lives of many who professed to administer his grace through Church sacraments. Luther, Zwingli, and later Calvin, so at least their critics would argue, sought to replace a sacramental *Deus ex machina* which purported to administer salvation through ritual observances, irrespective of any participant faith; but did they not replace it with the hardly more acceptable scenario of an arbitrarily predestinarian Deity whose selections for salvation seem equally mechanical?

It might well be argued that only the Radicals preserved the ideal of the actively consenting follower of Christ, striving so far as in him lay to obey Christ's injunctions within this world, to which ideal the *Enchiridion* above all had surely pointed the way. Admittedly, the excesses of the 'lunatic fringe' have no place within this pattern; yet such must surely be related to the ancestry of the dreaded late-medieval heresy of 'Spiritual Liberty' and to contemporary social ferment, rather than to Erasmus or even to the *Devotio Moderna*? The assertion that, although asked by Johann Cochlaeus in January 1528 to write against the Anabaptists, Erasmus was one of the very few reforming leaders who never did so,[85] must admittedly be qualified. Yet, all in all, there is a great deal to commend the claim that the major ethos of the Radical Reformation was a radicalisation not so much of the Magisterial Reformation as of an earlier, at once more ascetic and more lay-orientated, view of religious reform, and that the principal mediator of these ideas was Erasmus.[86]

THE RECEPTION OF ERASMUS

Nine

THE ENGLISH ERASMIANS

The first five chapters of this book were devoted to placing Erasmus and Erasmian ideas in the widest context of religious reform during the late fifteenth and early sixteenth centuries, while the three subsequent chapters examined relationships between Erasmus and that range of religious movements which may broadly be labelled 'the Protestant Reformation'. Our next four chapters will consider 'The Reception of Erasmus': interpreted, first, in a geographical sense and secondly in a widening religious perspective ranging from charges of heresy on the one hand to the case for 'Erasmus the Mediator' on the other. Finally we shall move in a longer time-perspective which considers the legacy of Erasmus to posterity. We have lately been concerned with a region distinguished both by predominantly Germanic characteristics and by the widespread emergence of avowedly Protestant 'state-churches'. The wider shores of these chapters will encompass a more peripheral range of nations, nearly all of which remained faithful to Rome, while one of them for long, at least officially, stopped short of a fully Protestant position. Despite the fact that the three 'Romance' nations – France, Spain and Italy – display greater mutual similarities of religious development than was the case in Britain, each of them affords its own individual example of the fortunes of Erasmianism within what was to remain a Catholic society.

We should at the outset remind ourselves that, with the exception of Spain, these wider shores were by no means unvisited by Erasmus himself. Moreover, for the most part we observe not fleeting visits but substantial periods of sojourn. Erasmus studied in Paris between 1495 and 1501 – with a fairly short excursus into England – and again in 1504–1505. Louvain, then second only to Paris in the repute of its university and culturally not far removed from the French orbit, was his main dwelling-place from 1502 to 1504 and again from 1517 to 1521. His long visit to Italy extended from 1506 to 1509. But pride of place in terms of number of visits – and probably in total length of residence –

must be accorded to England. In all four countries, including Spain, he made friendships, many of them enduring, as reflected in his letters long after any personal contact had ceased. Some of these relationships, most notably that with Colet, have been credited with a formative influence upon Erasmus. But now our chief concern, before moving still further into Central Europe, will be to trace the nature and the depth of his influence upon each of the four western nations, beginning with England.

The choice first of England has much to commend it. We have noted earlier the salient English influences brought to bear not only by Colet but also by other English scholars at a formative period in Erasmus' own development. The later visits, which occasioned about six years of actual domicile, gave rise to talk of England's becoming his permanent home. Nevertheless, a close reading of the correspondence casts doubt upon the enduring reality of any such wish on the part of Erasmus himself. Far more important is the suggestion that the English mirror of his complex ideals became the clearest and most informative of the four. Most crucially, it has been urged not only that the emergent Church of England became permeated through and through with Erasmian values and attitudes, but also that during the formative stages of the English Reformation the voice of Erasmus the Reformer may he heard as clearly as that of Luther or of Zwingli.

Erasmus' own recorded opinions about England ranged from glowing descriptions of its cultural ambience and his own desires for permanent residence, to expressions of distaste for its beer, and the dangers from cliffs, storms, and predatory customs officers while in transit. Yet as late as 1523 he could still declare that 'Britain is a far cry from Italy, but stands next to it in the value of its learned men'.[1] The same range of views is encountered in respect of the patronage bestowed: from real and repeated munificence to niggardly gifts and forgotten or broken promises. Certainly there is no dispute about the impressive array of figures in the first rank of the English cultural, religious, and court establishment which bulks largely in, and indeed almost dominates, Erasmus' letters during the first two decades of the sixteenth century.[2] His first brief visit in 1499[3] was followed by sojourns between late 1505 and June of 1506, from the summer of 1509 until July 1514 (with an absence between April and August 1511), then much more briefly in April–May 1515, in July and August of the following year, and finally in April 1517. His obstinate rejection of the English language reduced Erasmus to a social and cultural elitism markedly different from his more youthful immersion in the ebullient, almost classless life of the West Bank in Paris. Yet these visits, accompanied by frequent correspondence, make the 'English connection' of prime importance.

An introduction to him as a young prince led to a later exchange of not-insignificant correspondence with Henry VIII, while of that monarch's ministers Erasmus knew Wolsey, More and Thomas Cromwell.[4] Of the ecclesiastical hierarchy, we need but mention William Warham, Archbishop of Canterbury, John Fisher, Bishop of Rochester, and in the end Thomas Cranmer, to establish the level of Erasmus' credentials. Of Warham, 'my incomparable Maecenas', he declared on one occasion that 'he by himself would be enough to secure my felicity, if only fortune had placed him here [in Louvain] or if there were some bridge joining us to England: so much do I hate that Channel and those still more horrible sailors'.[5] Fisher gave him not only scholarly encouragement but sometimes also financial help. In return, it was apparently at Erasmus' instigation that Fisher undertook the study of Greek. In August 1516, writing to his friend Andreas Ammonio, an Italian in the service first of Mountjoy then of Henry VIII, Erasmus explained that he had stopped for ten days in Rochester to help its bishop in this endeavour.[6] Cuthbert Tunstall, who was to become Bishop of London in 1522, then of Durham in 1530, became a close friend during his residence in the Low Countries on diplomatic duties. Erasmus' letters testify in particular to the help and advice given – including suggested amendments – by the conservative Tunstall in the revision of the text of the New Testament, and to his reading of other works.[7]

Enough has been written about, and perhaps too much has been made of, the friendship between Erasmus and his 'dear More, whom I love best of mortal men'. The increasing religious conservatism and the high legal office of Thomas More, and indeed the very fact that they never met after 1521, all contributed to a widening divergence in their assessments of the action required in the face of ever more complex religious problems. There lay a world of difference between Erasmus and the keen heresy-hunter which More became in his years as Lord Chancellor of England. Indeed, one of More's last letters to Erasmus besought him, in effect, to get off the fence in unmistakable fashion.[8] Just such unequivocal action was soon to cost More his own life. We have already cited several English participants in what was a two-way exchange of ideas and scholarship. Erasmus was attracted not only to the versatile Thomas Linacre, but similarly to William Grocyn, 'who, to a professional knowledge of theology, added a competence in every branch of learning'. Again, Thomas Lupset, whom Erasmus met at Cambridge, is described in a letter of 1512 as 'helping me and delighting me greatly with his company every day and with the assistance he is giving me'. A few years later he played a somewhat equivocal part in the actual printing of *Julius exclusus*.[9]

Such brief illustrations of the duration and importance of Erasmus' personal connections with England might almost indefinitely be extended. But our prime concern must now be with the impact of Erasmian publications and ideas upon England's own religious development up to the middle decades of the century. As we have already noted, the seminal influence of Colet upon Erasmus' religious development has recently been queried. Conversely, the influence of Erasmus upon Englishmen has sometimes been described as exaggerated. Certainly there is validity in the warning that it will not do to assemble a 'rag-bag' of all progressive religious, social, educational, and political thought and then dub it 'Erasmian humanism', as the sole repository of all reforming ideas. Obviously, it seems even more perverse to ignore the evidence of personal contacts, of repeated translations of Erasmus' works, and of direct appeals to his moral authority. An evaluation of his impact may perhaps most conveniently and logically be accomplished by examining the evidence for a fairly extensive and eager adoption of Erasmian precepts, then the emergence of a minor but not inconsiderable body of opinion which discerned in his writings elements both of heresy and of subversion, and finally the quite substantial traces of Erasmian values and teachings which became incorporated in the emergent English Church during the decades up to and including the Elizabethan Settlement.

The first of these themes must take particular note of Erasmus' general influence upon religious, educational and social thought, of the 'anticlerical' element in his works which was eagerly exploited by supporters of Cromwell's religious policy, and of those aspects of his writings which were most enthusiastically appropriated by people who sought to welcome Erasmus as an essentially *Protestant* reformer. It has long been agreed that his influence extended into educational thought[10] through Elyot's *The Boke named the Governour* (1531), a masterly exposition of the Erasmian educational and political programme, worthily succeeded by Ascham's *Schoolmaster*. Erasmus is seen to be an inspirer of such socio-political concepts as the English version of the 'godly prince'.[11] But most notably, letters from Cambridge friends in 1516 assured him that 'your revision of the New Testament and your notes at the same time have thrown a wonderful flood of light on Christ', while Warham had written him a couple of months earlier on behalf of his brother bishops to commend him on such work which will surely secure him immortal fame among mankind. More mundanely, Colet told him that 'the copies of your new edition sell here like hot cakes'.[12] Admittedly, Erasmus' appeal for scriptural study by the laity met with but a tardy response, while any suggestion that the English Reformation, and indeed the whole ethos of mid-Tudor politico-social reform, may be described as Erasmian has not been without its critics. Yet an English translation of the book which has been identified in our present study as effectively the flag-bearer of Erasmian ideals, the *Enchiridion*, appeared no fewer than eight times between 1533 and 1549. To anticipate a conjecture made with less strength in a Spanish context, in so far as there was any slender prospect of successful liberal Catholic reform in England, then Erasmus was its prophet.

We propose only the briefest foray into the extensive field of English translations of Erasmus' works during the early and middle decades of the sixteenth century. Yet questions may usefully be asked about the identity and motivation of some of those who undertook this task. Love of scholarship *per se*; a perception of genuinely inspired guidance in the overlapping realms of religion, morality and education; an assumed identification of support for early Protestantism; or a wish to impress, directed in particular toward Thomas Cromwell: all have plausibly been suggested as variant English motives. Apparently first *translated* of Erasmus' works was the *Enchiridion*, the task of Tyndale between 1521 and 1523, but the first published version did not appear until 1533. Thus probably the earliest to appear in print, as *A devout treatise upon the Pater noster* (1525–26), was the work of Margaret Roper. While her motives were doubtless purely devotional, the suggested attribution to William Roy of a translation of the *Paraclesis* as *An exhortation to the diligent studye of scripture* (1529) would if accurate suggest a clearly Protestant motivation. Indeed, after rendering somewhat uncongenial assistance to the exiled Tyndale, Roy had then participated in the production of the scurrilously anti-clerical *Burial of the Mass*. The printing of *In laude and prayse of matrymony* (*c.* 1532) signalled the entry into the field of another, and far more temperate Protestant, Richard Taverner, who was to prove by far the most prolific populariser of Erasmus.[13]

Yet pride of place among the spate of translations which appeared in 1533 and 1534 must clearly be given to the work which was entitled first the 'manuell' and then *the hansom weapon of a christen knyght*. Tyndale's work – his claim thereto is accepted though not conclusively proven – was apparently much praised by More prior to his discovery of its provenance! This version of the *Enchiridion* is prefaced by some introductory verses confirming that this mortal world is a battlefield betwixt flesh and spirit, in preparation for which, scouring the spiritual battle-gear now cankered and rusted by neglect, 'Erasmus is the only furbisher'.[14] Almost contemporaneously appeared the epistle *Concernyng the forbedynge of eatyng of flesshe* and *An exhortacyon to the studye of the Gospell*, from Erasmus' *Paraphrases* on the New Testament. The publication of *A playne and godly exposition or declaration of the commune crede*, very probably by William Marshall, was accompanied by that of *Bellum Erasmi* – 'Warre is swete to them that know it not'[15] – and also by the much lesser-known *Epistle of Saint Paule unto . . . Titus*, by Leonard Cox.

We shall later encounter Cox in a wider context, for this cosmopolitan humanist held posts as schoolmaster and lecturer in Cracow, whence he corresponded with Erasmus, and also in what is now Czechoslovakia. After returning to England in 1528, again to the same vocation, he translated Erasmus' paraphrase and Latin version of the above epistle, which he presented to Thomas Cromwell in 1534, along with 'a goodly prologue' and a promise of further such translations. This was the first of several attempts, which ultimately succeeded, to secure ministerial favour.[16] William Marshall, another Cromwellian client, is best known for his initiative in the sphere of Poor Law reform. But he was also an industrious translator, whose output included works by Lorenzo Valla and Marsiglio of Padua, and it has been contended that his translation of Erasmus was undertaken on his own initiative, not at the behest of Cromwell, whose service he did not enter until *c.* 1536. Yet even if any picture of the minister's systematically procuring such translations should now be modified, it seems likely that in Marshall's case, as in that of Cox, genuine interest may well have been accompanied by a conscious choice of material calculated to win Cromwellian favour.[17]

Two translated versions of extracts from Erasmus' *Apothegmata* were published: *The garden of wysedom*, again by Taverner, in 1539, and *Apothegmes* by Nicholas Udall, the schoolmaster of erratic habits, in 1542. Despite his departure in disgrace from Eton, Udall was again to be involved in another major project toward the end of the reign of Henry VIII: the translation of the first volume of Erasmus' paraphrase of the New Testament, which so angered Gardiner.[18] More welcome to Gardiner might have been an anonymous translation (published *c.* 1538–47) of Erasmus' epistle *concernynge the veryte of the Sacrament of*

Christes body and bloude. In one of two clear mid-Tudor attempts to enlist his authority on the Catholic side in this controversial issue, its introduction asserts that Erasmus 'speaketh also very reverently of the mass in his book . . . *de sarcienda ecclesiae concordia* . . . and in many other places of his works besides as in his *Enchiridion* & in his *Paraphrasis*'.[19] Oddly enough, two of Erasmus' major works did not appear in English until well into the mid-century. *The praise of Folie*, translated by Sir Thomas Chaloner, who conceded the occasional tactful omission, lest he 'touch things which were better left unsaid',[20] appeared in 1549, and *The Complaint of Peace*, the work of Thomas Paynell, ten years later, whereas a version of *Julius exclusus* had been printed as early as 1533–34.

Not all of Erasmus' early friends and admirers in England became or remained 'Erasmian'. Thus one of his closest friends while at Cambridge, Henry Bullock, ceased to write to him after 1518, and three years later was a royal commissioner at that burning of Luther's books at St Paul's which so appalled Erasmus.[21] Nor did all those who remained Erasmian abandon the Roman Church, as we shall later find in the case of Richard Whitford. Yet a cursory glance at a list of the translators of Erasmus' works reveals an unmistakably Protestant bias. With due respect to William Tyndale, perhaps the most significant and rewarding case-study is that of Richard Taverner. A member of the original 'White Horse' circle of Lutheran sympathisers at Cambridge, Taverner was a zealous propagandist for the Protestant cause between 1535 and 1540. Not only did he translate work by Philip Melanchthon and Wolfgang Capito, but there is also clear evidence that his many translations of Erasmus were also pressed into service, not solely in their own right, but sometimes 'improved' by a little judicious amendment where necessary! From his *Prayse of Matrymony* in 1532, which included a call for 'some speedy reformation', until the final spate of his Erasmian translations in 1539 and 1540 – just prior to the fall of Cromwell, who had appointed him Clerk of the Privy Seal in 1536 – he pursued this purpose.[22]

Although he is usually accounted a Lutheran, it is worth noting that in some respects Taverner's was a very Erasmian Protestantism. Thus his version of the *Proverbes or Adagies* (1539) asserted that 'all that have the gospel hanging at their girdles be no gospellers. Nor again all that dispraise the lewd fashion of the Papists be not forthwith Heretics.' Yet again, while deriding such donors as would 'liever lash out their wicked Mammon on the dead, than on the quick, so little regard they have to the lively images of God', he also decries those whose excessive zeal for redress of ecclesiastical abuses would lead them to abolish 'all honest ceremonies'. His views with regard to the crucial issues of free will and the nature of the Sacrament of the Eucharist alike reflect Erasmus' influence. More generally, in Taverner the Erasmian pursuit of the golden mean of moderation which ultimately contributed to the Elizabethan Church Settlement may clearly be perceived.[23]

Before proceeding to widen our perspective to include the aid and comfort which a number of early English Protestant clerics professed to derive from Erasmus' writings, a page or so must be devoted to the thesis which James McConica advanced some thirty years ago: that Thomas Cromwell's programme of religious and social reform may be dubbed, overall, 'Erasmian', and that in its pursuit the minister embarked upon a policy of active recruitment of scholarly Erasmians to his cause in the years 1532 to 1534. Undeniably, a major spate of Erasmian translations occurred during the years of Cromwell's emerging dominance. Yet how far may one support the contention that in the five-year interval between the execution of More and that of Cromwell himself 'the Henrician commonwealth had been given a definite character. It was an Erasmian polity', because Cromwell had indeed accomplished 'the most complete fulfilment of the Erasmian programme which Europe had yet seen'?[24]

It is perhaps ironical that one of the first extensive appeals to Erasmian support made by a politico-social reformer, Thomas Cromwell, was in the context of his propaganda assault upon superstition and other alleged monastic shortcomings. Because while in itself this might well have pleased Erasmus, its context of an attack upon the Church of Rome as such assuredly would not. Yet, while hard-headed, Cromwell's approach was *not* irreligious. Although it could be presumptuous to identify his personality as a total embodiment of the Erasmian ideal of lay piety, many of his practical steps, together with the apparent enlistment to his cause of writers such as Taverner, Marshall and Thomas Starkey, appear to fall completely within that tradition. The very names in the title of Starkey's book, Pole and Lupset, reflect the *European* ambience within which such ideals flourished. Thomas Bedyll wrote informing Erasmus that Cromwell was an ardent friend of his name; more tangibly, along with Cranmer, Cromwell sent financial help for which the recipient returned his thanks. Whether or not we believe the story of his learning by heart the whole of Erasmus' Latin version of the New Testament, the appearance of Thomas Cromwell on the illustrated title page of the Great Bible may justly serve as his memorial. His Injunctions of 1536 and 1538, it has been urged, display Erasmian reform as their inspiration; but it is not necessary to concur with any concept of 'official Erasmianism' in order to concede the reality of the influence exerted.[25]

Within the avowedly Protestant ranks among the English clergy, a number cite the authority of Erasmus in their own attacks on superstitious abuses. John Hooper, later Bishop of Gloucester, declared that 'people should not be taught by images nor by reliques, as Erasmus Rotterdam . . . well declareth'.[26] This was written in 1547, but much earlier the 'Recantation of Thomas Topley' in 1533 confessed that 'I read in *Colloquium* [and] mused of these opinions so greatly, that my mind was almost withdrawn from devotion to saints'.[27] In a few years' time such sentiments proved of use to Cromwell in the context of his case for dissolution of the monasteries, for allegedly misguided adoration of 'relics' of saints and martyrs. A more general Erasmian scepticism as to the validity of worshipping externals in ceremonial is appealed to in Thomas Becon's *Comparison betwene the Lordes Supper, and the Popes Masse* . . . , and in his adjuration 'to worship him in mind that was crucified'![28]

We shall shortly return at greater length to the significance of Erasmus' views of the Eucharist. Meanwhile, surely the whole ethos of his approach to religion is succinctly set forth in another of Becon's earlier works, *The pathwai unto Prayer*: ' "The perpetual study of living godly," saith Erasmus, "is a continual prayer." ' Indeed, one passage in a work with a variant title, *The flower of godly prayers*, might have come straight out of Erasmus' own *Pseudevangelicos* in its assertion that

> the gospel of Christ begetteth and bringeth forth new life, and new manners, yea, and those pure, honest, and godly. If such fruits follow not the gospellers' profession, in vain do they brag of the gospel of the grace of God, of the christian liberty, of the justification of faith.[29]

Of the impact of Erasmus' scriptural scholarship, the testimony in a letter of 1531 to Cuthbert Tunstall, written by one of England's earliest Henrician martyrs Thomas Bilney, is a striking example:

> But at last I heard speak of Jesus, even then when the New Testament was first set forth by Erasmus; which when I understood to be eloquently done by him, being allured rather by the Latin than by the word of God (for at that time I knew not what it meant), I bought it even by the providence of God.

Thereby was Bilney converted. Thomas Garret, a later martyr, also testified to his reading of Erasmus' New Testament, together with works by Luther and Oecolampadius, while at Oxford *circa* 1526.[30]

In respect of Erasmian influence upon English Protestant thinking about the sacraments of the Church, Topley's 'Recantation' again contains the interesting testimony concerning his friend Coverdale, that 'they did commune together of Erasmus's works, and also upon confession. This sir Miles said, and did hold, that it was sufficient for a man to be contrite for his sins betwixt God and his conscience, without confession to a priest'.[31] This may well go beyond the avowed Erasmian position, but the influence of his distaste for merely formal enactment is clear. So too is the much later discussion by William Fulke, in 1583, of Erasmus on penance: 'Erasmus, finding the vulgar Latin insufficient, hath added *vitae prioris*, that is, "repent ye of your former life".'[32] Yet numerically such references are swamped by those upon the issue which, in England as across the Channel, became the focal point of debate: the nature of the Mass, Eucharist or Communion.

In his seminal work upon the evolution of this concept among the English Reformers, Professor Dugmore has set the great eucharistic debate within the wider context of a continuous tradition of 'Reformed Catholicism', stretching back to the early medieval theologian Ratramn of Corbie.[33] Erasmus also must surely be envisaged in that same context, for his own eucharistic opinions were *not* derivative from either Luther or Zwingli. Certainly his views were welcomed most eagerly by English Protestants. Becon, again, in *A new Catechisme*, dealing with 'The Lord's Supper', cites Erasmus at some length in his assault upon a custom by which the Sacrament was 'carried about like a puppet, as the manner is in the pope's wicked kingdom'. For it is meant

> to be meat unto the faithful, to be broken and eaten in the remembrance of Christ's passion and death, as Erasmus Roterodamus very godly writeth: 'Christ,' saith he, 'is in that sacrament, under this manner of meat and drink, that he should be received with high purity of mind; not that he should be shewed abroad, or carried about in plays and common pageants, or that he should be carried about the fields on horseback. This was not the manner of the primitive church, but in this the foolish affections of the multitude hath been too much served and obeyed.'[34]

John Hooper, also, in his *Answer unto my lord of wynchesters booke [on] the moost blessyd sacrament of the aulter*, 1546, appealed to Erasmus' authority on scriptural evidence about the matter.[35]

Yet it would be wrong to give the impression that Erasmus had no English opponents. Perhaps the most notorious names are those of Lee and Standish. An initially friendly scholarly acquaintanceship with

Edward Lee soon turned to bitter enmity. Despite Erasmus' avowed contempt for him, as ignorant, block-headed and venomous, his letters between 1518 and 1520 have rightly been described as choked with concern about his attacks. Indeed Lee's travels and career were such as to give him ample opportunity to press them – at Louvain, as ambassador in Spain between 1525 and 1530, and as Archbishop of York after 1531.[36] Dr Henry Standish, a lesser figure, invited and received considerable ridicule for his diatribes in a sermon at Paul's Cross and later, even more embarrassingly, at court in front of Henry VIII.[37] Standish was less comically involved in the harrying of Bilney, while more light is shed upon the position of one who almost certainly witnessed the court débâcle, Thomas More, if we examine his relations with William Tyndale. Tyndale, whose biographer is in no doubt about the significance of Erasmus' *New Testament* for his subject's own work, hurled at More, his vindictive enemy, the charge that he condemned in his writings things which he let pass when enunciated by 'his darling Erasmus'. More's reply, that 'I have not contended with Erasmus my darling, because I found no such malicious intent with Erasmus my darling, as I find with Tyndale, [for] I cannot take him for my darling, that the devil taketh for his darling', reads even less convincingly now than it would have done for Tyndale at the time. In this context it is of interest that Richard Marius clearly shares our scepticism about the identity of religious attitudes attributed to him and to Erasmus by some modern liberal Catholics.[38]

It seems clear that, from the outset, Erasmus' publications had always been subject to the criticism extorted from poor Topley in 1533, when he was prevailed upon to counsel that 'all Christian men beware of consenting to Erasmus's Fables, for by consenting to them, they have caused me to shrink in my faith'.[39] But it was during the middle decades of the century, against the background of the pendulum-like swings of policy of the Edwardian and Marian eras, that such doctrinal criticism was to receive its fullest expression. We have already cited Gardiner's concern about the effect of Erasmus' views in that grey area which so preoccupied the Tudor establishment: the religio-political issues of obedience. But in 1547 he also professed himself aghast at certain doctrinal aspects of Erasmus' writings, to a point at which he was ready to declare that

> I have favored Erasmus name as much as any other, but I never studied over this booke til now, and I now aggre with them that said Erasmus laid the eggs and Luther hatched them; adding further that, of al the monstrous

> opinions that have arysen, evil men had a wondrous occasion ministred to them of that booke.

Small wonder that he describes the *Paraphrases* as an 'abhomination', and pledges his life, if need be, to prevent its circulation.[40]

Small wonder, also, at developments under Mary Tudor, when Gardiner was a prime contributant to religious policy. Oddly enough, a Royal Proclamation of 1555, prohibiting a long list of works, does not include any books by Erasmus of Rotterdam – as distinct from Erasmus Sarcerius – and does not anticipate the ultimately sweeping decision of the continental Counter-Reformation. But in the same year, Nicholas Ridley, in *A Brief Declaration of the Lordes Supper* 'against the Error of Transubstantiation', relates how

> in the disputations, which were in this matter in the parliament house, and in both the universities of Cambridge and Oxford, they that defended transubstantiation said, that this part of Origen was but set forth of late by Erasmus, and therefore is to be suspected.[41]

By now, of course, Erasmus himself had been dead for nearly two decades. But it remains to attempt to evaluate his influence in the crucial mid-century upon the emergent 'Protestant' or at least non-Roman Church in England. Certainly such influence cannot simply be equated with the era of Cromwellian dominance; indeed the fact that Henry VIII's last wife sponsored the publication of an English edition of the *Paraphrases* which so infuriated Gardiner has been adduced to indicate the enduring prestige and influence of Erasmus in powerful circles at the end of the reign.[42] Catherine Parr was a crucial source of encouragement and patronage of Erasmian humanism during the years between the fall of Cromwell and the accession of Edward VI, into whose reign such influence continued. The printing of an English translation of Erasmus' *Paraphrases*, early in that reign, was undoubtedly her most significant contribution. Much of the work on the Gospel of John was that of the 'Lady Mary' herself – her eyes not yet opened to Erasmian dangers – at the direct invitation of Queen Catherine. Other contributors included Leonard Cox, again, but above all, Nicholas Udall. Udall's translation of the Gospel of St Luke, when presented to the Queen in September 1545, apparently made such an impression that he was then appointed general editor and subsequently oversaw the printing and publication of *The First Tome or Volume of the Paraphrase of Erasmus upon the Newe Testamente* in 1548.[43]

Udall's Preface, addressed to Edward VI himself, who is identified as destined to be the faithful Josiah who will extirpate the 'Romishe Hydra' and the worship of Baal, is crucial as an indication of the status of Erasmus in the eyes of English 'middle-of-the-road' reformers at this time. It recognises as a general virtue that 'Erasmus lyke as he is no where over vehemente, so is he everie where bothe full and syncere'. More specifically, in this long eulogy of his qualities, he is lauded for his leadership

> in repentance and purity of a Christian man's life, in detesting of imagery and corrupt honouring of Saints, in opening and defacing the tyranny, the blasphemy, Hypocrisy, the ambition, the usurpation of the See of Rome . . . in teaching obedience of the people towards their rulers and Governors . . . and finally in all other points or articles of our religion having now of late years been in controversy.

While he himself would hardly have accepted this attribution *in toto*, the passage is a splendid illustration of the dominance of Erasmus' priorities during the early stages of the emergence of the English Church.[44]

Significantly also, in a passage addressed to 'the moste vertuous Ladie Quene Catherine', Udall declares that

> in case any persons be enemies to Erasmus' writing, it proceedeth more of their envy, of their unquietness of mind, and of their hatred against the light and grace of the gospel . . . than of any fault or just defect in Erasmus . . . And truly whomsoever I perceive to be an eager adversary to Erasmus' writings, I . . . cannot but suppose the same to be an indurate enemy to the gospel . . .

One can hardly resist the speculation that Gardiner was in mind! Certainly the point is well-taken that the inclusion of Erasmus' *Paraphrases* in Royal Injunctions effectively incorporated his work in the official documents of the Church of England. Interestingly, Anne Seymour, wife of the Protector, was the patron of the second volume of the *Paraphrases* (1549), the translators being Miles Coverdale, Leonard Cox and John Olde.[45]

Thus the case has been made that alongside the dogmatic Protestantism which increasingly characterised the Edwardian regime, there still survived among the Erasmians at the court of the 'Young Josiah' the heirs of an established and positive tradition of evangelical Christian humanism.[46] Assuredly there is no dichotomy between Erasmian aims and the decision promulgated in the Royal Injunction of July 1547 that alongside an English Bible in the churches there must be placed, within twelve months, 'the paraphrasis of Erasmus also in English upon the Gospels . . . whereas their parishioners may most commodiously resort unto the same, and read the same'. Moreover, every clergyman was likewise enjoined that he furnish himself with the New Testament in Latin and in English, 'with the paraphrase upon the same of Erasmus, and diligently study the same, conferring the one with the other'. Injunctions for cathedral libraries, also in 1547, named Erasmus as the only modern author alongside a list of ancients to be placed therein. Cranmer's 'Articles for Canterbury Visitation', a year later, specifically enquired as to the presence of Erasmus' English *Paraphrases*.[47] Furthermore, the interesting point has been made that Erasmus' book on the Apostles' Creed became enormously popular in the England of Edward VI precisely because of its uncontentious nature.[48]

In this general context, the case of Thomas Cranmer himself, Archbishop of Canterbury, may now appropriately be examined at some length, as displaying many of the characteristics of English Erasmianism. Fittingly, it has been conjectured that Cranmer, some twenty years younger than the great humanist, may well have attended Erasmus' lectures when at Cambridge in 1511.[49] Certainly, according to a near-contemporary source, 'he gave himself to Faber, Erasmus, good Latin authors, iiii or v years together, unto the time that Luther began to write . . .'[50] 'Faber' is of course Lefèvre d'Étaples, the most famous French pioneer of a scriptural Christianity, whose contacts with Erasmus will concern us in the following chapter. It has shrewdly been observed that in the Cambridge of 1516 it is Erasmus' *Novum Instrumentum* rather than any Lutheran output that would have engaged attention at the White Horse Inn, followed two years later by his *Ratio verae theologiae*.[51] We know that Cranmer later owned and annotated a copy of the 1524 edition of Erasmus' *Enchiridion*, but in Cambridge he would have found no difficulty in obtaining a copy several years earlier. Significantly, in 1534 his correspondence includes his writing in quite peremptory fashion in support of a complainant who alleges that his own copy of the *Enchiridion* in English is wrongfully withheld from him. The offender, whose name is unknown, is directed forthwith to 'deliver unto him his said book', which has been approved by King and Council as meet to be read by all.[52]

It may thus be maintained with some confidence that Cranmer had become an Erasmian long before his encounter with Lutheranism, and indeed that in a meaningful sense he was to remain as such thereafter. Certainly Continental influences upon English reformers became intermingled in the 1520s and 1530s. Thus the movement toward a Bible in English, to which Cranmer gave his full support, should not be seen as a purely Lutheran or even Protestant concern. Cranmer fully understood the demand for a scriptural religion, based upon heartfelt devotion as opposed to pious outward observances and upon the imitation of Christ as opposed to the intellectual analysis of dogmas. Moreover, his personal affinities with Erasmus are not far to seek: Cranmer was by nature courteous, scholarly and pacific, not an avid seeker after controversy. In the last tragic crisis, he displayed an Erasmus-like shrinking from martyrdom and a readiness to temporise until that final surge of faith which gave him the strength for his famous act of defiance at the stake itself.

In middle life at Cambridge and Canterbury Cranmer became wholly abreast of the Christian humanist ideals of the earlier sixteenth century. This is being made clear by modern scholars as they enlarge and discuss the list of books bearing his name and his annotations. With his accession to the archbishopric in 1533 he obviously acquired the means to create a library said to be superior in 'modern' works to the university library of Cambridge. It shows that his new duties did not retard his eager study in several fields, especially his close textual, linguistic, historical examination of the Bible texts. The list at present includes a score or so volumes of Erasmus together with indirect evidence that he possessed others. They include not only patristic and classical commentaries but also the controversies waged by Erasmus against the conservatives Edward Lee and Josse Clichtove, together with his more popular works such as the *Enchiridion*, the *Paraphrases on the New Testament*, the *Paraclesis* and its attendant Greek–Latin Testaments, *The Immense Mercy of God*, *On Christian Marriage*, and the controversial works of 1524–6 against Luther on the issue of predestination versus human free will. Cranmer also owned several multilingual bibles, beginning with the famous Complutensian Polyglot, printed in 1514–17 – a reminder that Erasmus had not assumed the leadership of every modern branch of biblical scholarship.[53]

Thus, if we seriously wish to assess the character, objectives and achievements of Thomas Cranmer, his twenty-year period as Archbishop of Canterbury must be seen as a whole. The pliable careerist denounced by Hilaire Belloc and the infinitely 'shifting' mind diagnosed by Cardinal Gasquet were transparently superficial judgments. Cranmer was not only a laborious scholar but a very able ecclesiastical politician. While he executed Henry's 'divorce', even so sincere a Catholic as Thomas More recognised its necessity and its political implications. Time proved that Cranmer was no mere tool of the monarchy; indeed the reverse would seem nearer the truth, since he secured so many successes for ecclesiastical change both before and after Henry's death. Powerfully aided by his friend Thomas Cromwell, he installed the English Bible in the churches, and even in Henry's lifetime got permission to experiment with English liturgies. More important, the willow outlived the oak, since Cranmer went on to found a *via media* national Church and to integrate its ideology with astuteness and foresight. After all, his Edwardian Church of England not only survived both the Marian Reaction and extremist Protestantism, but with a minimum of modification has survived as a central core of modern English religion. Moreover, at least until he imported Zwinglian elements into the Prayer Book of 1552, Cranmer remained more of an Erasmian than a Protestant.

In noting specific evidence for the influence of Erasmus during the decades of Cranmer's leadership, we may commence with certain draft and unpublished proposed 'Injunctions' entitled 'All youthe to learne the Creade and Tenne commaundementes', which date from the late 1530s or early 1540s. These have been shown to bear an extremely close resemblance to Erasmus' recommendations in an English translation of *An exhortacyon to the studye of the Gospell* (*c.* 1534) in respect of religious teaching and the need to reaffirm the reality of baptismal vows in terms of Christian conduct. We have already noticed Erasmus' near-flirtation with certain Anabaptist contentions, and it is noteworthy that the 'official' English translation of his *Paraphrases* promulgated by Royal Injunction in 1547 omitted the passage about the renewal of baptismal vows. Intriguingly, a report in October 1547 has William Paget, a prominent Edwardian Councillor, asserting that Gardiner's opposition to the introduction of the *Paraphrases* into the churches derived in part from his opinion that Erasmus was an Anabaptist.[54]

Although unpublished, and of uncertain though clearly semi-official provenance, this draft surely finds its place in the efforts of Henrician church leaders, above all of Cranmer, to implement Erasmus' injunctions regarding the need for an educated and committed Christian congregation. Side by side with this went an equally Erasmian concern for genuinely pastoral preaching by the clergy. Admittedly, Cranmer himself has not left much sermon material, but three of the most important official 'Homilies' – those on faith, good works and salvation – are attributed to him. Colet had denounced clerical ignorance and demanded an effective performance of preaching and other duties. In the 1520s so had Fisher, for whom Erasmus himself published a book on preaching. These ideals were warmly shared by Cranmer: in his Visitation Articles of 1548 the clergy were enjoined to teach the people the Lord's Prayer, the Creed, and the Ten Commandments. It would be idle to pretend that his campaign to be rid of absentee or gambling and drinking clergy was not undermined by an excessive legacy of ordinations after perfunctory examination of the candidates. Likewise, too many patrons of livings still regarded parish priests as superior servants, much as in the time of the Pastons. Ironically enough, on the subject of diverted ecclesiastical funds, Cranmer himself inherited a pension-commitment directed by his predecessor Warham to Erasmus! Since this had been paid from the revenues of two English benefices, Cranmer was now unable to enforce payment by their incumbents. But he gave Erasmus the twenty pounds due from the living of Aldington in June 1533 and added a lesser gift in September 1535.[55]

Cranmer seems totally Erasmian in his conviction regarding the social duties of the Christian. At a personal level, his generous hospitality to all, even when he himself fasted, is praised by Foxe, while at his manor of Beaksbourne he maintained an almoner, a physician and a surgeon, while supporting sick old soldiers. More officially, his Visitation Articles of 1548 instructed the clergy not only to maintain a poor-chest but also to persuade their parishioners to donate and bequeath money to the poor.[56] He introduced new statutes for Canterbury Cathedral itself which specified the maintenance of twelve poor men, who were to attend the services and ring the bells. His prebendaries were ordered to show hospitality toward the poor. Unfortunately, he and several others had scant success in their efforts to persuade the Crown to create a national provision for the poor. His sympathies were in full accord, as we shall see, with the ideals of those who were sometimes accounted 'Commonwealth Men'.

Meanwhile it has also been suggested that indirect Erasmian influence increased during the reign of Edward VI as a result of the arrival in England of Continental Protestants – both as refugees and by invitation. One of the most notable, and quite possibly most cosmopolitan of all, was John à Lasco. His close and continued friendship with Erasmus will concern us in Chapter Eleven, and although he had moved on in a doctrinal as well as in a geographical sense, the continuity of Erasmian influence cannot be questioned. Now in 1548 this much-travelled Pole was invited to England by Cranmer and at the instigation of William Turner, once a fellow-exile of à Lasco in East Frisia. His first visit to England, lasting from September until the following April, proved influential and most notably upon Cranmer's developing opinions on the Eucharist. À Lasco's influence has been described as largely Zwinglian, but, as will appear, the element of Erasmian *adiaphora* persisted and was destined to find expression in the Elizabethan 'settlement' of this particular sacrament. He returned to England in 1550 and organised fully reformed churches in London before departing hurriedly after the accession of Mary Tudor.[57]

At this time the Marians exhumed and exposed to ignominy the remains of a still more eminent continental Protestant, Martin Bucer, recently buried at Cambridge. Remembering the personal hostility between Bucer and Erasmus, we may feel surprise at the contention that yet another boost had been given to Erasmus' influence in England by the arrival of Bucer in 1549. Even so, it must also be recalled that their quarrels masked many points of agreement on doctrinal and social issues. Both men might indeed have taken issue with a recent description of how 'the Erasmian protestant Martin Bucer' now joined the theological faculty at Cambridge.[58] Nevertheless Bucer there completed his *De Regno Christi*, a prescription for Christian humanist social reform which is unquestionably in the tradition of Erasmus' *Education of a Christian Prince*.[59] Although already in failing health, living only until February 1551, Bucer, who expressed his admiration for Colet's work, has been credited with considerable influence upon the *Homilies* and also upon the Second Prayer Book of Edward VI.[60] The very considerable *social* content of his *De Regno Christi* may point also to a major theme which most certainly bore the imprint of Erasmian ideas and of which a brief treatment is now appropriate: the ideal of the Commonwealth and the 'Commonwealth-men'.

Whatever one's views about any influence exerted upon governmental policy – particularly during the ministry of Thomas Cromwell and during the reign of Edward VI respectively – of those described, and sometimes describing themselves, as 'Commonwealth's Men', there can surely be no dispute about the prominence given to the ideal of the Commonwealth in mid-Tudor England. 'Commonwealth', in this context, was not merely a synonym for 'Realm', but conveyed a complex of ideas about the responsibility of governance within the social and economic aspects of life which derived directly from the concept of the God-given duties as well as powers of the Christian Prince. This ideal had long been replacing any notion of a country as constituting merely the estates of the monarch, had firm medieval roots, and may clearly be identified upon occasion in fifteenth-century England. Yet again, doctrinal Protestantism – in Europe also –

undoubtedly fed into certain lines of its growth and development. Yet if one work must be singled out as the earliest and most influential extended exposition of this ideal, it must surely be Erasmus' *Education of a Christian Prince*.[61]

Erasmus' ideal of the Christian Commonwealth was explored at some length in Chapter Four, and we need but reiterate that this was an integral part of his *philosophia Christi*. As to Erasmus' English influence on such issues, it is true that the *Christian Prince* itself, published in 1516, had to wait until 1550 for the production even of an unpublished manuscript English translation.[62] Yet nothing could be more explicit than the injunction to all governors in the *Enchiridion*, of which seven English versions appeared between Tyndale's first edition in 1533 and 1550, that they 'turn not to thine own profit things which are common, but bestow those things which are thine and thine own self altogether upon the commonwealth. The common people oweth very many things to thee, but thou owest all things to them.'[63] Again, *The booke whiche is called the body of Polycye*, translated from the French of Christine de Pisan in 1521, and much read in England, conveyed prescriptions which closely resemble those of Erasmus.

Quite certainly, most of those accounted Commonwealth sympathisers, or even in the late 1540s 'Commonwealth Men', whether their recommendations for social and economic amelioration remained conservative – as did those of Erasmus – or occasionally ventured into more innovative proposals, proffered their remedies for the ills of society as an integral part of a philosophy of the duties of the Christian ruler to his subjects which was completely Erasmian. Whether we look at such as Thomas Starkey and William Marshall in the Cromwellian era, or at a number of Commonwealth-minded divines in the mid-century, this remains true. For those Protestant bishops accounted Commonwealth sympathisers, such as Thomas Becon, John Hooper, Hugh Latimer, and Cranmer himself, who sometimes appealed to Erasmus' authority in matters doctrinal, also adhered to the principle enunciated by Tyndale, directly and through Erasmian translation, of the binding social and economic responsibilities of the monarch and his ministers.

To revert to mainstream doctrinal developments, although Mary Tudor had shared in the preparation of an English version of Erasmus' *Paraphrases*, we must not in general – remembering especially the forcefully expressed opinions of Stephen Gardiner – expect to find Erasmian views as welcome during her reign as they had been during that of her half-brother. Yet they were pressed into service when thought appropriate: in 1554 there was published an anonymous translation of the letter written by Erasmus to Conrad Pellican as long ago as 1525 which spurned any attribution of sympathy with heretical opinions on the Eucharist.[64]

The accession of Elizabeth opened the curtain on a far more favourable scene. Those whom it later became customary to describe as Anglicans, while regretting Erasmus' failure to break away from Rome, were in no doubt that on the practical issues of religion he was on their side, and they cited him accordingly. As for official policy, may we not discern in the basis and development of the Elizabethan Settlement a 'cool Erasmianism' to set alongside the 'cool Erastianism' so often described? The decision on the crucial wording in the Communion Service – to include phraseology from both the 1549 and the 1552 Prayer Books – may be taken to signify a studied ambiguity, hesitancy, recognition of the principle of *adiaphora*, or merely a hedging of one's bets. Yet was it not a device worthy of Erasmus himself? Thus we need hardly be surprised to find him lauded by sources as diverse as Foxe and Archbishop Whitgift during the reign of Elizabeth. Predictably, Archbishop Grindal's Injunctions for both York and Canterbury in 1571 besought the presence of 'the paraphrases of Erasmus in English upon the gospels . . . set up in some convenient place . . . according to the Queen's Majesty's Injunctions'.[65] But it is much more unusual to encounter a recent suggestion that the *Enchiridion* may well have contributed more to the origins of English Puritanism than any other book save the Bible itself.[66]

This pointer is worth following for a page or so. Admittedly, were one to equate Puritanism solely with doctrinal Calvinism, and in particular with a strictly enunciated doctrine of Predestination, then it would seem to indicate a very short blind alley. But if we concentrate instead upon a more widely valid touchstone of early English Puritanism, that is, a determination to apply Christ's teaching, in spirit as well as in the letter, to every aspect – religious, social and economic – of the Christian's life, then the suggested line of development becomes far more promising. A deeply held sense of personal commitment, of personal responsibility, in the conduct of one's life according to Christ's example and teachings, as established in the Scriptures, devoid of pseudo-academic gloss and free of the trammels of over-elaborate ritual or involvement in meaningless ceremonial: may not these surely agreed characteristics of the ideal of Puritan life be quite clearly descried in Erasmus' own teachings?

In general, does not a strain of the *Devotio Moderna*, a fundamental source of Erasmus' *philosophia Christi*, run straight through to several aspects of that radical Protestantism which contributed to the emergence of Tudor Puritanism? More specifically John Hooper – that model early Puritan – appealed to Erasmus' authority regarding relics and images, while Becon's approving citation of his injunction that 'the perpetual study of living godly is a continual prayer' might find its place as a text in any later Puritan conventicle. Or again, William Turner, whose involvement in the early Elizabethan 'precisian' controversy was to be cut short by his death, queried Erasmus' opinion on scriptural authority regarding baptism, yet remained distinctly Erasmian in his view that the Scriptures should stand as a prescription for Christian living rather than as a peg for doctrinal controversy. Likewise, his suspicion of any false or excessive ceremonial, and most certainly his concern for social amelioration – which places him firmly within the Commonwealth idealist tradition.[67] Later Elizabethan Puritans such as William Fulke, who cited Erasmus on penance and on the need for genuine repentance, were to hark back over over half a century to the great humanist's teachings.[68]

To move from doctrinal to social issues, a recent detailed exposition maintains that, despite certain obvious theological disparities, it was above all English Puritanism which continued to propagate Erasmian social teachings into Elizabethan and Stuart times. Regarding the elements of continuity between the ideals of mid-Tudor Puritans such as Robert Crowley and those of medieval social thought which Erasmus sought to preserve, the thesis is far from new, having been developed by M. M. Knappen and Ernst Troeltsch more than fifty years ago. More novel and debatable is the contention that after the breakdown of an acknowledged consensus on most social issues between Catholics, Anglicans and Puritans during the Elizabethan decades, it was, after the advent of Laud, to be Puritanism alone which became the residual legatee of the Erasmian tradition.[69] Pursuit of this issue is outside the remit of this present work. Yet much else hereabouts is distinctly Erasmian; for example, the Puritan emphasis not only upon the godly nature of the married state – proclaimed by Turner with some scurrilous thrusts at the pseudo-celibacy of Romanist clerics – but also upon the family as in effect a commonwealth in microcosm. In mid-Tudor England these concepts formed a consensus by no means limited to Protestants. Thus Richard Whitford, author of *The werke for housholders* (1537), enunciated a code of manners and conduct, but was and remained a Catholic.[70]

Yet more significant than any perceived 'line of descent' between

Erasmian and Puritan social thought, and indeed more important in regard to the general thesis of this book, is the suggestion that, from the time of its first impact right up to the Elizabethan Church Settlement, Erasmian moderation and irenicism were fundamental though perhaps not always dominant elements in the direction of development taken by the English Church. In the same tradition as Cranmer there stands Queen Elizabeth's first Archbishop of Canterbury. Matthew Parker plainly showed the lasting influence of Erasmus from the days of his friendship with Bilney right up to the years when Holbein's portrait of the great humanist was proudly displayed in his gallery.[71] It is suggested that very considerable similarities of character, including a distaste for extremes, were matched by a certain analogy in their careers, in that neither sought avidly for ecclesiastical advancement. Parker's irenicism had been perhaps oddly demonstrated in a risky attempt to preach to Ket's rebels on Mousehold Heath in 1549 about the error of their ways! He had been friendly with Martin Bucer during his all-too-short residence in Cambridge. Perhaps above all as evidence of a temperament which sought neither martyrdom nor conflict, he had contrived to remain safely if somewhat obscurely in England during the reign of Mary Tudor. Elizabeth's choice of Parker attests not only her sure grasp of the religious temper of the great majority of her subjects but also the enduring nature of the Erasmian impact in England.

Meanwhile, before we trace significant developments elsewhere in Europe we should recall that the last years of Erasmus' life witnessed the constitutional absorption of Wales into the English realm. The Erasmian spirit had already occupied the minds of certain educated Welshmen, but as to any such influence upon the great majority of the population whose native tongue was still Welsh, much care is needed. Indeed, most Welsh writers at this time published in a language – English, Latin or even Italian – which was not their own. But the evidence of Erasmian influence upon both the lay and the religious leaders of Welsh thought is incontestable, and this regardless of whether they ultimately followed a Catholic or a Protestant path.[72]

Perhaps the earliest recorded direct contact between Erasmus and a Welsh-born cleric is attested in a letter dated 1 May 1506 which he wrote 'to his delightful friend, the English [sic] scholar Richard Whitford', who was chaplain to Bishop Foxe. Erasmus' discussion of his work which accompanied the epistle is evidence of the mutual regard between its recipient and both More and Erasmus: 'two authors whom you used to describe as so similar in mind, character, outlook and pursuits that, you said, no pair of twins on earth could be more alike'.[73] Erasmus' allusion to his *English* friend is worth noting, for Whitford was a 'London Welshman'. Yet most significantly, in the general context of our theme of Erasmian influence, he has rightly been described as an outstanding representative of the *Devotio Moderna*. This is far from surprising, since Whitford's translation of à Kempis' *Imitation of Christ* was printed as early as 1530. This most celebrated of early Welsh humanists continued to display the warmest regard for saints, and never embraced radical Protestantism. He was, in short, an Erasmian humanist, not a religious revolutionary.[74]

Such lay representatives of the 'Anglo-Welsh establishment' as Sir Edward Carne and Sir John Price also demonstrated sympathy with the Erasmian reformist ideal. True, the first-named contrived to combine service of Henry VIII and the acquisition of monastic property at Ewenny with his retention of Catholic sympathies and indeed his later service as Queen Mary's ambassador at Rome, where he remained until his death in 1561. Sir John Price of Brecon, also an active and influential royal servant, participated both in monastic visitation and thereafter in monastic spoils. He left published evidence of his adhesion to Erasmian views, in particular in his condemnation of the short-comings of the contemporary clergy and of the mechanistic and superstitious approach to religion of the laity. Most notably, his concern for religious education in his native tongue was expressed in the form of the first book printed in Welsh, *Yn y Llhyvyr Hwnn* . . . (In This Book), which appeared in 1546. A basic religious primer, it deplored his countrymen's religious and educational darkness as attributable largely to the deficiencies of the clergy.[75]

Last but certainly not least in regard to the provision of a religious literature in Welsh, we turn to the literary lawyer who became converted to Protestantism while at Oxford, William Salesbury. Not only has his *Oll Synnwyr Pen Cymro* (The Welshman's Common Sense), 1547, been termed the first manifesto of Welsh Protestant humanism, by 'a perfervid admirer of Erasmus', but Salesbury also obeyed his mentor's injunction in publishing a translation of the epistles and the gospels of the prayer-book in *Cynnifer Llith a Ban* . . . (As Many Lessons as are Read) some four years later. Salesbury, who thought Erasmus to be the 'most learned, eloquent, and accomplished scholar in Christendom of our age and many ages before us', was later, in Elizabeth's reign, to continue his efforts to provide a translation of the New Testament and the Prayer Book into Welsh. Admittedly, one must ponder the observation that the peculiarities of his rendering prevented the great majority of the Welsh people from understanding it. Yet, all in all, these efforts of Welsh devotees of Erasmus to follow his precepts are far from unimpressive.[76]

Reverting finally to the mainstream developments of the English realm, is it justifiable to conclude that the English Erasmians constituted the most successful and permanent embodiment of their mentor's influence? Judged by the number and importance of leaders of religious reform who acclaimed his scholarship and teachings, together with the fact that the tendency of many Protestant humanists in Germany to turn away from Erasmus did not occur in England, there is much to commend this suggestion. Moreover, despite Stephen Gardiner's belated identification of dangerous trends in Erasmus' writings, it is significant that the Marian Royal Proclamation which listed so many heretical authors included Erasmus Sarcerius but not Erasmus of Rotterdam. Indeed, as we have already noticed, the mid-century witnessed the printing of translations of a couple of Erasmus' works by those who drew from them support for the Roman cause. Finally, we have alluded in some detail to Erasmian features in the emergent Church of England. Described by some as ambivalent or Janus-faced, the English visage of Erasmus belonged to a reformer and a mediator rather than to a revolutionary. Perhaps it was indeed in English soil that his propagation of the *philosophia Christi* found its most fertile seed-bed and put down its deepest roots.

Ten

FRANCE, SPAIN AND ITALY

It seems appropriate to shift our focus next to Erasmus and France. For as we have seen it was in France that he commenced his serious studies; he spent some half-dozen years domiciled in Paris and visited that city another six times. It is true that the Collège de Montaigu and the capital itself do not seem always to have furnished the happiest of recollections, but Erasmus continued to profess himself as always loving the land of France and wrote thereof a couple of glowing encomia. Indeed, on several occasions in later life he spoke of moving there – specifically to Besançon – though a major attraction appears to have been the quality of the wine![1] Much more seriously, we have already seen that the years in France were formative for Erasmus and that his sojourn in Paris contributed much to the evolution of the Christian humanist. Appropriately, we shall now consider the incontestable evidence of the impact of Erasmus himself upon French religious development. In any assessment of such impact, the suggestion that his permanent legacy consisted, first, of 'Erasmians who became Lutherans', and secondly and of quite a different category, of literary figures who remained Catholic or became free-thinkers, is an over-simplification.[2]

For a while at least, in the decade or so following the accession to the throne of Francis I in 1515, France furnished an example of an indigenous movement for religious and cultural reform, centred around Lefèvre d'Étaples and Guillaume Briçonnet, which apparently had more in common with Erasmus than any other. French Christian humanism received from Francis himself and his sister not only tolerance and protection but significant encouragement. Erasmian sympathisers in influential positions included not only a royal physician, Guillaume Cop, and the king's confessor, Guillaume Petit, but also the pre-eminent humanist and royal secretary, Budé, and indeed Étienne Poncher, Bishop of Paris. Such support was of crucial importance, for France was also to produce, in the shape of the Faculty of Theology at the Sorbonne, led by Noël Béda, one of the fiercest and perhaps most sustained assaults upon the teachings of Erasmus himself. Finally, one of the greatest French literary figures of the sixteenth century, François Rabelais, was a professed admirer.[3]

As early as 1495 Erasmus had been noticed by Robert Gaguin, a distinguished French Humanist,[4] but his most significant contact in such circles was with Jacques Lefèvre d'Étaples. Lefèvre had undergone a process of development in respect of letters, philosophy, theology, and religion not unlike that of Erasmus – whom he most closely resembled in his approach to scriptural studies and in his Christocentric religious teaching, with its stress on the primacy of genuine inner faith over externals and ceremonial. By the first decade of the sixteenth century he had established around himself a humanist circle. The two men did not in fact meet until 1511, but thereafter mutual admiration characterised their correspondence until the publication of Erasmus' *New Testament* in 1516. But after Lefèvre's criticism of Erasmus' rendering of Hebrews 2:7 as coldly literal, making Christ lower than the angels, things were said that must surely have been regretted. It has been suggested that an apparently trivial difference actually symbolised a profound divergence of spiritual outlook; but, as so often, one wonders at the part played once more by wounded *amour propre*. By April 1518 Erasmus was appealing to the 'most learned and excellent' Lefèvre, 'in the name of Christian charity, by our common love of sacred study', for a reconciliation. They were to meet again in Basel in 1526, but a certain wariness lingered.[5]

While it is impossible to discount the influence of Erasmus' writings and of his technique of textual analysis, within a wider context Lefèvre has also been seen as a quite independent case of reformist evangelism deriving from the *Devotio Moderna* and anticipating the Anabaptists.[6] Certainly his emphasis upon the 'imitation of Christ', his insistence that faith must lead to good works, and his rejection of any rigorously predestinarian element in theology, all have links with the *Devotio*, Erasmus and the sectarians. Yet the reformist circle around Marguerite d'Angoulême, sister of Francis I and later Queen of Navarre, looked to Lefèvre and not to Erasmus, of whose intellectual basis in humanism and religion Marguerite herself was sceptical, responding most coolly to his approaches. It has been suggested not only that Lefèvre himself proceeded to occupy a stance mid-way between Erasmus and Luther – attempting to reconcile the former's exegesis with the latter's theology – but also that, in common with Berquin and Farel, he only adhered to Erasmus in so far as he came close to Luther! The breach occasioned by an initial disagreement over translation which we referred to a page or so earlier seems to have widened after Lefèvre's move from Paris to Meaux. According to one contemporary this move had been hastened by his distaste for the increasingly anti-Lutheran feeling in the capital. By 1522–23 he is described as having become a convinced Lutheran in his emphasis on man's total incapacity without the gift of grace, in contrast with Erasmian confidence in the intrinsic resources of the human intellect.[7]

The 'Cercle de Meaux' itself – centred around its Bishop, Guillaume Briçonnet,[8] and including Lefèvre and for a while Guillaume Farel, prior to his departure on more extreme courses – also exhibited ambivalent attitudes toward Erasmus. It has rightly been stressed that in fact Briçonnet himself resembled Erasmus in his emphasis upon preaching, the simplification of the liturgy and the use of the vernacular. They also shared a certain scepticism concerning superfluous images. Yet despite the bishop's formal condemnation of Luther's doctrines in 1523, the influence of the German Reformer helped to produce in him what has been characterised as a 'uniquely ambivalent Christian humanism'. While stopping short of acceptance of basic Lutheran tenets such as the denial of transubstantiation, the 'gens de Meaux' moved steadily away from approaching Scripture with Erasmian confidence in man's innate ability to search for truth to a position of total denial of any such powers or hopes without divine intervention.[9] None the less, as late as 1524 there is testimony to some residual goodwill toward Erasmus among those at Meaux.[10]

Discounting Farel, who was ultimately to move to Calvinism and an utter rejection of Erasmus' position, the clearest example of a certain lack of empathy appears in Marguerite d'Angoulême. Again, although she has been engagingly described as 'Lutheran in her fashion', the basic reason why she never disguised her lack of sympathy with Erasmus was not identifiably doctrinal. The admiration expressed in a letter from Erasmus[11] which thanked her for her protection of sincere Christians and of good letters went unanswered and unreciprocated, not because Marguerite arrived at a hostile doctrinal position, but rather because she perceived in him the sin of intellectual pride in seeking to apply mere human reason to those things which are of God.[12]

Meanwhile King Francis himself, eager to be seen as a patron of scholarship, gave the humanist movement rather firmer support. His secretary Guillaume Budé[13] had already in 1516 begun a correspondence with Erasmus which endured for over a decade through some fifty often lengthy epistles. Though here again the exchanges alternated between warm friendship and jealous suspicion, it was to Budé that Erasmus confided that in his *Enchiridion* 'I have dared to differ widely from this age of ours, undeterred by any man's authority'. Writing in 1517 to Étienne Poncher, Bishop of Paris, he combined a tribute to Budé, 'most certainly the glory of France', with another to 'the most flourishing realm in the Christian world' whose monarch was 'most Christian in fact as well as title'. Francis, having resolved to establish a college for the study of classical languages, had in the same year invited Erasmus to take charge, offering him a rich prebend as an inducement to reside in France. Budé's respect for Erasmus was such that, although often himself considered France's greatest humanist, he did not bridle at being thus passed over, but wrote at some length commending both the choice and the invitation. Though obviously flattered, Erasmus penned a most courteous refusal on the grounds of his age and health. Even so, his commitment to Charles, from whom he was in receipt of a pension, must also have weighed quite heavily.[14]

Meanwhile Francis, always rejecting the Lutheran heresy, would have won Erasmus' approval in his determination not to allow his rejection to become a stick with which to beat good letters. Yet this crude weapon the Faculty of Theology at the Sorbonne, led by Noël Béda, now proceeded to use. Although not without his own early reformist tendencies, Béda, who may well have known Erasmus at the Collège de Montaigu in the mid-1490s, had now come to believe that the new exegetical methods of Erasmus and other humanists presented a danger to Church unity, especially when set alongside the emergent Lutheran heresy. He became the diligent spearhead of a movement which, in its attempts to impose censorship, its repeated attacks upon Erasmus, and finally in its successful procurement of the martyrdom of Berquin, was manifestly persecution.[15]

Erasmus himself became acutely sensitive to the danger from this quarter to his reputation and well-being. Between April 1525 and November 1527 he engaged in a prolonged and fruitless correspondence with Béda which may fairly be called a dialogue of the deaf. Fortunately, King Francis had from the outset warned the Sorbonne against using an anti-heretical pretext to cover a general attack on Christian humanism and on Erasmus in particular. This position he was not disposed to abandon. None the less, learning that the Faculty was exploring alleged errors and heresies in his *Paraphrases* – to be followed in June by a condemnation of the *Querela pacis* – Erasmus wrote to Béda in April 1525 to exculpate himself. The reply evoked one of his very longest missives in his own defence. In February 1526 he complained to the Faculty of Theology itself about Béda's 'calumnies', taking particular exception to being described as 'shamelessly opposed to good morals' and as schismatic. The following March he fruitlessly despatched to his chief assailant Part I of *Hyperaspistes*. Then in mid-June he sent off a trinity of letters. The Paris Parlement was bluntly told that Erasmus had discovered in Béda's censures on his *Paraphrases* 'more than an hundred lies and calumnies'. An appeal to King Francis persuaded him, to the rage of its author, to intervene to stop the circulation of Béda's book: the *Annotationes* which bracketed Erasmus with Lefèvre. The letter to the Faculty was scathing in its rebuttal of anything seditious or factious.[16]

In November 1527 news of a renewed assault evoked from Erasmus another letter to the Sorbonne, deriding Béda's praise of Lee, whom Erasmus deemed unfit to set foot in a School of Theology. The Parlement of Paris was again appealed to, while a letter to Béda himself contains some gems of impassioned invective: surely his manifest lying and impudent blasphemy must be clear to all, as is the abyss into which Satan is striving to drag him! Small wonder that Erasmus remarked to a Spanish correspondent that 'in one Béda there are three thousand monks'. Sadly, nevertheless, in December 1527 Béda procured from the Faculty a formal condemnation of his *Colloquies*, *Paraphrases* and other works.[17]

Writing directly to Francis I himself, Erasmus had claimed that that monarch was confronted with a conspiracy of theologians and monks, seeking to arrogate political power. Such a point was not likely to be missed by the King. Yet his power to protect Erasmus' name, at a safe distance, was not quite equalled by his ability to ensure repeated clemency toward a more obvious and intransigent heretic within France itself. Louis de Berquin, a nobleman of Flemish origin and a member of the Royal Council, may fairly be described as an Erasmian, in so far as he had already almost certainly translated several works, including the *Querela pacis*. Seizing the opportunity afforded by the enforced absence of Francis after his defeat and capture at the Battle of Pavia in February 1525, the Faculty proceeded to examine and condemn several of Erasmus' works, in translation. Their actual appearance in print in October provoked further action.[18]

Berquin had already been condemned in 1523 for possession of Lutheran books but had escaped, after royal intervention, by means of a humble abjuration. Béda's declared suspicion that he was the translator now involved evoked from Erasmus a disclaimer, while he complained to Berquin himself that his infuriating actions were assisting his enemies in their attacks upon his works. Between January and March in 1526 Berquin was imprisoned and condemned as a relapsed heretic, but the providential return of Francis saved him once more. However, his protestation to Erasmus at being condemned merely for faithful translation was weakened by the inclusion of *Lutheran* material. Erasmus, in fairness, despite his caveat to Berquin himself, defended him to the King, who was by now involved in a not-inconsiderable trial of strength with the Paris Parlement, which obstructed direct orders for Berquin's release from prison until November.[19]

Marguerite also had interceded for Berquin, and had taken him into her service. Erasmus commended royal intervention in saving Béda's intended victim from the flames and, although considering him imprudent, wrote to Berquin in friendly fashion. Berquin's reply repeated his denial of all charges, imitating Erasmus in a protestation that the Faculty would condemn the words of Christ Himself! Erasmus again replied in December 1528, but by the following March was again regretting Berquin's vehement and imprudent actions. His comment was just, for by now Berquin, apparently emboldened by royal favour, took the rash and disastrous step of making a formal appeal against his sentence and attacking Béda. This led only to a third trial which ended in mid-April in another condemnation, which was executed by burning within twenty- four hours while Francis was absent from the capital. It seems indeed likely that even the King had written off the foolhardy offender.[20]

In Erasmus' comments on this tragedy, fear jostles with sympathy and horror. He refers to Berquin's death in a letter to his old friend Pirckheimer in May 1529, and at greater length when writing in July to Charles Utenhove, apparently to discharge a promise made to Berquin himself. This letter includes his oft-cited distinction between honest error and obdurate heresy, together with a scathing condemnation of Béda's insensate procuring of Berquin's martyrdom. As for Berquin, happy is he 'if he died with a good conscience, as I trust'. Nearly four years later, Erasmus was still to allude to the 'example of Louis Berquin, who was destroyed for nothing more than honest free speech against monks and theologians, being a man in other respects most blameless'. Yet on 25 April 1533, four days later, he still deplores the fact that Berquin 'would never have perished if he had conformed to my counsels'. All in all, his sourly expressed pleasure at the eventual disgrace and public degradation of Béda is hardly surprising.[21]

A very different example of the impact of Erasmus in France is found in François Rabelais. Given their vastly different popular images, any juxtaposition of these two, who never met, may seem at first sight to be incongruous. Yet the only extant letter of Rabelais combines a warning about potential enemies with a lavishly respectful tribute, couched at one point in appropriately earthy terms.[22] Moreover, it has been urged that a descendant of Erasmus' picture of the 'holy fool', often attested in clear verbal parallels, may be discerned in Panurge, a comic character in *Pantagruel*. This work was published in 1532, to be followed by two editions of *Gargantua* in 1534 and 1535, straddling the notorious 'Affair of the Placards': the publication of broadsheets levelling a furious assault at the Catholic doctrine of the Eucharist.[23]

The *Colloquies*, *Enchiridion* and *Querela pacis* have all been identified as sources used by Rabelais, along with the *Praise of Folly*. Most notably of all, the *Adages* often supplied the authority which Rabelais embellished with humour in his satirical thrusts. While Erasmus could not have been much gratified by the coarse scurrilities of his admirer, Rabelais always retained a profound respect for the great humanist. It has been suggested that the version of Christianity which appealed to him was a Philosophy of Christ which recognised free will and counselled its exercise in a good life, with morality more important than doctrinal precision. Like Erasmus, he sought always the real meaning of the Scriptures, while the two men were as one in condemning war. Erasmian pacifism is evident in Rabelais' treatment of the Picrocholine Wars in *Gargantua*, while he quotes Plato via Erasmus to make the telling point that war between Christian states is in itself a variety of *sedition*.[24] Again, the notion of the 'philosopher-king' appears in both writers, while some passages in Rabelais have been seen as reflecting, in knockabout fashion, Erasmus' views on Utraquism in the Eucharist and above all on free will. On this vital issue Rabelais adhered to Erasmus, not to Luther. Indeed, Michael Screech points to a later interpolation in the 1559 edition of Calvin's *Institutes of the Christian Religion* as very probably a direct counter to the synergistic theology of Rabelais, who in turn alluded to the 'demoniac' and 'impostor' of Geneva.

Erasmus and Rabelais combined a genuine wish for religious reform with wickedly pointed satire on contemporary abuses within organised religion, though the former's mockery of the cult of relics and of pilgrimages was taken further by Rabelais, who also levelled derisory thrusts at the Sorbonne and at Béda in particular.[25] Yet the description of Rabelais as 'the last of the French Erasmians' begs the question. For another French literary giant, writing admittedly some decades after

Erasmus' death, is perhaps the closest by temperament of all his creative disciples, affording a genuinely closer parallel than Rabelais. Michel de Montaigne makes a solitary direct reference to Erasmus; but the influence of the *Adages*, *Colloquies* and *Praise of Folly* has been clearly discerned in his *Essays*. He was Erasmian in his derision of medieval formalism and note of irreverent jesting. But most notably Pierre Villey ascribed his 'philosophy of nature' to Erasmus' emphasis upon the power of human reason.[26]

The suggested inclusion among French Erasmians of John Calvin is in many respects a very much more doubtful proposition. For despite the much vaunted 'humanist phase' of Calvin – who also attended the Collège de Montaigu, and praised Erasmus, Valla, Budé, and Lefèvre in his early days – it is difficult to sense any real empathy between his theology and the essential ethos of Erasmus' teachings. Unlike Luther, Calvin very rarely attacked Erasmus by name. Yet references to the 'durability' of Calvin's humanism must surely be offset by the elements of discontinuity, sometimes of radical dichotomy, between its essential spirit and 'post-conversion' Calvinism. In particular, Calvin's rigorous predestinarianism and utter contempt for Man's own potential are poles apart from the humanist optimism which coloured so much of Erasmus' thinking.[27]

In Calvin's *Institutes*, while Erasmus is not personally refuted, the score of note-references to his *De libero arbitrio* by the editor of a modern translation are crucial pointers. In the text itself, Calvin attacks such as stop short of 'a frank confession of man's powerlessness', who dare to 'think nothing more inconsistent than that out of the common multitude of men some should be predestined to salvation, others to destruction', who 'usually say that after we have accepted the first grace, then our own efforts co-operate with subsequent grace'. They contend 'that no place is now left for merits if they do not have free will as their source', indeed that it is but folly to reprove sin unless a power to obey is conceded. Such thrusts make it well-nigh impossible not to descry Erasmus among his targets. His rebuttals, first of 'the notion that there is something in man's will and effort which, although feeble in itself, when aided by God's mercy does not fail to yield a favourable outcome', and secondly of 'the shamelessness of certain impious persons who slanderously charge us with abolishing good works . . . when we say that men are not justified by works', and thus with making the path to righteousness too easy, remind us almost irresistibly of *De libero arbitrio*, and of Erasmus' charge of 'opening a door to impiety of all sorts'.[28]

By 1536, when the *Institutes* appeared, Erasmus was dead, while Capito's hopeful cry of 1527 that 'the king favours the Word', followed by royal contacts with Bucer and an invitation to France of Melanchthon, had long been overtaken by events which had convinced Francis that religious orthodoxy and public peace went together.[29] Despite the efforts of Lefèvre and Briçonnet, an Erasmian-type of Catholic revival put down but shallow roots in France, while Protestantism's ultimate achievement of a secure if minority establishment owed much more to the disciplined canons of Calvin than to the gentler and tolerant piety of Erasmus. Yet, all in all, although its immediate influence was cut short, Erasmian humanism had as long a flowering in France as it did to the south, across the Pyrenees.

Indeed, an outline of Erasmianism in Spain might seem to be a depiction of a massive paradox, in that the nation which produced Caraffa and the Inquisition should also present the clearest evidence of a vivid, if all-too-brief efflorescence of Erasmus' religious ideals. Yet closer study may modify if not resolve such question-begging contrasts. Thus, Church *reform* as such within Spain neither began nor ended with Erasmus, while in the realm of ideals the Alumbrados or 'Illuminists' most emphatically ante-dated his influence. Again, it may well be argued that Erasmianism arrived in Spain as part of the retinue of Charles V, flourished above all during his residence there in the 1520s and under the protection of a couple of his pre-eminent statesmen and ecclesiastics, and waned thereafter. Assuredly, by the 1540s Spanish Erasmians had been scattered and silenced – or were dead. Yet parallels have been traced between the *Enchiridion* and the teachings of the man who initiated the Jesuit spear-head of the Counter-Reformation, Ignatius Loyola.

Perhaps we should remind ourselves that the Counter-Reformation itself had its roots not only in the repression of heresy but also, and indeed earlier, in Church reform. In terms of organisational and spiritual renewal the most notable Spanish figure of the late fifteenth century was Cardinal Francisco Ximénez. While not successful in his invitation to Erasmus to visit Spain, he was the founder of what was to be the great centre of Spanish Erasmianism, the University of Alcalá. Moreover, his patronage and leadership of the cause of scriptural reform led to the production of the six-volume 'Complutensian' Polyglot Bible, completed by 1517 although not published for five years. Yet alongside all this a determination to suppress heterodoxy was also already present, in the form of the Inquisition.[30]

Meanwhile the sect of Alumbrados, or Illuminists, was equally and totally indigenous in its origin. This soon fell foul of the Inquisition and by September 1525 had been condemned. Described by one authority as an aberration of mysticism, it has been seen by some as providing a 'reception area' for Lutheran Protestantism in Spain just as Lollardy had reputedly done in the case of England. Again, the fact that others have discerned a link between Illuminism and some Erasmians must be set alongside the irony of the fact that Loyola was jailed in 1527 under suspicion of Alumbradist inclinations! Given the often very emotional mysticism which characterised so many of the Alumbrados, and which was conspicuously lacking in the personality of Erasmus himself, the attribution of any connection is perhaps surprising. Yet the movements had in common a particular emphasis upon internal Christian faith as opposed to outward formalism and ceremonial. Indeed, Erasmianism in Spain has even been termed a far more sophisticated counterpart of Illuminism. Contacts undoubtedly existed between Erasmians such as Juan de Valdés and the Alumbrados. Naturally, the narrowly orthodox made use of the ploy of accusing Erasmians of Illuminism and of Lutheranism after both had been condemned in 1525.[31]

It is difficult to resist the contention that the fairly rapid establishment and the brief éclat of Erasmianism in Spain owed very much to the support of the entourage of Charles V, and that the years when Spain came within the Burgundian Flemish orbit were those when its ideas made significant penetration. Juan Luis Vives, a pre-eminent humanist in his own right and a friend of Erasmus, typifies both in his career and his travels the cosmopolitan milieu thus envisaged. But supremely important, as in effect an Imperial guarantee of the orthodoxy of Erasmus, was the favour of Charles himself and of his Chancellor, Mercurino Gattinara, until his death in 1530. Gattinara, a determinant influence upon Imperial policy during the third decade of the sixteenth century, first exchanged letters with Erasmus as early as 1520, expressing mutual regard. But it was in the middle of the decade, against the background of Gattinara's appeal for assistance against the Lutheran heresy which we noted in an earlier context, alongside Erasmus' almost simultaneous need of support against the attacks of his opponents in Spain, that the friendly relationship with Charles – who had, after all, appointed him councillor – and with his chief adviser became of crucial import.[32]

On 28 October 1525 Gattinara wrote from Toledo, in cordial terms, to acknowledge that Erasmus' attack upon Luther's 'pestiferous dogma' had made no small impression. The following April Erasmus complained to the Chancellor about the Lutheran growling against him, and, in default of an early receipt of any reply, expressed growing concern regarding the efforts of his Spanish adversaries in another letter to Gattinara on 3 September. In fact, a most reassuring missive from Charles V himself, expressing his joy and gratitude at Erasmus' endeavours, including the recent Part I of *Hyperaspistes*, against the impious Lutheran faction, had already been penned. This was followed on 1 October by a letter from Gattinara in what has been seen as the most important item in their entire correspondence. This pledged total support but also included a passage which will concern us later in the context of the debatable concept of Erasmus and the 'Third Church'. Nor were the Chancellor's efforts to defend Erasmus confined to Spain, as was to be demonstrated in a sharp rebuke addressed to his adversaries at Louvain which spoke warmly of the benefits conferred by him upon the *Christiana respublica* and included a specific assurance that among the Spaniards no name was more celebrated. Erasmus was simultaneously informed of its content and also advised to discount any effect of the calumnies of Edward Lee. Such reassurance, in February 1527, must have been doubly welcome in the light of the impending storm centred at Valladolid.[33]

Before examining this, it is time to stress that sincere Erasmians within Spain itself included several churchmen and humanists of the first rank. Amongst these, pride of place may be given to Alonso Manrique, Archbishop of Seville,[34] if only because he was also Inquisitor General, becoming a Cardinal in 1531, and as such took action against Lutheran and Illuminist heresies. Yet he defended Erasmus when Edward Lee, England's ambassador in Spain, fomented attacks upon him. Manrique, to whom one edition of a Spanish translation of the *Enchiridion* was dedicated, proved to be a faithful, resolute and effective defender of Erasmus' scholarship and orthodoxy. Indeed, Erasmus' *Apologia adversus articulos aliquot per monachos quosdam* was dedicated directly to this prelate. On 26 August 1527 Erasmus appealed to Manrique, retailing at some length his grievances, his services to the Catholic Church, and his resentment at the unjust calumnies currently directed at him. Perhaps he was emboldened to take this step in the light of a letter which had been sent to Manrique by Clement VII himself the previous month, which combined an exhortation to vigilance against unorthodoxy with a glowing tribute to Erasmus: 'an eloquent, learned, and most industrious man' who had written *summa cum laude* against the heresiarch Martin Luther.[35]

Here mention should also be made of Luis Núñez Coronel, of Segovia, who, after obtaining a doctorate in theology at the Sorbonne, became a councillor and confessor at the court of Charles in 1519 before returning to Spain and becoming secretary to Manrique. A declared Erasmian from 1522, he kept in touch and essayed a defence of the *Enchiridion* which is no longer extant. At Valladolid he played a major part in influencing both his master and Fonseca against Erasmus' assailants. Indeed, informing Manrique of the publication of his *Apologia*, Erasmus declares his awareness of how much he owes to 'the most accomplished theologian Ludovico Coronello'. Sadly, in 1531, Coronel was one of several Spanish Erasmians who were to fall before the Reaper's blade, thus gravely weakening their cause in Spain even before the Inquisition's attack in the late 1530s.[36]

When J. L. Vives wrote to assure Erasmus that he had the enduring favour of eminent personalities against the enmity of the Spanish monks, he certainly also had in mind Alonso de Fonseca, Archbishop of Santiago before becoming Archbishop of Toledo and Primate of Spain in December 1523. A patron of humanists in his own right, Fonseca's selection of Juan de Vergara as his secretary, and his personal interest in the well-being of the University of Alcalá, are clear indications of his sympathies. Indeed, Erasmus' appeal to Gattinara on 3 September 1526 was accompanied by a letter of the same date in which he thanked Fonseca for his help against his Spanish enemies. On 24 April 1527 Fonseca himself penned a brief but friendly letter, confirming his own and the Emperor's goodwill and counselling both fortitude and moderation. His offer of regular support should Erasmus decide to come to Spain was declined, but there followed despatch of financial help on the one hand and the dedication of an edition on the other. In all the circumstances, Erasmus' expression of concern for Fonseca's declining health was genuine, and the Archbishop's death in 1534 when the tide had already turned against the Erasmians was another heavy blow to their cause.[37]

Among those by then already arrested by the Inquisition and charged with heresy was Juan Vergara himself, and we must now go back to sketch a group of Erasmian politico-literary figures, as distinct from ecclesiastics of the first rank. Important as was Vergara, in terms of *general* significance the career of Alfonso de Valdés[38] who, together with his younger brother Juan, was a resolute Erasmian, must be accorded primacy. Not only was he a persistent supporter of Erasmus at the Imperial Court, where he became secretary to Gattinara, assuming at Augsburg his role of attempted moderation in personal contact with Melanchthon after his master's death, but he was also an Erasmian author of some repute. The *Enchiridion*, *Colloquies*, *Praise of*

Folly, and *Querela pacis* were all reflected in his two chief publications (1527, 1528) which attacked both clerical abuses and papal conduct. Moreover, some of the social comment of Erasmus, on the rights of the poor as well as of the rich, and on the duties of the prince, also found its way into his writing. But also evident, as in the case of his brother Juan, is some Illuminist influence. Sadly, Alfonso – described by Olivar at Valladolid as appearing 'more Erasmian than Erasmus' – did not long survive Gattinara. His death by plague in 1532 is yet another case of how mortality virtually ruined the Erasmian cause in Spain even before the death of its fountain-head in 1536. Alfonso de Valdés' death has rightly been termed an irreparable loss. Following a brief but friendly letter from Erasmus on 31 March 1527, he had performed the triple task of defending him against his Spanish adversaries, keeping him informed of their attacks, and counselling moderation in his writings. A letter sent him by Erasmus in March 1529 refers to the approaching tragedy which Berquin may have provoked by his excessive zeal.[39]

Meanwhile, if Alfonso was better known and indeed more important because of his political influence, his brother Juan probably attained a more profound significance through his literary and religious influence. Through his follower Peter Martyr and perhaps also through Bernardino Ochino, this extended to the English Church. Thus one contemporary English commentator ranked him alongside Martyr, Calvin, Melanchthon, Luther, and Knox as one of the great names of the Reformation. After entering the University of Alcalá he speedily became an Erasmian, and his *Dialogue on Christian Doctrine* (1529) as well as making brief reference to the great humanist's translation of the New Testament, reflected to the full his theology, his attitude toward Church reform, and above all the fundamental optimism of his humanity. His later work, unpublished during his lifetime, apparently moved beyond Erasmus. But what did appear in print was already enough to fall foul of the Inquisition, and Juan de Valdés was exiled from Spain for the rest of his life. We shall again encounter his influence in Italy. He was not the only distinguished exile. Pedro Lerma, Chancellor of the University of Alcalá, was imprisoned for heresy in 1537, made public recantation throughout Spain, and left the country.[40]

Hardly less important was the assistance given to Erasmus by Juan de Vergara,[41] supported by his brothers Francisco and Bernardino Tovar. After studies at Alcalá, participation in Ximénez' project of the Polyglot Bible, and a period as secretary to the Cardinal himself, Juan first met Erasmus at Bruges in 1520, then again at Louvain in 1521.

Thereafter he endeavoured, with total lack of success, to halt the attacks made upon Erasmus by a theologian of Alcalá, Diego López Zúñiga – Spain's very own Lee, according to Erasmus' unfair depiction. Indeed the Vergara–Zúñiga correspondence has been accorded the significance of separate treatment by the Toronto editors of Erasmus' letters. Certainly he was a fearsome adversary: Erasmus considered him as 'raving mad as any Orestes', and Vives as sounding 'like one of the Furies, not a human being'.[42]

In January 1521 Vergara became court chaplain to Charles V, and then, after returning to an increasingly Erasmian intellectual climate in Spain, secretary to Archbishop Fonseca. From this influential position he continued to defend and to warn Erasmus. At the outset of the Valladolid inquiry he despatched a long letter from that city to apprise him of the fact that, while there were indeed many eminent and erudite men who praised the name of Erasmus, there were others who dubbed him heretical, blasphemous, impious, and sacrilegious. Such critics, he continued, would prohibit his works as inciting disorder among the people and as insinuating doctrinal heresies. They would impute collusion with Luther and discover impiety even in the *Enchiridion*. The suspension of the Valladolid conference of theologians without recording any formal decision was greeted as a victory by the Erasmians, and the period 1527–30 is sometimes seen as a high-water-mark.

If so, most certainly the tide was soon to ebb with quite disastrous rapidity. In 1528 Juan Vergara defended Juan de Valdés' *Dialogue on Christian Doctrine* before a commission at Alcalá. But the departure of Charles V for Italy was followed during the early 1530s by a resolute counter-attack by those who opposed Erasmus. In September 1530 Juan Vergara's brother, Bernardino Tovar, was imprisoned on a charge of heresy, and was followed in June 1533 by Juan himself. His trial lasted until December 1535, and by then the death of Fonseca in February 1534 had ruinously weakened his position. In May 1534 Vives wrote to tell Erasmus that 'in Spain Vergara and his brother Tovar are captive, besides certain other learned men'. Such news would scarcely have furthered the accompanying wish that Erasmus might enjoy a tranquil old age! Although he publicly abjured his errors after contrition, Vergara did not regain his freedom until February 1537 and was by then a broken man.[43]

While Erasmus' connections with the Valdés and Vergara brothers were by far the most important links with influential Spanish humanists, these were far from being isolated. Relations with Alonso Ruiz de Virués,[44] of Olmedo and Burgos, whose published praise of

Erasmus was at first tempered by unwelcome criticism, were fairly cool until the intervention of such mutual friends as Juan Vergara. Thereafter, Virués publicly expressed his adhesion to the Erasmian cause. In June 1527 Alfonso de Valdés included a reference to the part played at Valladolid by 'the distinguished theologian Alonso Virués of Olmedo' in defending Erasmus against the calumnies of the monks. Virués also published, albeit anonymously, translations of some of the *Colloquies* in 1529. Becoming a court preacher he went with Charles V to Germany, but after his return to Spain in 1533 he paid the penalty for his allegiance. Despite giving evidence against Juan de Vergara in April 1534, by the end of that year he found himself in prison, where he remained until 1538.[45] Not all Erasmians remained loyal. Thus Juan Maldonado, a one-time admirer in the Erasmian circle at Burgos, the recipient of that long and perhaps over-frank letter from Erasmus we cited earlier, had by 1534 ceased his attachment, perhaps because he considered the *Colloquies* to be dangerous to the Christian faith, perhaps because discretion outweighed valour.[46]

If the years 1522–25 had marked the first sweeping inroads of Erasmus' thought in Spain, 1527 had seen the first determined but unsuccessful attempt at its rebuttal. The conference of theologians at Valladolid had in fact been summoned by Archbishop Manrique himself, perhaps in response to undoubted pressure or possibly in anticipation of the desired result: a failure to condemn Erasmus coupled with an injunction at least to desist from further assaults. One of the fullest accounts of the 'ridiculous' Articles which set forth the charges against Erasmus, in March 1527, was promptly despatched to him by the linguist Pedro Juan Olivar, of Valencia. Yet another courtier-Erasmian, Olivar was more than once a visitor to England where he had met Linacre, and also translated into Latin one work which Erasmus had edited in Greek. His letter assures Erasmus that Valdés and Coronel do not cease to influence the opinion of Fonseca and Manrique, while Chancellor Mercurino Gattinara makes daily and reverent reference to him. Vergara's support is also mentioned.[47]

In May and June a spate of letters attests the concern of Erasmus and his Spanish allies about the impending re-opening of the conference, which was to endure through the next three or four months. Erasmus' letter to Manrique on 26 August sets out his indignant rejection of the charges made against him, which we shall explore in detail in Chapter Twelve. This he followed with a clutch of letters in early September to Gattinara, to Charles V himself, to Fonseca, to Juan and Francis Vergara, and, at much greater length, to Alonso Manrique – in which he essays a numbered, point-by-point rebuttal of the Valladolid Articles. Another letter to Manrique, later in September, was in effect the preface to Erasmus' *Apologia* against his Spanish adversaries, an 'advance-copy' of which was sent in October. Alfonso Valdés and Juan Maldonado wrote back to him in late November, but at the end of that month he felt constrained to despatch yet another exculpatory missive, this time to Francis of Vitoria, Professor of Theology at Salamanca. Erasmus must have been vastly relieved to receive the letter sent from Burgos by Charles V himself on 13 December, commending his 'honourable, devoted, dear Erasmus . . . whose Christian piety we have explored', and who need fear nothing from examination of his writings.[48]

The substantive content of the *Apologia adversus articulos aliquot per monachos quosdam, in Hispaniis exhibitos* will concern us later. Meanwhile, we may round off our brief survey of Erasmianism in Spain. The surge of support after the qualified victory at Valladolid proved to be as short-lived as it was impressive. The conjunction of the departure of Charles V with the loss of favour by some crucial supporters and the deaths of others, had completely changed the position by the time that the monarch returned in 1533, and this time the tide proved to be irreversible. Erasmus himself, informing a correspondent of the news about imprisonment of the Vergara brothers, remarked that now 'we must expect a Franciscan reign'. His last years were saddened by the spectacle of the collapse of his cause in the country of which at one time he had written that 'I owe more to Spain than to my own country, or any other'.[49]

In retrospect, the brief brilliance of the 'Erasmian phase' in Spanish history is instructive in our wider context of the relationship between Erasmus and religious reform. It is surprising only if one accepts the ploy of its contemporary adversaries in denigrating it by heretical and above all Lutheran association. The influence of Erasmus was an import which, although undoubtedly assisted by friends at court, achieved such notable success only because of indigenous movements of reform. Criticism of church abuses, a nurturing of biblical scholarship, and an appeal to the inner life of the Christian as opposed to doctrinal formalism, had *preceded* and in several ways anticipated it. It is thus supremely ironical that an alleged association with doctrinal aspects of the Lutheran Reformation which he himself rejected should have been used as the chief weapon to crush his supporters in a country where it seemed, at one time, as if Erasmianism would be established and would flourish upon undoubtedly Catholic soil. Some historians have conjectured that an Erasmian-led wave of spiritual fervour might have produced a Spain with a reformed, but non-Lutheran, church which could have led the cause of European *reform* as opposed to Counter-Reformation. This may now appear fanciful, but would not have done so during the 1520s.[50] In the event, the legacy ranged only between a certain spiritual empathy between Erasmus and the Spaniard whose name to some epitomises the Counter-Reformation, Ignatius Loyola,[51] and a last flickering of Erasmian wit in that very different character, Cervantes.

In moving finally to consider Erasmus and Italy it is as well at first to set aside any retrospective temptation to accept the narrowly restrictive aspects of the Counter-Reformation as inevitable, or indeed as all-embracing even in the post-Tridentine era. Again, we must stress the genuinely cosmopolitan characteristics, in respect of their origins, travels, and contacts, of many of the leading Italian figures with whom he came into meaningful relationships. We have but to recollect the time spent in Italy by the interlocutors in Starkey's *Dialogue*, Pole and Lupset, or by Juan Valdés in permanent exile in Naples after 1530, or to recall the origins and career of Pope Adrian VI, in order to expunge any picture of an Italy obdurately closed to new ideas and the predestined home of Counter-Reformation. Erasmus himself spent some three years in Italy between 1506 to 1509. Some of the impressions received and contacts made remained long lasting. Yet it is also true, here as in the case of Spain, that some of the more crucially important links established were through the pen and the mind – most notably in the case of Sadoleto. Finally, in sketching the impact of Erasmianism in Italy we must start by pointing to a major similarity with Spain in that what has been variously described as Catholic Evangelism or as Liberal Catholicism ante-dated such an impact – and did so not in any Lollard-type obscurity but in significant figures of the Catholic Church.[52] It welcomed Erasmian pleas for reform of Church abuses, for an emphasis upon predominantly scriptural theology, and for an irenical approach to religious differences. But it must *not* be equated with an 'Erasmian party' and always existed alongside of the harsher spirit, personified by Aleander and Alberto Pio, which ultimately won the day.[53]

Since several of those who were not unsympathetic to Erasmian reform were in touch with, or even part of, the Papal curia, a word is needed about the pontiffs themselves at crucial junctures. We have already noticed the Papacy in institutional terms and also in the context of the Lutheran debate (in Chapters Four and Six respectively), but are now concerned with personal attitudes toward Erasmian ideas as such. Ignoring Julius II, his successor in 1513, Leo X, had been hospitable to Erasmus during his stay in Rome in 1509, a fact which may have caused him to overlook the new pontiff's involvement in his predecessor's military campaigns when he wrote such fulsome assessments of his scholarly, pious and pacific intentions. The realities of international diplomacy and political ambition soon supervened. Simultaneously, any prospect of a golden age for good letters, and of papal sympathy – expressed indeed in Leo's hope that Erasmus would visit Rome – was undermined by the emergence of the Lutheran heresy, which clouded other issues.[54]

Pope Adrian VI was a Dutchman from Utrecht, who had felt the influence of schooling by the Brethren of the Common Life and of the *Devotio Moderna* before becoming tutor to the future Emperor Charles V, and then an associate with Ximénez' movement for Church reform in Spain; his election in January 1522 closed no doors. Erasmus' personal contact with him had ceased when Adrian left Louvain, where he had been Professor of Theology, but overt friendship was speedily resumed when the new pope invited him to Rome and Erasmus in turn expressed, again in flattering terms, his admiration of his theology and also claimed that Adrian helped to check his assailants at Louvain. 'Take up Christ's psaltery', urged Erasmus, 'and play on it some truly apostolic melody which can unite the hearts of princes and people.' It has indeed been suggested that even such a brief tenure of the papacy made a significant contribution to the advent of Church reform. But while Adrian may well have envisaged some diminution of existing rampant malpractice his prime concern was inevitably Luther. We noted earlier Erasmus' willingness to submit a confidential scheme for achieving peace, an overture which was welcomed by Adrian who enjoined speed and secrecy and urged him to come to Rome. Well might Erasmus have conjectured as to the possibilities if only Adrian had lived.[55]

The accession of Clement VII betokened an element of continuity with his Medici cousin Leo. Erasmus once more professed a belief in the prospects of moderate reform and urged upon him a conciliatory approach. But the new Pope showed no eagerness for a General Council. Certainly Clement took action to silence one of Erasmus' most hostile critics in Italy, the Spaniard Zúñiga, and to stem the attacks of his Louvain adversaries. He accepted an Erasmian dedication and sent a substantial monetary gift. In turn papal urgings to Erasmus to write against Luther at last met with success, and the dedication of *De libero arbitrio* to Clement himself was contemplated. Yet ultimately for Erasmus all hopeful signals were wiped out by political ambition and papal involvement in war.[56]

Erasmus did not see much of the tenure of the next pope, Paul III. The content of a letter of congratulation sent on 23 January 1535 is important in its commendation of concord. This will surely best be achieved by deferring all definition of dogma to a Synod, with the crucial addendum that, following the principle set by the Pope's namesake, some latitude must be allowed to opinions and ceremonies whose variations will not shatter the unity of the Church. A letter from a correspondent in Rome at the end of March makes vague references to impending fortune and dignity, with rumours of a cardinalate, but that which followed from the Pope himself on 31 May, though very friendly, is also very vague as to promotion. Alas, on August 1 Paul offers not a Cardinal's hat but the provostship of Deventer. Whatever the prospects for Erasmus, in terms both of preferment and of acceptance for his views, had he lived, it is slightly ironical that the briefs to summon a special commission to consider reform of the Church were despatched only a week after his death in July 1536.[57]

Those briefs were sent out, after preparations for a General Council, by Sadoleto and Contarini, leading figures along with Pietro Bembo in the movement for genuine irenical reform. Jacopo Sadoleto, who joined the papal secretariat of Leo X in 1513 and became Bishop of Carpentras in southern France four years later, was of outstanding significance. A scholar in his own right – his address to Louis XII, *Contra Turcos*, has been likened to the *Querela pacis* – he played a crucial role not only in relation to Erasmus but also in a very real attempt at reform from within the Catholic Church. Oddly enough, although he became Erasmus' constant though not uncritical ally within the papal camp, and arguably the closest of his Italian friends, there is no evidence that the two men ever met. It was through Sadoleto that Pope Leo commended Erasmus to Henry VIII and put in train his exemption from certain personal disabilities. Thereafter he proved to be a consistent advocate of his cause in the curia of the Medici popes.[58]

An exchange of friendly letters in September and November of 1528 is typical in deploring the Sack of Rome and attesting their concurrence in wishing that reason might be permitted to lead to peace and concord. There were genuine similarities in both scholarship and religious purpose. Sadoleto has been seen as following both Colet and Erasmus in his adoption of an exegetical approach to Scripture which dispensed with scholastic devices and stressed the content of the text. During the years of the Lutheran crisis he spoke consistently for Erasmus against the hardly veiled imputations of Aleander and vouched for the goodwill of Pope Clement. In return Sadoleto received a copy of *De libero arbitrio*, followed in February 1525 by the interesting assertion that some have been thereby persuaded to abandon Lutheran dogma. Erasmus also praised him for his commentary on the Fiftieth Psalm, the first of a number of similar works. It has justly been observed that, like Erasmus, he saw both sides in the Lutheran crisis and recognised that toleration of corruption and failure of leadership within the Church had in effect nurtured the success of rebellious schismatics. He resembled Erasmus also in looking to Melanchthon as the most hopeful portent of compromise in the Protestant ranks and in evincing a less-than-generous reaction to the death of Oecolampadius. Their correspondence, which deplores the difficulties of rescuing the Church from its present convulsions and restoring its pristine vigour, persisted into the early 1530s. In one letter Erasmus' repeated allusion to medical treatment which rather serves to aggravate than to alleviate is here directed to his own encounter with a surgeon who would best be suited to the fierce Scythians![59]

Yet all this said, it is a mistake to think of Sadoleto as either simply or wholly Erasmian; he too was *homo per se*. Thus he counselled his friend against an over-contentious rounding on his critics. It is also true that he was personally involved in the drafting of papal edicts for action against Lutheran heretics in Germany. But he almost certainly sent warnings to Erasmus about Aleander and defended him against Zúñiga. In short, Erasmus' assertion that, had the whole matter been entrusted to people like Sadoleto, much bitterness would have been avoided, is indicative of a broad yet genuine meeting of minds. Sadly, as in other cases, and this time so shortly before the death of Erasmus, a misunderstanding which followed his criticism of one of Sadoleto's works led to a certain coolness, despite the usual polite protestations.[60] We should not leave Sadoleto without observing two fundamental aspects of his work which raise the intriguing possibilities of an Italianate Christian humanism triumphant in its own right. First, the philosophy of his religious exegesis, which asserted that man is 'not bond but free', resembles the stance of Erasmus as a hopeful assessment of the potentialities of human nature in co-operation with divine grace. Again, while assuredly less willing than Erasmus to compromise on doctrine, his address of November 1536 to an assembly of prelates, which included Aleander and the future Pope Paul IV, seems wholly

Erasmian in its bitter invective against the hierarchy for tolerating the corruption which had fomented heresy.[61]

Our justifiably extensive treatment of Sadoleto suggests far briefer allusions to Erasmus' other Italian friends, the number of whom was proudly adduced by him in a letter of March 1535. Among these, Pietro Bembo of Venice, a philologist in his own right, had entered the papal secretariat along with Sadoleto in 1513. Moving to Padua in 1521 he there embarked upon intensive literary work, the repute of which brought him to the attention of Erasmus and evoked an expression of concern after the Sack of Rome. Thereafter they became friendly correspondents and Erasmus acquired another distinguished ally.[62] Named also by Erasmus alongside Sadoleto and Bembo was the eminent jurist, Andrea Alciati. In fact the two never met but in 1521 a sporadic literary correspondence commenced, and when Alciati turned to literature the influence of Erasmus was evident. On more than one occasion Erasmus paid tribute to 'the ornament of this age'. Alciati in turn counselled prudence and restraint in response to Erasmus' complaint that, unlike Hercules, he has to contend not with one monster but with a phalanx of conspirators.[63]

Another notable Italian well-wisher was Gian Matteo Giberti, holder of several influential posts in the papal curia and in 1524 made Bishop of Verona, where he engaged in pastoral reform. His appeal to Erasmus during the Lutheran conflict was followed by receipt of a copy of *De libero arbitrio* – evoking his description of its author as the best antidote to Lutheranism. Unfortunately Erasmus' requests for protection against his Louvain assailants met with only partially successful endeavours. Significantly, Giberti was one of the commission of nine which in 1537 drafted the *Consilium de emendenda ecclesia*.[64] As for another member of the commission and leader of Catholic reform, Gasparo Contarini, there is no evidence of any contact with Erasmus, but Cardinal Cajetan, also an advocate of ecclesiastical reform, with whom late and infrequent contact was established, gave clear signs of respectful recognition of his virtues.[65] Finally, a high-ranking ecclesiastic with whom Erasmus had frequent contact from 1519 onwards was Lorenzo Campeggio, who rendered praise and the occasional gift. Erasmus in turn attempted through Campeggio in a quite voluminous correspondence to advocate moderation on the Lutheran issue and to enlist assistance against his own enemies in Rome.[66]

Such enemies assuredly existed, for his writings did not elicit universal admiration. Apparently some members of the so-called

Roman Academy found fault not only with his orthodoxy but also with his style and accuracy, dubbing him 'Errasmus'. Juan de Vergara informed him of Zúñiga's threat that 'a large and picked force of learned Italians is now mobilizing, who will make a sortie and bear down headlong on your writings'! Rather later, and more seriously, the report of the reform commission was to contain a recommendation that the *Colloquies* be suppressed, as engendering impiety in the young. Thus a strong anti-Erasmian threat was always present.[67]

Although their author was of Spanish origin, some of the earliest assaults upon Erasmus published in Italy were those of Diego López Zúñiga – the 'Stunica' of his letters. As early as August 1520 Erasmus had identified Spain's 'second Lee', and in 1521 Zúñiga presented the manuscript of his *Erasmi Roterodami blasphemiae et impietates* to Leo X, who refused him permission to publish it. A letter from Rome in February 1522 relates how his 'insufferable malevolence' is publicly displayed, the writer goes on to proffer the disquieting thought that, despite the defence put up by Paolo Bombace, 'the wrong side might have won, had not Leo died and left their virulence unsupported'. A couple of months later Vives reported that 'Zúñiga is preparing a long and savage attack on you' and by the summer of 1522 Erasmus is complaining how 'every month he spews forth a fresh pamphlet full of blasphemies' even though 'he has been forbidden by the cardinals to rant against your friend Erasmus'. The content of his polemics will concern us in due course.[68]

Meanwhile, the later attacks on the *Colloquies* in the *Consilium de emendenda ecclesia* evoked the scornful wrath of Luther and of Melanchthon, directed primarily by the last-named at Sadoleto, though presumably they represent the voice of Aleander.[69] Of formidable intellect, despite a patchy early career, Aleander became a doctor in theology, and had in 1508 actually shared a room with Erasmus in Venice. Moving to Paris, he there delivered enormously successful lectures. Thus far there developed a fairly amicable correspondence with Erasmus, but Aleander's move into the service of the future Clement VII and to the librarianship of the Vatican marked a switch in his attitude. His mission to Germany and the Low Countries to implement the bull *Exsurge Domine* against Luther was characterised by a ruthless and uncompromising stance which soon involved a total change in demeanour toward Erasmus. His position of central influence after the accession of Clement was followed by a number of anti-Lutheran missions. Admittedly, half-hearted expressions of reconciliation fended off overt confrontation in a personal quarrel with Erasmus.

Yet although the scathingly anti-Erasmian manuscript 'Racha' is now attributed not to Aleander but to Egidio da Viterbo, the denunciation of his former friend, on the one side, continued to be matched by the frequent expression of bitterly felt and totally justified suspicions of duplicity and enmity on the other. In April 1532 Aleander wrote to Erasmus in denial of the accusation that he had assisted both Alberto Pio, Prince of Carpi, and Julius Caesar Scaliger in their attacks. We need not agree with Erasmus in this example of his favourite 'conspiracy theory' to perceive that Aleander did not share Sadoleto's irenical approach toward the case for religious reform.[70]

Alongside Aleander in opposition to all things Erasmian stood Alberto Pio, who in effect devoted the last six years of his life to such attacks – provoking indeed an *Apologia* directed against him by name in the very year in which he died.[71] Alberto was defended posthumously by yet another but longer-lived anti-Erasmian, Juan de Sepulveda, who claimed that Clement VII had allowed Erasmus the freedom he enjoyed, not because he approved of his opinions, but from fear lest he be driven to join the Lutherans.[72] To conclude this brief sampling of the Italian opposition, Julius Caesar Scaliger of Padua possesses an unusual distinction in that his very existence was disputed by his victim, who persisted in asserting that this was but Aleander in disguise! Since Scaliger himself had fantasised about his origins, this may well be poetic justice, but he was in fact both philosopher and doctor at Agen, whose literary career commenced with a scurrilous attack upon Erasmus which was not published until 1531. Erasmus described this work as raving and slanderous, trying to have it suppressed. Even after being assured by Rabelais that Scaliger was real – and an able physician to boot – Erasmus shifted only from dismissing him as a pseudonym to dubbing him an agent suborned by Aleander.[73]

Any sketch of those trends in Italy which were for some time at least conducive to Catholic reform in an Erasmian sense would be incomplete without a reference to the influence of the 'Valdesiani'. Although it centred upon the Italianate Spaniard Juan de Valdés who became a permanent exile in Naples, this movement has been regarded as peculiarly Italian, since nearly all his followers were themselves Italians. While admittedly an intellectual influence rather than an organisation, many of the leading proponents of ecclesiastical reform felt its impact. Valdés' emphasis lay not only upon the authority of Scripture and the Fathers, but also on the concept of *adiaphora*. The last of these Erasmian characteristics enabled him to remain within the Catholic Church until his death in 1540. A much less orthodox

Erasmian was one of Valdés' associates, Bernardino Ochino, one-time Superior of the Capuchin Order. He fled Italy in 1542, visited the England of Edward VI, and there reputedly influenced the equally cosmopolitan early Puritan William Turner. His death much later amongst Italian Anabaptist exiles in Moravia is yet another supreme example of the swirling international currents of diffused Erasmian influence.[74]

The pattern of Erasmian success and failure in Italy invites instructive comparisons with Spain. In Italy also there existed a genuine and indigenous wish for religious reform which welcomed Erasmus' message. Several of those who were favourably disposed toward his influence occasionally gained the ear of the Popes. Accordingly, while the anti-Erasmian cause was sometimes most vigorously supported by several men of letters, the Curia itself proved more likely to intervene in any dispute in favour of Erasmus rather than in that of his adversaries. Yet the papal entourage also harboured some inveterate opponents of virtually everything for which Erasmus stood, while Charles V and his ministers were here quite unable to play the protective role which they performed in Spain. Dr Silvana Seidel Menchi's recent detailed analysis of the extent and depth of the popular influnce of Erasmus in Italy, prior to suppression by the Index and the Inquisition, has reinforced Renaudet's observation of forty years ago: that the shift from a humanist acclaim of *Erasmus noster* to a hostile identification of *Erasmo luterano* had commenced even before the Italian 'reception' of his works peaked about 1530. Thereafter the process accelerated.[75]

Indeed, the image of Erasmus derived by Menchi not only from the writings of such people as Aleander and Alberto Pio but also from the records of the Inquisition engaged in suppressing grass roots signs of heresy, becomes the ultimate depiction of a 'pestilential heretic'. Thus, although the quinquennium 1520–24 witnessed an impressive response to his ideas, most notably by an influential circle at Padua which included Fridericus Nausea, a future Bishop of Vienna, the phase of *Erasmus noster* is envisaged as but 'a prelude'.[76] The emergence of the figure of *Erasmo luterano* between 1520 and 1535 owed much to a suspicion of a heretical conspiracy between literateurs and grammarians, and also to a resolve on 'the defence of Italy' which introduced an ethnic element to the controversy. But above all, Erasmus was seen as the *fomes malorum*, the great source of Luther's heresy.[77] Intriguingly, given the papal pressures for its composition, Erasmus' anti-Lutheran *De libero arbitrio* made no great impact upon his Italian audience, despite the printing of an Italian edition in Venice and, infuriatingly, when it was not merely ignored it tended to arouse suspicion as heretical! Yet upon reflection this development seems in full accord with our own suggestion that the essentially optimistic ethos of the work would sometimes prove as offensive to the 'old guard' Catholics as to predestinarian Protestants. Conversely, his treatise *De immensa Dei misericordia*, also written in 1524, became popular and was printed in three independent translations in 1542, 1551 and 1554[78]

Moving thus into the second half of the century, we must ask how far Erasmian influence and values survived in Italy. The crushing impact of the Pauline Index of 1559, which banned all of Erasmus' works, would seem at first sight to be beyond debate. Whereas over ninety publications of works by Erasmus had occurred between 1520 and 1529, and twenty even between 1550 and 1554, after 1559 only two were printed throughout the remainder of the century.[79] Yet the Grendlers' study establishes a quite massive survival of Erasmus' works in libraries, schools, and sometimes – despite the dangers – in private hands, and shows that he remained attractive as a scholar and an educator even to those who found his religious opinions suspect and in some cases resorted to expurgations of varying severity.[80] As against this, Menchi, pointing to the 'durable sediment of hostility' deposited by the anti-Erasmian controversy of the period 1520–35, seems at least disposed to question whether we can predicate a survival of an Erasmian tradition in Italy, simply on the basis of the survival of his books, in face of the Inquisitors' systematic attempt to extirpate his teachings.[81] To evaluate the continuing popularity of a writer is notoriously difficult, yet in this context at least one other recent authority finds himself convinced that the 'popular legacy of Erasmus was permanently suppressed by the Inquisition, with an inestimable loss to Italian culture'.[82]

None the less, before concluding on this depressing note, we should indicate that, whereas Erasmianism in Spain had been virtually crushed by 1540, several leading Italian churchmen continued – as will appear in a later chapter – well into the mid-century to foster irenic policies deriving from Erasmus.[83] Moreover, one contention that his social values and those of pre-Tridentine Catholic reform survived within Italy points to recommendations by Contarini and Giberti expressed not only in general charitable precepts but also in specific plans for systematic and discriminating poor relief in Venice and Verona.[84] Finally, the Italian legacy of Erasmus has been traced in less orthodox circles. Ideas present in or at least attributed to Erasmus which proved attractive to 'heretics' included what was perceived as scepticism concerning the Trinity. Thus Beza, Calvin's successor at Geneva, declared him to be at heart an Arian. Again, his admirers and his critics noted his rejection of any rigorous form of predestination and adoption of a tolerant approach which verged on a respect for religious liberty. The suggested empathy between the Savoyard refugee Sebastian Castellio and the teachings of Erasmus has been raised in the context of Italian heretical thought.[85] But native-born Italians who looked to Erasmus became exiles for religion's sake: such as the Socinians, in Poland and Hungary, and Celio Secondo Curione, who while at Basel wrote a book on *The Wideness of God's Kingdom* which envisaged universal salvation.[86] To such issues we shall return in Chapter Twelve.

Eleven

ERASMUS IN CENTRAL EUROPE

At first sight, those scattered regions of Central Europe in which a notable Erasmian influence may be traced appear to have less in common than the three 'Romance' nations of our previous chapter. Yet upon reflection, the Habsburg dynasty and the Germanic language suggest two partly connective elements. Even in the cities of Poland German cultural influence was strong at this time. Certainly, no brief survey of the extent of Erasmus' influence would be anything like complete if it omitted developments not only at the Viennese Court of Ferdinand I and in several German principalities which cannot simply be categorised as Lutheran, Zwinglian or Roman, but also in another state of great significance in Central Europe, Poland. Ferdinand – reared in Castile, unlike his brother Charles – was effectively in charge of the Habsburg German lands after 1521, becoming King of Hungary and Bohemia in 1526 and prospective Emperor in 1531. His struggles against Turkish inroads evoked expressions of sympathetic concern in Erasmus' correspondence. The two men had met while Ferdinand was in the Netherlands in 1518–21 when Erasmus, although declining an invitation to become the young archduke's tutor, expressed anticipation of his enlightened rule. Fittingly, the *Education of a Christian Prince* was to become a handbook in the upbringing of the Habsburg children. A dedication by Erasmus of his paraphrase of John was followed by a sporadic exchange of letters, and in 1528 Ferdinand invited him to Vienna, promising both funds and scholarly freedom. Though this invitation also was declined, it was to Ferdinand's city of Freiburg that Erasmus moved in 1529, receiving substantial monetary help and on one occasion payment of his house-rent. Although Erasmian influence upon his brother Charles has been considered greater, his irenic principles were certainly at work in Ferdinand's readiness at least to consider making concessions to the Protestant Reformers. Indeed, Erasmus for long cherished hopes of a policy of religious moderation and judicious clemency, and in the mid-1520s he expressed his concern for its continuance. But the Anabaptist threat was to play a major role in the understandable shift toward severity both of Ferdinand and of Charles.[1]

Meanwhile, Ferdinand's sister Mary (1505–58), had married the unfortunate young Louis II, King of Bohemia and Hungary, who in 1526 was drowned after defeat by the Turks at Mohacs. Henceforth she exemplified both the extension of Habsburg power and the spread of Erasmus' influence. For Ferdinand now inherited the crowns of her childless husband, and the Dowager Queen encouraged reforming elements which were already active at the Hungarian Court. Indeed, a letter from Cracow in 1526 had already informed Erasmus that no one was held in higher esteem by the young King and Queen. His name is often heard, and 'there is no book of Erasmus which this prince does not have in his library'. Notably, what has been described as the cult of the national language in Hungary, manifested in translations of the Bible, has been ascribed to Erasmian influence, as has the emergence among the ranks of the clergy of the first Church reformers. The spread of reformist notions was such that Hungary was later to afford a refuge even to Anabaptists and to the anti-Trinitarian Servetus.[2]

A one-time tutor of King Louis, Jacobus Piso, has been identified as one of the complex channels through which Erasmian influence began to enter Hungary. Piso, who was destined to lose his estates in Transylvania after Mohacs, spent much time in Italy as an ambassador. He is mentioned as having been known to Erasmus some time ago at Rome, in an adulatory letter dated 20 June 1518 and sent from Breslau by John Thurzo. Despite becoming domiciled in Poland and made Bishop of Breslau in 1506, Thurzo had in fact come from an influential Hungarian family, and he typifies the Polish–Hungarian link we shall again encounter. In an epistle to Thurzo of April 1519, Erasmus expresses his pleasure at being reminded of his original encounter with Piso. Piso himself writes to Erasmus in February 1526 from Buda, referring to his embassy to the monarchs Ferdinand and Sigismund of Poland. Then in December 1527 a letter of Caspar Ursinus Velius – also mentioned by Piso as an acquaintance of Erasmus – informs the latter of Piso's death. Not in themselves momentous, these and other surviving letters illustrate the important fact that the notable people of Hungary and Poland were anything but detached from central and western Europe. Another Transylvanian and a prominent member of the Erasmian circle at Buda was Nicholas Olah, who in March 1516 had been appointed secretary to the ill-fated Louis II, and after Mohacs had remained in the entourage of the

Dowager Queen Mary. He was not known to Erasmus until he ventured to write to him in July 1530, expressing the vain hope that he would see him at the Diet, where his presence was very necessary. In March 1531 Olah was to accompany Mary of Hungary to the Netherlands when she became Regent, whence, as we shall see, further correspondence ensued. Thus the Hungarian-Habsburg connection with Erasmus continued, as it were, from a Brussels base.[3]

Certainly Erasmian influence endured at the Court of Vienna, personified by such confidants and ministers as Johannes Fabri, Fridericus Nausea, and Bernard of Cles, Bishop of Trent. Fabri (given as Faber by some editors) became an adviser to Ferdinand from 1523 and Bishop of Vienna from 1530. A noted patron of scholarship, he expressed a fervent admiration for Erasmus, with whom he corresponded as early as 1516, and whom in 1528 he sought to attract to Vienna so as to escape the malignant influence of Oecolampadius and Zwingli. Indeed Fabri took a very stern line against heresy in general and Anabaptism in particular, resisting his friend's appeals for leniency. Yet a pointer to Erasmus' continued respect for Fabri is seen toward the end of 1532, when he concludes a long letter regarding events in England with an unstinted tribute to the bishop's assiduous exercise of his episcopal duties, as an example which all should follow.[4]

Ostensibly a more whole-hearted exponent of Erasmian religious ideals was Fridericus Nausea. An able preacher and a considerable author, he became Papal Notary in 1524, attracted the notice of Fabri and, although not in fact created a Councillor to Ferdinand until 1539, succeeded Fabri as Bishop of Vienna in 1540. As early as 1524, amidst the Lutheran crisis, in his *Ad magnum Erasmum . . . oratio* Nausea published an appeal for support of the great humanist's conciliatory efforts. Erasmus in turn expressed his regard in a letter of May 1525, and soon afterwards he met his admirer. In July 1533 Erasmus wrote again to extend his thanks for a book received and to assure him of his continuing goodwill. Some three years later, Nausea accorded a glowing tribute to 'this most splendid ornament of the Catholic Church' in a funeral eulogy: *In Magnum Erasmum . . . Monodia.* At Trent in 1551 Erasmian irenicism endured in his support of Ferdinand's proposals to permit marriage to the clergy and also the taking of Communion in both kinds.[5]

An Erasmian sympathiser of still greater eminence was Bernard of Cles. Bishop of Trent in 1514, and Councillor to Maximilian I, Bernard later became adviser to Ferdinand and his Chancellor from 1527, as well as his candidate for the papacy itself in 1534. A notable patron of scholars such as Fabri and Nausea, it was through his hands that Erasmus' correspondence with the Viennese Court largely passed after 1523. A year later, Erasmus declined his invitation, which was repeated, to take up residence in Trent on generous terms, and it was Bernard who facilitated his move to Freiburg in 1529. Indeed, in February of that year, Erasmus' letter to him refers to Ferdinand's invitations and to the fact that Freiburg is nearer, 'although the town is cramped, and the people, as I hear, superstitious'. In June 1530 he complained to Bernard about the Strassburg publications of Geldenhauer and Bucer. In May 1532, after Bernard sent him the Emperor's offer of high office in the Church, Erasmus felt constrained to explain that he was by now useless for all of life's functions except for his studies, amid which he would be pleased to die. Understandably, nearly two years later, Bernard wrote to Erasmus that he had explained to Ferdinand that, being 'old and worn out', he was in no shape to reply to a new Lutheran attack. Finally, a letter dated 16 March 1536 expressed his poignant hope that God would liberate Erasmus from his anguish and restore him to full health. Significantly, Jedin includes the bishop among those statesmen who, after the death of Gattinara, still favoured a reconciliation on Erasmian terms.[6]

Still more wide-ranging in his persistent pursuit of conciliatory ideals – so much so that Froude thought he was a Protestant[7] – was Julius Pflug, who, as an adviser both to the Catholic Duke George of Saxony and to the Emperor Charles V, formed in some sense a link between the Habsburg and other German courts. It was Pflug who in May 1531 despatched to Erasmus an impassioned appeal to use his influence in the cause of religious concord that will concern us in the next chapter. A couple of months earlier, Erasmus had penned a glowing tribute to Pflug in a letter to George of Saxony, and it was to Pflug that he was to address his complaint about 'six hundred furies' and his regret that Pope Adrian had not lived longer, when he replied in August. In May of 1533 Pflug wrote much about the Eucharist in a letter to Erasmus. He persisted in fruitless efforts to reconcile the Lutherans to the Catholic Church, participating in negotiations at Leipzig (1534) and Regensburg (1541), where he was apparently an outstanding and determined supporter of a conciliatory approach. Becoming Bishop of Naumburg in 1542 he was also to attend the Council of Trent.[8]

In approaching the important topic of Erasmus' relations with German humanism, reference must be made to two broader contexts: the centrifugal structure of German politics and society, and the non-Erasmian elements of German humanism already apparent before the year 1500. The complex and inefficient constitution of the Holy Roman Empire was powerless to create a functioning central monarchy on the model of those now flourishing in France, Spain, England and elsewhere. The huge complex of princedoms maintained some sort of order, but had neither authority nor machinery to conduct the basic reforms needed in both the secular and the religious spheres. By contrast the numerous cities, many of them self-governing, conducted profitable trade, were ruled by efficient oligarchies and became increasingly receptive of new cultural forms such as humanism, book-printing and Renaissance art. Contrarily, declining wealth and social tension characterised both the knightly landlords and the oppressed peasantry, both of which staged disastrous rebellions during the earlier 1520s. Meanwhile the Catholic Church was widely considered to need disciplinary, liturgical and financial reforms. Even before Luther appeared, Erasmus was far from being the only publicist who proclaimed the urgency of spiritual revival and even the possibility of doctrinal adjustments. The long political struggle between Emperors and Popes had done much to destroy any love toward the latter, which many Germans already regarded as decadent recipients of unpopular taxes. Though during the fifteenth century the Papacy readily gave founding-charters to several German universities, the latter continued under the dominance of faculties teaching scholastic theology.

Both inside and outside academic life the ideas of German humanists were not altogether in harmony with those of Erasmus. A spirit of militant chauvinism in violent contrast with his pacifist and cosmopolitan outlook began to develop before the end of the fifteenth century. Rudolf Agricola (1444–85), regarded as the father of German humanism, was indeed little more than a genial Petrarchan as distinct from an exponent of new social and religious ideas. Those humanists slightly his juniors were moderates, in many cases clergymen, affected by the *Devotio Moderna* and even by Neoplatonism. Some, like Sebastian Brant (*c.* 1458–1521) castigated the follies of society and became conservatives, or like Mutianus (1471–1526) combined humanism with mild criticism of the Church. But Conrad Celtis (1459–1508), crowned the first German laureate poet in 1487 by the Emperor Frederick III, was fiercely nationalist. He also developed a bizarre mixture of contradictory cults. A Platonist nature-mystic, he often wrote like a pagan unbeliever, while yet retaining devout practices and exalting the cult of the Virgin Mary. He could work with attractive enthusiasm on German topography and conduct scholarly researches on medieval German history.[9]

Though Celtis died with exemplary piety in 1508, he inspired a much younger contemporary, who carried fanatical chauvinism even into the early campaigning of Martin Luther. With the confidence of noble birth, Ulrich von Hutten sought to intervene decisively into actual politics, yet he also became subject to incompatible passions. Thanks to his schooling in the abbey of Fulda, he became a genuine humanist and an eloquent writer in both Latin and German. After wandering between several universities, he studied in Italy from 1515 to 1517, learned Greek and aided Rubeanus to write the *Letters of Obscure Men*, which in particular savaged the Dominican persecutors of Reuchlin. In 1518 Hutten edited Valla's *Donation of Constantine*, equipping the text with a highly sarcastic dedication to the Pope. He again excoriated the Papacy with his manifesto *Vadiscus*. Having applauded Luther, Hutten encouraged Franz von Sickingen to initiate the Knights' Revolt of 1522–3, and would doubtless have joined the fighting had he not been disabled by syphilis, the same disease which had killed his predecessor Celtis. Not long afterwards, as a lonely fugitive on an island in Lake Constance, Hutten died amid total failure. During his flight Erasmus had refused to receive him: an unromantic but logical decision, since apart from their common devotion to humanist scholarship, he had very little in common with this unbalanced adventurer.[10]

The direct influence of Erasmus upon the German humanists became strong during the second and third decades of the sixteenth century. We observe this most distinctly in the upper Rhineland, ranging from Alsace in the west to the Black Forest in the east. The cities chiefly affected by Erasmian ideals were Strassburg, Schlettstadt (Sélestat), Freiburg-im-Breisgau and Basel. All these places were then overwhelmingly German in culture and thus remained until after Louis XIV annexed Alsace. It is as well to remind ourselves that the Rhine, in whose delta Erasmus was born, was at this time a principal artery of Europe's communications and commerce, linking its north-western coast to near-access to Italy. Admittedly, the city on its banks in which Erasmus was to spend so many years was Swiss; yet it might well have seemed a short step from hailing Erasmus as a Rhinelander to claiming him as a German. Such already was his repute in the Rhenish Oberland that his progress up the river in 1514 has been likened to the triumphal celebration of a national holiday. On the first of several visits to Strassburg he was fêted by an organised group of humanists. At Mainz he met von Hutten, whom he met again, as well as Reuchlin, at Frankfurt am Main in the following year. While Erasmus himself travelled to Basel in 1514 and in 1516 to work with his printer, Johann

Froben, he was enormously impressed, and gratified, by his general reception in 'Upper Germany'.[11] Significantly, it has been suggested that, while Rhenish humanists perceived in Erasmus a spearhead for their thrust toward religious reform, as he himself 'became a German, he also became a religious reformer in the earnest German style'.[12] Certainly, when he tired of reactionary Louvain, in 1521 he was to settle in Basel. Yet with the later progress of Lutheran and Zwinglian Protestantism he again felt his freedom constricted and in 1529 he transferred to the calmer atmosphere of Freiburg, only to return in 1535 to Basel, where he died.

Most of the many humanists in this area were natives of the region and had studied at one or more of its four universities: Heidelberg, Freiburg, Basel and Tübingen. At this stage of his career Erasmus had little reason to frequent these universities, which were in general dominated by scholastic theology and philosophy, whereas his own friends and supporters had become literary men, often prominent in secular life. In the four cities we have mentioned, humanist groups had existed even before 1500, most notably in Strassburg[13] and Schlettstadt, where by 1520 they had almost attained the status and repute of academies. Though much of their inspiration derived from Italy, only a small minority of their members had visited that country. Most however had travelled widely within western Germany and elsewhere within the provinces of the Empire and of the Swiss Confederation. Many had become priests, yet their ideas were seldom stereotyped or localised. Their interest in the ancient classics and in German history appears distinctly varied, while not a few had become, or aspired to become, original writers and publicists. Even those who belonged to religious orders do not seem to have been rigorously confined to the cloister or even precluded from demanding moral and educational reforms throughout the Catholic Church.

Another historical feature of this region was the rapid expansion of printing since its origins at Mainz in the mid-fifteenth century. By the second decade of the sixteenth, printer-publishers had become exceptionally numerous and active in Basel, where they had taken advantage of the local paper-mills and of the Rhine itself as a channel of transport. In Florence, Savonarola had used a Bible printed at Basel in 1491, while in 1509 Luther had another from the same city. Businessmen were now enjoying considerable profits as a result of their active co-operation with the humanists, who came to their shops and instructed them in the methods demanded by the new scholarship. Erasmus, Wimpfeling and Reuchlin afford prominent examples of this collaboration. Indeed even the artists of the time co-operated with the printers, notably when they came to publish their Reformation engravings, the prime example being that of Holbein, who resided at Basel from 1528 to 1531. Many of the clerical Reformers were natives of the region, with a mature knowledge of its potentialities before the Reformation began. Zwingli himself had attended the University of Basel from 1502 to 1506. This powerful blend of forces is well illustrated by the career of Froschauer, the young Bavarian who came to Basel, married the widow of an established printer, thus establishing his own business by 1518. Then he became acquainted with Zwingli's friend Leo Jud, who had translated some of the writings of Erasmus for Zwingli and in 1521 helped Froschauer to print Luther's famous manifesto *The Freedom of a Christian*.[14] The lack of any effective laws of copyright facilitated the rapid expansion of new religious and cultural ideas. In short, dynamic change arose in this area from technology, then from humanism and finally from the main branches of Protestantism, both Lutheran and Zwinglian. Very soon, Strassburg began to rival Basel in such activities. Though as yet having no university of its own, it attracted theologians, humanists and printers, who likewise co-operated in promoting humanism and the reform of the Church.

Not long after the visits of Erasmus in the years 1514–18, Luther's exploits resounded in all these cities and were soon followed by those of Zwingli. Thenceforth many admirers of Erasmus, especially those among his juniors who expected him to follow, moved over from his cautious reformism into Protestant doctrines. Indeed a few of them acquired an interest in the more radical views of the sectarians and spiritualists, lumped together in later years as Anabaptists. Confronted by this wide religious spectrum, we now propose to take a few hasty glances at certain individual Erasmians of this region. From the early 1520s some of these, however critical, refused to leave the Catholic Church. Others advanced only to waver and retreat, yet many found a permanent anchorage in one or other of the Protestant churches. Yet even amid this welter of change, the Erasmian heritage seems to have inculcated a degree of moderation on both sides. By far the majority of those who had followed Erasmus emerged as either liberal Catholics or else as cautious, non-fanatical Protestants. Most were doubtless restrained not merely by the moderate spirit of Erasmus but also by bourgeois caution, by the obvious need to preserve the rule of urban oligarchies, as opposed to the risk of misrule by the proletarian and sectarian forces then striving not only among the peasants but within the town populations of central Europe.

Of the senior humanists known to Erasmus two notable figures stood out: Sebastian Brant (1458–1501) and Jacob Wimpfeling (1450–1528). The former, having taken a doctorate at Basel, had by 1494 written in German that famous social satire *The Ship of Fools*, which showed distinct anticlerical tendencies. Indeed it appears in many obvious respects a forerunner of the *Praise of Folly*, and it likewise gripped both literate and popular opinion for many years.[15] Nevertheless its author settled down as a syndic of Strassburg, wholly opposed to radicalism in religion and politics. Wimpfeling, a native of Schlettstadt, had migrated to Strassburg in 1501, only to return and join the active humanist group in the lesser city. A German arch-patriot and a writer of dramatic dialogues, he sided with Erasmus in 1515 against the attacks of Martin Dorp, the former friend who had temporarily become a tool of the ultra-conservative theologians of Louvain.[16] A moderate also born at Strassburg was Wimpfeling's former pupil Ottmar Nachtigall (1487–1537), who resisted the claims of Luther but did not hesitate to criticise the clergy. He also earned the admiration of Erasmus by introducing the study of Greek into Strassburg. Yet another moderate was Hieronymus Gebwiler (*c.* 1473–1545), a successful teacher of the humanities at Schlettstadt before settling in Strassburg and meeting Erasmus there in 1514 and 1518. These and several likeminded humanists appear among the frequent correspondents of Erasmus, yet so do numerous figures who in the early twenties helped to guide Strassburg into Protestantism. Here they were ably led by the cultured politician Jacob Sturm and, of course, by Martin Bucer.

Unless he had special reasons for disliking a convert, Erasmus did not exclude him from his list of welcome correspondents. Some of these Protestants in due course regretted their deviation and returned to conformity. One such was the able jurist Zasius (1461–1535), who codified the laws of Freiburg and then benefited from the personal guidance of Erasmus within the humanities. At first Zasius saw Luther as an ally of Erasmus in the cause of church reform, but he then developed a strong antipathy toward the German prophet and wished that Erasmus possessed the courage to disown Luther outright.[17] Perhaps he exemplifies the calculation of James Tracy that of the German, Dutch and Swiss humanists born between 1450 and 1480 only five out of twenty-four became Protestants, as against eighty-four out of the 127 born between 1481 and 1510![18] Included in the number of determined Lutherans among the devotees of Erasmus who never forfeited his friendship was Nikolas Gerbel (*c.* 1485–1560) who helped to entertain him in Strassburg in 1514 and 1515, and soon afterwards met him again at the Frankfurt book-fair. Gerbel, a graduate of Cologne and a prominent supporter of Reuchlin against the Dominicans, went on to Basel as proof-corrector of Erasmus' Bible. Soon afterwards he relinquished his intention to become a priest, married and joined the Reformers. Erasmus continued to encourage his scholarly pursuits, which resulted in numerous publications, some historical in character. Rather different was the case of Wolfgang Capito, whom we have already encountered in the context of Erasmus' relations with Luther and with Bucer. A native of Hagenau near Strassburg and a former student at Ingolstadt and Freiburg, this friend of Zasius joined the humanist circle at Basel and exchanged heartfelt tributes with Erasmus, before his defection to Lutheran ideas and then to Bucer in Strassburg brought about an acrimonious cessation of correspondence.[19]

A number of the great body of Erasmians were members of religious orders, such as the Carthusian Otto Brunfels from Mainz (1488–1536), who ultimately denounced the Catholic Mass and became the Lutheran pastor of Neuenberg in the Breisgau. Brunfels not only admired the sectarian Andreas Karlstadt (*c.* 1480–1541), but entered into polemics in order to convince and recruit Erasmus, yet not to the point of a final rift. One warm admirer of the Dutch humanist did become an actual sectarian leader and was finally dismissed from the fellowship. This was the Swabian Sebastian Franck (1499–1543), a graduate of Heidelberg who was a Lutheran pastor in 1527 but joined the Anabaptists in 1528, whom we encountered in an earlier chapter.[20]

Again, even from the briefest list of Erasmians who became Lutherans, we must not omit the two leaders of the remarkable humanist society at Schlettstadt. One of these we have already noticed as a close associate of Erasmus and his first formal biographer: Beatus Rhenanus (1455–1547). The other, Paul Volz (1480–1544), became the recipient of a letter from Erasmus which emerged as one of the great manifestos of humanist Christianity. Volz had by then risen in the Benedictine Order to become abbot of the monastery at Hugshofen near Schlettstadt. Citing him as a living examplar of the ideals enunciated in the *Enchiridion*, Erasmus further immortalised Volz by utilising the letter as the preface to the decisive 1515 edition of the work. Nevertheless in 1526 Volz went over to Luther, yet he never forfeited the warm affection of Erasmus, who not only accepted gifts from Volz, but bequeathed him a sizeable sum by his will.[21]

Also among those closest to Erasmus during these years was Johannes Sapidus (1490–1561), another product of the excellent school at Schlettstadt, to which – after studying along with Beatus Rhenanus in the University of Paris – he returned to teach in 1517. Nine years later he transferred to Strassburg in order to direct the Latin school newly founded in the big city; and there he remained for the rest of his life. Meanwhile his friendship with Erasmus had begun in 1514, when he had courteously escorted the latter to Basel. Thenceforth a triangular friendship developed between the two and with Volz, which survived even when both disciples had deviated into the Protestant cause. The enthusiasm of Sapidus for the Lutheran Reformation displeased the patriarchal Erasmian Wimpfeling, and perhaps all the more because in 1520 Erasmus had dedicated the *Antibarbari* to Sapidus. In short, the humanist network within the upper Rhineland – and its history could be considerably extended – appears to have become distinctly influential, and most clearly so in its eventual recruitment to Protestantism. Under the direct leadership of Erasmus throughout so many years, the spectacle goes far to support the claim of his enemies that, whatever his eventual disapproval, he had contributed a great deal to the Lutheran cause *before* Luther himself emerged.[22]

Meanwhile, we must not give the impression that Erasmianism in Germany was restricted either to the Rhineland or to a 'city-state' milieu. Our sketch may now be extended further east as well as to certain princely courts. Admittedly, Erasmus personally does not have a high profile in Nuremberg, but religious developments in that city *were* much influenced by the Protestant leader with whom he felt most empathy, Melanchthon. Erasmus himself never visited the city, despite the repeated invitations of one of his most frequent and significant correspondents, over a period of many years. Willibald Pirckheimer, member of a patrician family and also of the Council of Nuremberg, was a notable humanist in his own right. Throughout a lengthy and cordial exchange of letters, Pirckheimer, like Erasmus, deplored the increasing virulence of the conflict between Roman obscurantism and Lutheran brashness, with its harmful impact upon good letters. Indeed, in attempting to dissuade Erasmus from too bitter a response to the attacks of Hutten and of Luther, he showed himself to be perhaps more irenic even than his mentor. Letters of Erasmus concerning the Oecolampadian interpretation of the Eucharist and resolute adherence to Church membership – two crucial issues – are especially revealing. In a letter in May 1531 to Duke George of Saxony, Erasmus expressed his particular regret at the news of the death of his friend – 'mi Bilibaldo', whose portraits hung upon the walls of his study – the previous year.[23]

In not far distant Augsburg, a scene of much tension in the 1520s between nascent Protestant and entrenched Catholic interests, there resided another important correspondent of Erasmus in his later years. Unlike Pirckheimer, Johann Koler (John Choler), priest, provost and canon at Augsburg, outlived Erasmus by a couple of years. Apart from mentioning invitations sent to Erasmus by the Fuggers, this correspondence ranges from Anabaptism in Holland and anti-Lutheran measures in France to the injustice of both Lutheran and Romanist attacks upon Erasmus and worrying developments in Augsburg itself. In June 1533 Choler complains about the 'Zwinglian faction', and in July of the following year about heretical opinions in the Augsburg Senate.[24]

Moving further north in Germany, we find that the city of Erfurt presents us with a virtual case-study of the complex development of relationships between Erasmianism and the early impact of Luther. The humanist circle in this city included the leader of the most renowned such group outside Alsace, Mutianus,[25] who had initiated a critique of scholasticism from the first decade of the century and had emerged as an early supporter of Reuchlin, Mosellanus, Heinrich Stromer, Eobanus and Jonas – names which figure in Erasmus' correspondence. Eobanus, who visited Erasmus in 1518, lectured on the *Enchiridion*, while Jonas, who travelled to the Netherlands a year later, was swayed by Erasmus to shift his interest from law to theology. But the group also included a friend of Luther from Wittenberg days, Johann Lang, whose arrival at Erfurt in 1516 led to the introduction of Lutheran ideas to the city's humanists.

The Erfurt circle had already responded in May 1520 to a plea for support against the attacks of the English theologian Edward Lee, by publishing a set of epigrams which were too vituperative even for Erasmus himself. Now in July its members produced a scurrilous dialogue directed against Eck, who had visited the city two years earlier. This intimated that the Erfurt humanists as yet, somewhat oddly, saw the attack upon Luther as but another assault upon humanist scholarship. Later on, an anonymous pamphlet upbraided traducers with the typically Erasmian charge of crying 'Heresy' on all occasions. Yet in December 1521 a visit of Melanchthon served in effect to propagate Luther's views and to shift the balance of opinion among the Erfurt humanists from 'Erasmian' to 'Martinist', if only in the sense that they now saw Luther's cause as an issue in itself, not simply as an extension of that of Erasmus. The shift was not sudden or uniform. Indeed, although Eobanus had produced a set of elegies in May 1521 which hailed Luther as restoring the pure Word of God in completion of the work of Erasmus, Justus Jonas had also written in June to Luther's protector Frederick the Wise, in terms which clearly demonstrate his identification of a new well-spring of truth. The humanist cause soon suffered a reverse in Erfurt, but these events in one urban milieu well illustrate the complexity of early Erasmus–Luther relationships and of the interpretations placed upon them by third parties.[26]

Justus Jonas (1493–1555) is himself of particular interest as an Erasmian who delayed his total surrender to Luther until 1527. The recipient of Erasmus' famous letter on Vitrier and Colet, this doctor of divinity and university rector tried as late as that date to reconcile Luther to Erasmus, such was his admiration of the great humanist. In this effort Jonas may be likened to Melanchthon. Erasmus for his part attempted to dissuade Jonas from what he saw as a particularly regrettable defection, without avail. For thereafter Jonas worked whole-heartedly for the Lutheran cause at Marburg and at Augsburg, translated works by Luther and Melanchthon, and helped to establish the Protestant Reformation in the cities of Leipzig and Halle.[27]

Meanwhile, in Saxony, the Catholic Duke George, despite his incessant goading of Erasmus to write against Luther,[28] was not devoid of irenical traits. Indeed, conscious of the need for church reform, the Duke encouraged debate upon Luther's initial emergence – though he soon detected signs of his adherence to Hussite doctrines which changed his tune! None the less, his court at Leipzig nurtured humanism, and between 1516 and 1531 he sent Erasmus ten letters and received double that number in reply. Joseph Lecler concluded that, of the courts of the German princes, the one which felt Erasmus' influence most profoundly was that of George of Saxony. Yet, significantly, George remained a devout Catholic and a virulent enemy of Luther until his death in 1539. He welcomed Erasmus' insistence that Rome must be carried along with any movement for church reform, preferably through an ecumenical council,[29] but his own vision of its outcome was probably far more favourable to the *status quo*. Nevertheless, recent contentions that he surrounded himself with conciliatory ministers find support in the presence alongside Pflug of Pistorius (Simon Pistoris) and Witzel. The much-travelled Georg Witzel returned from a brief sojourn within the Lutheran camp and after 1538 was briefly employed by Duke George to frame the basis of an acceptable conciliatory policy. He later became a consultant to both Charles V and Ferdinand I, and his name will recur when we discuss 'Erasmus the Mediator'.[30]

Another patron of humanism who corresponded with Erasmus was the immensely influential Prince-Bishop Albert of Brandenburg, Archbishop of Mainz and Cardinal. Again, this unreformed fund-raiser has more recently been seen as not altogether opposed to consideration of moderate, conservatively structured reform. Alongside the spectacle of his acceptance of Tetzel's indulgence-peddling, which triggered off Luther's declaration, must be set his appointment of Nausea as preacher in his Frankfurt-am-Main cathedral and of Julius Pflug as canon of his diocese in 1530. Among his one-time advisers who had felt Erasmian influence were Heinrich Stromer and Wolfgang Capito. It was to Albert that Erasmus dedicated his *Ratio verae theologiae* in 1518, and addressed his famous letter regarding Luther dated 19 October 1519. Whatever one's assessment of the depth of Albert's belief in humanist reform, Erasmian principles were at work in his efforts at negotiation at the Diet of Augsburg in 1530 and the religious colloquy at Leipzig in 1534, and also, arguably, in certain of his attempts at educational, administrative and juridical reform.[31]

Equally significant, although in a rather different way, was John III, Duke of Cleves-Mark-Jülich. A belated but none the less genuine and simultaneous realisation of the dangers of Lutheranism *and* of the need for religious reform is discernible after 1525. A link with Erasmus had commenced with his recommendation of Konrad Heresbach as tutor to the Duke's son William. Thereafter he was several times invited to visit and even to settle in Cleves – the last invitation accompanying Heresbach's account of the fall of Münster in July 1535 – while John awarded him an annuity of thirty gold pieces in May 1533. In terms of policy, his appointment of Heresbach and of Johann von Vlatten, the nature of the church ordinance which he issued in January 1532, the subsequent consultation with Erasmus on its implementation and interpretation, evoking his expressed approval of ducal policies, are all indicative of a genuine sphere of influence – in actuality as distinct from exhortation.[32]

Johann von Vlatten, doctor of civil and canon law, had met both Heresbach and Erasmus by at latest 1523, and in the following year became Councillor to Duke John, later attaining the post of Vice-Chancellor in 1530. Together with Heresbach he exercised a consistent influence in favour of an irenic church policy – though this did not extend to toleration of the neighbouring Anabaptist danger at Münster, in the suppression of which he played a crucial part. From the time (1523) of Erasmus' dedication of an edition of Cicero to Vlatten the two men corresponded until parted by death in 1536. Most notably, during the Diet of Augsburg in 1530, Vlatten was one of several who urged Erasmus to attend, in the interests of the Christian Commonwealth in general and of the 'unlucky and miserable Germans' in particular. In default of this, he kept him fully informed of events. Several letters were exchanged in the next few years. Most notably, on 3 May 1533 Vlatten wrote to render, in cordial terms, his own and his master's thanks. In July, Erasmus replied, reviewing the current religious dissension and in particular the diversity of opinions on the Eucharist, but most significantly expressing his approval of the religious ordinances of the illustrious duke. This commendation was repeated in a letter in August to an unidentified recipient which Allen and Garrod describe as effectively a near-recapitulation of the final pages of Erasmus' *De sarcienda ecclesiae concordia*.[33]

The reforms which Duke John had promulgated in January of 1532 demonstrated a debt to elements of medieval theology and indeed to the *Devotio Moderna* which makes it inaccurate simply to dub them Erasmian, while the mark of Georg Witzel has again been discerned. Yet without doubt they conveyed Erasmian principles in their demand that all preaching must be based upon the Scriptures and Holy Fathers, avoiding contentious polemics, while those who undertook it were to be well-educated priests not 'uneducated and rabble-rousing' monks. As to the Christian Faith which God in his Grace has offered, 'without good works it is dead and without love to one's neighbours it cannot exist'. Most indicatively, prior to the final draft of an 'Interpretation' designed to avoid uncertainty, a face-to-face consultation with Erasmus himself at Freiburg was undertaken by Heresbach in September 1532. The Interpretation as issued in April 1533 has been seen as Erasmian not only in its fundamental ideas but also because much of its phraseology echoes that of his writings. Assuredly, the letter of Erasmus just referred to attests his wish that the duke's pious example should be followed. Thus, despite the comparatively small extent of the state involved, recent research has rightly pointed to this rare case of direct Erasmian influence upon ecclesiastical policy.[34] Nor did such Erasmian tendencies disappear with his death. Vlatten and Heresbach persisted, both internally by way of educational reform in the shape of an Erasmian curriculum, and externally in demonstrating conciliatory attitudes at religious colloquies into the mid-century. Upon reflection, it might well be argued that Erasmian irenicism had a far longer run from its German, Austrian and perhaps also its Italian bases than was the case within France or Spain.

Next, though farthest of all removed from Erasmus' Rhenish and south German heartland, one other nation figures so largely in his correspondence as to demand inclusion in our brief survey: Poland. Indeed it is at the outset worthy of emphasis not only by reason of its record in terms of cosmopolitan humanism, but also in that its printing resources at this time were probably superior to those available in England. Oddly enough, two of the most important personalities involved – Leonard Cox and John à Lasco the younger – had direct connections with England. Cox[35] was himself a well-travelled humanist who pursued a not undistinguished though chequered career as schoolmaster, lecturer and author. After studies at Cambridge and visits to Paris and Germany, Cox established himself at the University of Cracow between 1518 and 1520, at first under the patronage of Justus Decius. That university had recently established an international repute, notably in respect of the study of languages and the newer humanities, together with its abandonment of fruitless scholasticism. Such Erasmian characteristics won fulsome praise from Cox, who spoke eulogistically of Cracow as 'the very Athens' in an oration which may well have helped to secure him a chair! His time in Poland has rightly been described as producing the highest achievements of his career.

More immediately significant in our own context is the fact that an eminent Polish authority[36] describes Cox as having commenced Erasmian lectures at Cracow and as gathering around him a number of Polish Erasmians, including Andrew Krzycki, John à Lasco junior, and Andrew Zebrzydowski, men whom we shall encounter later. An important patron was John Konarski, Bishop of Cracow and one of the first Polish humanist bishops, yet it was primarily by Justus Decius, to whom Erasmus himself dedicated one of his works, that Cox was established in this propagandist circle in Poland. To this process Cox undoubtedly made his own major contribution. Moreover, his departure for a sojourn in Hungary between 1520 and 1524 exemplifies still further the vigour of cosmopolitan Erasmianism. His new patron in the town of Levozca, John Henckel, had himself attended the University of Cracow and had now, significantly, become the confessor of Queen Mary and a great enthusiast for Erasmus. Cox apparently moved with Henckel to Kosice, again becoming the rector of a school and remaining there for nearly three years. In emphasising the contribution of 'the Cracow pleiad of Hungarian Erasmians' to the progress of their nation's culture, Henryk Zins points in particular to John Sylvester – a scholar of that university who translated the New Testament and produced the first book on Hungarian grammar – as taking over the Erasmian cult from Leonard Cox.[37]

Upon his return to Cracow, Cox again obtained a chair, which he held until 1527. Among his works was a poem in praise of à Lasco, now returned from visiting Erasmus. At this time Cox's stance remained anti-Lutheran, as did that of his new protector Andrew Krzycki (Latinised Cricius) despite his attempt to persuade Melanchthon to visit Poland. By this time, also, Piotr Tomiczki, Bishop of Cracow and Chancellor of Poland, had shown favour to Cox. Thus, concludes Professor Zins, 'the English humanist moved in the circle of the most outstanding Polish representatives of the Renaissance era', while his home 'became a live centre of Polish Erasmians'.[38] Indeed it was professedly on their behalf, referring specifically to how à Lasco among others performed the role of his Maecenas, that Cox wrote to Erasmus himself on 28 March 1527, recounting in adulatory terms how he dominated their lives and thinking. Erasmus despatched a polite, if brief, reply some seven weeks later.[39]

Included in Cox's letter was a commendation of a rich and well-connected pupil of his, one Andrew Zebrzydowski,[40] a nephew of the powerful bishop Cricius, who had conceived such an intense admiration of Erasmus that he was firmly resolved to pay him a visit. Whether or not Erasmus was later to concur with Cox's possibly over-inflated description of his pupil's talents, he wrote to the well-commended protégé (also on 21 May) referring to his sincere friendship with Cricius and expressing his hopes for such talents, nurtured by such a notable master as Cox himself. On 26 August of the following year Erasmus wrote to Cricius, in one of a batch of six letters destined for Poland, describing how his nephew was now living with him in Basel and pursuing his studies under his direction. Zebrzydowski's arrival would have been the more welcome in that, on leaving Poland in February, he had brought with him letters from à Lasco, Tomiczki and King Sigismund I, the king having also sent a gift of money. In late September, Zebrzydowski left for Paris, but returned for another brief period in the spring of 1529. His career after his ultimate return to Poland was apparently distinguished more by the successful pursuit of ecclesiastical preferment – he later himself became Bishop of Cracow – than by any personal demonstration of Erasmian talents. Yet he asked that his monument should describe him as disciple and pupil of 'the great Erasmus of Rotterdam'. Meanwhile his erstwhile tutor in Poland had himself left for England, in or soon after 1528. It is hard to dissent from the conclusion that, through his links with the two main Erasmian circles in Poland – that surrounding the younger à Lasco and the other grouped around

Justus Decius – Leonard Cox 'to a large degree helped to create in Poland one of Erasmus of Rotterdam's cult centres'.[41]

As for John à Lasco (Jan Laski), there were in fact two men who bore this name, both well-travelled and both correspondents with Erasmus! The elder, Primate of Poland and an influential statesman and diplomat, was somewhat reserved in his attitude, largely because of Erasmus' loyalty to the Habsburgs. But his namesake and nephew, whom he launched upon his cosmopolitan-educational travels in a career which took him to Basel, Paris, Friesland, England, Friesland again, then Frankfurt, before his final return to Poland, emerged thence as perhaps the most influential, and certainly the most widely travelled, of the Polish Erasmians. Ultimately he moved beyond Erasmian reformist religious positions, while politically his friend's Habsburg commitment proved an occasional irritant.[42]

The importance of his connection with Erasmus cannot be doubted. Visiting him in May 1524, à Lasco thereafter met Briçonnet and Lefèvre d'Étaples in Paris before returning to Basel to spend six months as Erasmus' house-guest. Included in his financial generosity was an arrangement in 1526 to buy Erasmus' library, while leaving to him its use during his lifetime. À Lasco came into contact with Baer, Amerbach and Froben, as well as meeting Zwingli, Oecolampadius and Farel, but at this time the paramount influence upon his religious development was that of Erasmus. After his return to Poland in 1526 he became the focal point of Erasmian influence, and continued to correspond with Basel. In March 1526 Erasmus wrote to him recounting his verbal exchanges with Pellican about the Eucharist, and in May of the following year, very probably at his friend's instigation, he wrote directly to King Sigismund I. He also kept à Lasco informed of events in Spain and in Louvain, as well as about the Berquin affair.[43] À Lasco's undoubted influence in England during the reign of Edward VI has been noted in our Chapter Nine.[44] It should not be forgotten that Poland, which together with Hungary retained reformist elements from a previous era and therefore leaned toward Erasmian ideas, was in mid-century to provide a refuge for such as Ochino and Sozzini, for both anti-Trinitarians and Anabaptists.[45]

Moving to Erasmian influence in Polish court and ministerial circles, the king's secretary, the Alsatian Justus Decius, had met Erasmus while in Basel on one of several diplomatic missions. A patron of the humanities, an economist, and highly respected in the annals of Polish cultural history, Decius' central position nurtured Erasmian influence, especially at Cracow. Indeed, as well as maintaining a friendly personal correspondence with Erasmus, Decius served as a clearing house for the transmission of news, correspondence and gifts. It was to him that Erasmus despatched that brief but most revealing letter of 8 June 1529 in which he confided his adiaphoric approach to disputed dogmas. Some years later, Decius received letters in which Erasmus referred to his maintaining 'no common friendship' with Melanchthon, and recounted events ranging from those in England to the Anabaptist troubles in lower Germany and the disgrace of Béda.[46]

Another recipient of frank Erasmian avowals was Andrew Cricius,[47] who sent him a long, admiring communication in December 1525. Nearly five years later, Erasmus wrote to Cricius deploring not only the continuing descent into doctrinal controversy but also the extent of contemporary social and economic hardship and injustice. Who can recall such furious agrarian tumult, and when was there such dearth of the necessities of life? A further letter to Cricius in the last year of Erasmus' life voices regret at the death of the Bishop of Cracow and refers to another Polish connection of outstanding importance. Piotr Tomiczki, Bishop of Cracow and Chancellor of Poland, who had been instrumental in Decius' promotion in 1520 and supported Cox's publication of some letters of St Jerome in 1529, was a major patron of Polish humanism. We should also recall the contention that yet again a fertile seed-bed for Erasmian ideas had been prepared by the survival of reformist ideas in the theological faculty at Cracow throughout the fifteenth century, so that the university and the cathedral chapter, as well as the court of Sigismund, welcomed and nurtured the new learning.[48]

Tomiczki's[49] commitment to Erasmian principles appeared in his suggestion that the upbringing of Prince Sigismund Augustus should be grounded on the *Education of a Christian Prince*. Direct correspondence between the two was initially brief, the first epistle being included in a small batch despatched (the way in which letters each way were usually sent) to Erasmus' 'Polish connection' in December 1527. But the Zebrzydowski who visited Erasmus was in fact Tomiczki's grand-nephew, and the substantive content of their letters increased. In the epistle to Tomiczki which was effectively the preface to his second edition of Seneca, Erasmus alludes to his ideal of *Christiana philosophia*, while later missives discuss religious developments, for example in Switzerland. From Freiburg, after reference to his new home, Erasmus expresses his hope that sectarian fury may yet abate 'and all return to Christian concord'; in March of 1533 a more mundane fear that the death of Warham will mean the loss of his pension is followed by reiterated hope that Emperor and Pope will restore the peace of the Church.[50]

In April 1535 Tomiczki wrote what is effectively an encomium of Erasmus' endeavours for the *respublica Christiana*, and at the very end of August Erasmus despatched one of the last of his long letters in which, repeating his wish to be with Christ, he recounts how, after ill-health accompanied by dreadful pain up until May, he has been carried back to Basel – a city now restored to a more tranquil state. After the scathing reference to the Anabaptists noted earlier, a comment on the 'Placards' affair in Paris, and the well-known affirmation that in the death of More he sees his own, he confides the rumour of proposals by Paul III to make him cardinal and includes the obvious objections. The final exchange of letters is not without a certain poignancy. For Tomiczki's reply, dated 25 October, congratulating his 'dearest friend' upon his appointment to Deventer, was apparently not then sent, for its author died three days later. On 1 February following, Erasmus himself wrote to Andrew Cricius regretting the news of the death of his friend, without having had a sight of Tomiczki's last letter, which was belatedly delivered to him only after his own death. On such a note we may perhaps not unfittingly conclude our sketch of Erasmian influence upon 'wider shores'; for surely there can be few better examples of the power of the mind and the pen of Erasmus to strike a chord with kindred spirits all over Europe.[51]

Finally, we may hardly end our survey of the reception of Erasmus without returning, if only briefly, to the land which had originally nurtured this essentially cosmopolitan humanist. In so doing we should perhaps reflect that the Low Countries in which, after all, Erasmus spent over thirty years of his life, were in themselves a sufficiently cosmopolitan milieu, with rulers who looked, at different times, to Austria and to Spain, and whose most prominent member spoke French as his first language. It may then be useful to relate our comments, first to what the Netherlands meant for Erasmus, and secondly, to the influence of Erasmus and his teachings upon the Low Countries and their history.

As we noted in our first chapter, the *Devotio Moderna*, which contributed so much to Erasmus' spiritual development, had its base in the northern Netherlands, while his significant discovery of Valla took place near Louvain. The considerable patronage received from certain Netherlands notables in the early stages of his career was followed by the maintenance of a number of long-term and genuine personal links. Jean le Sauvage, Chancellor to the Emperor Charles, obtained the appointment of Erasmus as Councillor in 1515; *Querela pacis* was written at his special request, and it has indeed been observed that a great deal of Erasmus' political writing took place against a Low Countries background. Relations with Erard de la Marck, Prince-Bishop of Liège, became increasingly tainted by mutual suspicion after Erasmus moved to Basel. At a rather less eminent level, Jacob Batt of Bergen op Zoom, tutor and administrator, remained a faithful friend and correspondent until he died in 1502. The humanist's namesake, Erasmus Schets, merchant and banker of Antwerp who became his agent, exchanged friendly letters with him for decades, not only on business matters but sometimes including gossip about religious developments.[52]

Among those who testified to the goodwill felt toward Erasmus in the Netherlands and to a genuine wish for his return we may include a trio of closely linked correspondents: Levinus Ammonius, Audomarus Edingus and Charles Utenhove. The first-named, a Carthusian monk of Ghent, received no reply to his first letter to Erasmus; but then in October 1528 a letter from Erasmus evoked an ecstatic response from his admirer which included the oft-cited declaration that 'Christ teaches me through Erasmus'. This letter to Ammonius also included a reference to Charles Utenhove, *procureur* to the Council of Flanders, at present staying with him, who was a kinsman of Audomarus Edingus, a Flanders humanist. In July 1529 Ammonius wrote to Erasmus associating himself with an invitation of Edingus (Omaar van Edingen) to settle in Flanders when he feels obliged to leave Basel, endeavouring to paint an alluring portrait of the tranquil freedom from tumult which he might there enjoy. Utenhove was the recipient, in the same year, of two long and discursive letters from Erasmus, including discussion of the fate of Berquin, while to Edingus, writing from Freiburg in April 1531, Erasmus was to profess himself sick of Germany 'to the point of vomiting' and to observe that Mary, quondam Queen of Hungary, was well-disposed toward him. To such urgings we may add that of Marcus Laurinus, from Bruges, in July 1527, assuring Erasmus that many people longed for his return and that Flanders would not be happy until it saw him again.[53]

More familiar are the names of Maarten van Dorp, whose friendship survived the clashes of opinion we have observed, and Gerard Geldenhauer of Nijmegen who, despite early amicable contacts was destined to become one of his *bêtes noires*, and most distinguished of all, Viglius Zuichemus. This last-named Dutchman pursued a glittering career in international administration and politics, becoming in mid-century President of the Privy Council in Brussels. After their first contact in 1529 he became a frequent correspondent of Erasmus, reporting from Italy and later relating the Münster episode while in the service of the Bishop. His admiration for Erasmus survived into the 1560s, when he strove in vain for reconciliation in the Netherlands. Of Erasmus' academic associates at Louvain, we have already noted some inveterate opponents, but Conrad Goclenius, Professor of Latin at the University and his closest friend there, continued loyal until his death. Nicolaas Everaerts, who also knew Erasmus at Louvain, later became President of the Council of Holland and again exemplifies the personal goodwill and the sympathy with his religious position in many official circles. We have noted the post held by Utenhove in Flanders, while a letter of Ammonius assured him that the whole of the Flanders Senate was 'heartily devoted' to him.[54]

What then was the extent of the Erasmian impact upon religious developments within the Netherlands? Certainly it differed from the situation just across the border, in Cleves-Jülich-Berg, where his ideas made their most notable mark in terms of official church policy. The political contrast with the Netherlands is crucially important, for here Charles ruled as an hereditary prince, and his personal patronage of Erasmus and admiration of his writings did not extend to the toleration of any Erasmian ideas which might surface in some quasi-Protestant garb. The mass-burning of Lutheran books at Louvain in October 1520 was followed by the establishment of a regional Inquisition in 1522 and by the first martyrdoms in Brussels the following year: all events deplored by Erasmus. By 1530 many leading 'evangelicals' had fled the country, following the execution of about thirty people during the decade.[55]

Against this background, the diffusion of Erasmian reformist trends – as in Ammonius' testimony that many monks were abandoning superstitious customs[56] – is sometimes difficult to separate from the evidence of the early impact of Lutheran ideas. Of those termed 'Biblical Humanists', of whom Erasmus himself is identified as the most representative figure, and 'Evangelicals', defined as those who preferred plain scripturally based preaching to speculative theology, the latter became progressively more and more identified with Lutheranism. 'Heresy' was at first largely confined to the intelligentsia, and even when popular religious dissent emerged, the direct Erasmian influence thereon was limited by the relatively late appearance of Dutch translation of his works. Nevertheless, it is suggested that the impact upon many Evangelicals of a translation of the *Enchiridion* which *was* published in 1523 may well have been greater than that of Luther's writings.[57]

As yet there was no clear division between Biblical Humanism and doctrinal Protestantism. Regarding the 'accepted' characteristics of Netherlands reformism – austere biblicism, scepticism as to the mediation of Our Lady and the Saints, a wish to define the true nature of Confession, and a sacramentarian approach to the Eucharist – it can be said that Erasmus was by no means unsympathetic. In particular, as to the assertion that the *focus* of the Reformation in Holland was 'the spiritualising of the sacrament of the Lord's Table',[58] we have already seen that the tract published by Zwingli but written by the Hollander Cornelis Hoen is perhaps the best-known early rejection of any corporeal version of the Real Presence. Yet by that time, 1524, Erasmus himself was already suspect of holding similar views.[59] As to the sacrament of Baptism, despite the delayed arrival of this issue as a cause of conflict until 1531, Erasmus' homeland was thenceforth to become a major base of Anabaptism.

From this relatively complex picture at least one eminent Dutch historian has deduced that in the Netherlands 'Erasmus' personal influence counted for more than anywhere else'.[60] Indeed, in assessing the depth and durability of that influence, one should beware of taking Erasmus' own abhorrence both of the obscurantism of Louvain at the one extreme, and of the spectre of Anabaptist-bedevilled Groningen at the other, as an indication of the whole panorama of the 1530s. Likewise suspect are exaggerated claims regarding the speed and the completeness of militant Calvinist success during the middle and later decades of the century. Thus we endorse the strong contention that amongst the leaders of anti-Spanish resistance in Holland and Zealand in the early days of the Revolt were the spiritual descendants not of Calvin but of Erasmus, who fought not for a Calvinist theocracy but for religious liberty. The spirit of Erasmus lived on in those who favoured 'a sacramentarian, biblical-evangelical, tolerant, anti-confessional form of religion'. Admittedly, in the wake of victory in the Northern Netherlands came domination by the Calvinists; yet even amid their ranks it has been reasonably argued that the Arminian deviation represents a survival of the Erasmian spirit.[61]

To conclude on an appropriately personal note, the possibility of a return by Erasmus to the Netherlands was never discounted by his contemporaries. It has been suggested that toward the end of his life he thought of himself no longer as a Hollander but as a Netherlander, who saw Flanders and Brabant as well as constituting his homeland.[62] The final invitations came from the very highest quarters, and again demonstrate to the last the essentially cosmopolitan quality of Erasmus' repute. In July 1532 Jean de Carondelet (Imperial Chancellor) wrote from Brussels, conveying the good wishes of the Queen Regent and of her confidant Nicholas Olah who had accompanied her from Hungary, and their combined desire for his return. In the spring months of the following year Imperial sanction was obtained and an official letter of invitation despatched. On 13 June 1533 no less a person than the Regent Mary herself wrote a personal letter which speaks in glowing terms of Erasmus' service to the Christian faith, makes financial promises, and ends with an urgent appeal for his return without delay. According to one modern authority, this missive, together with others and with funds for the journey, was conveyed to him in Freiburg by none other than Levinus Ammonius. Olah appealed to him again a year later. Whatever the parts played by ill-health, inclement weather, and the length of the journey, Erasmus – whatever his intentions – never got further than Basel. Yet in the last of his personal letters, despatched on 28 June 1536 to Conrad Goclenius, he uttered the plaint 'Oh that Brabant were nearer'; and on the point of death he cried out to God in his native tongue.[63]

Twelve

ERASMUS: HERETIC OR MEDIATOR?

In this chapter we shall consider variant assessments of Erasmus' contribution toward two crucial aspects of religious development. These relate to the problem of definitive establishment of Christian truths and to the contingent but far from precisely identical issue of religious concord. His own views on heresy and mediation – despite the pejorative overtones of the first – are in no way mutually exclusive. Erasmus' readiness almost to welcome 'grey areas' in respect of several issues of doctrine, while an obvious target for censure by rigorous dogmatists both Catholic and Protestant, has been applauded among his contemporaries and more frequently by succeeding generations of seekers after religious concord. This ideal they have often been ready to base upon the twin pillars of *adiaphora* in dogma and of toleration in respect of conduct.

To review the interpretations of Erasmus by those later historians who have made him *parti pris* to their own religious preferences[1] is hardly our business. Some would render him an eighteenth-century *philosophe*; others would gear him to some philosophy of religion untrammelled by dogmatic anchor-points, or even make him a modern liberal Catholic. Rather are we concerned with his influence within the sixteenth century, in a milieu within which the vast majority of thinking people devoutly believed that it was not only possible but indeed mandatory to display an established Christian credo. The modern concession that there may not exist any one authoritative source of religious truth would not for a moment have been entertained in that era.[2] Such certainty inevitably involves enforced compliance with an established creed, not only within the Church itself, but also in society as a whole, the two being generally regarded as co-extensive.

None the less, we may also discern the emergence of what modern sociological historians of religion, notably Ernst Troeltsch, have identified as 'sects'. These latter, while perfectly willing to enunciate strict codes of religious belief and conduct, seem concerned almost to exclude from membership the major part of a presumably unredeemed mankind.[3] Yet in the sixteenth century we also encounter rare cases of a less-than-dogmatic certitude about the doctrines, as distinct from the moral implications of religion, as with Castellio or Servetus. A common feature of both of these disparate trends is an unwillingness to enforce such beliefs upon others. Significantly, both looked quite avowedly to Erasmus for much of their inspiration, while simultaneously subjected to persecution by Catholics and Magisterial Protestants alike. The ground of such persecution was the accusation of religious heresy, which we must now examine in some detail.

In establishing the fundamental sixteenth-century belief in the necessity and the implications of a categorical definition of religious truth, it is worth repeating the assertion of Calvin's lieutenant Beza, that religious liberty means freedom for every man to go to hell in his own way. In this sense the Magisterial Protestants remained completely within the tradition of the late-medieval Catholic Church. That Church had assuredly been no stranger to what it identified as obdurate heresy. Indeed, although the identification of supposed heresies dates back almost to apostolic times, it was during the Middle Ages that the Church itself instigated systematic repression by the 'secular arm', sometimes even directing 'crusades', as against the Albigensian, Waldensian and Hussite heresies.

An attempt to define heresy as conceived by the sixteenth-century mind may well start with the orthodox assumption that salvation in the next world could be attained only in and through the Holy Catholic Church, this involving acceptance of its doctrines and its sacraments. Significantly, Luther, Zwingli and Calvin, and their churches adhered, broadly speaking, to the same principles. They justified their schisms by asserting that the Roman or 'Papist' Church had betrayed its trust by distorting certain dogmas of the Christian faith, by introducing sacramental definitions without any scriptural basis, and by condoning most un-Christian conduct by its clergy. But over and above this general position, both sides of the religious divide within the Christian Church identified specific doctrinal errors deemed not only so horrendous as to entail damnation to all holders but also all too likely to entice others along the primrose path. This double count fully merited the penalty of death.

In establishing the position of Erasmus it cannot be too strongly emphasised that he never departed from the notion of salvation in and through membership of the Catholic Church. The crucial points at issue between Erasmus and more orthodox religious voices involved the nature and definition of heresy itself, the actions appropriate to deal with heretics, and most crucial of all, the charge that he himself, in several aspects of his teaching, was guilty of heresy – or at least of a scepticism which encouraged heresy in others. In respect of the first, Erasmus did *not* equate error with heresy, holding that the nature and magnitude of the error, the obstinacy with which it was held or promulgated, and its likely impact upon the Christian faith in the widest context, should be the determinant factors. As to any punishment, this again must be related to the foregoing considerations; but assuredly, burning for a mere error was to him nothing short of criminal. Finally, the accusations made on several counts against Erasmus himself will need fairly detailed consideration.

On his firm belief in membership of the Church, his late work *De sarcienda ecclesiae concordia* ('On Mending the Peace of the Church', 1533) is repeatedly specific. Thus, 'outside the Church there is no hope of real blessedness', for even the good works and the charity of heretics are inevitably rendered fruitless. Or again, 'there can never be day unless in the Church. Those who are outside it are in night', and indeed reject 'the mystical body of Christ which is the Church'. This of course only confirms the stance which he had taken earlier, but at this final stage in his life Erasmus was also ready to write as follows: 'Do you wish then to be safe from every evil? Then do not be blown about by every wind of doctrine, but let us hold fast to what the Catholic Church has handed down to us from Holy Scripture. What it commands, let us carry out with simple obedience . . .' The categorical injunction of these last words is somewhat attenuated in a typically Erasmian fashion by the preceding qualification: 'from Holy Scripture'. But nothing could be less equivocal than the declaration that it is surely worse to withdraw from the Church and move to heresy or schism, than to live impiously but saved through belief![4]

Yet in truth these extracts from a latter-day Erasmus convey an over-simple impression of his position. With regard to the declaration of specific doctrines there is no doubt that, at least in spirit, he was a major contributor to the emergent concept of *adiaphora*, not scrupling on occasion to infer that this was the Church's own position. We have already encountered several statements of his belief that the required and definitive articles of the Christian faith should be as few and as simply expressed as possible. Beyond these, surely it is fruitless to essay complicated, and often heated, enquiry and debate merely in order to enunciate requirements which have little to do with a Christian faith of the inner spirit, and then to make them literally a matter of life and death. Years before, he had declared that 'there are some things on which it is impious for men to pronounce, for example, on the essential nature of God'. Such speculations could only produce a knowledge which is neither useful nor pious. 'There are men who string out frigid syllogisms and create articles of faith based on a passage insufficiently understood or from insignificant human institutions, with not the least bearing on Christian piety.'[5]

Erasmus' declaration that 'by heresy I mean, not error of any sort, but the *wilful* malice of those who for their own profit by *perverse* dogmas disturb the tranquillity of the Church' is crucially important. Clearly, he never advocated complete liberty, at least of expression, in the sphere of religious thinking; but the adjectives we have italicised and the end-result he envisaged are well-nigh conclusively indicative. Error in belief is one thing, and does not disturb him over-much; but the obdurate and malicious proselytising of others in order to lead them also into error, thereby wrecking both Church unity and Christian concord, is a very different thing. On all this, his views have not changed since the evidence of his correspondence a decade and a half earlier. In 1521, writing to a headmaster charged with heresy, he explains that 'the man who makes an honest mistake is deserving of mercy; but all heresy which is combined with obstinacy that will not learn must be abhorred by pious minds . . .' Interestingly, having declared that 'some heresies are more pestilent than others', he goes on to contend that 'those heresies seem least far removed from true religion which, from some excessive zeal for the full rigour of the Gospel, demand of men more than is right'. A year or so later he adds: 'I do not deny that heretical intransigence must be abhorred, if incurable. But meanwhile because of our hatred of one error we must beware of falling into another. I would have recommended that anyone in agreement with Arius be admonished and instructed, but I would not immediately have called him Satan or Antichrist.'[6]

It has indeed been contended that Erasmus' condemnation of heresy was based upon ethical rather than theological grounds.[7] Aggressive heresy, producing bitterness and quarrelling, was as unattractive as persecuting dogmatism. But in Erasmus' view such errors of the spirit should be corrected only by the weapons of the spirit. In his *Supputatio* or *Reckoning of the Errors in the Censure of Béda*, Erasmus defends the proposition that 'God does not wish Pseudo-Apostles & Heresiarchs destroyed, but tolerated, lest perchance they recover their senses, & from tares be turned to wheat'. Indeed, in the ancient Church the *ultimate* penalty was anathema. The task, therefore, of the bishops, 'in so far as in them lies, is to teach, correct, cure. But of what sort is a bishop who can do nothing other than fetter, torture, and deliver to the flames?' He disclaims any advocacy of milder treatment of heretics – *if only he could identify a genuine heretic with certainty*, as erring maliciously, as factious and incurable. Crucially, he declares his concurrence with Augustine's avowal that 'I am able to be in error. I am not able to be a heretic.' Yet, having earlier cited Augustine's intercession for the Donatists, seditious bandits as well as heretics, he poses the question of whether he, who deemed the servants of God's glory dishonoured by the blood of enemies, believed 'that the simple heretic, however obstinate, should be consumed in flames'?[8] Such passages are cited triumphantly by Sebastian Castellio in his *Concerning Heretics*, as is also the relevant section in Erasmus' reply to the accusations made at Valladolid (below, pp. 273–7). Thus, while heresy and schism are execrable, Erasmus cannot agree with contemporaries who 'on account of scholastic opinions, drag men to prison and the stake, as now we see priests burned because they would rather call a girl with whom they live a wife than a concubine'. Although his claim that for more than four centuries after Christ the orthodox bishops never besought the help of the emperors against heretics is inaccurate, Erasmus, citing Chrysostom and Jerome, concludes 'that in a case of unmistakable error we should not cut off hastily, and where the matter is dubious, never', but leave to God the task of gathering the tares for burning.[9]

Yet it is equally correct to emphasise that, although in general an opponent of religious persecution, Erasmus never enunciated a doctrine of absolute and unqualified toleration.[10] It is difficult to avoid the conclusion that, when action by the secular arm *was* sanctioned, indeed occasionally urged, by Erasmus, it is when we enter that 'grey area', so crucially important to the sixteenth-century mind, where religious, social and political considerations overlap. Thus 'let them burn, by all means, those who fight the teaching of the articles of the faith or something of equal authority by the consensus of the Church. But it is not right that an error of any kind be punished by burning unless it is linked with sedition or any other crime which the laws punish by death . . .'[11] Aggressive heresy, in short, invited repression when it led to schism within the religious, and sedition within the socio-political order. Speculation at a theological level was one thing; action which might lead to a splintering of the Church on the one hand, and the dissolution of the body politic amidst the questioning of all its correlative social assumptions on the other, was a very different thing. The use so often by Erasmus in this context of the Latin term *seditio* is fully indicative.

While Erasmus was at one with both the Catholic Church and the Magisterial Protestants in voicing condemnation of the more extremist positions of some of the Anabaptists, and indeed approval of the action taken by secular authorities against the excesses of the 'kingdom' of Münster, he was himself subjected to the charge of fomenting doctrinal heresy. Nor were the accusations limited to that of an over-liberal attitude which might open the gate to heresy. Very many facets of his own doctrinal position were deemed to be dangerously unorthodox. The range and stature of his assailants have already in part been reviewed in the previous chapters. But before now adopting an approach to the type of charges of heresy made against him which is conceptually and analytically rather than geographically based, we must perforce mention a fountain-head of such outbursts which angered Erasmus as much as any – Louvain.

An array of Louvain adversaries figures prominently in Erasmus' correspondence and published works, and their attacks, prior to his move to Basel, came not from far-distant opponents but from those close at hand. Nicolaas Baechem ('Egmondanus') equated Erasmus' *New Testament* with the arrival of Antichrist, apparently without the tiresome necessity of having read or even seen it. His insistent association of Erasmus' name with that of Luther ensured that controversy continued until his death in 1526, despite attempts by Popes Adrian and Clement to silence him. Relations between Erasmus and Jacob Hoogstraten, evocatively entitled 'Inquisitor for Heretical Depravity' for Cologne, were more equivocal, but were certainly soured by attempts to imply a Lutheran connection. Jacobus Latomus (Jacques Masson), identified by Erasmus himself as his principal and most unrelenting opponent in Louvain, took issue with him because he advocated the allegedly dangerous teaching of Greek and Hebrew. Another opponent whom Erasmus never wearied of denouncing was Vincentius Theodoric, Dean of the Faculty of Theology at Louvain, while Frans Titelmans received a warning letter in the course of a brief but bitter controversy.[12] Finally, the ubiquitous Edward Lee at one point stirred his own spoonful into the controversial pot. Persistent attacks from the Louvain Faculty were checked only by short-lived efforts at a truce. Together with the fact that the first major burning of Luther's books took place at Louvain in October 1520, these assaults did much to bring about Erasmus' move to Basel.[13]

The accusations made against Erasmus may conveniently be related first to his alleged views on the authoritative sources of religious truth – the Scriptures, the Ancient Fathers and the Church itself – and secondly to his opinions about the nature of the Godhead, specifically on the divinity of Christ, on the Trinity and on the Virgin Mary. Thirdly they relate to the sacraments of the Christian Church, and finally to the nature and ceremonies of that Church itself. Ironically, while one modern interpretation would, far too sweepingly, make Erasmus a precursor of a concept of religion as a code of ethics and morality devoid of mandatory doctrinal beliefs,[14] many opponents put forward the general criticism that his questioning of so much that was taken for granted by the contemporary Church actively encouraged anti-clericalism, scepticism, and impiety – especially among the young!

Early indications of suspicion appeared in the friendly warnings of Dorp and the relatively civilised disagreement with Lefèvre d'Étaples. Then came the much harsher strictures from such as Lee, Zúñiga, Béda and the Louvain critics, accompanied later by the assaults of Alberto Pio, Sepulveda and Scaliger, as well as the accusations put forward at Valladolid. As early as July 1522 Erasmus had despatched to 'the Theologians of Louvain' a full refutation of Baechem's allegations of heresy regarding eating of meat, fasting, indulgences and vows.[15] But the Valladolid charges are perhaps of most use for our purpose. For they were taken up for extended and methodical refutation by their target himself in his *Apologia adversus articulos aliquot per monachos quosdam, in Hispaniis exhibitos*, published at Basel in 1529. In a work of some two hundred pages, a frighteningly long list of over twenty specific charges of heresy is refuted, point by point. Its arrangement of the charges does not precisely correspond with that outlined in our previous paragraph, but such an authoritative 'check-list' is very useful.

Before exploring the allegations in some detail we must concede that his closest friends could hardly acquit Erasmus of occasionally indiscreet phraseology. In writing to Lefèvre as early as 1517 he himself conceded using words 'which, if obstinately adhered to, would make me a heretic'.[16] Nor is there any doubt that some of the attacks directed from both sides of the religious divide caused him to revise or rephrase some of his scriptural notes.[17] It is also worth citing a general attack made by perhaps the most cosmopolitan of his many enemies, Edward Lee. In a very long letter dated 1 February 1520 a couple of incisive passages inform Erasmus that 'you tear up the roots and opinions of our forefathers and do not allow even the decrees of the Church to remain inviolate; you appear to others besides myself to give superficial support to the ravings of heretics; you claim a special jurisdiction over theology'. Even worse, Erasmus appears to 'take pains to have texts befouled by heretics spread through the world [and] even seem more than once to take up the cause of heretics'.[18] If this is a fair sample of the 'sources' type of attack, that of Zúñiga, the Spaniard domiciled in Italy, typifies the 'range of heresies' assault in his accusation, in a letter to Juan Vergara in May 1522, that 'you will find him openly siding with Arius, Apollinaris, and Jovinian, also with the Wycliffites and the Hussites and indeed with Luther himself'.[19]

Scattered through Erasmus' *Apologia* against the Spanish monks are several headings which charge him with teachings contrary to 'the authority of holy scripture', directed against the Fathers and Scholastic Doctors, not to mention the Popes and Councils. His own position with regard to the sources of religious truth was reviewed at some length in our fifth chapter and need hardly be repeated. But it is worth emphasing that what Erasmus saw as a genuine attempt to establish philological accuracy in scriptural and other texts, in order to reveal the true meaning of the Christian faith, was not only questioned by Dorp and Lefèvre upon his own ground, but was then condemned by Lee, Latomus and Zúñiga as an assault upon the essentials of that faith as established by the wisdom of the Church over fifteen hundred years.

The crux of his opponents' case was indeed this accusation of fundamental heresy on issues which lay at the heart of the established Catholic faith. As listed in the *Apologia* these are: that Erasmus' teachings are 'against the divinity, dignity and glory of Christ', against the sacrosanctity of the Trinity and the divinity of the Holy Spirit, and against the honour of the blessed Virgin Mary. These charges we find repeated in individual attacks upon Erasmus, as are also his refutations in his own writings.[20] As early as 1517, in a letter to Wolfgang Capito he replies to criticism of what he has written on the nature of Christ: for 'who would deny that the name of Christ can be taken to be a substance subsisting out of two natures? . . . If anyone had said that Christ was composite, where was the peril in that?'[21] In general, Erasmus' critics argued that by his over-emphasis upon the example set for his followers by the humanity of Christ, he had become guilty of derogation of the *divinity* of Christ. As for the charges that Erasmus was sceptical about the divinity of the Holy Spirit and hence, inevitably, about the sanctity of the Trinity, we need only to refer again to the outline of his views given in our fifth chapter. But a little more detail is needed on the allegation that he had displayed a lack of respect for the Virgin Mary. The point at issue has been clearly, even bluntly, put in one modern treatment of this topic: 'Was the angel's greeting amorous?' For Lee, among others, argued that Erasmus' choice of words in conveying the angel's greeting to Mary in Luke 1 was vulgarly indiscreet.[22]

Whatever one's opinion on the justice of such strictures, we should certainly not overlook that lengthy general section of the *Apologia* devoted to his alleged attacks 'against the sacraments of the Orthodox and Catholic faith', and also against certain ceremonies, regulations and institutions of the Church. First listed is the charge that Erasmus is 'against Baptism'. We have already considered his views on this sacrament at some length, especially in our discussion of Erasmus and the Radical Reformation, and in fact he himself here devotes more space to the allegation that he is also 'against confession', re-emphasising that he has never denied that it was instituted by Christ.[23] Alberto Pio also makes the charge that in questioning the sacrament of Penance as decreed by the Church, Erasmus *is* rejecting acceptance of confession as instituted by Christ. Perhaps conscious of being on thin ice, Erasmus contents himself with the assertion that the contemporary practice is not necessarily Christ's legacy.[24] Earlier, in a very long letter to Johann von Botzheim, Erasmus had felt obliged to take issue with the repeated slanders of Baechem – over his wine, in the lecture room, and in public sermons alike – which included the assertion that 'Erasmus denies penitence' through a false and heretical reading of Scripture.[25]

Only slightly more space is devoted by Erasmus – perhaps not surprisingly, considering the even thinner ice involved – to the crucial issue that he is allegedly 'against the Eucharist'. Yet, taking one by one the specific charges made by his opponents, which include that of sympathising with the Bohemian errors, he is at pains above all to stress that he would never dare to question the wisdom and the decrees of the Church.[26] But to many, both Catholic and Protestant, the offence had long been given. Both Standish and Béda had already attacked him on this subject, the latter provoking a specific reply,[27] while we have noted Leo Jud's claim (1526) that Erasmus had anticipated opinions on the *symbolic* nature of the Eucharist.[28] The disclaimer in his *Apologia* and his subsequent rewording of certain notes did not avail to free him from suspicion. The contemporary censure of the Faculty of Theology in Paris need not surprise us. But as late as 1547 Stephen Gardiner, the scales now apparently removed from his eyes in respect of the danger of Erasmus' influence, was to declare that

> the Sacrament of the Altar is so wantonly talked of by him that, as the world is now, the reading of him were the whole subversion. Erasmus in his latter days, hath for the Sacrament of the Altar spoken as reverently and said as much for confirmation of it as may be, and crieth out of them that would

> take him otherwise. But this is in the end, when age had tempered him. In his Paraphrasis, which he wrote in his wanton age, the words and terms were able to subvert, if it were possible, as Christ saith, the elect. [Indeed], if the Paraphrasis go abroad, people shall be learned to call the Sacrament of the Altar holy bread and a symbol . . .[29]

As for the strictures on his views about ordination and clerical celibacy, Erasmus had never sought to deny the status of the priesthood: indeed, it could well be argued that all his criticisms of clerical hypocrisy were concerned to indicate the gulf that existed between the ideal and the reality, and certainly *not* to devalue the ideal itself. Similarly in respect of matrimony, which he was accused of slighting, it was its place within the life of a Christian that engaged his attention, while his apparent willingness to sanction divorce bespeaks a recognition that no contractual bonds can sanctify a husk which has become devoid of all vital significance, or which, as in some 'arranged' marriages, had never contained any.[30] Interestingly, Gardiner's complaints included his concern that 'by the Paraphrasis all men maye marrye, busshoppes and prestes', and indeed that 'the keeping of a concubine ys called a light fault', although, cryptically, 'that were good for Lankeshire'[31] – notoriously backward!

Next, several issues may be related to the general charge that Erasmus was opposed to Church ceremonies and regulations. In an oft-quoted passage he himself declared that 'to some men I seem to condemn ceremonies, but first of all I do not speak of all ceremonies nor do I categorically condemn those I speak of; I only indicate the underlying dangers'.[32] His best-known discussion of the relationship between a range of Church regulations and the promotion of real Christian piety is in his *Letter on the prohibition of eating of meat*. But equally vivid is his depiction in a letter to Udalricius Zasius (1523) of 'certain Pharisees who, having no true religion themselves, defend the semblance of religion with titles and colours and the shapes of vestments . . . What would these men have left in the way of piety if you removed their vestments and their discrimination between different foods?' Regarding dietary regulation for the laity, 'actually on Good Friday one is permitted to get so drunk that one vomits or has a fit, while for a sick man in peril of his life to eat chicken is a capital offence'.[33] Such passages predictably evoked the wrath of Alberto Pio. But the epistle on the eating of meat was also specifically attacked from yet another quarter: Josse Clichtove in Paris, who had moved from an earlier position of respect for Lefèvre to one of conservatism nearer to that of Béda.

Finally, in our list of Spanish charges against Erasmus, the unsurprising assertion that he opposed the authority of the Pope and of Councils is in fact preceded in its location and in its length by the claim that Erasmus was 'against the Holy Inquisition of heretics'. This theme takes pride of place immediately after the very lengthy discussion of the divinity of Christ and of the Holy Trinity.[34] We need scarcely rehearse the material surveyed in Chapter Eight in order to underline both the provenance and the crucial significance of this charge: that by the laxity of his approach to so many questions of doctrinal orthodoxy, and by his many expressions of guarded sympathy with the erroneous positions into which even well-meaning heretics had strayed, Erasmus was opening the door to a flood of apostates and schismatics which would inevitably sweep away all the foundations of Holy Church were it not penned in and drained away by the rigours of the Inquisition. Beyond question, Erasmus had so many times voiced his disapproval of those repressive methods which were popularly associated with that institution, and had so often deplored the appeal to the secular arm to carry out 'unchristian' physical punishments – prison and the stake – as positively to invite this charge.

If we may correlate and assess overall within the widest context the charges listed, and ask where in essence Erasmus' 'heresy' consisted, it is tempting to suggest that it lay above all in his emphasis upon the innate potentialities of humanity working in co-operation with God's call of the spirit and following the concrete example of Christ himself, the Godhead come down to earth. Of this stance his many references to a restoration of innocence and virtue are indicative. He rejected any assertion either that salvation might be attained solely through compliance with a number of prescribed rites and ceremonies, or alternatively through a totally arbitrary, incomprehensible and predestined decision, with whose consequences Man's noblest strivings might of themselves play not the tiniest part. His objections thus rested upon a common and consistent base: his dislike for the '*Deus ex Machina*' and his yearning for a '*Deus in Spiritu*'. It was what we may describe as the correlative optimism of so many of Erasmus' views that angered Roman Catholic and predestinarian Protestant alike.

Such considerations are not unrelated to our second principal concern in this chapter: to balance against the cries of heresy the claim of some admirers of Erasmus that he should more properly be conceived of as a mediator, and also the notion that his prescriptions and influence suggested the emergence of a 'third church'. At first sight the forthright, almost abrasive way in which he expressed his strictures and enunciated his principles, together with the incessant evidence of wounded *amour propre* and of personal vendetta, do not conjure up a mediating image. Again, the Erasmus of the *De sarcienda* in 1533, by which time (in Gardiner's phrase) age had tempered him, sounds more conciliatory than the younger man whose utterances had so delighted the emergent Protestant Reformers between 1516 and 1522.

It is not without irony that Erasmus himself had often justified his combative responses to his critics on the very ground that they were guilty of subjecting his reforming and mediatory suggestions to distortions which seemed designed to exacerbate the very schism which he was striving to avoid. Most significantly, the principle of *adiaphora* which he so consistently advocated in respect of dogma, and the degree of tolerance which he never ceased to enjoin toward those guilty solely of doctrinal error, emerged and have remained as essential bases for any reconciliation of the disparate factions of the Christian Church. But sadly, while Erasmus' perceived requisite of that Church during the first decades of the century was *reform*, by 1533 this had surely become yoked with, or even superseded by, the clamant need for prevention of *schism*. Thus, while Protestants like Luther and Hutten accused Erasmus of being a timid time-server, a number of Catholics, ranging from Duke George of Saxony to members of the Papal Curia, depicted him as sitting on the fence instead of defending the Catholic Church.

Before pursuing the theme of 'Erasmus the Mediator' in a specifically religious context, it must also be observed that his desire for peace and concord also shines through his writings on political and social themes. We have already noted his belief in both the desirability and the feasibility of negotiation to secure international peace, together with his reluctance to concede that even a 'just' war may be fully integrated within a code of Christian conduct. True, he was ready to contemplate condign punishment for the 'criminal scum' of mercenary forces active in the Netherlands, but in general he insisted on the avoidance of conflict if humanly possible. It is interesting that his rejection of a 'just war' attracted hostile comment – alongside the charges of heresy – by that formidable trio, Zúñiga, Béda and Alberto Pio.[35] More modern critics, as we have already observed, have shifted ground from heresy to *naïveté* and lack of political realism. In the context of the internal political and social order, and in common with other Christian moralists of the early sixteenth century, Erasmus remained certain that only a mediatory spirit throughout society could render tolerable and justify the many glaring social differences and violent tensions.

Yet it is against the background of increasingly bitter religious discord during the last twenty years of his life that Erasmus' stature as a mediator must be assessed. From some of his earliest writings on the Lutheran issue to the *De sarcienda* of 1533, he never wavered in his appeals for a conciliatory approach, designed to ascertain and preserve the essential bases of the Christian faith as the bed-rock of unity.[36] Admittedly, these appeals must be seen alongside his own abrasive polemics such as *Spongia* or *Pseudevangelicos*, which could hardly be characterised as a turning of the other cheek. We may well suspect that Erasmus loved all Christians in the generality, while finding many of them to be most unlovable individuals. More seriously, his perpetual search for and commendation of *adiaphora* and his plea for maximum tolerance – *not* to be equated with that unrestricted liberty which so often led to licence – are surely the clearest distinguishing marks of a mediatory approach.

Before we cite passages in support of these contentions we must reiterate a caveat against attempting to portray Erasmus as a mere religious libertarian. What he demanded was not a tolerant *recognition* of schism, but rather the adoption of the tolerance necessary to *prevent* it. Indeed, one recent interpretation has attributed to Erasmus the suggestion of 'a kind of sceptical basis for remaining within the Catholic Church'[37] – a notion not dissimilar to our own suggestion in Chapter Five, so long as we are clear that scepticism does not imply cynicism but rather a supension of judgment in the absence of incontrovertible evidence and fully agreed criteria. Certainly, Erasmus was dubbed a sceptic both by Luther and his orthodox Catholic opponents, while in some respects he has been likened to Castellio. Yet it might be wiser to regard Erasmus' resort to 'doubtful scepticism' as his taking refuge when pushed too far in debate rather than as a positive canon of his thought. A recent identification of Erasmus as the originator of an '*ars dubitandi*',[38] whose works promoted the habit of religious doubt, has met with the compelling counter-suggestion that, if labels must be applied, '*modus quaerendi*' is surely preferable.[39]

Perhaps an equally intriguing field of debate concerns Erasmus' contribution – whether by design or inadvertently through those who read into his works what they themselves wished to see – to the cause of religious freedom.[40] Yet here again Erasmus' own identification of religious liberty needs careful evaluation. His purpose was to free the individual Christian soul in its search for God, and for a Christian way of life, from the distracting and clogging trammels of often meaningless and actually misleading external rituals: the emphasis was on *Christian* liberty not libertarianism. The object of rejecting many superstitious rote observances was not to undermine but rather to reinforce the ethical consequences of Christ's teaching and example. Nor was Erasmus ever willing to grant to human whim the right obdurately to reject the combined authority of Church and Scripture.

Admittedly, writing in 1526 to Johann Fabri, minister to Archduke Ferdinand, he conceded the possibility that 'it would be better to secure that in cities where the evil has increased, both parties keep to their quarters and everyone be left to his conscience until time brings the opportunity of some agreement'. But the last phrase is crucial: for in the meantime any sedition must be punished and the evils which have helped produce this position should be corrected, pending a general synod. A letter in August 1530 addressed to Campeggio – which, though perhaps undelivered was eagerly pirated and printed – is even more pessimistic. Reviewing the spread of disorder and of sects in a chain of evil from Frisia to Switzerland, Erasmus warns the Emperor, of himself 'inclined toward peace, clemency, and tranquillity', lest his piety lead to an over-hasty enforcement of papal edicts. Admittedly, 'it is to be feared lest this tumult tends to the total subversion of the Church'. Yet the need for peace supersedes what the wickedness of the sects clearly merits. Connivance at their toleration, as in Bohemia, is an evil less than that of war.[41] Again, Preserved Smith cites Erasmus' memorandum in reply to Basel's Town Council in 1525 as of supreme importance in the history of liberty in that 'it actually proposed, for the first time, a plan to allow for differences of religious practices, and freedom for arguing opposite opinions, within the same territory'.[42] Erasmus' irenicism, and that of like-minded individuals on either side of the sadly widening divide, consisted of a search for such agreement about the basic realities of the Christian faith which would lead to genuine religious concord. Within this context, we must remind ourselves that he died in 1536. With hindsight, many would argue that the Rubicon had by that date been crossed and all bridges burnt, yet this could have been by no means clear at the time. The contention of one scholar that 'Christian humanism appears to be diametrically opposed to the spirit of the Reformation'[43] begs many questions. For surely the latter may not be simply equated with the intransigence of Luther and Calvin. We have indeed sought to make it clear that Christian humanism formed a vital ingredient of the Reformation. This is surely exemplified by the case of Melanchthon and also by that of Capito, who, although regarded by Erasmus as an apostate from his cause, published a German translation of *On Mending the Peace of the Church*.

De sarcienda has been discerned by more than one historian as effectively Erasmus' last will and testament.[44] Published in 1533, and only a couple of years before the failure of French negotiations approved by Pope Paul III ruined yet one more hope of concord, the work is notable not so much for new ideas as for the expression of residual hope, much tempered by sadness at the spectacle of an age most fertile of sects. The early pages are distinguished by a repetition of Erasmus' social ideals, but also and more particularly by a repeated emphasis upon the need for continued membership of the Church. Typically, he later derides those who intemperately shout 'Heresy! To the flames!' and misconstrue harmless assertions, preferring destruction to reconciliation. Thereafter, the *desiderata* of concord are reviewed.[45]

Here one cannot fail to notice what may be termed a toning down or at least a careful rephrasing of some of his own earlier assertions. Thus, those who rage against the images of saints have been somewhat immoderate. Admittedly, the superstitious element must be eliminated; 'but do not disturb those who, short of superstition, revere images' for love of what they represent. Again, concerning the question of whether 'sacramental confession was instituted by Christ himself . . . our principal concern should be to detest what is admitted to, and return to our pristine state'. He still suggests some reduction in the present 'plethora of feast days' and is willing to keep an open mind in respect of fasting and dietary regulations. In such areas, the concept of *adiaphora* is clearly dominant.[46]

A similar spirit is manifest in Erasmus' discussion of the two crucial issues of free will and the Eucharist. While the ideas expressed are in no way new in his writing, his summation on the first of these is surely a masterpiece of compromise:

> Concerning *freedom of the will*, argument is truly more thorny than fruitful. If anything may be sought for here, let it be soberly discussed in theologians' debates. Meanwhile it is enough to agree among ourselves that man of his own power can do nothing, and if he can accomplish anything, all such is owed to grace . . . Let us agree that most must be attributed to faith, provided that we acknowledge that this is a special gift of the Holy Spirit, and that it is more widely accessible than the ordinary person believes . . . Let us vouchsafe that we are justified by faith, that is, that believers' hearts are purified, provided we admit the necessary works of love as accompanying salvation. Nor indeed can true faith be inoperative, since it is the fount and seed-bed of all good works.[47]

'As to the Mass, if any superstition or vulgarity had crept in, it is reasonable to correct it. Why the Mass itself should be so execrated I do not see,' although the number of 'special Masses' is too great. As to its nature and meaning, certain problems should be set aside as matters of opinion pending a Synod. Admittedly, 'Christ having once died, will die no more, but that one Sacrifice is renewed daily in sacred rites, so long as we draw from that inexhaustible spring a grace continually new for us'. As for participation in communion in the Mass, this was the way in which it was instituted by Christ and formerly was customarily observed. Yet again, 'if Christ is wholly present in the Eucharist, why should it not be adored?' Divergences of opinion persist, but those who are not clear about it should surely acquiesce in what the Church has handed down, namely, 'that the body and blood of the Lord are truly there, unquestionably living', and leave the detail to a Synod.[48] It could well be argued that here Erasmus is not saying anything that he has not said before; yet his critics might plausibly urge that whereas in his younger days he had been eager to pose questions, he now seems more concerned to postpone answers!

A concluding passage accords praise to Charles V, Ferdinand I, Francis I, Henry VIII and Pope Clement VII: all poised to pursue political and religious peace.[49] Perhaps this should not too readily be dismissed as evidence of utter lack of realism. Not one of those named – even if they were motivated primarily by a recognition of the baleful political and social implications of religious schism – had as yet quite written off all hope of peaceful concurrence. Even Henry VIII, not everyone's embodiment of Erasmian sweetness and light, was to appeal for 'perfect love and concord' in his well-known speech to Parliament in December 1545, adjuring its members to consider 'what love and charity is amongst you, when the one calleth the other, Heretic and Anabaptist, and he calleth him again Papist, Hypocrite and Pharisee'.[50] Moreover, many of the most prominent ministers of the monarchs listed, some of whom we encountered in the previous chapters, cherished Erasmian ideals of irenical negotiation. During what has been discerned as 'the humanist attempt at religious conciliation' the principles advocated by Erasmus were, as we have seen, active in several German courts, not only in the 1530s from the Diet of Augsburg onward but also in the efforts put into religious colloquies after 1540. Indeed, within the ranks of the Catholic negotiators acting on behalf of the Pope, both at such conferences and at the Council of Trent itself, were several Erasmians, notable by reason of their intellectual and social standing.[51]

There remain for discussion the issues of Erasmus and the 'Third Church', and 'Erasmus the Modernist'. The first of these relates to a case which has been entertained by a very few twentieth-century historians and roundly rejected by most of their peers. The notion that Erasmus pointed the way, however inadvertently, to a *third* Church – that is, non-papal or perhaps non-Roman, but equally clearly non-Protestant, and in effect forestalling the Protestant schism by transforming the existing Church – has been floated most notably by the distinguished scholar Renaudet.[52] To be fair, no one would contend that Erasmus consciously envisaged, much less sought to establish, a separate 'third' Church; indeed, he was upon occasion at some pains to disavow the existence of any 'Erasmian party' or of identifiable 'Erasmians'. Yet here again we must beware of imposing upon the 1530s, as if by then inevitable, those ecclesiastical battle-lines which had become all-too-well entrenched by the end of the century. Neither the continuance of the Roman Church in its existent form, nor the secession and permanent establishment of so many disparate Protestant Churches can have appeared as ineluctably determined at that time.

Indeed it is significant that *contemporary* evidence of a belief that Erasmus' teaching and influence would lead at least to a re-orientation of ecclesiastical development may be culled from very different sources, some favourable and one most hostile. First in point of time, and also in respect of the stature of the correspondent involved, is a letter from no less a personality than Gattinara. One very recent assessment interprets a crucial passage therein as presenting Gattinara's diagnosis of the *Christiana respublica* as fragmented into Romanists, Erasmians, and Lutherans, before identifying himself with the second of these as proffering the only solution to current ills. A close reading of the text of the letter, dated from Granada 1 October 1526 and in fact quite short, confirms this impression. Most certainly, of the three parties into which the Christian *respublica* has been torn by the tempest, infinitely preferable in Gattinara's opinion either to that of the Roman Pontiff, with deaf ears and blind eyes, or to that into which the Lutherans have got their teeth, is the one which seeks only the glory of God and the public well-being.[53]

Alongside this testimony from within the Imperial court in Spain we may now set that expressed by Julius Pflug, writing from Leipzig on 12 May 1531. To Erasmus, he urges, are turned the eyes of all who hope for peace. He must use all the authority which immortal God has given him to persuade our princes that, if our religious controversies are to be removed, which God himself would applaud, then the Church must be willing to relax and to moderate merely human laws and institutions. If this can be done, then probably those on the other side who do not abhor Christian concord, such as Melanchthon, may reciprocate.[54] To this Erasmus replied at some length on 20 August, in a letter containing his well-known allusion to an age in which one might think that six hundred Furies had rushed out of Hell, and also his opinion that had Adrian occupied Peter's throne for ten years Rome might have been purified. He reiterates his views on the need of Church reform, especially for a better clergy, in default of which the people wander in different paths like scattered sheep without a shepherd, and for 'one hundred and fifty men of saintly life and singular erudition' to settle disputed doctrines. He nevertheless believes that opinions need not in any way be made articles of faith. Yet his estimates of any mediating influence which he might himself exert, and indeed the prospects for mediation in general, are pessimistic. Alas for Melanchthon's efforts at Augsburg; Pflug knows what came of it. The whole epistle bespeaks the near-despairing apostle of mediation and concord, but it gives no hint whatever of any wish for a 'third Church'.[55]

A year or so later the German humanist theologian, Georg Witzel, wrote two letters to Erasmus, alas unanswered, in which he still expressed the hope of achieving the unity of a reformed Church through an ecumenical council. In September 1532, having voiced his intense admiration of Erasmus, Witzel urges continuance of his struggle to fend off schismatics on the one side and 'sophists' on the other in order to restore the old theology. In March of the following year Witzel assures him that neither Luther nor 'the Sophists' will be listened to, but that it is Erasmus and his like who will be heard by those who favour no particular faction, but seek Christianity with a sincere spirit.[56] Testimony from a very different source is cited by Erasmus himself in a letter to John Choler on 19 February 1534. Deploring, typically, that 'the Franciscan reign flourishes', he alludes to one of that Order, Nicolaus Herborn, as having published in Antwerp a work which includes the assertion that 'Luther has drawn to himself a large part of the Church; no less have Zwingli and Oecolampadius; most of all, Erasmus. And [Herborn] adds that it would be well if that man had never been born.'[57]

While varied in their provenance, such extracts suffice to demonstrate that, whatever his own protestations to the contrary, a specifically Erasmian approach to the problem of Church reform was for long identified by friend and foe alike. Admittedly what his supporters saw as conducive to genuine concord and unity was identified by his detractors as yet another ingredient of schism. Yet it is, surely, stretching the evidence to read into Erasmus' undoubted wish for real reform – as against schism and religious revolution – any concept of a Third Church. While never ceasing to long for the emergence of a *better* Church, Erasmus himself always believed that this could only take place with the agreement of the Holy See, in Rome itself amidst an ambience reflecting his values rather than those of Aleander. Sadly, this was rendered increasingly improbable by the hardening of Roman intransigence on the one hand and of narrowly doctrinal certainty within each Protestant Church on the other. The despatch, in May 1534, of his *De sarcienda* – which he had dedicated to Julius Pflug – to Cardinal Cajetan, together with a lost letter to the Pope, is totally symbolic of his lingering but waning hopes.[58] His combination of a fervent wish for peace-keeping mediation with a genuine percipience regarding future developments is often impressive. He has been credited with foreseeing that the outcome of the Diet of Worms would lead inevitably to the Council of Trent,[59] while we have noted earlier his suggestion of precisely that type of compromise settlement which, after the bloodshed of religious war, was ultimately to be conceded at Augsburg in 1555. But another modern admirer is saddened by the fact that, both at Worms in 1521 and at the Diet of Augsburg in 1530, 'this born mediator' failed to appear because he was not prepared to hazard his person for his faith.[60]

The name of the French historian Augustin Renaudet is also linked with the contention that 'Erasmian modernism' or even 'Erasmian agnosticism' sought to establish an 'evangelism without dogma and a religion purely of the spirit'. The contention is that, not content with his destruction of a Judaic system of prescribed dogmas and obligatory observances, Erasmus went on to become a stranger to all doctrinal rigour, in his realisation that dogma was powerless to define that which is essentially indefinable.[61] This assertion, which antedated and indeed went far beyond the thesis that Erasmian philosophy represented a Major, as distinct from a narrowly doctrinal Minor Reformation, need hardly detain us for long. It can surely glean only the most tenuous support from a reading of the sources. Erasmus sought indeed a religion of the spirit: but it was always and insistently the spirit of Christianity,[62] impelled by the example of Christ himself within this world, and sealed by the promise of eternal salvation through the grace of God in the hereafter. Erasmus the Mediator sought to establish and to purify – not to erode – the fundamental tenets of the Christian faith.[63] After all, the *Enchiridion militis Christiani* is much more than an exposition of a code of ethics!

CONCLUSION: THE LEGACY OF ERASMUS

The dissemination of Erasmus' writings and influence throughout Western Christendom is enormously impressive. Any tendency to attribute this to the fact that his works and letters were all written in the *lingua franca* of the age must be counter-balanced by the massive evidence of translation into the vernaculars. 'Little Bilney', the English Protestant martyr, was indeed at first 'allured rather by the Latin', but to him as to so many others it was the content which assumed supreme importance. Looking back on the European expansion of Erasmian ideas, we now attempt a few generalisations about the varying depth and duration of this impact.

Of those regions in which Erasmus spent a significant proportion of his life – his native Low Countries, France, the Rhineland, south Germany and England – a fellow-Dutchman has recently asserted that 'only in the England of Henry VIII did Erasmianism win a dominating position'.[1] Most certainly, its moderation exactly coincided with the *via media* aspirations both of the political nation and more crudely of the monarch himself. Nevertheless, in the very different milieu of the Netherlands, this aspect of Erasmianism has also been credited with contributing a significant thread to some of the diverse doctrinal confessions, including Mennonite Anabaptism. Later on it re-emerged in the shape of 'liberal' Arminianism within the Calvinist ranks. Further up the Rhine, the tendency to identify a 'Germanisation' of Erasmus indicates not only an enthusiastic reception of his works and teachings in their own right, but also a wish in some quarters to capture him for the nationalist and anti-Roman cause. Elsewhere indeed similar efforts were made to enlist him for emerging Protestantism; but only in Germany did his resolute resistance evoke a backlash of such savage criticism as almost to cast him in the role of renegade.

As for France, which we might of course include alongside Spain and Italy within a superficial category of the three 'Romance' nations, we encounter widely disparate opinions as to the formative impact upon

Erasmus of his years in Paris. The reception in France of his ideas came later through his publications and his epistolatory contacts with scholars such as Lefèvre d'Étaples. Thereafter, the extent, the depth, and the duration of Erasmian influence were all diminished by the polarisation of religion between intransigent Catholicism and militant Calvinism. The more immediate influence on England developed before the mid-century when Erasmianism fed into a 'middle-way' Church, exercising a far deeper religious influence than it did in France among the moderate spirits, the 'politiques' of the French Wars of Religion. At all events, the cynical observation of Henry IV that Paris was well worth a Mass could hardly be associated with any Erasmian principle!

Turning to Spain and Italy, the first was never visited by Erasmus, while in the case of the second, his sojourn there influenced his scholarship and his evaluation of the Papacy, but exerted little influence upon his developing religious thought. Yet both countries invite intriguing case-studies of the varying impacts of Erasmian ideology upon both politico-religious developments and of the existence of 'reception areas' for his works and influence. In Spain, the reformist activities of both Church and monarchy had preceded and prepared for Erasmianism by creating a genuinely indigenous movement for ecclesiastical reform and scriptural scholarship. These native influences, together with the Alumbradist movement, found in Erasmus a notable ally and led to the brief but vivid flowering of Spanish Erasmianism. But the quite literal removal, at a crucial stage, of monarchical protection, and the attribution of heresy both to the Alumbrados and to incipient Lutheranism – with which Erasmus could plausibly be bracketed – produced an equally rapid decline and left a meagre legacy.

Italy, where we noted the depressingly rapid transition from *Erasmus noster* to *Erasmo luterano*, presents a different case, and suggests some infuriating 'might-have-beens'. Although specifically anti-Erasmian elements, vividly personified by Aleander,[2] were present from the outset, an equally representative segment of the ecclesiastical establishment – and that at the highest level – both recognised the clamant need for Church reform and saw Erasmus as a cogent advocate. The conjecture as to what might have happened during the tenure of an even moderately reformist Pope is not ours but that of Erasmus himself in his oft-quoted reference to the death of Adrian.[3] The report of the Council of Cardinals appointed to consider reform, made in 1538, has not unjustly been regarded as a belated and restricted Erasmian programme. Doubtless one should also recall that, with his tendency to perch upon an adiaphoral fence, Erasmus never dismounted to deliver a categorical attack upon the doctrines of the Catholic Church. Yet in the last analysis, despite the survival of irenic tendencies for longer with Italian than with Spanish ecclesiastics, the Counter-Reformation ultimately marked the triumph of an anti-Erasmian ethos.

As to Erasmus' impact on certain parts of East-Central Europe – Austria, Bohemia, Hungary and Poland – our information precludes any firm verdict upon its long-term significance. In the case of Switzerland it has been felt realistic to subsume the influence of Erasmus within a Zwinglian rather than in a purportedly geographical context. Indeed, in the context of the extent and nature of the territorial influence of Erasmus, one crucially important point must be made. Despite his extensive fame, at no time did Erasmus command any strong politico-religious bases upon which his reformist principles could have been translated into actualities. Some of his admirers were sectarians, who simply misunderstood his liberalism. Others whom we have listed were scholars, office-holders, aristocrats and prelates: in general they were conservative people, widely dispersed across the map of Europe. They had much to lose by becoming social and religious visionaries, or even by creating pressure groups in order to spiritualise the Church along the lines of the *Enchiridion*. In so far as the Reformation may be equated with the foundation of 'territorial' churches, based in part upon national feelings, Erasmus had no part therein.

By contrast, Martin Luther not only arose on a surge of German nationalist emotion, but also achieved a fairly strong territorial base in central and northern Germany, where he created a new church under the protection of rulers led by the Electors of Saxony. He did not however create the historical forces which had carried him into this situation and which are well-documented across the previous three centuries of German history. These ranged from such conflicts between Empire and Papacy as the Investiture Contest, the Conciliar Movement, and criticism of the popes by the Imperial Diet, to the nearby Hussite revolution in Bohemia. There thus developed a broad antipathy between Central Europe and Italy. At a popular level, German prophets and propagandists[4] conveyed the picture of simple, good-hearted Germans, bamboozled by sponging, supercilious Italians and victimised by the financial demands of the Papacy.

Erasmus was a level-headed Dutchman, never carried away by such heavy passions, yet we detected more than a trace of them when we observed his sometimes hostile emotions both in Venice and in Rome. A decade later Luther exploited this factor to the full in denouncing the greedy and doctrinally suspect sale of indulgences. His cause was to flourish, helped by German antipathy against the Spanish and Burgundian descent of the young Charles V, Holy Roman Emperor from 1519, and by his many distractions elsewhere. Confusion became more confounded throughout the 1520s, Habsburg–Papal rivalry leading to the brutal Sack of Rome itself by the German troops of Charles, many of them now Lutherans! Amid this nightmare of political and religious confusion, while Erasmus still figured as a councillor of the Emperor, Luther was rapidly building up a separate church upon Saxon territory. In later decades the Lutheran Church was to expand from its Saxon base over much of central and northern Germany, not stopping there. Adopted by Denmark, Norway, Sweden and Finland, it meanwhile exercised strong effects upon England.

Of course the nationalist factor to which we allude was not confined to the Lutheran sphere of influence: Zwingli's Protestantism was based in part upon a conscious appeal to Swiss national feeling. Yet nowhere did it assist the Erasmian cause as such. Indeed we have noted that at least one strand of anti-Erasmian propaganda in Italy deliberately sought to harness protective national sentiment against Erasmus. He did not found, and did not seek to found, a territorial or 'Erasmian' church. This limitation detracts little from his seminal importance. For his influence is to be found *within* the development of certain churches rather than in their *establishment*, though sadly the universal Catholic Church to which he always clung was for a while to reject him. To these issues we now turn.

In attempting to assess Erasmian factors in the development of Christianity in early modern Europe, one should first recall what he set himself to do. Erasmus sought to rediscover the Christ of the Gospels, to clarify and then expound the written record of Christ's message. This done, by means of a rigorous and scholarly approach to the Scriptures themselves, he was then prepared to evaluate Church and society not only in terms of doctrinal, ritual and organisational issues, but also in those of individual Christian conduct. He never attacked the Catholic Church as such, nor in the last resort did he seek deliberately to undermine the unique position of the Papacy. His many real or apparent attacks on certain rituals may in general be related to abuses therewith associated, and in particular to the contention that mechanical observances served to obscure rather than to further the Christian message. Similar criteria were applied to some teachings of the early sixteenth-century Church concerning its doctrines and its sacraments. No 'Third Church', in institutional terms, ever existed in Erasmus' mind. But he sought a way forward which eschewed both Protestant brashness and innovation on the one hand and Roman obduracy in unscriptural error on the other. This process, he believed, demanded a clear re-establishment of the principles of early Christianity.

Such notions of rediscovery and re-establishment are of crucial importance. Erasmus saw his first task as the re-affirmation of the essential Christian message.[5] Again, he envisaged that message as designed to re-establish and to nurture those original and innate aspects of human character which were pleasing to the Godhead. Herein lies the key to his readiness ever to identify values and virtues within pre-Christian teachings and philosophy which were in themselves both laudable and conformable to Christian doctrine. Herein also lies the explanation of his yearning to evolve a concept of grace which would leave room for some contribution, however small, to be made by conscious human effort, and which would also yield unmistakable fruits in terms of human conduct. If any one brief passage of Scripture encapsulates Erasmus' grasp of the Christian message, it may well be found in the Epistle of Paul to Titus,[6] in those verses which declare that

> the grace of God that bringeth salvation hath appeared to all men; Teaching us that, denying ungodliness and worldly lusts, we should live soberly, righteously, and godly, in this present world; Looking for that blessed hope, and the glorious appearing of the great God and our Saviour Jesus Christ; Who gave himself for us, that he might redeem us from all iniquity, and purify unto himself a peculiar people, zealous of good works.

Alongside such a yardstick, we need hardly labour the rationale of Erasmus' rejection of the rigours of predestination, of the imputation of utter and total depravity, and of the denial of any validity to good works as putative evidence of salvation. Hence his revulsion against so much of the Protestant Reformation.

Yet if, essaying a different approach, we seek to identify those things in Erasmus which attracted so many of the Protestant Reformers and made them so determined to claim him, willy-nilly, for their cause, what would these be? Still to be accorded primacy of place stands his biblicism, closely allied with the Christocentricity of his theology. More particularly, his attacks upon what he saw as ritual and sacramental misrepresentations and abuses endeared him at one stage to Luther and to Zwingli, while his vision of the social prescriptions of Christianity seems most closely reflected in Bucer. His emphasis upon the spiritual significance of the Eucharist was seized upon by a wide range of Protestants, whose opponents of course lumped them all together as 'Sacramentaries'. His stress upon the implications for fellowship in sacramental participation was to endure above all in the Reformed Churches. Erasmus' concession of a generous range of doctrinal *adiaphora* and even of tolerance to well-meaning left-wingers, together with his insistence on the inescapable corollaries of conversion in terms of Christian conduct, these endeared him to very many of the Anabaptists. An exaggerated interpretation of certain of his utterances made him a source of comfort even to anti-Trinitarians, while the combination of his insistence upon the essential spirituality of the Christian faith with his adiaphoristic doctrinal tendencies proved particularly attractive to such as Castellio, who asserted what seemed almost a right to heresy.

At this point we may hardly avoid discussing the long-term importance of Erasmus for that Catholic Church which he so steadfastly refused either to condemn or to abandon. It is much too fanciful to suggest that this Church, had it but adopted and implemented Erasmian reforms in time, would successfully have preserved the ecclesiastical unity of Western Christendom in face of the assaults of Luther, Zwingli and Calvin. For by the middle decades of the sixteenth century far too many political and national forces stood all too ready to adopt and exploit the Protestant message – indisputably spiritual as it was in itself – for a variety of motives. Yet such a Church might just conceivably have become both more willing and more able to effect the reconciliation, or at least perhaps an irenic toleration, for which significant religious and political leaders continued to hope until much of Europe was plunged into the 'Wars of Religion'. As late as the turn of the present century an eminent Dutch Calvinist theologian contemplated with retrospective horror the possibility that the spirit of a 1540s 'Interim' might well 'have succeeded, by way of a Romanized Protestantism, in reducing Northern Europe again to the sway of the old Hierarchy', had not the star of Calvinism suddenly arisen.[7]

Dismissing such thoughts as hopeless dreams, are we left with any positive Erasmian legacy within the Catholic Church? For after devoting several chapters to relationships between Erasmus and the emergent Protestant 'sects', we may hardly conclude without considering his place in the eyes of the Catholic Church, at least in the context of developments up to the close of the Council of Trent in 1563. We may recall his notorious remark that he would perforce put up with that Church for want of a better, and that in turn it would have to put up with him.[8] Did its attitudes in fact 'improve' in an Erasmian sense, and how far did it continue to recognise its somewhat ambivalent defender? These questions may appropriately be related to the issues on which Erasmus had been at once a proponent of reform and a centre of controversy: reform of the clergy; the position and the quality of the Papacy; the primacy of Scripture in the Church's teaching; ritual and doctrine, most notably problems concerning the Mass and the definitions of grace and justification. Yet transcending such particular themes, many historians would give pride of place to the fate of Erasmian irenicism, confronted by the shift of emphasis within the Church itself from Catholic Reform to Counter-Reformation.

Erasmus' appeals for lenient treatment of 'heresy', in his never abandoned though increasingly tenuous hope of an irenic reconciliation, which should stretch without tearing for ever the seamless robe of Church unity, had been addressed at least as often to princes and to statesmen as to ecclesiastics. Fittingly then, perhaps the last credible, if in the event illusory, attempt at reunion took place under the auspices of the Emperor Charles, in the form of the Colloquy of Regensburg or Ratisbon, alongside the Imperial Diet of 1541. Indeed, Nicolas Granvella, Imperial minister and one of the presidents of the discussions, has been identified as quite Erasmian in his principles and objectives and as the guiding influence. Participants with pacific inclinations included, most notably, Melanchthon and Bucer from the Protestant ranks, and Julius Pflug, now Bishop of Naumburg, and Cardinal Gasparo Contarini of Venice, who had headed the *Consilium de emendenda ecclesia* in 1536, among the Catholics. Initially, the agreements about original sin and free will seem most impressive. So does the adoption of a formula on 'double justification' closely resembling Erasmus' position in his *De sarcienda* of 1533, which combined total dependence on grace with an equal emphasis on its fruits in works of charity. But the intransigence of both political elements and doctrinal hard-liners on either side vitiated any reasonable prospect of success. Contarini himself would not yield on transubstantiation, nor would the Protestants accept the *necessity* of Confession, while the Papacy all too readily administered the *coup de grâce*. Alike symbolic are the failure of the Colloquy of Regensburg and the death soon afterward of Contarini himself, a figure already considered suspect by the many conservatives.

Thereafter, the cause of Catholic Reform, though never abandoned, became increasingly subsumed within a Counter-Reformation[9] comprising the militantly orientated Jesuit Order, the expanded Inquisition, and the Index of Prohibited Books. The central drama was played out in three acts: the sessions of the Council of Trent in 1545–49, 1551–52, and 1562–63. Yet some of the principles of Erasmian reform did not sink rapidly or without trace. More than one historian has alluded to a generation of Catholics, among both ecclesiastics and statesmen, who saw themselves as the heirs of Erasmus. These included a number of reforming bishops both from Italy and among the Habsburg entourage, while even as late as the final session of the Council the Cardinal of Lorraine and the Emperor Ferdinand I himself both submitted an unrepentantly Erasmian list of desirable reforms. Many of these were blocked by the obdurately intransigent Papacy as representing doctrinal innovation; yet clear signs of the survival, or even triumph, of certain aspects of the Erasmian programme are not far to seek. Some of the new and 'reforming' Religious Orders, often regarded as vigorous early signs of Catholic Reformation, shifted their emphasis away from cloistered seclusion, while yet retaining saintliness of life and austerity of conduct. Such Orders moved out into a socially conscious performance of missionary, charitable and educational work. Of these, the Capuchins – established in about 1528–9 and confirmed in the year of Erasmus' death – have been described as the chief Italian agents in keeping the masses loyal to the Church. Yet their Vicar General, Bernardino Ochino, fled the country in about 1541, rightly suspected of heterodox views. As for empathy between Erasmus and Ignatius Loyola, founder of the most famous instrument of the Counter-Reformation, divergent opinions are expressed; yet a distinction is justly made between those spiritual forces which led to the genesis of the Jesuit Order, and the direction later imposed on its activities by papal edict. In respect of the standards of the secular clergy, while the line was held prohibiting matrimony, it may well be that no decrees of the Council of Trent were to produce more decisive effects than those enforcing residence and enacting the establishment in each diocese of a seminary for the training of priests. Moreover, Catholic educators used Erasmian methods and texts (if often expurgated) in an effort to improve the religious knowledge of the laity, so that in this respect the aftermath of Trent did not entail total failure.

On other issues, and indeed on the central question concerning the devotional ethos of the Church, no realistic assessment can fail to conclude that Trent was a major defeat for the Erasmian cause. Among the Popes themselves, Paul III (1534–49) was a papal Janus, standing between Renaissance and Counter-Reformation: admittedly, having set up the Commission which produced the recommendations for reform in 1537, he issued the Bull which led to the Council of Trent. Yet in 1542 he also set up the Holy Office or Inquisition. This was immediately implemented by Caraffa who, as Paul IV (1556–59) was to display fanatical zeal in the enforcement of values from which Erasmus would have recoiled. Indeed the establishment of an Inquisition in Italy has been seen as a major landmark in the transition from Erasmian reformism to a dual policy of reform plus repression. Under Paul IV, such leaders of Catholic reform as Morone and Pole, two of the three legates who opened the Council of Trent in 1542 – while Pole had been considered a powerful candidate for the Papal throne in 1549 – found themselves under attack. Apart from more recent flirtations with concessions, they, like Contarini, had shown some sympathy with the Italian evangelism associated in the 1530s with the Erasmian Juan de Valdés! The climax arrived when in 1559 the Index Librorum Prohibitorum included all the works of Erasmus within a frighteningly comprehensive list; five years later even the revised Index of Pius IV still thought him profoundly suspect.

In retrospect, the 1550s had marked a watershed not only in regard to antagonism toward Erasmus, but also for any prospects of liturgical and doctrinal reform together with adiaphoristic compromise. By the 1560s the last Erasmian generation had passed away. During the last session of Trent in 1562–63, the proposals of the Cardinal of Lorraine for the permission of clerical marriage, the abolition of superstitious observances, and a wider use of the vernacular, together with the demands of the Emperor Ferdinand for recognition of a married clergy and of communion in both kinds, had no hope of success. Effectively, the relentless pressure of the Spaniards for ecclesiastical reform was only equalled in its success by their determined resistance to all innovation in matters of ritual and of doctrine. Moreover, within Italy itself – and no fewer than 189 of the 255 prelates who signed the Council's decrees were Italian – *Erasmo luterano* had long displaced *Erasmus noster* as the prototype associated with 'Catholic Reform'. Thus, of Erasmian emphases, any appeal to Scripture as a sole authority was totally constrained by insistence that the Church alone had the right of interpretation. Erasmian opinions on orginal sin and on the sacraments were considered suspect, while one canon of the Council of Trent has been seen as avowedly anti-Erasmian in its condemnation of what were taken to be his neo-Anabaptist views on the significance and implications of the sacrament of Baptism. The seven sacraments were confirmed, and on the test-case of the Mass communion for the laity in one kind only and the doctrine of Transubstantiation were both upheld. Yet in respect of justification, the doctrine as defined in 1547, described as settling midway between the declared errors of Pelagianism on the one hand and of Lutheran solifidianism on the other, seems very close to the position of Erasmus, even though Pole apparently considered it insufficiently scriptural. All in all, Trent was not only a declaration of war upon Protestant heresies, but also a defeat for the humanist neo-Pelagianism of Erasmus and for his *philosophia Christi* which avoided overmuch dogmatic definition, as well as a victory for the medieval concept of the priesthood.

Any attempt to trace the fortunes of Erasmian ideas and influence through the centuries which followed would clearly require another book. More accurately, Bruce Mansfield's admirable study of changing *Interpretations of Erasmus* has recently extended to a second volume.[10] Yet before closing it seems desirable at least to indicate those general aspects of Erasmus' thinking which have stood the test of time. True, one must distinguish between those commentators who have sought to project back upon Erasmus their own particular amalgam of ethics and religion, and those others who seem genuinely to reflect what he actually taught and believed. Yet in both cases, selection of facets of his thought for comment has tended to reflect contemporary preoccupations. It is interesting to encounter allusions to his pacifism in the literature of the conflicts of mid-seventeenth-century England. His emphasis upon international negotiation as the way to peace found a ready welcome in the 'peace movements' of the early decades of the present century. Not surprisingly, Erasmus' insistence on the moral implications of Christ's teaching for Man's social conduct, together with his adiaphoric approach to dogma, has been seized upon by those who would make him a precursor of the eighteenth-century *philosophes*.[11] But this will not do, especially in the light of the scepticism about all revealed religion which was so often a feature of their thought. Erasmus sought to purify Christian teaching, not to erode its base. He did not wish to replace the salvation offered by Christ with a simple moral code.

An Erasmian insistence also upon the duty of the Christian to make direct pronouncements in the social, political and international sphere has resurfaced most strikingly – and sometimes provocatively – in the later decades of the twentieth century. Again, the current enthusiasm for an ecumenical approach to Christianity has been seen as in harmony with the tolerant approach of Erasmus to doctrinal differences, together with his realisation that a 'unity in diversity' might be preferable to the threat of total disintegration. Indeed his expression of the fear that pharisaism may be succeeded by paganism now seems to be uncomfortably relevant. Erasmus was ahead of his time when, as a professing Christian, he was ready to concede that certain aspects of Old Testament religion had been 'given us for a time'. Taken together with his admiration for some features of pre-Christian philosophy, and his abhorrence of what he referred to as 'Judaic' rigidities, this might be interpreted as opening the door to modern concepts of *evolving* religious beliefs and practices. But his own insistence upon a fundamental bedrock of the Christian faith never faltered. No indiscriminate bible-thumper, he found in the New Testament the pure Word of God.

For Erasmus, the promise of salvation through Christ remained definitive. He held fast to the Christ of the Gospels, not only as man's hope of redemption in the next life but also as the Teacher of Righteousness in this. If we may look for any unifying element which informs his positive prescriptions for the Christian life, his often acerbic critiques of contemporary religion, and his approach to doctrine, it is surely his emphasis upon the *spirit*. Here we find the unifying factor. To Erasmus, conversion to the Christian faith was necessarily reflected in one's conduct. He was ready to compromise on details of ritual and often of dogma, but not on the need for direct and personal involvement in the living out of the Christian message. It was in this sense that he believed that the letter killeth but the spirit giveth life. Over and above the specific contributions of Erasmus to those different visions and denominations of the Christian faith which we have outlined above, this surely is his enduring legacy. He attacked in scathing terms the doctrinal and sectarian wrangling of his own time. Yet in the context of modern ecumenical Christianity, at grass-roots level, his spirit has rarely been better expressed than in the following words: 'mere respect for the faithful members of the different denominations is totally inadequate. We must love them and what they do.'[12]

Finally, in the widest context of what, at the outset, we termed the liberation of religious thought, it seems significant that the issue on which Melanchthon was accused of revisionism within the Lutheran camp was almost precisely that on which the 'heresy' of Erasmus' compatriot, Arminius, emerged within the Calvinist ranks half a century later. Whether we speak of 'Synergism' or of a denial of double predestination, this distaste for a totally arbitrary selection of souls for salvation – which would utterly abase the stature of the human race by denying any particle of innate natural goodness – seems quintessentially Erasmian. Erasmus did not strive to free the human soul, in its conscious quest for the Christian life, from the deadweight of a mechanical and often superstitious ritual, only to welcome a theology which would render this quest a meaningless exercise. Nor would we question the contention that the theological assumptions involved were profoundly philosophical. It was surely the combination of Erasmus' *adiaphora* in doctrine with his optimism in philosophy which alienated the 'hard-liners' in both ecclesiastical camps. Erasmus did not write for the 'free-thinkers' of the eighteenth century; but perhaps he came nearer to writing for the Ecumenical Christian movement of the twentieth.

GLOSSARY OF THEOLOGICAL TERMS

Some may welcome the following brief and basic definitions of certain terms as employed in this book. Those seeking fuller and more sophisticated expositions are directed to the *Oxford Dictionary of the Christian Church* and the *New Catholic Encyclopedia*.

Adiaphora	Literally, 'things indifferent'; beliefs or articles of faith which some religious thinkers do not consider to be a necessary condition of salvation.
Arian	A follower of the doctrines of Arius (d. 336), ascribing true Divinity to God the Father only.
Asceticism	A wish to conform to the behaviour, and if need be the sufferings, of Christ in this world,
Communion, Holy	The ceremony or Sacrament relating to Christ's Last Supper, involving Christian fellowship. But see also: Eucharist, Last Supper, Mass, Real Presence, and Transubstantiation.
Confession	A practice of the Catholic Church relating to the Sacrament of Penance, involving admission of the penitent's sins to and through a priest.
Confirmation	The Sacrament of admission to full Church membership.
Doctrine or Dogma	Broadly speaking, an article of faith, prescribed by the authority of the Church.
Eucharist	Literally, 'thanksgiving'; participation of the bread and/or (according to interpretation) the wine as in the Lord's Supper.
Extreme Unction	The Sacrament of anointing the dying – *in extremis* – with consecrated oil.
Free Will	The concept that in some sense the individual has a real freedom of choice affecting his destiny, as opposed to determinism (in a philosophical) and predestination (in a theological sense).
Grace	The gift of sanctification, leading to eternal life or salvation, given through the gratuitous and quite unmerited mercy of God.
Indulgence	Remission to a penitent sinner (a) of the *temporal*

punishment for sin, but (b) sometimes distorted and made a source of revenue in purporting to secure remission of the pains of Purgatory.

Justification — The doctrine that, despite their sins, men are justified, and thus redeemed in an after-life, (a) by Faith in Christ Alone (Solifidianism), or (b) by some meaningful combination of Faith and Works.

Last (or *Lord's*) *Supper* — Christ's meal with his disciples, before his Crucifixion; sometimes taken to refer to the Sacrament of Communion.

Mass — Latin 'missa'; a Sacrament of the Catholic Church involving a particular interpretation of the Eucharist; see Real Presence and Transubstantiation.

Original Sin — The notion of the innate depravity of all men, consequent upon the Fall of Adam.

Pelagian — Pertaining to the teaching of Pelagius, a fifth-century British monk, who denied man's total depravity; usually associated in the sixteenth century with a belief that man has Free Will to contribute something toward his salvation, as against the notion of Predestination.

Predestination — Divine pre-determination of each individual's fate in respect of eternal salvation or damnation; usually associated with, but in fact preceding in Luther and in Zwingli, Calvin's teaching on the Elect and the Reprobate.

Real Presence — The real or substantial presence of Christ – more narrowly, that of his body and blood – in the Eucharist.

Sacerdotal — Pertaining to the belief that an ordained priesthood is endowed with special authority and powers – most notably in celebration or administration of the Sacraments.

Sacraments — Religious rites of particular significance as a means of Grace. The Seven Sacraments of the Catholic Church are: Baptism, Confirmation, Matrimony, Penance, Mass, Extreme Unction, and Holy Orders (for the clergy).

Socinian — Adhering to the teachings of the sixteenth-century Italian brothers Sozzini, in not professing a belief in the Divinity of Christ; analogous to modern Unitarianism.

Transubstantiation — The doctrine that, when blessed by the priest, the bread (or host) and the wine in the celebration of the Eucharist become in some real or substantial, though not in an externally apparent, sense transformed into the flesh and the blood of Christ.

Trinity — The three-in-one or triune God of orthodox Christians: Father, Son, and Holy Spirit.

Utraquist — A believer in the right of the laity to participate 'in both kinds' (that is, in bread and wine) at Communion.

NOTES

1. *The Inheritance*

1. On scholasticism the books approachable by historians include F. Copleston, *Medieval Philosophy* (London, 1952) and E. Gilson, *History of Christian Philosophy* (London, 1955). For explanatory accounts, see *NCE*, xii, 1145–70, noting especially those on scholastic terms and axioms, ibid., 1147–53, and the article 'Scholastic Theology', ibid., 1153; see also *ODCC* s.v. scholasticism. For a sad example of Aristotle's influence upon the extremist antifeminism of Thomas Aquinas, see R. L. Camp, 'From Passive Subordination to Complementary Partnership', *Catholic Historical Review*, lxxvii (1990), 508–9.
2. A .E. McGrath, *The Intellectual Origins of the European Reformation* (Oxford, 1987), pp. 69–93. On the traditional methodology, see e.g. H. A. Oberman, *The Harvest of Medieval Theology, Gabriel Biel and late Medieval Nominalism* (Cambridge, Mass., 1963). For a general survey of the classical legacy to the Middle Ages see W. G. De Burgh, *The Legacy of the Ancient World* (Pelican, 1953 edn.), II, ch. 11.
3. On Christian Platonism, see De Burgh, II, 443–64, and A. E. Taylor, *Platonism and its Influence* (London, 1925), especially ch. 4: 'Plato the Theologian'; R. Klibansky, *The Platonic Tradition during the Middle Ages* (London, 1929); refs. in *NCE* and *ODCC*, s.v. Platonism, Neoplatonism, Origen, Gemistos Plethon. Further refs. below, notes 15–21.
4. *Adages*, pp. 376–8.
5. *NCE*, s.v. Transubstantiation.
6. A. Hyma, *The Christian Renaissance. A History of the 'Devotio Moderna'* (2nd edn., Hamden, Conn., 1965).
7. On the influence of the *Devotio* and parallel movements in France, see A. Renaudet, *Préréforme et Humanisme à Paris* (Geneva, 1981 reprint of 2nd edn.), pp. 67–78; W. L. Gundersheimer (ed.), *French Humanism 1470–1600* (London, 1969), pp. 65–8, 74–80; A. Hyma op.cit., n. 8 below, often refers to the activities of the Brethren outside the Netherlands, but much remains to be explored in Germany, France and elsewhere: note e.g. R. K. Davis, *Anabaptism and Asceticism*, pp. 57, 246–9, 262–3. For early English translations of the *Imitatio Christi* and related writings, see *Short Title Catalogue of Books printed in England*, &c., (1963), nos. 23955–23993; *Early*

English Text Society, Extra Ser., lxiii (1892); *DNB*, s.v. Atkinson, William; Beaufort, Margaret; Whitford, Richard.

8. On Erasmus and the Brethren see below, ch. 2; R. L. DeMolen, *Spirituality*, ch. 2 and index, s.v. Brethren. A. Hyma, *The Youth of Erasmus*; P. Mestwerdt, *Die Anfänge des Erasmus* (Leipzig, 1917); Preserved Smith, *Erasmus. A Study of his Life, Ideals, and Place in History*, ch. 1. For a general account of the Order, see A. Hyma, *The Brothers of the Common Life* (Grand Rapids, Mich., 1950); *NCE*, iv, 831–2, is scholarly, with good general bibliog. on the *Devotio*.
9. R. R. Post, *The Modern Devotion: Confrontation with the Reformation and Humanism*. Despite our reservations, this work remains essential reading, especially on the Dutch *Devotio*. It surveys the later continuities in chs. 14–15.
10. On Windesheim, see especially R. R. Post, op. cit., chs. 7, 12, 15: *NCE*, xiv, 956 and also ibid., ii, 78–80, under 'Brethren of the Common Life'; A. Hyma, op. cit., ch. 4.
11. On Thomas à Kempis see R. R. Post, op. cit., ch. 13; refs. in *ODCC* and *NCE*. s.v.; A. Hyma, op.cit., ch. 5.
12. On Ascetical Theology see *NCE*, i, 142–4; *ODCC*, pp. 93–4.
13. R. R. Post, op. cit., passim, rightly stresses the doctrinal conservatism of the *Devotio*, but appears too absolute in excluding it as a factor toward the Reformation.
14. Cited by A. Hyma, *The Christian Renaissance* (n. 5 above), pp. 213–14.
15. See e.g. the parallel situation in England: Jo Ann Hoeppner Moran, *The Growth of English Schooling, 1340–1548* (Princeton, N.J., 1985), especially chs. 6, 7; N. Orme, *Education and Society in Medieval and Renaissance England* (London 1989), especially ch. 2, 'The Laicisation of English School Education'. A continental comparison appears in Jean Rott, 'L'humanisme et la réforme pédagogique en Alsace' in *L'humanisme en Alsace, Congrès de Strasbourg 20–22 Avril, 1938* (Paris, 1939), pp. 64–82.
16. General treatment: Nesca A. Robb, *Neoplatonism of the Italian Renaissance* (London, 1935); P. Shorey, *Platonism: Ancient and Modern* (Berkeley, Cal., 1938). L. Miles, *John Colet and the Platonic Tradition* (London, 1962) has a useful bibliog. (pp. 221–6) on Neoplatonism to *c.*1960. Other items cited in *NCE*, s.v. Platonism and Neoplatonism; *ODCC*, p. 960. See n. 3 above and notes 18, 20, 21, below.
17. Cited from *NCE*, xi, 435.
18. On Ficino see e.g. P. O. Kristeller, *The Philosophy of Marsilio Ficino* (New York, 1943); S. R. Jayne (ed. and trans.), *Marcello Ficino's Commentary on Plato's Symposium* (Columbia, Mo., 1944). The bibliog. in L. Miles (n. 16 above) gives (pp. 225–6) numerous refs. to both Ficino and Pico.
19. Profuse factual refs. to Grocyn, Linacre and their 'Italianate' friend William Latimer are in A. B. Emden, *Biographical Register of the University of Oxford*, ii (1958), pp. 827–30, 1147–9, 1106–7, together with a full list of refs. made to them by Erasmus. Emden here adds much to *DNB*. The three corresponding biographies in *Contemporaries* add a little, but are largely based upon Emden, who also (op. cit., i (1957), pp. 462–4) deals efficiently with their associate John Colet, to be treated in our ch. 2, below.

In this context we can name S. R. Jayne, *John Colet and Marsilio Ficino* (Oxford, 1963).

20. L. Miles, op. cit. (n. 16 above) is informative (pp. 234–6) on Colet's uses of both Ficino and Pico. On the background see E. Cassirer, *The Platonic Renaissance in England*, trans. J. P. Pettegrove (London 1956).
21. For bibliog. on Pico, see L. Miles, op. cit., p. 22; *NCE*, xi, 247–8; *ODCC*, p. 1089.
22. B. Castiglone, *Il Libro del Cortegiano*, bk 4, sections 65–70: several Italian edns. are available. The famous English translation by Sir T. Hoby (*Everyman*, n.d.), has Bembo's speech, pp. 316–22.
23. On the general characteristics of humanism, see J. E. Siegal, *Rhetoric and Philosophy in Renaissance Humanism* (Princeton, N.J., 1968); E. Cassirer, P. O. Kristeller and J. H. Randall, *The Renaissance Philosophy of Man* (Chicago, 1948). Naturally the general works on the Renaissance contain relevant discussions. Note e.g. Denys Hay, *The Italian Renaissance in its Historical Background* (London, 1961) and *The Renaissance Debate* (London, 1966); also Myron P. Gilmore, *The World of Humanism, 1453–1517* (*Torchbook* 3003).
24. On the earliest humanists see R. Weiss, 'The Dawn of Humanism in Italy', *Bulletin of the Institute of Historical Research*, 42 (1969). On Petrarch's role, J. H. Whitfield, *Petrarch and the Renaissance* (London, 1943) is still useful.
25. Refs. on Chrysoloras: *NCE*, iii, 676ff.
26. A good example occurs in Colet's refs. to Suetonius in his lectures on *Romans* (ed. J. H. Lupton, London, 1873), p. 95. For modern discussions on the application of humanist methods to the Scriptures, see A. E. McGrath, *The Intellectual Origins of the European Reformation* (Oxford, 1987), chs. 4, 5, 6, 7; also E. H. Harbison, *The Christian Scholar in the Age of the Reformation* (New York, 1956).
27. See especially J. E. Seigal, *Rhetoric and Philosophy in Renaissance Humanism . . . Petrarch to Valla* (Princeton Univ. Pr., 1968). For Valla's work and thought see A. E. McGrath, ch. 2, and S. L. Camporeale, *Lorenzo Valla: Umanesimo e Teologia* (Florence, 1922), esp. pp. 227–403. On Valla and Erasmus, see Harbison, pp. 43ff, 143–9.
28. A short account of his career with some further refs. is in *NCE*, s.v. For a good select bibliog. see *ODCC*, p. 1424, which cites some English translations of the *Donation*. A better one is that by W. L. Gundersheimer in his *The Italian Renaissance* (Englewood Cliffs, N.J., 1965), pp. 55–68.
29. A previously unpublished recension of his *Collatio Novi Testamenti* – as distinct from Erasmus' printed version – is edited by A. Perosa (Florence, 1970).
30. On Valla and the Vulgate, see A. E. McGrath, op. cit., pp. 124–33.
31. The letter to Christopher Fisher (Allen, i, Ep. 182; see esp. 410, and compare *CWE* 2, No. 182) was written from Paris about March 1505.
32. Refs. in *ODCC*, s.v. 'Complutensian Polyglot' and 'Ximenes', Complutum was the Roman name of Alcalá.
33. *NCE* and *ODCC*, s.v., have select bibliogs. on Reuchlin. Ludwig Geiger, *Johann Reuchlin, sein Leben und seine Werke* (Leipzig, 1871) is still valuable for

facts and documents. The account of Reuchlin by H. Scheible in *Contemporaries*, iii, 145–50, is scholarly and informative on his relations with Erasmus. The more recondite aspects of Reuchlin are summarised by L. W. Spitz, 'Reuchlin's Philosophy: Pythagoras and the Cabala for Christ', *ARG*, 47 (1956), reprinted in his *The Religious Renaissance of the German Humanists* (Cambridge, Mass., 1963).

34. On the problem of German anti-Semitism see H. A. Oberman, *Würzeln des Antisemitismus* (Berlin, 1981), which was translated by J. I. Porter, *The Roots of Anti-Semitism in the Age of Renaissance and Reformation* (Philadelphia, 1984). On this theme see S. H. Hendrix, 'Toleration of the Jews in the German Reformation', *ARG* 81 (1990).
35. For a judicious review of recent writing on these issues see James Tracy, in *The Catholic Historical Review*, LXXIII (1987), 462–3.
36. *CWE* 5, No. 713 (15/11/1517).
37. *CWE* 2, No. 290, 3, Nos. 300, 305, 324, 326B, 4, No. 457.
38. See below, p. 120.
39. Reuchlin's highly reverent letter to Leo X is printed in Ludwig Geiger (ed.), *Johann Reuchlins Briefwechsel, Bibliothek des Litterarischen Vereins in Stuttgart*, cxxvi (Tübingen, 1875), pp. 267–75.

2. *The Formation of Erasmus*

1. Allen, i, pp. 46–52; *CWE* 4, pp. 400–410; also trans. J. C. Olin, *Christian Humanism and the Reformation* (New York, 1965 – hereafter, Olin), pp. 22–30. On the parentage and early life of Erasmus see Allen, i, Appendices i–iii, and recent guidance in the following: J. K. Sowards, 'The Youth of Erasmus: some Reconsiderations', *Yearbook* 9 (1989), pp. 1–33; R. L. DeMolen, *Spirituality*, especially ch. 2, 'Erasmus as Adolescent'; R. J. Schoeck, *Erasmus Grandescens: The Growth of a Humanist's Mind and Spirituality* (Nieuwkoop, 1988).
2. Allen, ii, Ep. 447; *CWE* 4, No. 447.
3. Allen, i, pp. 56–71, trans. Olin, pp. 31–54. On Beatus, see P. Adam, *L'Humanisme à Sélestat* (Sélestat, 1962), pp. 51–67.
4. Sowards, op. cit., p. 5, n. 22; DeMolen, op. cit., pp. 15–16; P. Smith, *Erasmus*, p. 8; H. Vredeveld in *Nederlands Archief voor Kerkgeschiedenis*, n.s.71 (1991), p. 105, forecasts a return to 1466.
5. Manuscript copies by Gerard have survived. Details in Sowards, op. cit., p. 9, n. 35, who also discusses rival theories on his life and travels.
6. Sowards, op.cit., p. 10.
7. Biographical details on Peter Gerard in *Contemporaries*, i, 441–2. Erasmus' letter to him is in Allen, i, Ep. 3; *CWE* 1, No. 3.
8. See P. Smith, *Erasmus*, pp. 76–7; below, p. 51. On Leo's relationship with Erasmus, see *Contemporaries*, especially ii, 319–23.
9. Allen, i, Ep. 1; *CWE* 1, No. 1.
10. *Contemporaries*, ii, I 173. At this time he taught only the senior forms at Deventer and Erasmus probably met him only on special occasions.
11. Ibid., i, 15–17.
12. In the Grunnius letter and the *Compendium Vitae*, *CWE* 4, pp. 406–7.

13. Above, n. 2.
14. R. R. Post, *The Modern Devotion*, pp. 365–6 discusses such direct entries.
15. Allen, i, Ep. 3; *CWE* 1, No. 3, probably from Steyn.
16. Above n. 7.
17. Sowards, op.cit., pp. 17–20.
18. Allen, i, Epp. 4–9; *CWE* 1, Nos. 2–9.
19. Sowards, op. cit., p. 18.
20. Ibid., p. 19; R. Bainton, *Erasmus of Christendom*, pp. 16–17. See DeMolen, *Spirituality*, ch. 5, which also discusses the *De Contemptu Mundi*.
21. Refs. in Sowards, op. cit., pp. 23–4.
22. See DeMolen, op. cit., ch. 8: 'Erasmus' Commitment to the Canons Regular of St. Augustine'.
23. Sowards, op. cit., pp. 21–2.
24. Charles Béné, *Érasme et Saint Augustin* (*Travaux d'Humanisme et Renaissance*, ciii) Geneva, 1969, cites many relevant examples.
25. *Contemporaries*, i, 132–3; Allen, i, App.v: 'Erasmus with the Bishop of Cambray'.
26. On the ms. copy at Gouda (*c.*1519 from an earlier copy) see A. Hyma, *The Youth of Erasmus*, ch. 15 and Appendix B, where he prints it and collates passages with the later published version. Hyma concludes that Erasmus' anti-monastic views became markedly severer in his later years.
27. A good translation of the *Antibarbarorum Liber* is in *CWE* 23, 1–122, trans. and ed. by M. M. Phillips (note pp. 8–15 of her Introduction). On different interpretations of its precise aims and priorities see, e.g., B. Bradshaw in *Journal of Ecclesiastical History*, 33 (1982), pp. 596–610, and at somewhat greater length in *Journal of Theological Studies*, 30 (1982), pp. 411–47.
28. For the relevant members of the House of Burgundy: see *Contemporaries*, i, 223–32.
29. On David: *ibid.*, 226–7 and on the ordination, Sowards, op. cit., p. 22.
30. On their financial relations see Allen, i, Epp. 75, 77, 81, 128; *CWE* 1, Nos. 75, 77, 81 and 128; and on the cooling of their friendship, *Contemporaries*, i, 132–3.
31. On Erasmus' contacts with members of the Bergen family, see *Contemporaries*, i, 129–34, passim.
32. *Contemporaries*, iii, 281–2.
33. Craig R. Thompson (trans. and ed.), *The Colloquies of Erasmus* (hereafter *Colloquies*), pp. 312–56. An earlier complete translation exists: that by N. Bailey (1887).
34. On the medieval university of Paris and its colleges, see H. Rashdall, *The Universities of Europe in the Middle Ages*, ed. F. M. Powicke and A. B. Emden (3 vols., London, 1936), i, ch. 5; A. E. McGrath, *Life of John Calvin* (London, 1990), ch. 2.
35. Cf. N. M. Sutherland, 'Parisian Life in the Sixteenth Century' in W. L. Gundersheimer (ed.), *French Humanism 1470–1600* (London, 1969), pp. 51–64.
36. G. Duby and R. Mandrou, *History of French Civilisation* (London 1968), p. 186.

37. On Clamanges: *Dictionnaire de Biographie Française*, viii, 1347.
38. On Fichet: ibid., xiii, 1283–4.
39. Cf. A. Renaudet, 'Paris from 1494 to 1517' in Gundersheimer, op. cit., pp. 65–89, which summarises much of his major work *Préréforme et Humanisme à Paris pendant les Premières Guerres d'Italie* (2nd edn., Paris, 1953). A general account of Erasmus' relations with French scholars is in Margaret Mann, *Érasme et les Débuts de la Réforme Française 1517–1536* (Paris, 1934), ch. 1.
40. On Gaguin: *Dictionnaire de Biographie Française*, xv, 55–6, and the bibliog. in *Contemporaries*, ii, 69–70.
41. *Contemporaries*, ii, 315–18.
42. Ibid., 447–8.
43. Ibid., i, 53–6; Allen, xii, Index of Correspondents, p. 426; Cf. below, n. 51.
44. Ed. Craig Thompson (above, n. 33).
45. Cf. ibid., pp. 623–37. The *De Utilitate* was published in the 1526 edn. of the *Colloquies*.
46. Craig Thompson, op. cit., p. 623. An outstanding brief account is that by Margaret Mann Phillips in *Erasmus and the Northern Renaissance* (1949 and later edns.), pp. 102–22.
47. Craig Thompson, op. cit., p. xxii, especially the refs. in n. 22.
48. Ibid., loc. cit.; further guidance in Preserved Smith, *A Key to the Colloquies of Erasmus* (Harvard U.P., 1927).
49. On W. Blount, fourth Lord Mountjoy, see *Contemporaries*, i, 154–6; *DNB*, ii, 721–2. Erasmus lamented his death (1534) in the dedication of his *Ecclesiastes*, addressed to the Bishop of Augsburg (1535), and again in his dedication to the fifth Lord Mountjoy, in the 1536 edn. of his *Adagia*. For the extant letters between Erasmus and William, see Allen, xii, Index of Correspondents, p. 433. It is apparent that William wrote competent humanist Latin.
50. These points are well illustrated by our two earliest birds' eye view maps of London, both dated *c.*1558–9. The first is the coloured engraving attributed to Frans Hogenberg. The second consists of two contiguous copper-plates (lately discovered) depicting the City and Moorfields, on which latter the citizens are disporting themselves. All the above are reproduced in F. Barker and P. Jackson, *The History of London in Maps* (London, 1990), pp. 12–15.
51. Allen, i, Ep. 103; *CWE* 1, No. 103.
52. On the relations of Erasmus with Grocyn, Linacre and Latimer, see respectively *Contemporaries*, ii, 135–6; ii, 331–2; ii, 302–3. On early English students and their teachers at Padua, see C. Sturge, *Cuthbert Tunstall* (London, 1938), ch. 3.
53. R. Weiss describes this situation in *Humanism in England during the Fifteenth Century* (3rd edn., London, 1967), pp. 179–86.
54. Richard Pace, the diplomat and eventually Colet's successor at St Paul's, spent many years in Italy where in 1508 he first met Erasmus (*Contemporaries*, iii, 37–9). On the relationship of Erasmus with Thomas More and his family, see *ibid.*, ii, 451–9. On Tunstall, later Bishop of Durham, see Sturge, n. 52 above, and *Contemporaries*, iii, 349–54. On their contacts with Erasmus, see Index of Correspondents in Allen, xii, pp. 434, 436.

55. The letter to Prince Henry: Allen, i, Ep. 104; *CWE* 1, no. 104.
56. J. R. Gleason, *John Colet* (Univ. of California, 1989). Of the earlier biographies, the most generally useful is still that by J. H. Lupton, *Life of John Colet* (1887, 1909). Lupton also translated most of Colet's works: listed in *Brit. Mus. Cat. of Printed Books to 1955*, v, 1168.
57. Allen, i, Ep. 108; *CWE* 1, No. 108. His known contacts with Ficino are described in Sears Jayne, *John Colet and Marsilio Ficino* (Oxford, 1963), chs. 1–3, also by Gleason, op. cit., pp. 47–52.
58. Allen, i, Ep. 107; *CWE* 1, No. 107.
59. Allen, i, Ep. 159; *CWE* 2, No. 159. Here he probably refers to the confiscation of his money by the customs men of Dover in 1500.
60. Allen, i, Ep. 108; *CWE* 1, No. 108.
61. For the justified dismissal of 'The Oxford Reformers', as understood in F. Seebohm's work of that title (1867), see Gleason, op. cit., pp. 3–4, 8–10. There are however some good things in Seebohm, e.g. his generalisations on Colet's Oxford lectures, pp. 34–42.
62. For Gleason's character of Colet, see e.g. his pp. 62–4. For Erasmus' all-important account of Vitrier and Colet in his long letter to Justus Jonas (13 June 1521), see Allen, iv, Ep. 1211; *CWE* 8, No. 1211; Olin, pp. 165–91; *CWE* 7, No. 1053.
63. For these calculations, see Gleason, op. cit., ch. 4, especially pp. 71–92.
64. *DNB*, iv, 778–9.
65. J. H. Lupton (ed.), *Ioannis Coleti Enarratio . . . An Exposition of St Paul's Epistle to the Romans* (London, 1873), pp. 95–6. Gleason (op. cit.), pp. 126–32, denies that Colet was historically minded.
66. 'Though he had neither obtained nor sought for any degree in divinity, yet there was no doctor there, either of divinity or law, no abbot or other dignitary but came to hear him and brought his text-books with him as well.' Erasmus to Justus Jonas, above n. 62.
67. R. Pfeiffer, *History of Classical Scholarship, 1300–1850* (London, 1976); ch. 7 concerns Erasmus and pp. 72–3 Colet; E. H. Harbison, *The Christian Scholar in the Age of the Reformation*, pp. 55–62.
68. C. A. L. Jarrott, 'Erasmus's Annotations and Colet's Commentaries on Paul', in DeMolen: *Essays*, pp. 125–44.
69. P. A. Duhamel, 'The Oxford Lectures of John Colet' in *Journal of the History of Ideas*, 14 (1953).
70. P. I. Kaufman, 'John Colet and Erasmus' *Enchiridion*' in *Church History*, 46 (1977).
71. J. H. Lupton, op. cit., pp. 13–19.
72. Romans, 2, 25–9.
73. For the relevant passage in Erasmus, see R. Himelick, *The Enchiridion of Erasmus* (Gloucester, Mass., 1970), p. 107.
74. Gleason, op. cit., pp. 168ff; on his preaching see ibid., pp. 179–84.
75. *STC*, 5550 (1530). The sermon is translated in J. H. Lupton, *Life of John Colet* (1887), pp. 293–304 and thence in C. H. Williams (ed.), *English Historical Documents*, v, (1485–1558), pp. 652–60. Comment in C. Harper-Bill, 'Dean Colet's Convocation Sermon' in *History*, 73 (1988).
76. *STC*, 17806 (*c.*1510). On Melton and his sermon see A. G. Dickens, 'The

Writers of Tudor Yorkshire', *Transactions, Royal Hist. Soc.*, 5th ser., xiii (1963), pp. 53–5, reprinted in *Reformation Studies*, pp. 221–2.

77. Olin, p. 178.
78. Ibid., pp. 189–91.
79. On Colet's Platonism and Neoplatonism, note especially S. R. Jayne, op. cit., pp. 47–9 and L. Miles, *John Colet and the Platonic Tradition* (London, 1962). An important element was the *Hierarchies* of Dionysius, then almost universally accepted as the work of St Paul's Athenian convert. Cf. J. B. Trapp, 'John Colet and the Hierarchies of the Pseudo-Dionysius' in *Studies in Church History*, 17 (1981) and the same author's 'John Colet, his mss and the Pseudo-Dionysius' in R. R. Bolgar (ed.), *Classical Influences in European Culture, 1500–1700* (London, 1976).
80. On Fitzjames and Colet see Gleason, op. cit., pp. 87–90, 235–60. For general background: H. C. Porter, 'The Gloomy Dean and the Law: John Colet 1460–1519' in G. V. Bennett and J. D. Walsh (eds.), *Essays in Modern Church History in Memory of Norman Sykes* (London, 1966).
81. See on this 'true fellow-work' Gleason, op. cit., pp. 233–4.
82. Edns. from 1514: *Bibliotheca Erasmiana*, 1st. ser., pp. 51–3.
83. On the struggle of Erasmus to attain proficiency in Greek, see Allen, i, pp. 592–3.

3. *The Philosophy of Christ*

1. Of the several scholarly biographies covering this middle period of Erasmus, that by Preserved Smith conveys a steady flow of references to Allen and might well to this day be regarded as the most generally useful biography. We have of course used also the lives by J. Huizinga, C. Augustijn and R. H. Bainton. In addition L. E. Halkin, *Érasme parmi Nous* is lively and sensitive. It has now appeared in English, trans. and ed. J. M. Tonkin (1993).
2. See Bibliography for editions of *Adages* cited.
3. A compact summary of the English visits is in P. Smith, op. cit., ch. 3.
4. On Lucian see refs. in ibid., pp. 193–7. Some commentators regard Aristophanes as also a significant influence.
5. Erasmus' edns. of these Greek authors are listed in F. Van der Haeghen, *Bibliotheca Erasmiana*, 2nd. ser., pp. 25–7, 49.
6. On his best-known secretary, Gilbert Cousin, see *Contemporaries*, i, 350–2.
7. For Erasmus on inns: *Colloquies*, pp. 147–52.
8. Though primarily concerned with the long-term impacts of Erasmus upon Italy, A. Renaudet, *Érasme et l'Italie*, has also (livre ii, pp. 41–109) a full account of the journey itself. On the latter, see also the pioneering work by P. de Nolhac, *Érasme en Italie* (Paris, 1898).
9. Cf. the accounts of his relations with both artists, respectively in *Contemporaries*, i, 413–15 and ii, 194–7. Note also E. Panofsky, 'Erasmus and the Visual Arts', in *Journal of the Warburg and Courtauld Institutes*, 32 (1969).
10. On Bologna and Julius II, see Allen, i, Ep. 203; Renaudet, op. cit., pp. 75, 97; for the *Julius Exclusus*, below, pp. 71–2.

11. *Opulia Sordida*, in *Colloquies*, pp. 488–90. On the stay of Erasmus with Aldus, see Renaudet, op. cit., pp. 83ff.
12. Alexander Stuart made a deep and lasting impression on Erasmus: Allen, iii, Ep. 604, vii, Epp. 1824, 1992, viii, Ep. 2283, x, Epp.2856, 2874. Also *Contemporaries*, iii, 285.
13. Erasmus in Rome: Renaudet, op. cit., pp. 90–9; Nolhac, op. cit., ch.3; and Erasmus' own recollections, especially in Allen, i, Ep. 253 (*CWE* 2, No. 253).
14. On superficial religiosity and the secular atmosphere in Rome, see Renaudet, op. cit., pp. 95–8; P. Smith, op. cit., p. 114, based on E. Rodocanachi, *Courtisanes et Bouffons* (Paris, 1894) and the same author's *La première Renaissance, Rome au temps de Jules II et de Léon X*, (Paris, 1912).
15. On Mountjoy: above, p. 33 and n. 49. His letter recalling Erasmus (Allen, i, Ep. 215 and *CWE* 2, No. 215) may have been drafted by Ammonius, then acting as Mountjoy's secretary. It adds that Warham has promised to give Erasmus a benefice, if he comes to England.
16. The standard edn. of the Latin text of the *Folly* was for long that by J. B. Kan (The Hague, 1898); but now see that by Clarence Miller (*ASD*). A sound and readily available English trans. by B. Radice is in *Penguin Classics* (1971) and reappears in *CWE* 27. In the Penguin volume both the Introduction and the annotations by A. H. T. Levi are valuable: we cite this edn, as 'Levi' below. The chapter-divisions of the *Folly* are not Erasmian, but were introduced in the edn. by A. G. M. de Querlon, 1765.
17. Full details in Maria Dowling, 'John Fisher and the Preaching Ministry', *ARG* 82 (1991), pp. 287–309.
18. Allen, i, Ep. 241 and *CWE* 2, No. 241.
19. Allen, i, Ep. 244a and *CWE* 2, No. 244A. For the subsequent detail on his personal finances see Eckhard Bernstein, 'Money Connection: The Antwerp Banker Erasmus Schets and Erasmus of Rotterdam', in *Erasmus in English*, 14 (1985–6); also D. F. S. Thomson and H. C. Porter, *Erasmus and Cambridge*, pp. 68–71.
20. Ammonius (Andrea Ammonio of Lucca) worked as Latin secretary to Henry VIII in 1511 and became an English subject in 1514. At this period he was the closest friend of Erasmus and over forty letters between them (1511–17) have survived (*Contemporaries*, i, 48–50). Note especially Allen, i, Epp. 239, 240, 295.
21. By far the best account of his life in Cambridge is the Introduction by H. C. Porter in *Erasmus and Cambridge* (n. 19 above). *Inter alia* it reconstructs the impressive range of his varied scholarly tasks there (pp. 47–53), which included the important educational treatise *De Ratione Studii*.
22. On Johann Froben, see *Contemporaries*, ii, 60–3.
23. How Erasmus from 1514 exerted a powerful influence on German scholars we shall discuss in ch. 11 below.
24. On Johann Amberach, see *Contemporaries*, i, 47.
25. Van der Haegan, op. cit., 1st. ser., pp. 111, 116.
26. For the striking *Axiomata* sent by Erasmus, see below, page 119.
27. Allen, ii, Ep. 474 and *CWE* 4, No. 474; see also Allen, ii, Ep. 470 and *CWE* 4, No. 470 – 'I cannot . . . both clothe myself and keep horses'; yet again,

CWE 2, No. 282, to Ammonio. See R. H. Bainton, *Erasmus*, p. 111.

28. Standard Latin text ed. Hajo Holborn, *Ausgewählte Werke des Erasmus von Rotterdam* (Munich, 1933). English editions, see Bibliography. Some leading commentaries: R. Stupperich in *ARG*, 69 (1978); O. Schottenloher in *ARG*, 45 (1954); E.-W. Kohls in DeMolen, *Essays*, pp. 61–82; F. L. Battles, 'Erasmus' *Enchiridion*', in M. Spinka, ed., *Advocates of Reform*, *Library of Christian Classics*, xxv (Philadelphia, 1953).
29. *Contemporaries*, iii, 114–15.
30. On Anna van Borssele, see *Contemporaries*, i, 173–4, noting the role played by Jacob Batt in the relations between Anna and Erasmus: ibid., 100–01.
31. John, i, 14. On these extreme dualist sects in southern France, stamped out with great ferocity in the thirteenth century, see *ODCC*, pp. 31, 864–5; also Cathars, p. 251.
32. Lust, like Avarice and Ambition, is a favourite topic of Erasmus in the *Enchiridion* (ed. R. Himelick, pp. 72–83, 157–60, 171–2, 177–84) but not in the *Folly*. Conversely, preaching does not figure in the *Enchiridion* but in the *Folly*. This comparison admirably illustrates the contrast of approach between the two works, the one personally directed, the other concerned with 'public' religion.
33. Himelick edn., pp. 155–6. On smug theologians, p. 53; laxity of monasticism, p. 54; misuse of saint-worship, p. 99.
34. Ibid., pp. 85–6; but in regard to this and n. 35, the passages are quoted from the livelier if often freer translation by J. P. Dolan, *The Essential Erasmus* (hereafter, Dolan), p. 53.
35. Ibid., p. 86.
36. R. Stupperich, 'Das Enchiridion Militis Christiani . . . nach seiner Entstehung, seinem Sinn und Charakter', *ARG*, 69 (1978), 5–23. For Auer and Kohls, ibid., 6, nn. 4, 5.
37. *Contemporaries*, iii, 408–9; Allen, iv, Ep. 1211.
38. For sixteenth-century *Lucubrationes* and *Lucubratiunculae* see Van der Haeghen, op. cit., 1st ser., pp. 119–20.
39. For early edns. of the *Folly* see s.v. *Moriae Encomium* in ibid., 1st ser., pp. 122–9.
40. For early edns. of *Enchiridion*, see ibid., 1st ser., pp. 79–84.
41. Levi, pp. 135–6.
42. Ibid., pp. 154–5.
43. Ibid., p. 157.
44. Ibid., pp. 164ff.
45. M. A. Screech, *Ecstasy and the Praise of Folly*; see Index, s.v. Ecstasy, pp. 261–2. On the interpretations added in the 1514 edn., see App. A, pp. 214ff.
46. Olin, pp. 55–91.
47. Levi, pp. 211–52. On Dorp, see *Contemporaries*, i, 398–404, and Rummel, *Catholic Critics*, I, ch. 1.
48. E. F. Rogers, *The Correspondence of Sir Thomas More* (Princeton, 1947), pp. 27–74.
49. Edns. in Van der Haeghen, op. cit., pp. 57–8. Erasmus' *Annotations on the New Testament (the Gospels)*, are ed. in facsimile by Anne Reeve (1986) with valuable Introduction by M. A. Screech.

50. On the Polyglot, see *NCE*, xi, 540–2; on the reforms of Ximénes, the Polyglot and contemporary Spain, *Érasme et l'Espagne*, chs. 1 and 2. On a different level see also Basil Hall in *Cambridge History of the Bible*, iii (1963), 50–63 passim. Also above, p. 17 and below p. 225.
51. Good technical account of the task in F. H. Scrivener, *A Plain Introduction to the Criticism of the New Testament*, 2nd edn., 1874, pp. 380–5.
52. Ibid., p. 383. Note the charitable comment of Ximénes when his own editor Stunica (Zúñiga) ridiculed the performance of Erasmus! For a balanced account of his achievement in the field of biblical studies, see L. Bouyer in *Cambridge History of the Bible*, ii (1969), pp. 492–505. For contemporary conservative reactions, see Rummel, *Catholic Critics*, I, chs. 2 and 3.
53. For comments on the *Paraclesis* and a translation, see Olin, pp. 92–106.
54. Ibid., pp. 96–7.
55. Ibid., p. 97.
56. Ibid., p. 98.
57. See *CWE* 24, 25, 26 for some characteristic 'educational' works.
58. Van der Haeghen, op. cit., 1st ser., p. 9. The bibliogs. give an edn. of 1518, not inspected by us. For edns. of works by Erasmus, see Anon., *Bibliotheca Erasmiana, Répertoire des Oeuvres d'Erasme*, (Nieuwkoop, 1961).
59. See James McConica's *Erasmus*, ch. 2: 'The educational mission'.

4. *The Christian Commonwealth*

Abbreviation/short-title specific to this chapter:
Christian Prince: Erasmus' *The Education of a Christian Prince*

1. See J. K. McConica, *English Humanists and Reformation Politics*, for a full but perhaps overstated survey of Erasmian influence in England.
2. R. W. Green (ed.), *Protestantism and Capitalism* (Boston, 1959) is one introduction to a vast body of literature.
3. See J. H. Elliott, *Imperial Spain 1469–1716* (London, 1963), p. 181.
4. R. H. Bainton, *Erasmus of Christendom*, p. 150.
5. *Paraclesis* (Olin), p. 100; on the general contrast between Erasmus and Machiavelli, see A. Renaudet, *Érasme et l'Italie*, pp. 178–85.
6. *Julius exclusus*, *CWE* 27, p. 196: see M. J. Heath's Introductory Note, pp. 155–60, for the still contentious issue of authorship – though the balance of probability is very heavily inclined toward Erasmus. W. K. Ferguson, *Erasmi opuscula* (The Hague, 1933), pp. 38–124, has an important edition of the Latin text, with Introduction.
7. *Defensor Pacis* (trans. W. Marshall as *Defence of Peace*, 1535) and (trans.) *The Governance of England* – early fourteenth and late fifteenth centuries respectively.
8. *Colloquies*, trans. Craig R. Thompson.
9. M. M. Phillips, *Adages*, pp. 29, 35–6.
10. A. H. T. Levi, *CWE* 27, Introduction, p. xxvi.
11. *Adages*, p. 183.
12. Ibid., pp. 312, 338, 346.

13. *CWE* 6, No. 932.
14. J. D. Tracy, *The Politics of Erasmus.*
15. J. P. Whitney, *Reformation Essays* (London, 1939), p. 58.
16. *CWE* 4, No. 586 (to Dukes Frederick and George of Saxony, 5/6/1517), p. 382.
17. J. D. Tracy, op. cit., p. 8; see also A. Renaudet, *Érasme et l'Italie*, p. 192.
18. M. M. Phillips, *Erasmus and the Northern Renaissance*, p. 101.
19. *Praise of Folly, CWE* 27, p. 139.
20. *Panegyric, CWE* 27, pp. 54–6.
21. *CWE* 2, No. 288.
22. Ibid., 4, Nos. 541, 566.
23. *CWE* 5, Nos. 796, 825, 832.
24. *Dulce bellum inexpertis*, in *Adages*, pp. 315–16, 319, 323, 343.
25. *CWE* 2, No. 288. On this theme see especially Robert P. Adams, *The Better Part of Valor.*
26. *Adages*, pp. 344–5; *LB*, v, 345–68 (359A, 365B–C); E. Rummel (ed.), *The Erasmus Reader*, pp. 315–33, includes a part of *De bello turcico*. Below, p. 244, for Louis II.
27. M. M. Phillips, *Erasmus and the Northern Renaissance*, p.103.
28. *Christian Prince, CWE* 27, p. 286.
29. *Querela pacis, CWE* 27, pp. 308, 314–15.
30. *Adages*, pp. 280, 337–8, 340, 348–9. See Rummel, *Annotations*, pp. 163–7.
31. *Adages*, pp. 336–7.
32. H. S. Bender, 'The Pacifism of the Sixteenth-Century Anabaptists', in *MQR*, 30 (1956), 17–18.
33. *Querela pacis, CWE* 27, pp. 293, 300, 313, 317.
34. 'Peace Book Club' edn. of *Institutio principis Christiani*, ed. J. A. Joyce (London, n.d.), pp. 12–13.
35. R. P. Adams, *The Better Part of Valor*, pp. 63, 112. See also A. Renaudet, *Érasme et l'Italie*, pp. 187–9.
36. M. M. Phillips, *Adages*, p. 105.
37. *CWE* 2, No. 288.
38. *Adages*, pp. 285–6, 339, 353.
39. J. D. Tracy, *The Politics of Erasmus*, pp. 29–31.
40. *Julius exclusus, CWE* 27, pp. 169, 173, 178, 180, 189–90.
41. Ibid., pp. 186–7, 191–4.
42. *Adages*, p. 353.
43. 'Letter to Paul Volz' (Olin), p. 113.
44. *Christian Prince, CWE* 27, p. 212.
45. M. M. Phillips, *Erasmus and the Northern Renaissance*, p. 105.
46. *Christian Prince, CWE* 27, pp. 216–18, 229, 233, 237–9, 274.
47. *Adages*, pp. 280, 341.
48. *Querela pacis, CWE* 27, p. 312.
49. R. H. Bainton, *Erasmus of Christendom*, p. 219.
50. *The Letters of Stephen Gardiner*, ed. J. A. Muller, pp. 381, 383–4, 422.
51. S. Gardiner, *Answer to Bucer* (1541), in *Obedience in Church and State*, ed. P. Janelle (Cambridge, 1930), pp. 175, 179, 183, 193, 205, 209.
52. *Adages*, p. 220.

53. *Christian Prince*, *CWE* 27, p. 231.
54. Thomas Starkey, op. cit., p. 7.
55. J. D. Tracy, *The Politics of Erasmus*, p. 35.
56. *CWE* 7, No. 1001.
57. *Panegyric*, *CWE* 27, pp. 43–5.
58. *Christian Prince*, *CWE* 27, p. 235.
59. Ed. *Utopia*, pp. 349.
60. *Praise of Folly*, *CWE* 27, p. 100.
61. *CWE* 3, No. 393.
62. M. M. Phillips, *Adages*, p. 37; see also Preserved Smith, *Erasmus*, pp. 44, 200.
63. *Adages*, pp. 235, 238–9.
64. Ibid., pp. 284, 295.
65. Ibid., p. 223.
66. Ibid., pp. 220–2.
67. *Praise of Folly*, *CWE* 27, pp. 135–6.
68. *Querela pacis*, *CWE* 27, p. 302.
69. *Panegyric*, *CWE* 27, pp. 41, 43.
70. *Praise of Folly*, *CWE* 27, pp. 136–7.
71. *Adages*, pp. 132, 212.
72. *Querela pacis*, *CWE* 27, pp. 305–6.
73. *Adages*, pp. 219, 222.
74. See M. M. Phillips, *Erasmus and the Northern Renaissance*, p. 97, and J. D. Tracy, *The Politics of Erasmus*, pp. 6–8, 53–4, 112.
75. *CWE* 5, Nos. 670, 688.
76. *CWE* 8, No. 1148.
77. See Betty Radice, in *CWE* 27, p. 290.
78. *Adages*, p. 349.
79. Allen, v, Ep. 1352.
80. *CWE* 8, No. 1202.
81. *Adages*, p. 340.
82. *Christian Prince*, ed. L. K. Born, p. 178.
83. *Concerning the Eating of Fish*, in Dolan, pp. 303, 306–7.
84. *Christian Prince*, *CWE* 27, pp. 215, 268.
85. *Adages* pp. 130–1.
86. See Marjorie O. Boyle, *Erasmus on Language and Method in Theology*, p. 114, and Margo Todd, *Christian Humanism and the Puritan Social Order*, (Cambridge, New York, 1987), pp. 180–2. Albert Rabil (*Renaissance Humanism: Foundations, Forms and Legacy*, Philadelphia, Vol. 2, 237–8) observes that for Erasmus 'society changed by example from the top'.
87. *Adages*, pp. 284, 310.
88. *Querela pacis*, *CWE* 27, p. 307.
89. *Letter to Paul Volz* (Olin), p. 120.
90. *Christian Prince*, ed. L. K. Born, pp. 148, 150.
91. Ibid., pp. 219, 227.
92. Ibid., pp. 212, 217, 227, 228.
93. Ibid., p. 215.
94. *Panegyric*, *CWE* 27, p. 44.

95. *Adages*, pp. 227, 283.
96. *Christian Prince*, *CWE* 27, pp. 260–2.
97. T. More, *Utopia*, ed. Surtz and Hexter, pp. 90–1.
98. *Enchiridion* (Dolan), pp. 73, 68.
99. *CWE* 6, No. 959.
100. Cited by E. Surtz, op. cit., p. 273.
101. J. C. Olin, *Christian Humanism and the Reformation* (1987 edn.), p. 21.
102. *On Mending the Peace of the Church* (*LB*, v, 505D; Dolan, pp. 386–7, and R. Himelick p. 96). Margo Todd's assertion (op. cit., p. 132) that 'clearly, for Erasmus, a strictly ordered communism was the ideal economic order', begs many questions.
103. Dolan, pp. 323–4.
104. *LB*, v, 471E–F, 472A; Dolan pp. 334–5; Himelick, p. 32.
105. *Praise of Folly*, *CWE* 27, p. 121.
106. *Adages*, pp. 132, 185.
107. *CWE* 6, No. 916.
108. *Julius exclusus*, *CWE* 27, pp. 192–3.
109. *Adages*, p. 332.
110. *On Mending the Peace of the Church* (*LB*, v, 474B–C, 490E–F; Dolan, pp. 338, 365; Himelick, pp. 37, 68).
111. *Concerning the Immense Mercy of God* (Dolan), p. 233.
112. *Contra quosdam, qui se falso iactant Evangelicos*, A4 verso–A5 recto, Bi recto–Bi verso.
113. See below, Chapter Six, p. 143.
114. See N. Birnbaum, 'The Zwinglian Reformation in Zurich', *Past and Present*, 1959, pp. 34–5, 40–5.
115. See W. R. D. Jones, *The Tudor Commonwealth 1529–1559* (London, 1970), pp. 20–1, 78–9.
116. *Christian Prince*, ed. L. K. Born, pp. 225–6.
117. *Concerning the Immense Mercy of God* (Dolan), pp. 269–70.
118. See, for example, J. L. Vives, *De Subventione Pauperum*, 1526, translation in F. R. Salter, ed., *Some Early Tracts on Poor Relief* (London, 1526), and Martin Bucer, *Christian mens Almose*, English translation *c.*1557. We shall later meet with the interesting attribution to Erasmian influence of projects of poor relief, including the discriminatory principle, in one or two Italian cities (below p. 241).
119. *Julius exclusus*, *CWE* 27, p. 187.
120. Dolan, p. 316.
121. *Enchiridion* (Dolan), p. 54.
122. R. de Roover, 'Scholastic economics . . .', in *Quarterly Journal of Economics*, 69 (1955), 177.
123. J. T. Noonan, *The Scholastic Analysis of Usury* (Cambridge, Mass., 1957), pp. 2, 121, 199, 279, 361–2.
124. *Adages*, p. 226.
125. See Myron P. Gilmore, *The World of Humanism 1453–1517* (New York, 1962), p. 45.
126. M. M. Phillips, *Erasmus and the Northern Renaissance*, p. 104.
127. *Adages* pp. 184–5, 213.

128. *Praise of Folly*, *CWE* 27, p. 121.
129. See J. T. Noonan, op. cit., p. 89.
130. *Concerning the Immense Mercy of God* (Dolan), p. 268.
131. *Adages*, pp. 130, 153.
132. M. M. Phillips, *Adages*, p. 112.
133. Richard Marius, *Thomas More* (London and Melbourne, 1985), p. 236.
134. Thomas Starkey, *A Dialogue Between Reginald Pole and Thomas Lupset*, ed. K. M. Burton, Dust-jacket.
135. Thomas Becon, 'The flower of godly prayers', in *Prayers and other pieces*, ed. J. Ayre (Parker Society, Cambridge, 1843), p. 5.
136. Hugh Latimer, *Sermons* (Everyman edition), pp. 242, 248.
137. Richard Morison, *Remedy for Sedition*, 1536, F.iii–F.iv.
138. J. K. McConica, *English Humanists and Reformation Politics*, p. 160.

5. *The Problem of Theology*

Abbreviation/short-title specific to this chapter:
Payne, *Sacraments*: John B. Payne, *Erasmus. His Theology of the Sacraments*

1. See C. R. Thompson, Introduction to *Colloquies*, p. xviii; C. A. L. Jarrott, 'Erasmus' Biblical Humanism', *Studies in the Renaissance*, 17(1970), p. 146; and Marjorie O. Boyle, *Erasmus on Language and Method in Theology*, pp. 36, 53, 57, 63, 68–9, 71, 118–19.
2. H. A. Enno van Gelder, *The Two Reformations in the Sixteenth Century* (The Hague, 1961).
3. Ernst-W. Kohls, 'The Principal Theological Thoughts in the *Enchiridion Militis Christiani*', in DeMolen, *Essays*, p. 73 – though more recently Cornelis Augustijn (*Erasmus*, pp. 44–5) has deemed it 'questionable whether the theology he sees is Erasmian'.
4. See J. B. Payne, 'Towards the Hermeneutics of Erasmus', in *Scrinium Erasmianum*, ed. J. Coppens, II, 13–49, especially 23–4.
5. *Adages*, p. 267.
6. *Colloquies*, p. 473. See M. O. Boyle, op. cit., pp. 94, 97.
7. Above, pp. 57–8. Rummel, *Catholic Critics*, I, 1–13, deals fully with Dorp.
8. *CWE* 3, Nos. 347, 373 and 421. See Rummel, *Annotations*, pp. 30, 33.
9. *CWE* 5, No. 769, 6, No. 855, and 7, No. 1007.
10. See Georges G. Chantraine, 'The *Ratio Verae Theologiae* (1518)', in DeMolen, *Essays* pp. 179–85; also C. Augustijn, *Erasmus*, pp. 77–9, 84–5, 99, 103–6, 117, 191–4.
11. *CWE* 7, No. 1062. For the reception accorded his *New Testament*, and Erasmus' efforts to forestall or reply to criticism, see Rummel, *Catholic Critics*, I, Chaps. 2 and 3.
12. *Contemporaries*, iii, 285–6; Rummel, *Catholic Critics*, II, 135–9.
13. Allen, ix, Ep. 2513.
14. Payne, *Sacraments*, pp. 12–14; see also C. J. de Vogel, 'Erasmus and his attitude towards Church dogma', in *Scrinium Erasmianum*, II, 103–4, 119–22.
15. M. M. Phillips, *Erasmus and the Northern Renaissance*, p. 63.

16. *Colloquies*, p. 41.
17. See E.-W. Kohls, in DeMolen, *Essays*, p. 65.
18. Payne, *Sacraments*, pp. 16–17.
19. *CWE* 5, No. 798.
20. Payne, *Sacraments*, p. 17.
21. In what Marjorie Boyle (op. cit., p. 36) identifies as 'pedagogical reform of theology'.
22. J. Huizinga, *Erasmus and the Age of Reformation*, p. 112.
23. *CWE* 5, No. 769, and 6, No. 844.
24. See above, pp. 55–6.
25. See Rummel, *Annotations*, pp. 74–7, 84–5.
26. See Payne, *Sacraments*, pp. 23, 25, 30.
27. *Adages*, p. 281. On these issues see J. K. McConica, 'Erasmus and the Grammar of Consent', in *Scrinium Erasmianum*, II, 84–7, and, more recently, *Erasmus*, pp. 77–80, as well as C. Augustijn, 'The Ecclesiology of Erasmus', in *Scrinium Erasmianum*, II, 140–1, and *Erasmus*, p. 152.
28. Allen, vi, Ep. 1893.
29. Bruce Mansfield, 'Erasmus of Rotterdam: evangelical', in *Erasmus in English*, 6 (1973), 3–4.
30. R. H. Bainton, *Erasmus of Christendom*, p. 239.
31. A. Rabil, Jnr, op. cit., p. 141, and 'Erasmus's *Paraphrases of the New Testament*', in DeMolen, *Essays*, pp. 147–9, 155.
32. Preserved Smith, *Erasmus*, pp. 52–55, 170–1.
33. Op. cit., Book IV, Chapter XVIII.
34. See below, pp. 182–3.
35. *CWE* 7, No. 1039.
36. *CWE* 9, No. 1334; Allen, v, Ep. 1365.
37. Allen, xi, Ep. 2988.
38. Regarding the contention that the Christocentric piety of Erasmus 'is the culmination of the present understanding' of scholars and that 'Erasmus found his life's vocation in a scriptural, Christocentric theology' (Manfred Hoffman, *Yearbook*, ix (1989), pp. 120–1), see *inter alia* C. A. L. Jarrott, in *Studies in the Renaissance*, 17 (1970), p. 146; E.-W. Kohls, in DeMolen, *Essays*, pp. 65, 69, 72–3; Olin (1987 edn.) pp. 18–19; J. B. Payne, *Erasmus: His Theology of the Sacraments*, Chap. IV, 'Christology'.
39. A. Rabil, *Erasmus and the New Testament*, pp. 93, 146.
40. Payne, *Sacraments*, pp. 58, 67.
41. Dolan, 80–1; Bainton, op. cit., pp. 127–8.
42. *CWE* 1, No. 108.
43. E.-W. Kohls, in DeMolen, *Essays*, p. 73.
44. See R. H. Bainton, op. cit., pp. 178, 230.
45. Below, pp. 133–5.
46. *The Imitation of Christ*, Book I, Chapter 1.
47. For Lee, *Contemporaries*, iii, 311–14 and below, pp. 202–3.
48. *Colloquies*, pp. 420–1.
49. See Payne, *Sacraments*, p. 101, and C. Augustijn, *Scrinium Erasmianum*, II, 145–6.
50. See Rummel, *Annotations*, pp. 146–9.

51. *Colloquies*, pp. 47, 68–9.
52. E.-W. Kohls, in DeMolen, *Essays*, p. 61.
53. R. H. Bainton, op. cit., pp. 313–14. See below, pp. 174–5 and 184–5.
54. On Confession and Penance, see above, p. 15.
55. See below, pp. 273–5.
56. Allen, ix, p. 298 note 393.
57. See C. A. L. Jarrott, 'Erasmus' Biblical Humanism', pp. 125–8, and Rummel, *Annotations*, p. 152.
58. See R. H. Bainton, op. cit., pp. 70–1, 276.
59. Payne, *Sacraments*, p. 109.
60. *Colloquies*, p. 59.
61. Allen, vii, Ep. 1868; see also vii, Ep. 1782 (2/2/1527) from John Botzheim.
62. Latin verse in J. A. Froude, *Life and Letters of Erasmus*, p. 116.
63. *Praise of Folly*, p. 127. On Transubstantiation, above, pp. 7, 56.
64. Payne, *Sacraments*, Chapter VIII.
65. See M. A. Screech, *Ecstasy and the Praise of Folly*, pp. 117–18.
66. *Contemporaries*, i, 233–4.
67. *CWE* 8, No. 1126.
68. Allen, viii, Ep. 2175.
69. M. A. Screech, op. cit., pp. 119–20.
70. Allen, v, Ep. 1523.
71. Allen, vi, Epp. 1539, 1616 and 1624.
72. Cited by R. H. Bainton, op. cit., p. 204.
73. Allen, vi, Ep. 1637.
74. Allen, vi, Epp. 1638, 1639 and 1640. On Pellican and Oecolampadius, see below, pp. 157–8.
75. *Contemporaries*, iii, 90–3.
76. Allen, vi, Ep. 1717.
77. On Ludwig Baer (Louis Ber), Basel theologian and humanist, see *Contemporaries*, i, 84–6.
78. Allen, viii, Ep. 2136.
79. Allen, viii, Ep. 2175.
80. *Contemporaries*, ii, 434–5.
81. Allen, viii, Ep. 2284. See below, pp. 198–9.
82. *Contemporaries*, i, 42–6.
83. Allen, ix, Ep. 2631.
84. Allen, viii, Ep. 2284.
85. Allen, ix, Ep. 2375. For Cricius, see below, pp. 259, 261.
86. See Payne, *Sacraments*, pp. 134–5, and M. A. Screech, op. cit., p. 118, among others.
87. See above, p. 7.
88. Payne, *Sacraments*, p. 145.
89. *The Imitation of Christ*, Book IV, Chapter XVIII.
90. Bruce Mansfield identifies several nineteenth-century historians for whom Erasmus was, above all, the 'founder of theological rationalism': *Man on His Own*, pp. 286–90.
91. See R. H. Bainton, op. cit., pp. 224–6, and E.-W. Kohls, in DeMolen, *Essays*, p. 69.

6. *'This Lutheran Tragedy . . .'*

1. Allen, iv, Ep. 1489, to John Fisher, Bishop of Rochester (4/9/1524).
2. E. G. Rupp, in *Contemporaries*, ii, 361.
3. *CWE* 4, No. 501 and *Luther's Works*, Vol. 48, pp. 23–6. On Frederick and Spalatin, see *Contemporaries*, iii, 203–5 and 266–7 respectively.
4. E. G. Rupp, loc. cit.
5. *Luther's Works*, Vol. 48, p. 40.
6. *CWE* 6, No. 939 (14/4/1519).
7. *CWE* 8, No. 1225.
8. *Luther's Works*, Vol. 48, pp. 52–3, 306.
9. *CWE* 6, No. 933.
10. *CWE* 6, Nos. 858, 872.
11. *CWE* 7, No. 1003 (19/10/1519). For Albert of Brandenburg see *Contemporaries*, i, 184–7.
12. *Luther's Works*, Vol. 48, p. 150.
13. *CWE* 7, Nos. 1041, 1102.
14. *CWE* 6, No. 980.
15. *CWE* 7, Nos. 1119 and 1127.
16. *CWE* 8, No. 1167. For Campeggio (Lorenzo Campeggi) see *Contemporaries*, i, 253–5 and below, p. 237.
17. *Axiomata* printed in Olin, pp. 146–9.
18. *CWE* 6, No. 947.
19. *CWE* 7, Nos. 1071 and 1113.
20. *CWE* 8, Nos. 1141, 1156, 1166.
21. *CWE* 8, Nos. 1185, 1191, 1192A.
22. *CWE* 8, No. 1218.
23. *CWE* 3, Nos. 305, 335, 418, 432, and 5, No. 636. For Reuchlin, above pp. 17–18.
24. *CWE* 7, No. 1041.
25. *CWE* 8, No. 1155.
26. *CWE* 8, No. 1161 (13/11/1520).
27. *CWE* 6, Nos. 939 and 961.
28. *CWE* 6, No. 967.
29. *CWE* 6, No. 1003.
30. *CWE* 8, Nos. 1153 (for Nicolaas Baechem of Egmond see *Contemporaries*, i, 81–3, and below, p. 272), and 1144 respectively.
31. *CWE* 8, No. 1157.
32. See E. Gordon Rupp, *The Righteousness of God* (London, 1953), p. 267.
33. *CWE* 8, No. 1164. On Godschalk Rosemondt see *Contemporaries*, iii, 171–2.
34. *CWE* 8, No. 1167.
35. *CWE* 8, No. 1188. For Tommaso de Vio, Cardinal Cajetan, see *Contemporaries*, i, 239–42, and below, p. 237.
36. See below, pp. 226–7, for Gattinara.
37. *CWE* 8, No. 1195.
38. *CWE* 8, Nos. 1197 and 1198.
39. *CWE* 8, No. 1212.

40. *CWE* 8, Nos. 1217 and 1218.
41. *CWE* 9, No. 1269.
42. *CWE* 8, Appendix, No. 4. On Zúñiga (Erasmus' 'Stunica'), see below, pp. 238, 274.
43. *CWE* 6, No. 938. See below, p. 162, for Erasmus and Capito.
44. *CWE* 8, No. 1202 – below, p. 255, for Jonas.
45. *CWE* 8, No. 1241.
46. *CWE* 9, Nos. 1259, 1265, 1268.
47. *CWE* 9, No. 1275.
48. *CWE* 9, No. 1342.
49. *CWE* 6, No. 983.
50. *CWE* 8, No. 1202.
51. *CWE* 8, Nos. 1205 and 1244 respectively.
52. *CWE* 9, No. 1348.
53. *CWE* 7, No. 1003.
54. *CWE* 8, No. 1127A.
55. *CWE* 8, Nos. 1153, 1156, 1166, 1183, 1188 and 1191.
56. *CWE* 9, No. 1342.
57. *CWE* 8, Nos. 1203 and 1202 respectively.
58. *CWE* 8, No. 1156. For Johannes Faber, see *Contemporaries*, ii, 4–5. See also P. Smith, *Erasmus*, pp. 237–8.
59. *CWE* 8, No. 1225.
60. *CWE* 9, No. 1352.
61. *CWE* 8, No. 1180. For Sadoleto, see below, pp. 235–7.
62. *CWE* 8, No. 1213. On Paolo Bombace of Bologna, see *Contemporaries*, i, 163–5.
63. *CWE* 8, No. 1219.
64. *CWE* 9, No. 1268.
65. *CWE* 9, No. 1275.
66. *CWE* 8, No. 1228.
67. *CWE* 9, Nos. 1267, 1298, 1324.
68. *CWE* 9, No. 1340.
69. *CWE* 9, No. 1342.
70. Allen, v, Ep. 1369 headnote, Ep. 1367.
71. Gordon Rupp, *The Righteousness of God*, p. 269.
72. Allen, v, Epp. 1381 and 1385.
73. Allen, v, Ep. 1380.
74. Allen, v, Ep. 1376.
75. *Spongia adversus aspergines Hutteni*, *LB*, x 1631B, 1632B.
76. *Spongia*, Basel edition, a.2 recto.
77. *Spongia*, *LB*, x 1635A–1644E, 1645A–B, 1645E.
78. Ibid., 1650D–F, 1651D–E, 1654A–B.
79. Ibid., 1654D, 1661B.
80. Ibid., 1663A–B.
81. Allen, v, Ep. 1397.
82. Allen, v, Epp. 1410, 1411, 1415.
83. Allen, v, Epp. 1418 and 1430.
84. *Inquisitio de fide*, translation printed in Dolan, pp. 208–21, and in *Colloquies*

and as *Inquisitio de Fide*, both ed. C. R. Thompson whose Introductions (pp. 177–8 and 1–47 respectively) are valuable.

85. *Luther's Works*, Vol. 48, pp. 76–81.
86. Allen, v, Ep. 1452.
87. Allen, v, Ep. 1445.
88. Allen, v, Epp. 1448 and 1459; for Caspar Hedio, see *Contemporaries*, ii, 169–70.
89. Allen, v, Epp. 1466, 1469, 1477.
90. Allen, v, Epp. 1481, 1482, 1486, 1487, 1488, 1489, 1493, 1495 & 1496; letter to Melanchthon below, pp. 151–2.
91. B. A. Gerrish, 'De Libero Arbitrio . . .', in DeMolen *Essays*, p. 192. Marjorie O. Boyle, in *ARG* 75 (1984), 71, defines *Diatriba* as 'a classical mode of philosophical disputation'. See also J. F. Tinkler, 'Erasmus' Conversation with Luther', in *ARG* 82 (1991), 59–81.
92. *De libero arbitrio*, trans. and ed. E. Gordon Rupp, pp. 36, 37–41.
93. Ibid., pp. 43, 45, 47–9, 51–4. For Pelagius, above p. 5. Georges Chantraine, *Érasme et Luther: libre et serf arbitre*, proffers perceptive insights into grace and freedom in Erasmus' thinking: op. cit., pp. 124, 407, 449.
94. *De libero arbitrio*, p. 54.
95. B. A. Gerrish, op. cit., p. 194.
96. *De libero arbitrio*, pp. 60–1, 64, 74.
97. *De libero arbitrio*, pp. 74, 76, 80, 84. On Synergism, see Gerrish, p. 198, and Émile G. Léonard, *A History of Protestantism*, trs. T. L. Westow (London, 1969), I, 248.
98. *De libero arbitrio*, pp. 85–8. Chantraine (op. cit., pp. 219–20, 225–6, 239) traces Erasmus' pursuit of this theme in his two *Hyperaspistes*.
99. *De libero arbitrio*, pp. 89–95.
100. J. Huizinga, *Erasmus and the Age of Reformation*, pp. 164–5.
101. Bernard Lohre, *Martin Luther*, trs. R. C. Schultz (Edinburgh, 1987), p. 69.
102. Harry J. McSorley, *Luther: Right or Wrong?*, pp. 277–93. By contrast, the verdict of Chantraine is very much more favourable to Erasmus.
103. R. H. Bainton, *Erasmus of Rotterdam*, pp. 228, 230.
104. M. M. Phillips, *Erasmus and the Northern Renaissance*, p. 120.
105. Léon-E. Halkin, *Érasme Parmi Nous*, pp. 237–8.
106. A. H. T. Levi, Introduction to Penguin Classics edn. of *Praise of Folly*, p. 30, suggests that 'much more than Eucharistic theology, it was the driving force behind the schism', while Chantraine devotes Chapter II to 'L'affrontement spirituel' between Erasmus and Luther.
107. Indeed, Peter I. Kaufman (*Augustinian Piety and Catholic Reform. Augustine, Colet and Erasmus*, p.vii) suggests that Erasmus' 'rather peculiar brand of synergism . . . appeared initially and nearly in full a quarter of a century earlier in his *Enchiridion*'.
108. B. Lohre, *Martin Luther*, p. 65.
109. A. H. T. Levi, Introduction (n. 106), pp. 30–1, suggests that 'the dilemma was rigid . . . Luther chose one of its horns and Erasmus the other'; but James D. Tracy, 'Two Erasmuses, Two Luthers: Erasmus'

Strategy in Defense of *De Libero Arbitrio*', *ARG* 78 (1987), 37, suggests that Erasmus was conscious of the ambiguity of his position, while Chantraine credits him with propounding a balanced attribution which 'avoids the Scylla of arrogance, without falling into the Charybdis of despair' (op. cit., p. 157; see also p. 263).

110. See Walther von Loewenich, *Martin Luther. The Man and His Work*, trs. L. W. Denef, (Minneapolis, 1986), p. 267.
111. See A. G. Dickens, *Martin Luther and the Reformation* (London, 1967), pp. 83–6, on Luther's 'most sustained essay in systematic theology'.
112. P. S. Watson, *Luther and Erasmus: Free Will and Salvation*, (see n. 129), pp. 13–17.
113. See both Lohre and von Loewenich, op. cit., p. 274.
114. W. von Loewenich, op. cit., p. 269.
115. See Levi (op. cit., n. 106), p. 20, Kaufman (op. cit., n. 107), p. 127, and Tracy (op. cit., n. 109), p. 37, on this issue.
116. Both Kaufman, p. 133, and Marjorie O. Boyle, 'Erasmus and the "Modern" Question: Was He Semi-Pelagian?', *ARG* 75 (1984), 73–4, would do so; but Tracy (op. cit. n. 109), is not convinced.
117. J. D. Tracy (op. cit., n. 109), p. 45.
118. See above, Chapter 3, p. 26; also Levi (op. cit., n. 106), pp. 24–8.
119. *De servo arbitrio*, translated as *The Bondage of the Will* (by P. S. Watson and B. Drewery), *Luther's Works*, Vol. 33, pp. 295, 16, 24, 61, 176.
120. As would he consider Albert Rabil's summation (in *Renaissance Humanism: Foundations, Forms and Legacy*, ed. A. Rabil, Philadelphia, 1988, Vol. 2, 253–4) that 'for Luther the most important thing was that God be God, for Erasmus that God be good'! See C. Augustijn, *Erasmus. His Life, Works, and Influence*, p. 144, for a similar conclusion.
121. Thus E. G. Leonard, (op. cit., n. 97), I, 248, and W. von Loewenich (op. cit., n. 110) p. 269.
122. See Gordon Rupp, *The Righteousness of God* (London, 1953), p. 270 and J. D. Tracy (op. cit., n. 109), p. 56.
123. Allen, v, Epp. 1513 and 1525.
124. Allen, v, Epp. 1531, 1520 and 1526.
125. Allen, v, Ep. 1528.
126. Allen, vi, Epp. 1555, 1589 headnote, 1643.
127. Allen, vi, Epp. 1624, 1633 and headnote, 1653 and 1677.
128. Allen, vi, Epp. 1678 and 1688.
129. See J. D. Tracy, op. cit., n. 109, p. 57, and E. G. Rupp, 'The Erasmian Enigma', in *Luther and Erasmus: Free Will and Salvation*, E. G. Rupp and P. S. Watson, p. 2. Chantraine devotes two chapters (op. cit, Chaps. V and VI) to detailed analysis of the significance of the two *Hyperaspistes*.
130. *Hyperaspistes Diatribae adversus servum arbitrium Martini Lutheri*, *LB*, x, 1423B–C, and J. Huizinga, *Erasmus and the Age of Reformation*, p. 165.
131. Allen, vi, Epp. 1670, 1716, 1717.
132. Allen, vi, Ep. 1731.
133. Allen, vi, Ep. 1743.
134. Allen, vi, Ep. 1770.
135. A. G. Dickens, *Martin Luther and the Reformation*, p. 86. Chantraine (pp.

125–7) finds Luther obsessed with continued resentment against Erasmus.

136. Allen, vii, Epp. 1804 and 1805.
137. Allen, vii, Epp. 1846 and 1847.
138. Allen, vii, Epp. 1869, 1872.
139. Allen, vii, Epp. 1873, 1874, 1875, 1876 and 1877; below, pp. 231–2, 273–7.
140. Allen, vii, Ep. 1924 and headnote.
141. Allen, vii, Ep. 1983.
142. Allen, vii, Ep. 1981 and headnote. Chantraine, p. 191, remarks that 'of the two *Hyperaspistes*, the first, though arduous, is readable . . . the second is almost unreadable'.
143. Allen, vii, Ep. 1987.
144. Allen, vii, Ep. 2013.
145. Allen, viii, Ep. 2134.
146. Allen, viii, Ep. 2175; for Decius, see below, pp. 260–1.
147. Allen, viii, Epp. 2328 and 2329. For Alberto Pio, below p. 239 and n. 71, Chap. 10.
148. Allen, ix, Ep. 2403.
149. Allen, ix, Epp. 2411, 2445 and 2448.
150. Allen, ix, Epp. 2492 and 2513.
151. Allen, ix, Ep. 2522; for Pflug, see below, p. 246.
152. *Luther's Works*, Vol. 54, *Table Talk*, pp. 77, 81, 84, 136. See also P. Smith, *Erasmus*, p. 367.
153. Allen, x, Epp. 2715 and 2786; on Witzel, see *Contemporaries*, iii, 458–9, and below, p. 284.
154. Allen, x, Ep. 2918 and headnote.
155. See M. M. Phillips, 'Some Last Words of Erasmus', in J. C. Olin et al., eds., *Luther, Erasmus and the Reformation*, pp. 96–103 for a full resumé and analysis.
156. *Adversus calumniosissimam epistolam Martini Lutheri*, *LB*, x, 1537B–C, D; 1539A.
157. Ibid., 1544C–D (also 1555B) & 1545C–E; 1545E–1550C.
158. Ibid., 1553C–D; 1556B–D; 1557B.
159. Allen, x, Epp. 2936, 2937 and xi, Ep. 2947. For Johann Koler, below, p. 254.
160. Allen, xi, Epp. 2970 (note 17) and 2976.
161. Allen, x, Ep. 2906 and xi, Ep. 3004.
162. Marjorie O. Boyle, *Rhetoric and Reform. Erasmus' Civil Dispute with Luther*, p. 155. To Preserved Smith also, 'it was natural that the battle should be joined on precisely the issue taken, that of the free will, for both to the dogmatic and to the ethical mind this question is fundamental' (*Erasmus*, pp. 337–9).
163. Chantraine points to Erasmus' fear that Christian humanism would be harmed as much 'by Lutheran negation as by pharisaical tyranny'. Indeed he discerns 'two types of Christology' as at issue: with the difference between 'origenism' and 'augustinianism' reflected in that between Erasmus' '*philosophia Christi*' and Luther's '*theologia crucis*' (op. cit., pp. 49, 86–7, 101 and 445–6).

7. *Protestant Humanism: Lost Leader or Errant Disciples?*

1. Heinz Scheible, in *Contemporaries*, ii, 424–9.
2. Clyde L. Manschrek, *Melanchthon. The Quiet Reformer* (New York and Nashville, 1958).
3. See Robert Stupperich, *Melanchthon*, trs. R. H. Fisher (London, 1966), pp. 14–15, 31, 34, and *CWE* 4, Nos. 454, 563 and 5, No. 605.
4. *CWE* 6, Nos. 910, 947.
5. *CWE* 7, Nos. 1113, 1119, and 8, No. 1168; on Lee, Standish, Latomus, below pp. 202–3, 272.
6. *CWE* 8, No. 1202; for Justus Jonas, see below, p. 255.
7. *Loci communes theologici* (trs. L. J. Satre), pp. 22–30.
8. Ibid., pp. 33, 46–7, 105–6.
9. Ibid., pp. 130, 152. Interestingly, for Cornelis Augustijn (*Erasmus. His Life, Works, and Influence*, p. 196) this 'first systematic theological work of Protestant origin . . . clearly shows Erasmian influence'.
10. Allen, xi, Ep. 3120.
11. *Loci communes theologici*, pp. 105–7.
12. Allen, v, p. 545, n. 26–7; see also C. L. Manschreck, *Melanchthon*, p. 115.
13. See Allen, v, Epp. 1429, 1437 and 1477, also R. Stupperich, *Melanchthon*, pp. 63, 66.
14. Allen, v, Ep. 1496 and headnote.
15. Allen, v, Ep. 1500, and Manschreck, p. 118.
16. See L. C. Green, 'The Influence of Erasmus upon Melanchthon, Luther and the Formula of Concord', in *Church History*, 43 (1974), 183–200, also Manschreck, p. 121.
17. Allen, v, Epp. 1523 and 1531.
18. See Manschreck, pp. 120–1.
19. Allen, viii, Epp. 2343 and 2355.
20. Allen, viii, Epp. 2357 and 2358.
21. Ibid., Epp. 2363 and 2365.
22. *Epistola ad fratres Germaniae inferioris*, Ii recto, G5 verso.
23. Allen, x, Epp. 2732, 2937, xi, Epp. 2947 and 2970.
24. Allen, xi, Epp. 3120 and headnote, 3127.
25. R. Stupperich, *Melanchthon*, p. 103.
26. See Fritz Büsser, in *Contemporaries*, iii, 481–6.
27. See G. W. Bromiley, *Zwingli and Bullinger* (Philadelphia and London, 1953), p. 16; Ulrich Gabler, *Huldrych Zwingli*, trs. Ruth C. L. Gritsch (Edinburgh, 1987), pp. 32–3; 38–9; W. P. Stephens, *The Theology of Huldrych Zwingli* (Oxford, 1986), pp. 49–50; and G. R. Potter, *Zwingli* (Cambridge, 1976), p. 15. For Glareanus see *Contemporaries*, ii, 105–8.
28. *CWE* 3, Nos. 401 and 404.
29. Printed in B. J. Kidd, *Documents Illustrative of the Continental Reformation* (Oxford, 1911), II, 378–9.
30. On these issues see U. Gabler, pp. 40, 72–4, and Gottfried W. Locher, 'Zwingli and Erasmus', pp. 4, 12–13.
31. G. W. Locher, loc. cit., also his *Zwingli's Thought. New Perspectives* (Leiden, 1981), pp. 53, 76–7.

32. See G. R. Potter, *Zwingli*, p. 75, and Fritz Busser in *Contemporaries*, iii, 482–4.
33. *CWE* 9, Nos. 1314 and 1315.
34. *CWE* 9, No. 1327; see U. Gabler, *Huldrych Zwingli*, pp. 54, 58–9.
35. Allen, v, Epp. 1378 and 1379; see P. Smith, *Erasmus*, pp. 332–5.
36. Allen, v, Ep. 1384 and n. 2.
37. Allen, v, Epp. 1496 and 1523, vi, Ep. 1620.
38. Cornelisz Hoen, 'A Most Christian Letter', in *Forerunners of the Reformation*, H. A. Oberman (London, 1967), pp. 268–76.
39. Allen, vi, Ep. 1644.
40. On Pellican, see Hans R. Guggisberg, in *Contemporaries*, iii, 65–6.
41. See Henri Meylan, *D'Érasme à Théodore de Bèze* (Geneva, 1976), pp. 56, 58–9, and W. P. Stephens, op. cit., n. 27, p. 98.
42. Allen, vi, Epp. 1674 (8/3/1526) and 1723 (23/6/1526).
43. Allen, vii, Ep. 1901.
44. Allen, viii, Ep. 2341.
45. *Epistola ad fratres Germaniae inferioris*, A8 verso.
46. Allen, ix, Epp. 2561 and 2579. For Amerbach and Oecolampadius, see *Contemporaries*, i, 43–5, and iii, 24–7 respectively.
47. Allen, ix, Epp. 2593 and 2607. See *Contemporaries*, iii, 220–1 on Schets, and below, pp. 244–5, for Olah.
48. See Ulrich Gabler, *Huldrych Zwingli*, pp. 72–4.
49. Above, pp. 105–110.
50. J. T. McNeill, *The History and Character of Calvinism* (New York, 1954), pp. 46–7; see also G. R. Potter, *Zwingli*, pp. 292–3.
51. See W. P. Stephens, *The Theology of Huldrych Zwingli*, pp. 16, 218, 227, 236–9, 252–3, 256–7; on Leo Jud, *Contemporaries*, ii, 248–50.
52. On these issues, McNeill, p. 76, G. W. Locher, 'Zwingli and Erasmus', pp. 7–8, and *Zwingli's Thought. New Perspectives*, pp. 76–7, and Stephens, op. cit., pp. 90, 100 n. 84, 103 n. 95, 147 and 153.
53. See Heinz Scheible in *Contemporaries*, iii, 484–5, Ulrich Gabler, op. cit., p. 46, and Rupert E. Davies, *The Problem of Authority in the Continental Reformers* (London, 1946), pp. 84–9.
54. See Miriam U. Chrisman in *Contemporaries*, i, 209–12, as well as her *Lay Culture, Learned Culture* . . . for the background of Strassburg; also W. P. Stephens, *The Holy Spirit in the Theology of Martin Bucer* (Cambridge, 1970), pp. 5–6, Nicole Peremans, *Érasme et Bucer*, p. 30, and Hastings Eells, *Martin Bucer* (New Haven, 1951), pp. 3, 9.
55. N. Peremans, op. cit., pp. 32, 46. For Hubmaier, et al., below, Chapter Seven.
56. See James M. Kittelson, *Wolfgang Capito. From Humanist to Reformer* (Leiden, 1975), and in *Contemporaries*, i, 261–4.
57. Above, pp. 122–3.
58. Allen, v, Epp. 1290 and 1308.
59. Allen, v, Ep. 1374.
60. Allen, v, Epp. 1437, 1459 and 1485.
61. Kittelson, op. cit., pp. 110–11, and Eells, op. cit., p. 41.

62. Translation from 'Selected Letters' in J. Huizinga, *Erasmus and the Age of Reformation*, pp. 243–6.
63. For Geldenhauer see *Contemporaries*, ii, 82–4.
64. See N. Peremans, op. cit., pp. 71–3, H. Eells, op. cit., p. 127, and Smith (*Erasmus*, p. 393) who points out that the last two words of Geldenhauer's title, *Erasmus's Annotations on Ecclesiastical and Imperial Laws Concerning Heretics* became the display line of the title page!
66. *Epistola contra quosdam qui se falso iactant evangelicos*, a2, A5 recto, B1 recto and verso.
66. Eells, pp. 128–9 and *Contemporaries*, i, 210.
67. Allen, viii, Ep. 2326 (6/6/1530).
68. *Epistola ad fratres Germaniae inferioris* . . ., A6 verso, A8 recto.
69. Ibid., B3 recto–verso.
70. Ibid., C4 recto–C5 verso.
71. Ibid., D2 verso.
72. Ibid., G5 verso, H2 verso, and I1 recto.
73. Allen, ix, Epp. 2365, 2371 (29/8/1530) and 2383 (7/9/1530).
74. Allen, ix, Ep. 2441.
75. Allen, ix, Ep. 2587. For Erasmus' persistent suspicions of Heinrich Eppendorf, a relatively minor figure, see *Contemporaries*, ii, 438–41.
76. Allen, ix, Ep. 2615, pp. 445–50.
77. Ibid., pp. 451–2.
78. Ibid., pp. 452–5.
79. Ibid., pp. 455–7.
80. See J. M. Kittelson, *Wolfgang Capito*, p. 207, N. Peremans, *Érasme et Bucer*, pp. 31, 151–2, and W. P. Stephens, *The Holy Spirit in the Theology of Martin Bucer*, p. 11.
81. Peremans, pp. 33, 154; Stephens, p. 15. On Calvin's debt to Bucer, see F. Wendel, trs. P. Mairet, *Calvin* (London, 1965), pp. 329–55.
82. See Bucer's *De Regno Christi*, trs. W. Pauck, in *Melanchthon and Bucer*, especially pp. 183, 227; 341–2, 360–1; 256–9, 306–15; 337, 324–5, and 383.
83. Peremans, p. 154.
84. Kittelson, p. 3.
85. See J. M. Stayer, 'Zwingli before Zurich', in *ARG* 72 (1981), 61–2.

8. *The Radical Reformation*

Abbreviations/short-titles specific to this chapter:
Davis (1): K. R. Davis, *Anabaptism and Asceticism*
Davis (2): 'Erasmus as Progenitor . . .'
Deppermann: Klaus Deppermann, *Melchior Hoffman*, trs. Malcolm Wren, ed. Benjamin Drewery (Edinburgh, 1987)
Harder: Leland Harder, ed., *The Sources of Swiss Anabaptism* (Scottdale, Pa., and Kitchener, Ontario, 1985)

1. Williams, pp. 2–3.
2. Heinold Fast, 'The Dependence of the First Anabaptists on Luther, Erasmus and Zwingli', *MQR*, 30 (April 1956), 109.

3. G. H. Williams and A. M. Mergal, eds., *Spiritual and Anabaptist Writers*, pp. 20–24.
4. Deppermann, pp. 2–5.
5. Above, pp. 7–11.
6. See H. A. Enno van Gelder, *The Two Reformations in the Sixteenth Century*, p. 251; R. Kreider, 'Anabaptism and Humanism', *MQR*, 26 (April 1952), 123, 138; above all, Davis (1), pp. 26–7, 30–1, 244–9, 266–73, and Davis (2), pp. 163–4.
7. See Deppermann, p. 165.
8. See H. Fast (loc. cit, n. 2), pp. 109–10, and R. H. Bainton, *Studies in the Reformation* (London, 1964), p. 123.
9. *Mennonite Encyclopaedia*, II, 239.
10. See Williams, pp. 34, 85, and Deppermann, pp. 191, 244, 263, 269.
11. See Robert Kreider (loc. cit., n. 6), pp. 131, 174–5, and Williams and Mergal (op. cit., n. 3), p. 21.
12. Allen, v, Ep. 1369.
13. See R. H. Bainton, *Erasmus of Christendom*, pp. 313–14, and Harder, pp. 345, 718–19 n. 13.
14. *Mennonite Encyclopedia*, II, 239.
15. Harder, pp. 444, 448, 516, Davis (2), pp. 173–4, and Deppermann, p. 171.
16. Printed in R. H. Bainton, *The Age of the Reformation*, p. 128.
17. See Thor Hall, 'Possibilities of Erasmian Influence on Denck and Hubmaier in their views on the Freedom of the Will', *MQR*, 35 (April 1961), 149–70, also Deppermann, pp. 185–7.
18. John Denck, *Whether God is the Cause of Evil*, 1526, printed in Williams and Mergal (see n. 3), p. 100, and Balthasar Hubmaier, *On Free Will*, 1527, in Williams and Mergal, pp. 114–15, 124–8, 131. For Hubmaier, *Contemporaries*, ii, 210–11.
19. On this crucial issue, see H. J. Hillerbrand, 'Anabaptism and the Reformation: Another Look', *Church History*, 29 (1960), 407–8, and 'The Origin of Sixteenth-Century Anabaptism: Another Look', *ARG*, 53 (1962), 161; Deppermann, p. 224; Williams, pp. 156–7; Davis (1), pp. 102, 145–9, 224; Davis (2), pp. 164–70; Hubmaier, pp. 124–8.
20. R. H. Bainton, *Hunted Heretic* (Boston, 1960), p. 58. See above, pp. 101–2.
21. Earl M. Wilbur, trs. of *On the Errors of the Trinity*, by Michael Servetus, Introduction, p.xvii; *CWE* 9, No. 1334 (to Jean de Carondelet, preface to edn. of St Hilary).
22. See H. Fast (loc. cit., n. 2), p. 110.
23. Harder, pp. 274–9, 516.
24. Deppermann, p. 219.
25. See R. Kreider (loc. cit., n. 6), pp. 125, 138, also Davis (1), pp. 74–5, 97–8, 109, and Davis (2), pp. 170–3.
26. Claus-Peter Clasen, *Anabaptism. A Social History, 1525–1618* (Ithaca and London), p. 9. See also Davis (2), pp. 169–70.
27. See Davis (1), pp. 64, 66–7, 122–8, Williams and Mergal, op. cit., p. 20, and R. H. Bainton, *The Reformation of the Sixteenth Century* (London, 1961), pp. 96–7.
28. Bainton, loc. cit., n. 16.

29. J. Denck, *Whether God is the Cause of Evil*, in Williams and Mergal, p. 108.
30. H. J. Hillerbrand, in *Church History*, 29 (1960), 413.
31. Harder, p. 382.
32. *The Letters of Stephen Gardiner*, pp. 383, 386; below, pp. 203–4.
33. H. S. Bender, 'The Pacifism of the Sixteenth Century Anabaptists', *MQR*, 30 (Jan. 1956), 5–6, 16–17.
34. H. Fast (loc. cit., n. 2), p. 110 and n. 32.
35. Harder, pp. 118–19, 290, 608 n. 11.
36. See R. Kreider (loc. cit., n. 6), p. 136.
37. H. J. Hillerbrand, in *ARG*, 53 (1962), 158, and Harder, p. 536.
38. See James M. Stayer, *Anabaptists and the Sword* (Lawrence, Kansas, 1972), pp. 55, 312.
39. Davis (2), pp. 171–2, and Harder, pp. 343–5.
40. N. Cohn, *The Pursuit of the Millenium* (London, 1957), pp. 274–5, 262.
41. C.-P. Clasen (op. cit., n. 26), pp. 324–7, and Deppermann, pp. 198–9.
42. Printed in R. H. Bainton, *The Age of the Reformation*, pp. 129–30. See also F. H. Littell, *The Anabaptist View of the Church* (American Society of Church History, 1952), pp. 27 n. 44, 53, and Kreider (loc. cit., n. 6), p. 138.
43. *CWE* 9, No. 1334 – see note 21.
44. See W. K. Ferguson, 'The Attitude of Erasmus toward Toleration', in *Persecution and Liberty. Essays in Honor of G. L. Burr* (New York, 1931), p. 171, and J. Lecler, *Toleration and the Reformation*, trs. T. L. Westow (London, 1969), I, 339, 343–4, 417.
45. See J. K. Zeman, *The Anabaptists and the Czech Brethren in Moravia 1526–1628* (The Hague/Paris, 1969), p. 138. On Maarten Lips of Brussels, see *Contemporaries*, ii, 333–4.
46. *CWE* 7, No. 1021 and p. 373 n. 14.
47. *CWE* 7, No. 1039 and headnote.
48. *CWE* 7, No. 1039 headnote.
49. *CWE* 8, Nos. 1154 and 1183. For Arkleb of Boskovice see *Contemporaries*, i, 174–5.
50. Allen, v, Ep. 1292 headnote; Williams, p. 65; J. K. Zeman, pp. 125, 139; P. Smith, *Erasmus*, p. 382.
51. Harder, pp. 165, 633 n. 10.
52. Allen, v, Ep. 1522, vi, Ep. 1644.
53. Allen, vi, Ep. 1574. For Johann von Botzheim see *Contemporaries*, i, 177–8.
54. Allen, vii, Epp. 1805, 1901. For Juan Maldonado, below, p. 231.
55. Allen, vii, Epp. 1959, 1977.
56. Allen, viii, Ep. 2134.
57. Ibid., Ep. 2149. See *Contemporaries*, i, 84–6, on Ludwig Baer of Basel.
58. Ibid., Ep. 2341.
59. Above, p. 165; Allen, ix, Ep. 2615 headnote.
60. On Franck, see *Contemporaries*, ii, 53–4, and Williams, pp. 265–7.
61. See Rufus M. Jones, *Spiritual Reformers in the 16th & 17th Centuries* (London, 1924), p. 51.
62. Allen, ix, Ep. 2587.
63. *The Forbidden Fruit*, p. 39.

64. For Servetus, see *Contemporaries*, ii, 242–3, Williams, pp. 16, 198–9, and R. H. Bainton, *Hunted Heretic*, pp. 9, 32.
65. Earl M. Wilbur, *A History of Unitarianism* (Cambridge, Mass., 1946), I, 58 n. 35.
66. *On the Errors of the Trinity*, p. 33.
67. Allen, xi, Ep. 2956.
68. See Deppermann, p. 341.
69. Allen, xi, Ep. 2957; for Zuichemus, who was born in Friesland, *Contemporaries*, iii, 393–5.
70. Allen, xi, Epp. 2961 and 2962.
71. Allen, xi, Epp. 2965 (*Contemporaries*, ii, 461–2 for Morillon) and 2981.
72. Allen, xi, Ep. 2990; *Contemporaries*, ii, 125–6, for Tielmann Gravius.
73. Allen, Ep. 2992; Deppermann, pp. 341–2, contrasts grandiose plans with meagre efforts.
74. Allen, xi, Ep. 2999.
75. Allen, ix, Ep. 3000; for Tomiczki see below, pp. 261–2.
76. Allen, xi, Ep. 3004. See Deppermann, pp. 341–2, and O. Chadwick, *The Reformation* (London, 1964), pp. 190–1.
77. Allen, xi, Ep. 3029; see below, p. 272, for Latomus.
78. Allen, xi, Epp. 3031, 3031a, and 3041. On Conrad Heresbach, below, p. 256.
79. Ibid., Ep. 3043.
80. Ibid., Ep. 3048.
81. Ibid., Ep. 3049.
82. See Davis (2), pp. 163, 173.
83. *The Complete Writings of Menno Simons*, trs. L. Verduin, ed. J. C. Wenger, (Scottdale, Penn., 1956), pp. 248, 270.
84. See Davis (1), p. 277.
85. Ibid.
86. Davis (2), p. 178.

9. *The English Erasmians*

1. *CWE* 2, No. 159, 4, No. 552, 9, No. 1347.
2. Ibid., 2, Nos. 189, 215, 227, 240A, 243, 3, No. 333, 9, No. 1347; above pp. 33–5.
3. Ibid., 2, No. 185, 3, Nos. 333, 334; for Mountjoy see *Contemporaries*, i, 154–6.
4. *CWE* 2, Nos. 284, 295, 297, 3, No. 348, 4, No. 577.
5. Ibid., 2, Nos. 208, 240A, 243, 252, 295, 3, Nos. 334, 396, 413, 4, No. 558; see *Contemporaries*, iii, 427–31.
6. *CWE* 2, Nos. 229, 242, 295, 4, No. 452; *Contemporaries*, ii, 36–9.
7. *CWE* 3, No. 332, 4, No. 584, 6, No. 886; *Contemporaries*, iii, 349–55.
8. *CWE* 5, No. 654; Allen, vi, Ep. 1770.
9. *CWE* 2, Nos. 194, 241, 270, 3, Nos. 388, 431, 9, No. 1347; *Contemporaries*, ii, 135–6, 331–2, 357–9.
10. On this, and indeed on the Erasmian legacy in Shakespeare, see Emrys Jones, *The Origins of Shakespeare* (Oxford, 1977), pp. 9–13, 96–7, 159–60, 216, 266.

11. For this, within 'the perspective of a pan-Erasmian movement of humanist reform' in England, see particularly J. K. McConica, *English Humanists and Reformation Politics*; significant if perhaps overstated. Yet still more recently Augustijn (*Erasmus*, p. 199) concludes that 'only in the England of Henry VIII did Erasmianism win a dominating position'.
12. *CWE* 3, Nos. 423, 425, 4, Nos. 449, 450. One third of all sales recorded by one Oxford bookseller in 1520 were of works by Erasmus (Preserved Smith, *Erasmus*, p. 158).
13. See E. J. Devereux, *A Checklist of English Translations of Erasmus to 1700* (Oxford Bibliographical Society, 1968) and A. W. Pollard and G. R. Redgrave, *Short Title Catalogue of Works printed in England, 1475–1640*, I (London, 1986).
14. *Erasmus. Enchiridion Militis Christiani: An English Version*, ed. Anne M. O'Donnell (EETS, 1981), pp. xxvi, xxxvi, xlviii-liii; *A booke called . . . the manuell of the christen knyght*, 1533, a.i.verso.
15. *Bellum Erasmi*, 1534, p. 2.
16. *Contemporaries*, i, 353–4.
17. See G. R. Elton, *Reform and Renewal* (Cambridge, 1973), pp. 26, 62, 76.
18. *DNB*, lviii, 6–9.
19. *Concernynge the veryte of the Sacrament*, A.ii.verso; see above, pp. 107–8.
20. *The praise of Folie*, 1549, A.iv.recto.
21. *Contemporaries*, i, 220.
22. See John K. Yost, 'German Protestant Humanism and the Early English Reformation: Richard Taverner and Official Translation', in *Bibliothèque d'Humanisme et Renaissance*, xxxii (1970), 613–25. His 'Taverner's Use of Erasmus and the Protestantization of English Humanism', *Renaissance Quarterly*, 23 (1970), 266–76, surveys the same ground.
23. J. K. Yost, pp. 618–19, 621–2, 624–5.
24. J. K. McConica, *English Humanists and Reformation Politics*, pp. 133, 143, 199, 235; see G. R. Elton, *Reform and Renewal*, pp. 3–5, for an incisive critique.
25. See Craig R. Thompson, 'Erasmus and Tudor England', in *Actes du Congrès Érasme* (Amsterdam/London, 1971), pp. 29–68, also McConica, pp. 120, 124, 144, 148, 160, 199, and G. R. Elton, *Reform and Renewal*, pp. 31, 34; Erasmus' letters in Allen, xi, Epp. 3036, 3058, 3107.
26. J. Hooper, *A Declaration of Christe. . .*, in *Early Writings* (Parker Society, Cambridge, 1843), p. 46.
27. John Foxe, *Acts and Monuments*, v (London, 1838), 40.
28. T. Becon, in *Prayers and other pieces* (Parker Society, Cambridge, 1843), pp. 359–60.
29. T. Becon, in *Prayers and other pieces*, pp. 5, 170.
30. J. Foxe, *Acts and Monuments*, iv (London, 1837), 633–5, and v, 421–3.
31. Ibid., v, 40.
32. William Fulke, *A Defense of the sincere and true Translations of the holie Scriptures* (Parker Society, Cambridge, 1843), pp. 154–5.
33. C. W. Dugmore, *The Mass and the English Reformers* (London, 1958), pp. 58, 130, 156–8; see also P. N. Brooks, *Thomas Cranmer's Doctrine of the Eucharist* (London, 1965), pp.xvi, 38–9, 60, 64, 68–9, 98.

34. T. Becon, in *The Catechism . . . with other pieces* (Parker Society, Cambridge, 1844), p. 253. Erasmus' *De sarcienda* (Dolan, p. 384) suggests a probable source for this.
35. J. Hooper, in *Early Writings*, pp. 240–1.
36. *Contemporaries*, ii, 311–14.
37. Ibid., iii, 279–81; Allen, viii, Ep. 1126.
38. J. F. Mozley, *William Tyndale* (London, 1937), pp. 84, 87, 91–4, 211, 217; Richard Marius, *Thomas More* (London and Melbourne, 1985), pp.x, 237–87, 289, 331; see also R. J. Schoeck, 'The Place of Erasmus Today', *Trans. Royal Soc. of Canada*, 4th.Ser., VIII, 1970, 288–298.
39. J. Foxe, *Acts and Monuments*, v, 40.
40. *The Letters of Stephen Gardiner*, ed. J. A. Muller (Cambridge, 1933), pp. 403, 412, 418.
41. 'Enforcing Statute against Heresy', 13 June 1555, No. 422 in *Tudor Royal Proclamations*, ed. P. L. Hughes and J. F. Larkin (New Haven and London, 1969), II, 57–60; N. Ridley, in *Works* (Parker Society, Cambridge, 1843), p. 29.
42. Craig R. Thompson, 'Erasmus and Tudor England', pp. 49–51.
43. John R. Wall, Introduction to *The First Tome or Volume of the Paraphrase of Erasmus upon the Newe Testamente*, ed. N. Udall (Delmar, New York, 1975), pp. 9–14.
44. Ibid., Text, A.v.recto, A.vi.verso, A.viii.recto, B.iii.recto.
45. Ibid., C.ii.recto; Introduction, pp. 7, 24 n. 21.
46. See J. K. McConica, op. cit., pp. 199, 235, 280; also C. R. Thompson, op. cit., p. 53.
47. *Miscellaneous Writings and Letters of Thomas Cranmer* (Parker Society, Cambridge, 1846), pp. 154–6, 498–501.
48. R. Marius, *Thomas More*, p. 444.
49. P. N. Brooks, *Cranmer in Context* (Cambridge, 1989), p. 1.
50. J. G. Nichols, *Narratives of the Days of the Reformation* (Camden Society, old series, lxxvii, 1859), pp. 418–19.
51. P. N. Brooks, op. cit., pp. 52–3.
52. T. Cranmer, *Miscellaneous Writings . . .*, p. 288.
53. Here we are greatly indebted to David G. Selwyn's Catalogue of the printed books in Cranmer's library.
54. Philippa Tudor, ' "All youthe to learne the Creade and Tenne commaundementes": Unpublished Draft Injunctions of Henry VIII's Reign', in *Historical Research*, lviii (No. 151, June 1990), 212–7.
55. See Maria Dowling, 'Cranmer as Humanist Reformer', kindly made available prior to publication.
56. T. Cranmer, *Miscellaneous Writings . . .*, pp. 159–60; G. K. A. Bell, *Statutes of the Cathedral Church of Canterbury* (London, 1920), pp. 62–5.
57. Ubbo Emmius, *Rerum Frisicarum Historia* (Emden, 1616), II, 925; see A. G. Dickens, *The English Reformation* (2nd edn.), p. 210, also W. R. D. Jones, *William Turner* (London and New York, 1988), pp. 19, 21–2.
58. Margo Todd, *Christian Humanism and the Puritan Social Order* (Cambridge and New York, 1987), pp. 43 n. 63, 196.
59. Martin Bucer, *De Regno Christi*, trs. W. Pauck, and P. Larkin (in

Melanchthon and Bucer, ed. W. Pauck, London and Philadelphia, 1969), especially on such issues as Poor Relief (pp. 306–15), education and the avoidance of idleness (pp. 333–7), the need for control of greedy merchants (pp. 337–45), and Magistrates' responsibility (pp. 361–74).

60. C. Hopf, *Martin Bucer and the English Reformation* (Oxford, 1946), pp. 52, 194.
61. On these issues see A. G. Dickens, *The English Reformation* (2nd edn.), pp. 249–51, 272; W. R. D. Jones, *The Tudor Commonwealth 1529–59* (London, 1970); G. R. Elton, *Reform and Renewal*, and in P. Clark et al., (eds.), *The English Commonwealth 1547–1640* (London, 1979), pp. 23–38; S. B. Chrimes, *English Constitutional Ideas in the Fifteenth Century* (Cambridge, 1936); and D. Starkey, in *Revolution Reassessed*, ed. C. Coleman and D. Starkey (Oxford, 1986), pp. 13–27, 208.
62. E. J. Devereux, op. cit., p. 20.
63. *Enchiridion*, ed. Anne M. O'Donnell (above, n. 14), p. 162.
64. C. R. Thompson, 'Erasmus and Tudor England', pp. 56, 60–1; Pollard and Redgrave, *STC* 10491 – see Allen, vi, Ep. 1637, and above, p. 107.
65. *Remains of Edmund Grindal* (Parker Society, Cambridge, 1843), pp. 134, 157.
66. R. Marius, *Thomas More*, p. 82.
67. See W. R. D. Jones, *William Turner*, pp. 179, 187–8.
68. Above, n. 32.
69. Margo Todd, *Christian Humanism and the Puritan Social Order*; M. M. Knappen, *Tudor Puritanism* (Chicago, 1939), pp. 401, 406; M. Todd, pp. 97–116.
70. R. Whitford, op. cit., A.ii.verso and F.iii.recto, on works and work.
71. Edith W. Perry, *Under Four Tudors* (London, 1964 edn.), pp. 36, 62–3, 115–16, 208.
72. Glanmor Williams, 'Religion and Welsh Literature in the Age of the Reformation', in *Proceedings of the British Academy*, lxix (1983), 372.
73. *CWE* 2, No. 191.
74. See Glanmor Williams, *Welsh Reformation Essays* (Cardiff, 1967), p.75, and *The Welsh Church from Conquest to Reformation* (Cardiff, 1962), p. 504.
75. See Glanmor Williams, *Recovery, Reorientation and Reform. Wales c.1415–1642* (Oxford, 1967), pp. 132–3, 137–8, 275, 280, 289–91, 303, 306; also David Williams, *A History of Modern Wales* (London, 1951), pp. 35, 55, 58. His treatise on the coinage is printed by W. A. J. Archbold (ed.), 'A manuscript treatise . . .', in *EHR*, xii (1898), 709–10 – Price was related, through marriage, to Thomas Cromwell.
76. Glanmor Williams, *Welsh Reformation Essays*, p. 195; *Wales c.1415–1642*, pp. 298, 314–15, and *The Welsh Church . . .*, p. 409; D. Williams, *History of Modern Wales*, pp. 60, 67, 76.

10. *France, Spain and Italy*

1. *CWE* 5, No. 529; Allen, ix, Epp. 2514, 2553, x, Epp. 2733, 2778, 2895, xi, Ep. 3103.

2. Margaret Mann, *Érasme et les Débuts de la Réforme Française (1517–1536)*, pp. xv-xviii.
3. Ibid., pp. 4–6. On the Faculty of Theology of Paris and its 'active pursuit of heretics without overt invitation' see James K. Farge, *Orthodoxy and Reform in Early Reformation France* (Leiden, 1985).
4. *CWE* 1, No. 43; above, pp. 30–1.
5. *Contemporaries*, ii, 315–18; *CWE* 5, Nos. 659, 778, 814; M. Mann, pp. 23–74, 155; above p. 31; see also Rummel, *Catholic Critics*, I, 48–58.
6. K. R. Davis, *Anabaptism and Asceticism*, pp. 263–5.
7. See M. Mann, pp. xvii, 70–3; Lucien Febvre, 'The origins of the French Reformation: a badly-put question?', in *A new kind of history from the writings of Febvre*, ed. Peter Burke (London, 1973), pp. 52–3, 58; R. J. Knecht, 'The Early Reformation in England and France: a Comparison', in *History*, 57 (1972), 10; and E. G. Leonard, *A History of Protestantism*, I, 228.
8. *Contemporaries*, i, 198–9, J. K. Farge (op. cit., pp. 171, 181–5) notes that Briçonnet and the Meaux reformers were attacked by the Paris Faculty of Theology.
9. See M. Mann, Chap. IV, especially pp. 81, 89, and Knecht, loc. cit., p. 11.
10. Allen, v, Ep. 1407.
11. Ibid., vii, Ep. 1854.
12. M. Mann, pp. 80–1, 88–9, 96–103; Lucien Febvre, *Autour de l'Heptaméron* (Paris, 1944), pp. 53–73.
13. *Contemporaries*, i, 212–17.
14. *CWE* 3, Nos. 403 (and headnote), 421, 4, No. 529, 6, No. 906, 7, No. 1004 (and headnote).
15. For a full survey of the Faculty's range of targets see Farge, op. cit., pp. 160–208; also R. J. Knecht, *Francis I* (Cambridge University Press, 1982), pp. 142–3; J. H. Salmon, *Society in Crisis. France in the Sixteenth Century* (London, 1965), pp. 85–6; for Béda, see *Contemporaries*, i, 116–18, and Rummel, *Catholic Critics*, II, Chapter 2.
16. Allen, vi, Epp. 1571, 1579, 1581, 1596, 1609, 1610, 1620, 1642, 1664, 1679, 1685, 1721, 1722, 1723; R. J. Knecht, *Francis I*, p. 203; Farge, pp. 184–94.
17. Allen, vii, Epp. 1902, 1905, 1906, 1911, 1969; Farge, p. 195.
18. M. Mann, Chap. V; for Berquin, see *Contemporaries*, i, 136–9; Farge, pp. 173–4, 186–7.
19. Allen, vi, Epp. 1692, 1721, 1722, 1723; R. J. Knecht, *Francis I*, pp. 202–3; Farge, pp. 259–60. Margaret Mann's detailed examination of the French translations of Erasmus which were apparently involved led her to conclude that it is highly probable that Berquin was indeed their author, but also that 'his religious ideas appear to have derived more from Luther than from Erasmus' (op. cit., pp. 121–49).
20. Allen, vii, Epp. 1821, 2027, 2048, 2066, 2077, viii, Ep. 2126; R. J. Knecht, p. 205.
21. Allen, viii, Epp. 2158, 2188, x, Epp. 2796, 2800.
22. Ibid., x, Ep. 2743 (30/11/1532).
23. See Walter Kaiser, *Praisers of Folly* (London, 1964), pp. 104–5; M. A. Screech, *Rabelais* (London, 1979), pp. 202–5; E. G. Leonard, *A History of Protestantism*, I, 225.

24. M. A. Screech, pp. 10–11, 43, 134–6, 165, 175; W. Kaiser, p. 109; M. Mann, p. 185; Dorothy Gabe Coleman, *Rabelais* (Cambridge University Press, 1971), pp. 18–22, 173–4.
25. W. Kaiser, pp. 123–4; M. A. Screech, pp. 18, 62, 185–6, 188–9, 201, 204, 348; M. Mann, p. 184.
26. R. Lebègue, 'Rabelais, the last of the French Erasmians', in *Journal of the Warburg and Courtauld Institutes*, 12 (1949), 91–100; Michel de Montaigne, *Oeuvres Complètes*, ed. R. Bassal and P. Michel (Paris, 1967), p. 329; R. A. Sayce, *The Essays of Montaigne* (London, 1972), pp. 25, 33, 40, 128, 315; Pierre Villey, *Les Sources et l'Évolution des Essais de Montaigne* (Paris, 1933), I, 138–9, II, 7, 10–12, 15–16, 214–17.
27. See W. J. Bouwsma, *John Calvin* (Oxford and New York, 1988), pp. 13–14, 117, 270 n. 86; F. Wendel, *Calvin*, trs. P. Mairet (London and New York, 1963), pp. 41, 44–5, 130, 248–9, 257, 351; M. Mann, op. cit., pp. 168–71, 188; Alister McGrath, *The Intellectual Origins of the European Reformation* (Oxford, 1987), pp. 55–6.
28. *Calvin: Institutes of the Christian Religion*, trs. F. L. Battles, ed. J. T. McNeill (Philadelphia, 1967), 2 vols., consecutive pagination, 259, 291, 305–6, 318, 320, 336–7, 797.
29. R. J. Knecht, *Francis I*, p. 204; E. G. Leonard, I, 231.
30. See J. Lynch, *Spain under the Habsburgs, I, Empire and Absolutism 1516–1598* (Oxford, 2nd edn., 1981), pp. 64–7, 70; above, pp. 17, 59.
31. Ibid., pp. 68–9; J. H. Elliott, *Imperial Spain 1469–1716* (London, 1963), p. 207.
32. Marcel Bataillon, *Érasme et l'Espagne*, pp. 89, 111, 150, 167; J. Lynch, pp. 70–1; for Gattinara, see *Contemporaries*, ii, 76–80.
33. Allen, vi, Epp. 1643, 1700, 1731, 1747, 1757, 1784A, 1785, 1791 headnote, vii, Ep. 1815; Karl Brandi, in *The Emperor Charles V*, trs. C.V. Wedgwood (London, 1960 reprint), p. 258, gives prominence to Gattinara's letter of 1/10/1526.
34. *Contemporaries*, ii, 373–5.
35. Allen, vii, Epp. 1864, 1846.
36. *Contemporaries*, i, 342–3; Allen, vi, Ep. 1581, vii, Epp. 1836, 1847, 1980.
37. Allen, vi, Epp. 1747, 1748, vii, Epp. 1813, 1847; on Fonseca, *Contemporaries*, ii, 42–3.
38. *Contemporaries*, iii, 366–7; see E. M. Wilson, in *Romance Philology*, Vol. XXVII, No. 2 (1973), 189–93, on the historiography of Valdés studies.
39. See Lynch, pp. 71–2; Manuel F. Alvarez, *Charles V*, trs. J. A. Lalaguna (London, 1975), pp. 66–7; J. B. Trend, *The Civilisation of Spain* (London, New York, 1944), p. 123; Allen, vi, Ep. 1791, vii, Epp. 1807, 1839, 1907, viii, Epp. 2126, 2163.
40. John E. Longhurst, *Erasmus and the Spanish Inquisition: The Case of Juan de Valdés* (Albuquerque, 1950), especially Chapter X, 'The *Doctrina Christiana*'; G. H. Williams and A. M. Mergal, eds., *Spiritual and Anabaptist Writers of the Radical Reformation and Evangelical Catholicism* (London and Philadelphia, 1957), pp. 297, 300–9, 328; *Contemporaries*, iii, 368–71; M. Bataillon, pp. 343–93.
41. *Contemporaries*, iii, 384–7.

42. *CWE* 8, No. 1128 and pages 335–46, 9, Nos. 1271, 1305.
43. Allen, vii, Ep. 1814, x, Ep. 2932, xi, Ep. 2965.
44. *Contemporaries*, iii, 400–1.
45. Allen, vii, Epp. 1838, 1839, ix, Ep. 2523, x, Ep. 2641.
46. *Contemporaries*, ii, 370–1; Allen, vii, Epp. 1805, 1908; J. E. Longhurst, p. 76.
47. M. Bataillon, p. 167; Allen, vi, Ep. 1791 and headnote; *Contemporaries*, ii, 31.
48. Allen, vii, Epp. 1830, 1836, 1838, 1839, 1864, 1872, 1873, 1874, 1875, 1876, 1877, 1879, 1888, 1907, 1909, 1920; see M. Bataillon, pp. 253–99.
49. M. Bataillon, pp. 298–9; J. Lynch, p. 71; Allen, ix, Ep. 2955; Rummel, *Catholic Critics*, II, 81–105; see also H. Kamen, *The Phoenix and the Flame. Catalonia and the Counter Reformation* (Yale, 1993), pp. 406–20 passim.
50. J. B. Trend, op. cit., pp. 121, 124–7.
51. John C. Olin, 'Erasmus and St. Ignatius Loyola', in *Luther, Erasmus and The Reformation*, ed. J. C. Olin, J. D. Smart and R. E. McNally (New York, 1969), pp. 114–33; Terence O'Reilly, 'Erasmus, Ignatius Loyola, and Orthodoxy', in *Journal of Theological Studies*, New Ser., XXX Pt. 1, April 1979, 115–127.
52. See Dermot Fenlon, *Heresy and Obedience in Tridentine Italy* (Cambridge Univ., 1976), pp. 18–19.
53. R. M. Douglas, *Jacopo Sadoleto. 1477–1547. Humanist and Reformer* (Cambridge, Mass., 1959), p. 21. Augustin Renaudet's *Érasme et l'Italie*, of course, remains a classic in this field – and on wider issues.
54. *CWE* 3, Nos. 335, 384, 4, Nos. 446, 518, 566; for Leo X, *Contemporaries*, ii, 319–22.
55. *CWE* 9, Nos. 1304, 1310, 1324, 1329, 1338; Allen, x, Ep. 2522; see A. Renaudet, *Érasme et l'Italie*, pp. 159, 176, R. M. Douglas, *Sadoleto*, pp. 30–1, and on Pope Adrian VI, *Contemporaries*, i, 5–9.
56. *Contemporaries*, i, 308–9; Allen, v, Epp. 1408, 1418.
57. Allen, xi, Epp. 2988, 3007, 3021, 3033, 3034; *Contemporaries*, iii, 53–6; Renaudet devotes a chapter (op. cit., pp. 238–42) to 'La Politique Érasmienne de Paul III'.
58. R. M. Douglas, *Sadoleto*, pp. 11, 21 n. 34, 74; *Contemporaries*, iii, 184–5.
59. Allen, vi, Ep. 1555, vii, Epp. 2059, 2074, viii, Epp. 2315, 2443, x, Ep. 2648; R. M. Douglas, pp. 47–8, 74.
60. See A. Renaudet, pp. 217–18.
61. R. M. Douglas, pp. 86, 116.
62. Allen, xi, Ep. 3005, vii, Epp. 2059, 2290; *Contemporaries*, i, 121–3.
63. Allen, viii, Ep. 2329, ix, Epp. 2394, 2468; *Contemporaries*, i, 23–6.
64. *Contemporaries*, ii, 94–6; Allen, vi, Ep. 1716.
65. *Contemporaries*, i, 334–5, 239–42; Allen, x, Ep. 2690 and headnote.
66. *Contemporaries*, i, 253–5; Allen, viii, Epp. 2328, 2341, ix, Epp. 2366, 2411, 2579 – among many others; see Renaudet, pp. 231–2.
67. *CWE* 9, p. 313 n. 115, No. 1277; R. M. Douglas, p. 108; Rummel, *Catholic Critics*, I, Chapter 7, and II, Chapter 5.
68. *CWE* 8, No. 1128, 9, No. 1260 and p. 32 n. 45, Nos. 1271, 1305.
69. *Contemporaries*, i, 28–32.
70. Allen, x, Epp. 2638, 2639, xi, Ep. 3032 headnote; H. Jedin, *A History of the*

Council of Trent, I, trs. Dom Ernest Graf (London, 1957), p. 198; Renaudet (p. 143) dubs Aleander 'le grand ennemi'; for authorship of 'Racha', see Silvana Seidel Menchi, *Erasmo in Italia 1520–1580* (Turin, 1987), pp. 44, 60–1.

71. *Contemporaries*, i, 86–8; Allen, vi, Ep. 1634, viii, Ep. 2329, ix, Epp. 2371, 2522, 2579; M. P. Gilmore, 'Italian Reactions to Erasmian Humanism', in *Itinerarium Italicum*, ed. H. A. Oberman (Leiden, 1975), pp. 70–81, gives a full account of Pio's allegations.
72. *Contemporaries*, iii, 240–2; Allen, x, Ep. 2637 and headnote.
73. *Contemporaries*, iii, 212–14, Allen, x, Ep. 2743. S. Seidel Menchi, op. cit., pp. 43–7, 60–1, gives a useful summation of the charges of Erasmus' Italian critics.
74. See Delio Cantimori, 'Italy and the Papacy', in *New C.M.H.*, II, 258, 264–6; Celia Hughes, in *Bulletin of the John Rylands Library*, lxvi (1983), 123, 132.
75. S. Seidel Menchi, *Erasmo in Italia*, which seeks to delineate Erasmus through the eyes of his Italian readers (p. 19), and to explore his *grass-roots* impact – thus Sadoleto is mentioned but twice. Renaudet's Chapter IV, 'Antiérasmiens d'Italie', traces the emergence of savage criticism in the 1520s and early 1530s.
76. S. Seidel Menchi, pp. 15 (also 230), 33, 35–6.
77. Ibid., Cap. 2, especially pp. 41–3, 46, 53–6, 61. On Pietro Corsi's *Defensio pro Italia ad Erasmum Roterodamum*, 1534, see also Renaudet, pp. 233–4.
78. Menchi, pp. 95–9, 142, 155; above, pp. 135, 145.
79. Menchi, pp. 79, 339.
80. Marcella and Paul Grendler, 'The Erasmus Holdings of Roman and Vatican Libraries', in *Erasmus in English*, 13 (1984), 2–10 – also in *Erasmus in English*, 8 (1976), 2–22.
81. S. Seidel Menchi, *Erasmo in Italia*, pp. 227, 235, 347–53.
82. Peter G. Bietenholz, *ARG*, Jahrgang 80 (1989), 318 (review of Menchi's book).
83. See H. Jedin, *Council of Trent*, I, 363–4.
84. Brian Pullan, *Rich and Poor in Renaissance Venice* (Cambridge, Mass., 1971), pp. 226–7, 270–1, 388.
85. Menchi, pp. 201–2; Delio Cantimore, *Eretici italiani del Cinquecento* (Florence, 1939/1967), p. 197.
86. Cantimori, op. cit., p. 184; Menchi, op. cit., pp. 216, 268; R. H. Bainton, *The Reformation of the Sixteenth Century* (London, 1953), p. 219; and G. H. Williams, pp. 628–9, who places Curione among the 'Italian Evangelical Rationalists in Diaspora'.

11. *Erasmus in Central Europe*

1. *Contemporaries*, ii, 17–20; A. Wandruszka, *The House of Habsburg*, trs. C. and H. Epstein (Westport, Connecticut, 1975 reprint), pp. 91–2, 112; Allen, vi, Epp. 1608, 1690, vii, Ep. 1924, ix, Ep. 2462 and headnote.
2. See Laszlo Makkai, in *A History of Hungary*, ed. Ervin Pamlenyi (London

and Wellingborough, 1975), pp. 118, 122, 140–1; *Contemporaries*, ii, 399–401; Allen, vi, Ep. 1660.

3. *Contemporaries*, iii, 94–5, 29–31; Allen, iii, Epp. 850 (and headnote), 851, 943, 944, iv, Ep. 1206, vi, Epp. 1662, 1754; vii, Ep. 1917, viii, Ep. 2339; below, p. 266.
4. *Contemporaries*, ii, 5–8; Allen, vii, Ep. 2000, x, Ep. 2750; J. Lecler, *Toleration and the Reformation*, trs. T. L. Westow, I (London, 1969), 225–6.
5. Lecler, loc. cit.; *Contemporaries*, iii, 7–8; S. Seidel Menchi, *Erasmo in Italia 1520–1580*, pp. 35–6; Allen, vi, Epp. 1577 (and headnote), 1632 (and headnote), x, Ep. 2847 (oddly, although six letters written to Nausea are extant, none received from him by Erasmus survive); *In Magnum Erasmum . . . Monodia*, A.4 verso.
6. *Contemporaries*, i, 313–15; Allen, viii, Epp. 2107, 2326, x, Epp. 2651, 2921, xi, Epp. 2941, 3110; H. Jedin, *A History of the Council of Trent*, trs. Dom Ernst Graf, I (London, 1957), 261.
7. J. A. Froude, *Life and Letters of Erasmus*, p. 406.
8. Allen, ix, Epp. 2452, 2492, 2522, x, Ep. 2806; *Contemporaries*, iii, 77–8; J. Lecler, op. cit., I, 227.
9. See A. G. Dickens, *The German Nation and Martin Luther* (London, 1974), Chapter Two, 'Humanism and the National Myth', especially pp. 27–38; also L. W. Spitz, *The Religious Renaissance of the German Humanists* (Cambridge, Mass., 1953), Chapter 5.
10. A. G. Dickens, op. cit., pp. 34, 45–50; above, pp. 127–9; H. Holborn, *Ulrich von Hutten and the German Reformation*, trs. R. H. Bainton (New Haven and London, 1937; New York, 1966); L. W. Spitz, op. cit., Chapter 6.
11. See Preserved Smith, *Erasmus*, pp. 129–33.
12. See James D. Tracy, 'Erasmus Becomes a German', in *Renaissance Quarterly*, 21 (No. 3, Spring, 1968), 281–88.
13. Strassburg's Humanism and Reformation are both far better covered by recent scholarship than those of any other city; see especially Miriam U. Chrisman, *Lay Culture, Learned Culture. Books and Social Change in Strasbourg 1480–1599* (New Haven, 1982), pp. 44–5, 92–3, 99, 151–2, 195.
14. On Froschauer see G. R. Potter, 'Zwingli and his Publisher', *The Library Chronicle*, 40 (1974), 108–9.
15. An excellent English version of Brant's *Ship of Fools* is that translated and edited by E. H. Zeydel (New York, 1944).
16. For Jacob Wimpfeling see *Contemporaries*, iii, 447–50.
17. *Contemporaries*, iii, 469–73.
18. See J. D. Tracy, 'Erasmus the Humanist', in *Erasmus of Rotterdam*, ed. R. L. DeMolen (New York, 1971), p. 125 n. 3.
19. Above, p. 162.
20. Above, p. 185.
21. *Contemporaries*, iii, 417–18; J. C. Olin, *Christian Humanism and the Reformation*, pp. 107–33, prints the letter to Volz (with good notes) – the first English translation since that of Tyndale! See Allen, iii, 361–77.
22. See A. G. Dickens, 'Luther and the Humanists', in P. Mack and M. C. Jacob (eds.), *Politics and Culture in Early Modern Europe* (London, 1987), pp. 199–214; Ch.2 of Alister McGrath's *The Intellectual Origins of the European*

reformation (London, 1987), despite the stature of the book, perhaps underrates the debt of Luther to Erasmus.

23. See Gerald Strauss, *Nuremberg in the Sixteenth Century* (New York, 1966), p. 236; on Pirckheimer: *Contemporaries*, iii, 90–4, Allen, especially vi, Epp. 1717 (6/6/1526) and 1729 (30/7/1526), vii, Ep. 1893 (19/10/1527), ix, Ep. 2493.
24. *Contemporaries*, ii, 269–70; Allen, x, Epp. 2814, 2868, 2936, 2937, xi, Epp. 2947, 2953, 2983, 3032.
25. On Mutianus and Erfurt see L. W. Spitz, *The Religious Renaissance of the German Humanists*, pp. 130–54; also *Contemporaries*, ii, 473–4.
26. On Humanism and the Reformation in Erfurt, see above all the works of R. W. Scribner, most notably 'The Erasmians and the Beginning of the Reformation in Erfurt', *Journal of Religious History*, xii (1976), 3–31; also *Reformation, Society and Humanism in Erfurt, c.1450–1530* (London University Ph.D. thesis, 1972) – main points summarised in R. H. Fife, *The Revolt of Martin Luther* (New York, 1957), pp. 51–6, and A. G. Dickens, *The German Nation and Martin Luther*, pp. 169–76.
27. *Contemporaries*. ii, 244–6.
28. Above, pp. 127, 131.
29. *Contemporaries*, iii, 205–8; also Gunther Wartenberg, 'Zum Erasmianismus am Dresdener Hof Georgs des Bärtigen', in *Nederlands Archief voor Kerkgeschiedenis*, 66 (1986), 2–6; see J. Lecler, *Toleration and the Reformation*, I, 226.
30. *Contemporaries*, iii, 458–9; below, p. 284.
31. Ibid., i, 184–7; above, p. 117.
32. Ibid., i, 315–16; Allen, v, Ep. 1390 headnote, x, Ep. 2804 and headnote, xi, Ep. 3031; Erasmus' *Early Liberal Education for Children*, 1529, was dedicated to Prince William, John's son, with specific mention of Heresbach: *CWE* 26, pp. 295–6. On Heresbach, *Contemporaries*, ii, 183–4.
33. Ibid., iii, 414–16; Allen, v, Ep. 1390, viii, Epp. 2335, 2346, ix, Epp. 2360, 2386, 2454, x, Epp. 2804, 2845, 2853 and headnote.
34. Allen, x, Epp. 2728, 2804, 2845; see John P. Dolan, *The Influence of Erasmus, Witzel, and Cassander in the Church Ordinances and Reform Proposals of the United Duchies of Cleve during the Middle Decades of the Sixteenth Century* (Münster, 1957), pp.iii, vii, 5–7, 8; though Preserved Smith (*Erasmus*, p. 395) observed the impact and significance of Erasmus' participation in ecclesiastical reform by temporal authority.
35. *Contemporaries*, ii, 353–4.
36. For much of the material in these pages we are greatly indebted to Henryk Zins, *Leonard Coxe and the Erasmian Circles in Poland, Annales Universitatis Mariae Curie-Sklodowska, Lublin Polonia*, xxviii (No. 8, 1973), 153–80.
37. H. Zins, op. cit., pp. 171–2, 176.
38. Ibid., p. 175.
39. Allen, vii, Epp. 1803, 1824.
40. *Contemporaries*, iii, 473–4.
41. H. Zins, op. cit., pp. 176–9; Allen, vii, Epp. 1826, 2030.
42. *Contemporaries*, ii, 296–7 and 297–301.
43. Allen, vi, Ep. 1674, vii, Epp. 1819, 1821, x, Ep. 2862. P. Smith, *Erasmus*, p.

260, prints the carefully worded contract of sale of the library.
44. Above, pp. 209–10.
45. See R. R. Betts, 'Poland, Bohemia and Hungary', in *New C. M. H.*, II, 186, 192, 194, 198, 206–7.
46. Allen, viii, Ep. 2175, x, Ep. 2874, xi, Ep. 2961; for Decius see *Contemporaries*, i, 380–2, for Sigismund I, ibid., iii, 249–51.
47. For Andrea Krzycki (Cricius), see *Contemporaries*, ii, 275–8; letters referred to in Allen, vi, Ep. 1652, ix, Ep. 2375, xi, Ep. 3039.
48. See R. R. Betts, op. cit., II, 187, 192–3, 201.
49. Piotr Tomiczki, in *Contemporaries*, iii, 327–9.
50. Allen, vii, Epp. 1915, 1918, 1919, viii, Ep. 2091 (Jan., 1529), and Ep. 2173 (8/6/1529), x, Epp. 2713, 2776.
51. Ibid., xi, Epp. 3014, 3049, 3066, 3089.
52. Above, pp. 7–10, 16–17: *Contemporaries*, i, 100–1, ii, 325–6, 383–5, iii, 220–1.
53. For Ammonius, see *Contemporaries*, 50–1, Allen, v, Ep. 1463 and headnote, vii, Ep. 2062 and headnote, viii, Epp. 2082, 2197; Utenhove, Allen, viii, Epp. 2188, 2209; Edingus, Allen, vii, Ep. 2060 and headnote, ix, Ep. 2485; Laurinus, Allen, vii, Ep. 1848 – see also *CWE* 9, No. 1342.
54. Above, p. 58; *Contemporaries*, i, 446–7, ii, 109–11, iii, 393–5; for Ammonius' letter, Allen, viii, Ep. 2197.
55. See Alastair Duke, 'The Face of Popular Religious Dissent in the Low Countries, 1520–1530', in *Journal of Ecclesiastical History*, 26 (No. 1, Jan 1975), 43, 66, and Pieter Geyl, *The Revolt of the Netherlands (1555–1609)* (2nd edn., London, 1962), pp. 55–6.
56. Allen, viii, Ep. 2197.
57. Geyl, p. 51; Duke, pp. 44, 62–3.
58. Duke, pp. 52, 54–5; Geyl, pp. 56–7; R. H. Bainton, p. 81.
59. Above, pp. 105–110.
60. Geyl, p. 52. Preserved Smith ascribed 'the peculiar character of the Reformation in the Netherlands, neither Lutheran nor Zwinglian' but humanistic and moral, to the influence of Erasmus: *Erasmus*, p. 431.
61. Ibid., pp. 140, 205, 289; David Friedman, in *The Netherlands*, ed. B. Landheer (Berkeley and Los Angeles, 1946), pp. 206–7.
62. Geyl, pp. 52, 64.
63. Allen, x, Epp. 2689, 2820 and headnote; *Contemporaries*, ii, 399–401; Allen, xi, Ep. 3130.

12. *Erasmus: Heretic or Mediator?*

1. Bruce Mansfield demonstrates how 'the divisions in Christianity . . . fixed attitudes about Erasmus': *Man on His Own*, p. 3 (also p. 347).
2. Rupert E. Davies, *The Problem of Authority in the Continental Reformers* (London, 1946), p. 12.
3. Ernst Troeltsch, *The Social Teaching of the Christian Churches*, trs. O. Wyon, 2 vols., (London, 1931), I, 329–63.
4. *LB*, v, 484E, 485E, 494E, 495D, 497C, 498B; Dolan, pp. 355, 357, 371–2, 375, 376; Himelick, pp. 57–8, 76, 77, 81, 82.
5. Translation quoted in Erika Rummel, *Annotations*, p. 149.

6. *CWE* 8, No. 1232, and 9, No. 1330.
7. W. K. Ferguson, 'The Attitude of Erasmus Toward Toleration', in *Persecution and Liberty. Essays in Honor of G. L. Burr* (New York, 1931), pp. 175–7.
8. *Supputatio Errorum in censuris Beddae*, *LB*, ix, 580C, 580F, 581B, 581D–E, 582F. For Béda, above, pp. 220–1.
9. Sebastian Castellio, *Concerning Heretics*, pp. 171–2, 175–7, 180–2.
10. W. K. Ferguson, in *Persecution and Liberty*, pp. 171, 178–9.
11. Allen, v, Ep. 1526 (12 December 1524, to Duke George of Saxony).
12. See *Contemporaries*, i, 81–3, ii, 200–2 and 304–6, and iii, 317–18 and 326–7, for Baechem, Hoogstraten, Latomus, Theodoric and Titelmans respectively. On Latomus see Rummel, *Catholic Critics*, I, 63–93, and on the Louvain group, ibid., II, 1–22.
13. R. H. Bainton, *Erasmus of Rotterdam*, pp. 197, 209.
14. Below, p. 285.
15. *CWE* 9, No. 1301.
16. *CWE* 5, No. 659.
17. Rummel, *Annotations*, pp. 124–7.
18. *CWE* 7, No. 1061, pp. 178, 192–3; see Rummel, *Catholic Critics*, I, 95–120.
19. *CWE* 8, No. 4 in Appendix.
20. *Apologia adversus . . . monachos*, pp. 55–83, 7–55, 83–94, 169–77. Rummel, *Catholic Critics*, II, 89–98, considers the Valladolid Articles and Erasmus' *Apologia*.
21. *CWE* 5, No. 734.
22. *Apologia adversus . . . monachos*, pp. 169–77; E. Rummel, op. cit., pp. 167–71; see also above, pp. 15–16.
23. *Apologia adversus . . . monachos*, pp. 107–11, 111–17.
24. Rummel, *Annotations*, p. 156; also *Catholic Critics*, II, 115–23 on Pio.
25. *CWE* 9, No. 1341A, pp. 332–3.
26. *Apologia adversus . . . monachos*, pp. 117–24.
27. Rummel, *Annotations*, pp. 157–8; see *Catholic Critics*, I, 122–7 on Standish.
28. Above, p. 160.
29. *The Letters of Stephen Gardiner*, ed. J. A. Muller, pp. 385–6.
30. *Apologia adversus . . . monachos*, pp. 124–9, 183–4, 129–35.
31. S. Gardiner, loc. cit.
32. Rummel, *Annotations*, p. 147.
33. *CWE* 9, Nos. 1293, 1353.
34. *Apologia adversus . . . monachos*, pp. 177–81, 94–107.
35. Rummel, *Annotations*, pp. 163–7.
36. See Mansfield (*Man on His Own*, pp. 299–300) for a nineteenth-century assertion that, far from withering, Erasmus' mediatory influence flourished *c.*1530.
37. R. H. Popkin, *The History of Scepticism from Erasmus to Descartes* (Assen, 1960), p. 5.
38. S. Seidel Menchi, *Erasmo in Italia*, p. 197.
39. Ibid., p. 214; see P. G. Bietenholz (review) in *ARG, Jahrgang* 80 (1989) 317, and Erika Rummel (review) in *Catholic History Review*, 75 (Jan., 1989), 164.
40. S. Seidel Menchi, op. cit., p. 112; Peter Bietenholz concurs (as n. 39, p.

316) that in Italy at least, via translation and exposition, 'Erasmus' message, as filtered out in such religious popularisers, overwhelmingly was one of religious freedom'.

41. Allen, vi, Ep. 1690 (16/4/1526), ix, Ep. 2366 (18/8/1530) and headnote.
42. P. Smith, *Erasmus*, pp. 386–8.
43. J. Lecler, *Toleration and the Reformation*, I, 141.
44. H. Jedin, *A History of the Council of Trent*, I, 358; John P. Dolan, *The Essential Erasmus*, p. 327.
45. *De sarcienda*, *LB*, v, 469A, 499C; Dolan, pp. 331, 377; Himelick, pp. 29, 84.
46. Ibid., *LB*, v, 501B, 501E, 502A, 502B, 504D, 504E–F; Dolan, pp. 380–1; Himelick, pp. 88–9.
47. Ibid., *LB*, v, 500B–D; Dolan, pp. 378–9; Himelick, p. 86.
48. Ibid., *LB*, v, 502D, 503C, 503D, 503F, 504C; Dolan, pp. 382–5; Himelick, pp. 90–4.
49. Ibid., *LB*, v, 506B; Dolan, p. 387; Himelick, p. 97.
50. Henry VIII's Speech of 1545 is printed in A. G. Dickens and Dorothy Carr, *The Reformation in England to the Accession of Elizabeth I* (London, 1967), pp. 118–19.
51. See J. Lecler, *Toleration and the Reformation*, I, ch. 4; H. Jedin, *A History of the Council of Trent*, I, 363–4. Bruce Mansfield, in *Phoenix of His Age*, p. 7, refers to 'the generation of Catholics who considered themselves his heirs', and Manuel F. Alvarez to the plans of Charles V, 'inspired by Erasmus, for a general concord at Regensburg in 1541' (*Charles V*, p. 20).
52. A. Renaudet, *Érasme et l'Italie*, p. 175 and Livre IV: 'Le problème de la troisième Église'; see also G. H. Williams, p. 11.
53. Allen, vi, Ep. 1757; see *Contemporaries*, ii, 78–9.
54. Allen, x, Ep. 2492.
55. Ibid., x, Ep. 2522.
56. Ibid., x, Epp. 2715 and 2786.
57. Ibid., x, Ep. 2906.
58. A. Renaudet, op. cit., pp. 175, 201, 208, 247, 265.
59. Ibid., pp. 150, 176, 212.
60. Stefan Zweig, *Erasmus*, trs. E. and C. Paul (1979 reprint, London), pp. 112, 156–60.
61. A. Renaudet, *Études Érasmiennes (1521–1529)*, pp. 145–6, 176, 188–9. See Bruce Mansfield, *Man On His Own*, pp. 311–14, for a recent critique of Renaudet's position: 'Erasmus was for Renaudet advancing an alternative form of Christianity'.
62. Preserved Smith was on somewhat firmer ground when he 'discovered in Erasmus the champion, in his own day, of that "undogmatic Christianity" now first coming to its own four hundred years after he proclaimed it' (*Erasmus*, p. xi).
63. Raymond Himelick, identifying 'the basic consistency of the Erasmian message which virtually nobody wanted to hear', insists that Erasmus 'did not intend to emancipate men from the old Christian pieties, but to return to them' (*Erasmus and the Seamless Coat of Jesus*, pp.viii, 5).

Conclusion: The Legacy of Erasmus

1. C. Augustijn, *Erasmus*, p. 199.
2. See above, pp. 238–9 (and n. 70 of Chapter 10). *Contemporaries*, i, 28–32 has a valuable short account of Girolamo Aleandro.
3. Above, p. 234.
4. For references on the antipapal propagandists see A. G. Dickens, 'Intellectual and Social Forces in the German Reformation', *Stadtbürgertum und Adel in der Reformation* (German Historical Institute, London, 1979), pp. 11–24. See also the same writer's *The German Nation and Martin Luther*, chs. 1 and 2.
5. Mansfield cites several nineteenth- and twentieth-century historians (notably Paul Wernle, R. H. Murray and Preserved Smith) who explored the theme of an Erasmus who recognised that 'any Christian renaissance requires a reform in theology' and who sought above all 'an inner piety largely free of dogma and ceremony' (*Man On His Own*, pp. 239, 290–1, 295, 367).
6. 2: Verses 11 to 14.
7. Abraham Kuyper, *Calvinism*, London, 1932 ('Stone Lectures', Princeton, 1898), p. 70.
8. Above, p. 139.
9. J. W. O'Malley (ed.), *Catholicism in Early Modern History. A Guide to Research* (St Louis, Missouri, 1988) has the most elaborate recent bibliographies. More readily accessible to some readers is A. G. Dickens, *The Counter Reformation* (London, 1968), pp. 203–6.
10. *Phoenix of His Age: Interpretations of Erasmus c.1550–1750*, and *Man On His Own: Interpretations of Erasmus c.1750–1920*.
11. See ch.3, 'Erasmus and Enlightenment', of Mansfield's *Man On His Own*. He concludes that 'to identify his "philosophy of Christ" with the outlook of the eighteenth-century *philosophes* would be a great distortion' (pp. 14–15), despite a verdict of Wilhelm Dilthey in the nineteenth century that Erasmus was 'the Voltaire of the sixteenth century' (p. 285).
12. Roger Phillips, *Basilican*, March 1985 (Bassaleg, Gwent).

TIME CHART

DATE	CAREER AND DOMICILES	SELECTED WRITINGS AND PUBLICATIONS	CONTEMPORARY EVENTS
1467	Born, Rotterdam (?1469)		
1475	School, Deventer		
1487	Augustinian Canons, Steyn		
1488	Takes his vows	Commences *Antibarbarorum Liber*	
1492	Ordained priest		
1493	Secretary to Bishop of Cambrai		
1495	Paris, Collège de Montaigu		
1497	Tutor to William Blount, Baron Mountjoy		Colet's Oxford Lectures
1498			Louis XII, King of France
1499	In England, for *c.*8 months		
1500	Returns to Paris	*Adages* first published	
1501	Leaves Paris; St Omer	Writes *Enchiridion militis Christiani*	
1502	Settles in Louvain		
1503		*Enchiridion* published	Julius II Pope
1504	Returns to Paris in Dec.	*Panegyric* addressed to Archduke Philip	
1505	Second visit to England, late 1505 until June 1506	Prints Valla's *Adnotationes in novum testamentum* (Paris)	
1506	Goes to Italy for *c.*3 yrs. Doctorate, Univ. of Turin		Reuchlin's *Rudiments of Hebrew*

1507	In Bologna, then to Venice in December		
1508	8 months in Venice, then Padua later in year	Aldine edn. of *Adages* published in Venice	
1509	Rome, then leaves for England: 1509–1514	Starts writing *Moriae encomium* (*Praise of Folly*)	Henry VIII, King of England
1510			
1511	April–August, out of England	*Praise of Folly* published in Paris	
1512	Chair of Theology, Cambridge, for 2½ years.	*De copia* and *De ratione studii* published	
1513			Leo X, Pope
1514	Leaves Cambridge. London, and then Rhineland journey	*Julius exclusus* circulates in ms.	Complutensian Bible printed (1514–17); published 1522.
1515	Leaves Basel to visit England (April–May)	Expanded edn. *Adages* includes *Dulce bellum inexpertis* and *Sileni Alcibiadis. Letter to Martin Dorp*	Francis I, King of France
1516	Visits England, July–Aug. Councillor to Charles	*Institutio principis Christiani. Novum instrumentum. Paraclesis.* Edn. of Jerome	Charles I, King of Spain More's *Utopia*
1517	Papal dispensation; England (April), then Antwerp, Anderlecht, and Louvain	*Paraphrases of New Testament. Querela pacis*	Luther's 95 Theses
1518	Settles in Louvain until November 1521	First edn. of *Colloquies. Letter to Paul Volz. Ratio verae theologiae. Julius exclusus* published	
1519		*Letter to Albert of Brandenburg*	Charles V, Emperor. Zwingli denounces Indulgences
1520	At coronation of Charles V, Aachen	*Axiomata. Antibarbari,* Froben edn.	Papal Bull against Luther. *Babylonian Captivity*

1521	Leaves Louvain for Basel where he stays until 1529		Edict of Worms against Luther. Melanchthon's *Loci communes theologici*
1522		The major editions of *Colloquies* published by Froben commence	Adrian VI, Pope. Knights' War. Reuchlin died
1523		Publishes *Spongia* against Hutten	Clement VII, Pope. Hutten died. Zwingli's 'Articles'
1524		*Inquisitio de Fide. De libero arbitrio. De immensa Dei misericordia*	Peasants' War
1525			Luther's *De servo arbitrio* Battle of Pavia
1526		*Concerning the Eating of Fish.* Part I of *Hyperaspistes*	Ferdinand becomes King of Bohemia and Hungary
1527		*Hyperaspistes*, Part II. *Reckoning of the Errors in Béda's Censure*	Sack of Rome. Valladolid Articles and Conference
1528		*Ciceronianus*	
1529	Moves to Freiburg im Breisgau	*Apologia adversus . . . monachos. Contra quosdam, qui se falso iactant evangelicos*	Berquin burnt at Paris. Protestant control in Basel. Turks besiege Vienna
1530		*Epistola ad fratres Germaniae inferioris.*	Diet and Confession of
1531		*De bello Turcico*	Augsburg. Zwingli killed at Kappel. Ferdinand becomes Emperor
1532			
1533		*De sarcienda ecclesiae concordia*	
1534		*Adversus calumniosissimam epistolam Martini Lutheri*	Paul III, Pope
1535	Returns to Basel		Anabaptists seize Münster
1536	Died, 12 July		Calvin's *Institutes*

SELECT BIBLIOGRAPHY

Only those works which have proved of special relevance are included; very many others are identified in full where appropriate in the Notes.

Secondary Works

Adams, Robert P., *The Better Part of Valor*, Seattle, 1962

Allen, P. S., *The Age of Erasmus*, Oxford, 1914 (Ann Arbor and London, 1980)

Augustijn, Cornelis, 'The Ecclesiology of Erasmus', in *Scrinium Erasmianum*, ed. J. Coppens, II, 135–55.

— *Erasmus. His Life, Works, and Influence*, trans. J. C. Grayson, Toronto, Buffalo, London, 1991

Bainton, Roland H., *The Age of the Reformation*, New York, 1956

— *Erasmus of Christendom*, New York, 1969 and London, 1970

Bataillon, Marcel, *Érasme et l'Espagne*, Paris, 1937 (1991)

Bietenholz, P. G., *History and Biography in the Works of Erasmus of Rotterdam*, Geneva, 1966

Bietenholz, Peter G., and Deutscher, Thomas B., eds., *Contemporaries of Erasmus*, 3 vols., Toronto, 1985, 1986, 1987

Bouyer, Louis, *Erasmus and the Humanist Experiment*, trans. F. X. Murphy, London, 1959

Boyle, Marjorie O., *Erasmus on Language and Method in Theology*, Toronto and Buffalo, 1977

— *Rhetoric and Reform. Erasmus' Civil Dispute with Luther*, Cambridge, Mass. and London, 1983

— 'Erasmus and the "Modern" Question: Was He Semi-Pelagian?', *ARG* 75 (1984), 59–77

Chantraine, Georges S., 'The *Ratio Verae Theologiae* (1518)', in DeMolen, *Essays*, 179–85

— *Érasme et Luther: libre et serf arbitre*, Paris, 1981

Chrisman, Miriam U., *Lay Culture, Learned Culture. Books and Social Change in Strasbourg, 1488–1599*, New Haven, 1982

Coppens, J., ed., *Scrinium Erasmianum*, 2 vols., Leiden, 1969

Davis, Kenneth, R., 'Erasmus as Progenitor of Anabaptist Theology and Piety', in *MQR*, 47 (July 1973), 163–78

— *Anabaptism and Asceticism*, Scottdale, Pa. and Kitchener, Ontario, 1974

DeMolen, Richard L., ed., *Essays on the Works of Erasmus*, New Haven and London, 1978
— *The Spirituality of Erasmus of Rotterdam*, Nieuwkoop, 1987
Devereux, E. J., *A Checklist of English Translations of Erasmus to 1700*, Oxford Bibliographical Society, 1968
Dickens, A. G., *The English Reformation*, 2nd edn., London, 1989
— *The Age of Humanism and Reformation*, New Jersey, 1971
Dolan, John P., *The Essential Erasmus*, New York, 1964
Erasmus in English, University of Toronto Newsletter
Erasmus of Rotterdam Society Yearbooks
Ferguson, Wallace K., 'The Attitude of Erasmus toward Toleration', in *Persecution and Liberty. Essays in Honor of G. L. Burr*, New York, 1931, 171–81
— 'Renaissance Tendencies in the Religious Thought of Erasmus', *Journal of the History of Ideas*, 15 (October 1954), 499–508
Froude, J. A., *Life and Letters of Erasmus*, London, 1916
Gelder, H. A. Enno van, *The Two Reformations in the Sixteenth Century*, The Hague, 1961
Gerrish, B. A., '*De Libero Arbitrio* (1524): Erasmus on Piety, Theology, and Lutheran Dogma', in DeMolen, *Essays*, 187–209
Gilmore, Myron P., 'Italian Reactions to Erasmian Humanism', in H. A. Oberman, ed., *Itinerarium Italicum*, Leiden, 1975, 61–115
Halkin, Léon-E., *Érasme parmi nous*, Paris, 1987
Hall, T., 'Possibilities of Erasmian Influence on Denck and Hubmaier . . . on the Freedom of the Will', in *MQR*, xxxv (April 1961), 149–70
Himelick, R., *Erasmus and the Seamless Coat of Jesus*, Lafayette, Indiana, 1971
Huizinga, J., *Erasmus and the Age of Reformation*, New York, 1957
Hyma, A., *The Youth of Erasmus*, Ann Arbor, 1930 (New York, 1968)
— *The Life of Desiderius Erasmus*, Assen, 1972
Jarrott, C. A. L., 'Erasmus' Biblical Humanism', in *Studies in the Renaissance*, 17 (1970), 119–52
— 'Erasmus' Annotations and Colet's Commentaries on Paul', in DeMolen, *Essays*, 125–44
Kaiser, W., *Praisers of Folly*, London, 1964
Kaufman, Peter I., *Augustinian Piety and Catholic Reform. Augustine, Colet and Erasmus*, Macon, 1982
— 'John Colet and Erasmus' *Enchiridion*', in *Church History*, 46 (1977)
Kleinhans, R. G., 'Luther and Erasmus, Another Perspective', in *Church History*, 39 (1970), 459–69
Kohls, Ernst-W., 'The Principal Theological Thoughts in the *Enchiridion Militis Christiani*', in DeMolen, *Essays*, 61–82
Locher, Gottfried W., 'Zwingli and Erasmus', in *Erasmus in English*, 9 (1979–80), 2–11
Longhurst, John E., *Erasmus and the Spanish Inquisition: The Case of Juan de Valdés*, Albuquerque, 1950
McConica, James K., *English Humanists and Reformation Politics*, Oxford, 1965
— 'Erasmus and the Grammar of Consent', in *Scrinium Erasmianum*, II, 77–99
— *Erasmus*, London and New York, 1991

McSorley, Harry J., *Luther: Right or Wrong?*, New York, London and Minneapolis, 1969

Mann, Margaret, *Érasme et les débuts de la réforme Française (1517–1536)*, Slatkine Reprints, Geneva, 1978 (Paris, 1934)

Mansfield, Bruce, 'Erasmus of Rotterdam: evangelical', in *Erasmus in English*, 6 (1973), 1–5.

— *Phoenix of His Age: Interpretations of Erasmus c.1550–1750*, Toronto, 1979

— *Man on His Own: Interpretations of Erasmus c.1750–1920*, Toronto, 1992

Menchi, Silvana Seidel, *Erasmo in Italia 1520–1580*, Turin, 1987

Mennonite Encyclopaedia, Scottdale, Pa., 4 vols., 1955–9.

Mestwerdt, P., *Die Anfänge des Erasmus*, Leipzig, 1917.

New Catholic Encyclopaedia, New York, 1967

Olin, John C., *Christian Humanism and the Reformation: Desiderius Erasmus: Selected Writings*, New York and London, 1965 (3rd edn., New York, 1987)

— J. D. Smart and R. E. McNally, *Luther, Erasmus and the Reformation*, New York, 1969

Oxford Dictionary of the Christian Church, 2nd (revised) edn., eds. F. L. Cross and E. A. Livingstone, Oxford, 1974.

Payne, John B., 'Towards the Hermeneutics of Erasmus', in *Scrinium Erasmianum*, II, 13–49

— *Erasmus: His Theology of the Sacraments*, Richmond, Va., 1970

Peremans, Nicole (Haesenne-), *Érasme et Bucer*, Paris, 1970

Phillips, Margaret Mann, *Erasmus and the Northern Renaissance*, 2nd edn., London, 1981

— *The 'Adages' of Erasmus*, Cambridge, 1964

— 'Some Last Words of Erasmus', in J. C. Olin, et al., *Luther, Erasmus and the Reformation*, New York, 1969, 87–113

Porter, H. C., and Thomson, D. F. S., *Erasmus and Cambridge*, Toronto, 1963

Post, R. R., *The Modern Devotion*, Leiden, 1968

Rabil, Albert, Jnr., *Erasmus and the New Testament*, San Antonio, 1972

— 'Erasmus's *Paraphrases of the New Testament*', in De Molen, *Essays*, 145–61

Renaudet, Augustin, *Érasme, sa pensée religieuse d'après sa correspondance (1518–1521)*, Paris, 1926

— *Études Érasmiennes (1521–1529)*, Paris 1939

— *Érasme et l'Italie*, Geneva, 1954

Rummel, Erika, *Erasmus' Annotations on the New Testament*, Toronto, Buffalo, London, 1986

— *Erasmus and his Catholic Critics*, 2 vols., Nieuwkoop, 1989

Rupp, E. Gordon, and Watson, Philip S., eds. and introdn., *Luther and Erasmus: Free Will and Salvation*, London and Philadelphia, 1969

Schoeck, R. J., *Erasmus Grandescens: The Growth of a Humanist's Mind and Spirituality*, Nieuwkoop, 1988

Schottenloher, O., 'Erasmus, Johann Peppenruyter und die Entstehung des Enchiridion militis christiani', *ARG* 45 (1954), 109–16

Screech, Michael A., *Ecstasy and the Praise of Folly*, London, 1980

Scribner, R. W., 'The Erasmians and the Beginning of the Reformation in Erfurt', in *Journal of Religious History*, 12 (1976), 3–31

Smith, Preserved, *Erasmus. A Study of his Life, Ideals and Place in History*, New York, 1962 (1923)

Sowards, J. K., 'The Youth of Erasmus: some Reconsiderations', in *Yearbook*, 9 (1989), 1–33

Stupperich, R., 'Das Enchiridion militis christiani des Erasmus', *ARG* 69 (1978), 5–22

Thompson, Craig R., 'Erasmus and Tudor England', in *Actes du Congrès Érasme*, Amsterdam and London, 1971, 29–68

Tracy, James D., 'Erasmus Becomes a German', in *Renaissance Quarterly*, 30 (Spring 1968), 281–8

— *Erasmus: The Growth of a Mind*, Geneva, 1972

— *The Politics of Erasmus*, Toronto and London, 1978

— 'Two Erasmuses, Two Luthers: Erasmus' Strategy in Defence of *De Libero Arbitrio*', *ARG* 78 (1987), 37–60

Van der Haeghen, F., *Bibliotheca Erasmiana*, Nieuwkoop, 1961

Vogel, C. J. de, 'Erasmus and his attitude towards Church Dogma', in *Scrinium Erasmianum*, II, 101–32

Williams, G. H., *The Radical Reformation*, London, 1962

Zins, Henryk, 'Leonard Coxe and the Erasmian Circles in Poland', *Annales Universitatis Mariae Curie-Sklodowska*, Lublin, 28 (1973), 153–80

TEXTS AND COLLECTIONS CITED

Bucer, Martin, *De Regno Christi*, 1550, trans. Wilhelm Pauck and Paul Larkin, in *Melanchthon and Bucer*, ed. W. Pauck, London and Philadelphia, 1969
Calvin, John, *Calvin: Institutes of the Christian Religion*, ed. J. T. NcNeill, trans. F. L. Battles, Philadelphia, 1967
Erasmus, Desiderius,
Collections and Selections
DeMolen, R. L., *Erasmus*, London, 1973
Dolan, John P., *The Essential Erasmus*, New York, 1964 (hereafter, Dolan)
Olin, John C., *Christian Humanism and the Reformation: Desiderius Erasmus: Selected Writings*, New York & London, 1965 (3rd edn, New York, 1987) (Olin)
Editions
Abbreviations or short-titles indicated where appropriate.
Collected Works of Erasmus (*CWE*), Toronto, Buffalo, London, 1974–
The Correspondence of Erasmus (1484 to 1523), vols. 1–9. Texts cited, vols. 23, 26, 27, 31
Desiderii Erasmi Roterodami Opera Omnia (*LB*), ed. J. Leclerc, Leiden, 1703–6, reprinted, Hildesheim, 1961
Omnia opera Desiderii Erasmi Roterodami (ASD), Amsterdam, 1969–
Opus Epistolarum Des. Erasmi Roterodami (Allen), ed., P. S. Allen, H. M. Allen, and H. W. Garrod, Oxford, 12 vols., 1906–58
Individual Works
Anglicised titles and/or short-titles employed in text or Notes indicated where appropriate. Editions cited as indicated in specific notes.
Adagia: Adages M. M. Phillips, *The 'Adages' of Erasmus*, Cambridge, 1964, and the *Adages, CWE* 31 (1982) ed. M. M. Phillips and R. A. B. Mynors are cited.
Adversus calumniosissimam (non sobriam) epistolam Martini Lutheri, 1534, *LB*, x, 1537–58
Antibarbarorum Liber: Antibarbari, 1520, trans. and ed. M. M. Phillips, *CWE* 23.
Apologia adversus articulos aliquot per monachos quosdam, in Hispaniis exhibitos: Apologia adversus . . . monachos, Basel 1529, and *LB*, ix, 1015–94
Axiomata, 1520, trans. Olin, 146–9
Colloquia: Colloquies, trans. Craig R. Thompson, Chicago and London, 1965
Contra quosdam, qui se falso iactant evangelicos: Pseudevangelicos, 1529

De libero arbitrio, 1524, trans. and ed. E. Gordon Rupp, London, 1969 – also by E. F. Winter, New York, 1961.

De immensa Dei misericordia: Concerning the Immense Mercy of God, 1524, trans. Dolan, 225–70

De sarcienda (amabili) ecclesiae concordia: On Mending the Peace of the Church, 1533, *LB*, v, 469–506; trans. Dolan, 327–86, also Raymond Himelick, in *Erasmus and the Seamless Coat of Jesus* (Lafayette, Indiana, 1971), 29–109

Enchiridion militis Christiani: Enchiridion, 1503 and many subsequent editions. English translations by R. Himelick,, Gloucester., Mass, 1970, J. W. O'Malley in *CWE* 26 (1988), and M. Spinka, Philadelphia, 1953

Hyperaspistes Diatribae adversus servum arbitrium Martini Lutheri: *Hyperaspistes*, I, 1526; II, 1527, *LB*, x, 1249–1336 and 1337–1558

Inquisitio de fide, 1524, trans. and ed. Craig R. Thompson, New Haven, 1950

Julius exclusus, 1518, English translation in *CWE* 27 (1986)

Institutio principis Christiani: *Education of a Christian Prince*, 1516, trans. and ed. Lester K. Born, New York, 1968 reprint (1936), and by M. J. Heath in *CWE* 27 (1986)

Moriae encomium: Praise of Folly, 1512, trans. Dolan, 94–173, and by Betty Radice, in *CWE* 27 (1986), the Introduction by A. H. T. Levy to the Penguin Classics edition is very valuable.

Novum Instrumentum, 1516, later editions: *Novum Testamentum*. Erasmus' *Annotations on the New Testament (the Gospels)*, facsimile edn., Anne Reeve, introd. M. A. Screech, London, 1986

Panegyricus, 1504, trans. Betty Radice, in *CWE* 27 (1986)

Paraclesis, 1516, trans. Olin, 92–106

Querela pacis: *The Complaint of Peace*, 1517, trans. Dolan, 174–204, and M. J. Heath, in *CWE* 27 (1986)

Responsio ad . . . fratres Germaniae inferioris, & Phrysiae Orientalis, Freiburg, 1530.

Spongia adversus aspergines Hutteni: *Spongia*, Basel, 1523, and in *LB*, x, 1631–1672

Supputatio Errorum in censuris Beddae: *A Reckoning of the Errors in Béda's Censure*, 1527, in *LB*, ix, 515–702

English translations of Erasmus (anonymous, and by Chaloner, Marshall, Taverner, Tyndale, and Udall) are cited in Notes where appropriate.

Foxe, John, *Acts and Monuments*, ed. G. Townshend and S. R. Cattley, Vols. III, IV, and V, London, 1887–8

Gardiner, Stephen, *The Letters of Stephen Gardiner*, ed. J. A. Muller, Cambridge, 1933

Harder, Leland, ed., *The Sources of Swiss Anabaptism*, Scottdale, Pa., and Kitchener, Ontario, 1985

Kempis, Thomas à, *The Imitation of Christ*, many editions

Luther, Martin, *De servo arbitrio*, translated as *The Bondage of the Will* by Philip S. Watson, in collaboration with Benjamin Drewery, in *Luther's Works*, Volume 33, Philadelphia, 1972

— *Works*, Vol. 48, *Letters*, I, trans. and ed. G. G. Krodel, Philadelphia, 1963

— *Works*, Vol. 49, *Letters*, II, trans. and ed. G. G. Krodel, Philadelphia, 1972

— *Works*, Vol. 54, *Table Talk*, trans. and ed. T. G. Tappert, Philadelphia, 1986

Melanchthon, Philip, *Loci communes theologici*, 1521, trans. Lowell J. Satre, revised Wilhelm Pauck, in *Melanchthon and Bucer*, ed. W. Pauck, London and Philadelphia, 1969

More, Thomas, *The Correspondence of Sir Thomas More*, ed. E. F. Rogers, Princeton, 1947

— *Utopia*, Vol. 4 of *Complete Works*, ed. Edward Surtz and J. H. Hexter, New Haven and London, 1965

Parker Society: Sermons and Remains of Becon, Cranmer, Grindal, Hooper, Latimer, Parker, Ridley, Cambridge, 1843–

Starkey, Thomas, *A Dialogue between Reginald Pole and Thomas Lupset*, ed. K. M. Burton, London, 1948

Servetus, Michael, *On the Errors of the Trinity*, trans. Earl Morse Wilbur, in *The Two Treatises of Servetus on the Trinity*, Cambridge, Mass., 1932

Williams, G. H., and Mergal, A. M., eds., *Spiritual and Anabaptist Writers of the Radical Reformation and Evangelical Catholicism*, London and Philadelphia, 1957 (includes: Denck, John, *Whether God is the Cause of Evil*, 1526, and Hubmaier, Balthasar. *On Free Will*, 1527)

INDEX

Adiaphora 99, 100, 109, 110–11, 129, 132, 136, 147, 212, 239, 267, 278, 279, 281, 292, 295, 299
Adrian VI, Pope 80, 117, 126, 127, 142, 233, 246, 272, 284, 288
Agricola, Rudolf 22, 247
Albert of Brandenburg, Elector Archbishop of Mainz, 100, 117, 120, 125, 256
Albigenses 51, 268
Alcalá de Henares, University of 59, 225, 228, 229, 230
Alciati, Andrea 237
Aldington 46, 209
Aldus Manutius 43
Aleander, Girolamo 121, 122, 131, 186, 233, 236, 238–9, 240, 285, 288
Alexander VI, Pope 71
Allen, Percy S. xiv, 127, 144, 257
Alsace 48, 248, 254
Alumbrados (Illuminists) 225–6, 227, 229, 288
Alvarez, Manuel F. 340 n. 51
Amerbach, Boniface 108, 159, 260
——, Johann 48
Ammonio, Andrea 47, 49, 195, 309 n. 20
Ammonius, Levinus 263, 264, 266
Amsdorf, Nikolaus von 143
Amsterdam 187–8
Anabaptists 87, 103, 144, 145, 158, 160, 162, 164, 171–2, 173, 174–5, 176, 177–82, 184–5, 186–90, 208, 218, 240, 244, 245, 250, 252, 254, 256, 260, 261, 262, 265, 272, 287, 292, 295
Andrelini, Fausto 32, 34
Anti-Trinitarianism 143, 171, 176–7, 185–6, 260, 292
Antwerp 48, 76, 183, 263, 284
Apostles' Creed 97, 129, 206
Aquinas, St Thomas 5, 6, 15, 16, 35
Arius, Arianism 100–1, 102, 144, 186, 242, 270, 274, 299
Aristotle 4, 5, 6, 7, 42, 60
Arkleb of Boskovice 183
Arminianism 265, 287, 297
Asceticism 9, 172, 299
Ascham, Roger 196
Augsburg, Bishop of 153
—— City of 144, 254, 255
—— Confession of 134, 285
—— Diet of 142, 153, 165, 228, 245, 256, 257, 282, 284, 285
—— Treaty of 285
Augustine, St 4, 5–6, 11, 14, 26, 42, 96, 116, 137, 271
Augustinianism, *Schola Augustiniana Moderna* 5
Augustinians, Order of 21, 22, 25, 26, 49, 124
Augustijn, Cornelis 287, 315 n. 3, 323 n. 9, 329 n. 11
Austria 262, 289

Baechem, Nicolaas (Egmondanus) 121, 272, 273, 275
Baer, Ludwig 107, 125, 184, 260
Bainton, Roland H. 25
Baptism, Infant: Sacrament of 56, 103–4, 165, 167, 174–5, 265, 295

see also Anabaptists
Basel 48, 49, 59, 62, 121, 128, 129, 142, 151, 152, 156, 158, 162, 165, 166, 172, 175, 179, 185, 242, 248, 249, 250, 251, 252, 253, 259, 260, 262, 263, 273, 280
Batt, Jacob 26, 27, 263
Beatus Rhenanus 20, 22, 161, 252, 253
Beaufort, Lady Margaret, mother of Henry VII 45, 46
Becker, Jan, Dean of Veere 66
Becon, Thomas 91, 201, 202, 211, 213
Béda, Noël 218, 220, 221, 222, 223, 261, 273, 275, 276, 278
Bedyll, Thomas 200
Beghards (Pygards) 182–3
Belloc, Hilaire 207
Bembo, Pietro 235, 237
Bender, Harold 70, 179
Benedictines, Order of 252
Bergen, Hendrick van, Bishop of Cambrai 26, 27, 28–9, 33
Berquin, Louis de 109, 218, 220, 221–2, 229, 260, 263, 332 n. 19
Besançon 217
Beza, Theodore 181, 242, 268
Biblical Humanists, Netherlandish 264–5
Bietenholz, Peter 241, 339–40 n. 40
Bilney, Thomas 201, 203, 214, 287
Binns, Leonard Elliott xiv
Birnbaum, Norman 87
Blaurock, Georg Jacob 175
Blount, William, Lord Mountjoy 34, 44, 46, 47, 127, 195, 306 n. 49
Boccaccio, Giovanni 14
Boethius 4
Bohemia 182–3, 243, 280, 289
Bohemian Brethren 171, 172, 182–3, 275
Bologna 43, 129
Bombace, Paolo (Bombasius, Paulus) 126, 129, 238
Borssele, Anna van, of Veere 50
Botticelli, Sandro 12
Botzheim, Johann von 184, 275
Boyle, Marjorie O. 146, 316 n. 21
Brabant 46, 265, 266
Bradshaw, Brendan 305 n. 27
Brant, Sebastian 247, 251
Breslau 244
Brethren of the Common Life 8–9, 10, 14, 22, 23–4, 29, 97, 234
see also Devotio Moderna
Briçonnet, Guillaume, Bishop of Meaux 217, 219, 225, 260
Bruges 79, 229, 263
Brunfels, Otto 252
Brussels 48, 79, 245, 264
——, Burgundian Court at 27, 245, 264, 266
Bucer, Martin 64, 75, 87, 89, 110, 144, 148–9, 154, 159, 161–8, 177, 184, 185, 186, 190, 210, 214, 225, 246, 251, 252, 292, 293
Buda 244
Budé, Guillaume, 74, 95, 217, 219–20, 224
Bugenhagen, Johann (Pomeranus) 157
Bullock, Henry 199
Burgos 230, 232
Burgundy 290
——, House of 27–8
——, David of, Bishop of Utrecht 28
——, Philip of, 'the Good' 28, 65
Busch, Hermann 106

Cajetan, Tommaso de Vio, Cardinal and Legate 121, 237, 285
Calais 79
Calvin, Jean 5, 101, 147, 161, 167, 181, 186, 190, 223, 224, 225, 229, 242, 265, 268, 280, 292
Calvinism 182, 212, 219, 224, 265, 287, 288, 292, 297
Cambridge 34, 45, 196, 199, 210, 214
——, University of 45, 46–7, 204, 206, 207, 210, 258
Queen's College, 46, 47
Campeggio, Lorenzo, Cardinal and Legate 96, 118, 121, 129, 153, 158, 159, 185, 237, 280
Canterbury 207, 209, 212
Capito, Wolfgang 98, 117, 122, 123, 134, 149, 162, 165, 166, 167, 168, 199, 225, 252, 256, 274, 280
Capuchins, Order of 240, 294

Carlstadt (also Karlstadt), Andreas Bodenstein 106, 107, 152, 157, 160, 173, 184, 252
Carne, Sir Edward 215
Carondelet, Jean de 100, 266
Castellio, Sebastian 171, 182, 242, 268, 271, 279, 292
Castiglione, Baldesar 13
Catholic Evangelicals 233, 295
Celtis, Conrad 247, 248
Central Europe 194, Chapter Eleven passim, 289
Cervantes, Miguel de 233
Challoner, Thomas 199
Chantraine, Georges 320 n. 93 and n. 102, 321 n. 109, 322 n. 163
Charles 'the Bold', of Burgundy 28
Charles V, Holy Roman Emperor (Charles I of Spain) 28, 49, 50, 68, 76, 79, 122, 123, 127, 128, 140, 141, 142, 153, 156, 188, 220, 225, 226, 227, 228, 230, 231, 232, 234, 240, 243, 244, 246, 255, 263, 264, 280, 282, 290, 293
Choler (also Koler), John 144, 254, 284
Chrisman, Miriam U. 324 n. 54
Chrysoloras, Manuel 14
Chrysostom, St John 271
Cicero 13, 33, 53, 60, 256
Clamanges, Nicolas de 30
Clement VII, Pope 129, 141, 227, 234–5, 236, 238, 239, 272, 282
Cles, Bernard of, Bishop of Trent 165, 245–6
Cleves-Mark-Jülich-Berg, Duchy of 256, 257, 264
——, John III, Duke of 256, 257
——, William, later William V, Duke of 256
Clichtove, Josse 207, 276
Cochlaeus, Johannes 190
Cohn, Norman 180–1
Colet, John 11, 12, 34–40, 47, 49, 51, 100, 101, 194, 196, 197, 208, 210, 235, 255, 307 n. 66
his 'Oxford Lectures' 35–9
Cologne 62, 125, 138, 187, 188, 252, 272
Commonwealth, Ideal of, in mid-Tudor England 63, 87, 91, 209, 210–11, 213
Communion, Holy, Sacrament of, 108, 109, 160, 202, 245, 282, 299
see also Eucharist, Lord's Supper, Mass
Complutensian Polyglot Bible 17, 59, 207, 225, 229
Conciliarism 289
Confession, Practice of 103–4, 129, 152, 165, 202, 265, 275, 281, 293, 299
see also Penance
Confirmation, Sacrament of 167, 299
Consilium de Emendenda Ecclesia 237, 238, 288–9, 293, 295
Constance 184, 248
Contarini, Gasparo, Cardinal 235, 237, 241, 293, 295
Cop, Guillaume 217
Coronel, Luis Núñez 227–8, 231
Counter-Reformation, Catholic Reformation 8, 31, 53, 204, 225, 233, 289, 293–6
Coverdale, Miles 202, 205
Cox, Leonard 198, 204, 205, 258–60, 261
Cracow 198, 244, 258, 259, 260
——, University of 258, 261
Cranmer, Thomas, Archbishop of Canterbury, 195, 200, 206–10, 211, 214
Cricius, Andrew: *see* Krzycki
Cromwell, Thomas, 91, 195, 196, 197, 198, 199, 200–1, 204, 208, 210, 211
Crowley, Robert, 213
Curione, Celio Secundo 242
Czechoslovakia 182–3, 198

Davis, Kenneth R. 172
Decius, Justus 106, 107, 142, 186, 258, 259–60, 260–1
Denck, Hans 162, 175–6, 178, 180, 185
Deppermann, Klaus 187

Deventer 8, 22, 235, 262
Devotio Moderna 3, 7–11, 22, 29, 30, 31, 38, 52, 171–2, 182, 188, 190, 212–3, 215, 218, 234, 247, 257, 262
Dolan, John P. 310 n. 34
Dominicans, Order of 5, 18, 24, 248, 252
Donatists 271
Dorp, Marten van (Martin) 58, 95, 251, 263, 273, 274
Dowling, Maria xiv
Dugmore, C. W. 202
Duhamel, P. A. 37–8
Duns Scotus, John 4, 56
Dürer, Albrecht 43
Düsseldorf 188

Eck, Johann Maier von 96, 254
Ecumenicism 143, 296–7, 298
Edingus, Audomarus (Omaar van Edingen) 263
Edward VI, King of England 168, 204–5, 206, 209, 210, 240, 260
Egmond: *see* Baechem, Nicholaas
Elizabeth I, Queen of England 212, 215
——, Religious Settlement of 196, 210, 212, 214
Elyot, Sir Thomas 196
England 80, 118, 120, 193, Chapter Nine passim, 240, 245, 247, 258, 259, 260, 261, 287, 288, 290, 298
——, Church of 194, 196, 200, 204, 205, 208, 214, 216, 288
English Channel 45, 195
Eobanus, Helius Hessus 254–5
Epicurus, Epicures 137, 144
Eppendorf, Heinrich 165
Erasmus, Desiderius
- birth 20, 21
- family 20–4
  - Gerard 20–2, 24
  - Margaret 20–2
  - Peter 21, 22, 23, 24
- character 24–6, 30, 32, 40, 42–3, 44, 47, 95, 96, 99, 116, 120, 121, 148, 168, 183, 207, 218, 278, 279, 289
- health 29, 44, 45, 47, 142, 236, 246, 262, 266
- education 19, 21–5, 31, 44
- monastic sojourn 21, 24–5
- travels and domiciles 42, 45, 48, 248, 290
  - Paris 5, 29–33, 40, 41, 216, 288
  - England 33–40, 42, 45–8, 49, 194–214, 215
  - Italy 42–4, 193, 233
  - Louvain 41, 47, 193, 249
  - Basel 127, 173, 184, 249, 262, 263, 266, 272
  - Freiburg 142, 158, 187, 243, 246, 249, 261, 263, 266
- appointments 26, 46, 49, 79, 226, 235, 262
- income 42, 44, 45, 46–7, 49, 228, 234, 243, 256, 259
- printers 43, 47, 48, 54, 62, 248–9
- scholarship 3, 40, 59–60, 130, 173
- debt to Valla 16–17, 49
- attitude toward pagan antiquity 26, 27, 42, 48, 137, 291
- concern for liberal studies and good letters 97, 98, 118, 119, 120, 131, 155, 157, 219, 220
- his 'Philosophia Christi' 41, 50, 58, 60–2, 63, 64–5, 74, 90, 93, 98, 100, 102, 110, 115, 135, 136, 145, 146, 149, 156, 159, 160–1, 211, 213, 216, 223, 261, 296
- social and political opinions:
  - the Christian Commonwealth Chapter Four passim, 167, 168, 211
  - the state, forms of government 67, 73–4, 75, 77
  - society, organic analogy of 66, 67, 74, 77, 80, 82
  - social hierarchy 80–2
  - obedience, duties and limitations of 74–7, 80
  - the prince, his education and duties 65, 73, 74–9, 82, 91, 211, 229
  - nobility 81
  - commons, democratic notions 74–7, 80–2, 83, 91

peasantry 88–9
merchants and marketing 88, 89–9, 168
interest, usury 64, 72, 88–90, 168
property, rights of 84–6, 180
property, community of 84–5
equity, 82–3, 168
equality, 83
government, social obligations of 74–5, 80, 211, 229
poverty, charity, begging, poor relief 64, 83, 84–8, 90, 168
taxation 83–4
marriage and divorce 51, 104–5, 276
his pacifism 32, 39, 47, 49, 63, 67–71, 109, 169, 179–80, 185, 223, 278, 296
on international relations 64, 66–71, 79, 92, 278, 296
the Turks 69
his alleged anti-semitism 17–18
as religious reformer:
as critic of:
the Catholic Church 41, 55, 73, 85, 128, 272, 284, 290–1
the clergy 54–5, 57, 62, 85–6, 94, 190, 284
images and pilgrimages 55, 201, 205, 219, 281
'Judaic ceremonial' 51, 93, 102–3, 117, 146, 167, 201, 212, 213, 273, 276, 277, 279–80, 285, 290, 291, 297, 298
friars 56–7, 117
monastic orders 24–5, 51, 53, 56–7, 62
scholasticism 6, 31, 35, 51, 53, 55, 56, 57, 58, 93, 98
obscurantism, superstition 27, 51, 55, 166, 200, 201, 281
the papacy and popes 43, 56, 57, 71–3, 99, 110, 119, 124, 128–9, 205, 233–5, 288, 290
as theologian: Chapter Five passim
on theology and theologians 7, 62, 63, 90, 93–7, 110, 145
his Christocentricity 100–1, 147, 155, 156, 161, 177, 179, 218, 291, 316 n. 38
on doctrinal and ecclesiastical authorities 6–7, 95, 97, 98–9, 107, 109, 131–2, 136, 144, 156, 159, 165, 167, 183, 269, 271, 272, 274, 277, 280, 282, 289
his own position:
adherence to the Catholic Church 94, 103, 121–2, 139, 253, 268–9, 275, 279–81, 285, 290–1, 292, 293
the Church, true nature of 94, 98–9, 121–2, 139, 177, 182
consensus, belief in 99, 109, 271
deity, concept of 101, 110, 134, 137, 139, 270, 273
adiaphora, belief in 99, 100, 110, 129 132, 136, 147, 181–2, 185, 210, 261, 267, 269, 278, 279, 281, 284, 289, 292, 296, 298
on the Sacraments 102–10, 129, 141, 146, 158, 160, 165, 167, 173–4, 175, 183, 202, 212, 265, 273, 275–6, 281, 282, 290, 292
on sacerdotalism 99, 102–3, 146, 173, 174, 178, 276
on the Trinity 101–2, 110, 176–7, 186, 242, 273, 274, 277
on Scripture 7, 17, 37, 52, 61, 94, 95, 96, 97–8, 99, 102, 104, 110, 131, 133, 136, 257, 269, 272, 274, 275, 280, 290, 295
Old Testament 18, 97, 98, 297
New Testament 3, 7, 18, 49, 53, 55, 59, 61, 94, 96, 97, 99, 100, 101, 102, 181, 195, 198, 297
as neo-Pelagian 6, 117, 123, 136–7, 160, 296
on religious toleration 181–2, 185, 235, 242, 270–1, 278, 279–80, 292, 293
as 'heretic' and on heresy 56, 80, 100–1, 102, 106, 116, 120, 121, 122, 123, 128, 130, 131, 141, 145, 163–4, 165, 184–5, 196,

208, 222, 230, 240–1, 242, 267–77, 281, 293
as mediator 118–19, 125, 126, 127, 130, 134, 136, 140, 141, 142, 152, 153, 163, 166, 193, 200, 216, 243, 257, 277–82, 283–5, 339 n. 36
as so-called advocate of a third church and of modernism 94, 145, 227, 273, 277, 283–6, 291
see also Free Will, Grace, Justification, Predestination
as educator 10, 40, 62, 90, 196, 241, 243, 257, 261, 294, 337 n. 32
as grammarian and philologian 16–17, 59–60, 94, 95, 96–7, 240, 274
his legacy:
to the Catholic Church 292–6
to Protestantism 291–2
to Ecumenicism 297–8
his influence in:
Austria 243, 245–6
England Chapter Nine passim, 287
France 217–25, 287–8
Germany 48, 166, 246–57, 289–90
Hungary 244–5, 258
Italy 233–42, 287, 288–9
Netherlands 262–6
Poland 258–62
Spain 225–33, 287
his works:
Adages 6–7, 41, 43, 65, 66, 69, 74–5, 77, 78–9, 81, 83, 84–5, 86, 88–9, 95, 199, 223, 224
Adversus . . . epistolam Martini Lutheri 143–4
Annotations 104
Antibarbari 26–7, 62, 253
Apologia adversus . . . monachos 163, 227, 232, 273, 274–7
Axiomata 119
Colloquies 29, 32–3, 42, 43, 65, 80, 95, 102, 104, 129–30, 201, 221, 223, 224, 228, 231, 238
Pseudevangelicos/Contra quosdam, qui se falso iactant evangelicos 86, 164, 165, 178, 201, 279
De bello turcico 69
De contemptu mundi 25
De libero arbitrio 129, 130–7, 140, 149, 151, 152, 153, 158, 162, 167, 176, 224, 234–5, 236, 237, 240–1
De immensa Dei misericordia 87, 207, 241
De sarcienda ecclesiae concordia 85, 154, 166, 199, 257, 269, 278, 279, 280, 281, 285
Enchiridion 13, 26, 32, 38, 39, 41, 50–4, 65, 66, 84, 88, 95, 101, 103, 117, 156, 160, 173, 177, 178, 190, 197–8, 199, 206, 207, 211, 212, 220, 223, 225, 227, 228, 230, 252, 254, 264–5, 286, 289, 310 n. 32
Hyperaspistes 139–40, 141, 146, 153, 221, 227, 322 n. 142
Inquisitio de fide 129–30
Institutio principis Christiani 49, 65, 69, 74, 76, 81, 82, 83–4, 87, 168, 210, 211, 243, 261
Julius exclusus 43, 70, 71–2, 86, 196, 199
Moriae encomium/Praise of Folly 42, 45, 50, 53, 54–8, 65, 76, 77, 78, 85, 89, 105–6, 185, 199, 223, 224, 228–9, 251, 310 n. 32
Novum Instrumentum/Novum Testamentum 40, 49, 50, 52, 58–60, 101, 102, 104, 200, 201, 203, 206, 218, 229, 272
Paraphrases 75, 98, 99, 150, 198, 199, 204, 205, 206, 207, 208, 211, 212, 220, 221, 275
Panegyricus 65, 67–8, 76, 83
Paraclesis 59, 60–2, 197, 207
Querela pacis/The Complaint of Peace 49, 65, 69, 70–1, 75, 77, 78, 81–2, 179, 199, 220, 221, 223, 229, 235, 263
Ratio verae theologiae 96, 206, 256
Responsio ad . . . fratres Germaniae inferioris 159, 164–5
Spongia 128–9, 130, 157, 279

Supputatio Errorum in censuris Beddae 270
Erasmus Sarcerius 204, 216
Erfurt 150, 254–5
Eucharist 105–10, 141, 148, 152, 154, 157, 158, 159–60, 162, 165, 167, 168, 173–4, 182–3, 200, 201, 202, 212, 223, 246, 253, 260, 265, 275–6, 281, 282, 292, 299
see also Communion, Lord's Supper, Mass
'Evangelical Rationalists' 171
Evangelicals 86, 151, 164, 166
——, Netherlandish 264–5
Everaerts, Nicolaas 264
Extreme Unction, Sacrament of 103, 299

Faber, Johannes (John) 126, 129
Fabri, Johannes, Bishop of Vienna 245, 246, 280
Falk, Swiss Anabaptist martyr 178
Farel, Guillaume 218, 219, 260
Farge, James K. 332 n. 8
Fast, Heinold 179
Fathers, Christian 3, 11, 34, 97, 98, 102, 133, 239, 257, 272, 274
Ferdinand I, King of Bohemia and Hungary (1526), 'King of the Romans' (1531), Holy Roman Emperor (1556) 28, 184, 243–4, 245, 246, 255, 280, 282, 294, 295
Ferguson, Wallace K. 145
Ferrara 186
Fichet, Guillaume 30
Ficino, Marsilio 12, 13, 35
Fisher, Christopher, 16
Fisher, John, Bishop of Rochester, Cardinal 45, 46–7, 79, 131, 195, 208
Fitzjames, Richard, Bishop of London 39
Flanders 182, 263, 264, 265
Flodden, Battle of 44
Florence 11, 35, 43, 249
——, Platonic Academy of 11–12
Fonseca, Alonso de, Archbishop of Toledo, Primate of Spain 184, 228, 230, 231
Fortescue, Sir John 65
Foxe, John 91, 209, 212
France 39, 47, 68, 154, 193, 217–25, 247, 254, 257, 287–8
Francis I, King of France 68, 122, 217, 218, 219, 220, 221, 222, 282
Francis of Vitoria 232
Franciscans, Order of 5, 24, 138, 232, 284
Franck, Sebastian 165, 176, 185, 252
Frankfurt am Main 143, 151, 248, 256, 260
Frederick III, Holy Roman Emperor 247
Frederick III, 'the Wise', Elector of Saxony 49, 116, 118–19, 255
Free Will, Controversy regarding 5, 101, 123–4, 128, 129, 130–7, 139, 145–6, 147, 150, 152, 154, 156, 158, 167, 168, 175–6, 189, 200, 207, 223, 224, 236, 281, 293, 299
Freiburg im Breisgau 172, 243, 246, 248, 251, 252, 257
Frisia 187, 260, 280
——, East 164, 187, 209
Froben, Johann 48, 49, 248–9, 260
Froschauer, printer 250
Froude, James Anthony 246
Fuggers, Bankers, of Augsburg 88, 254
Fulke, William 202, 213

Gaguin, Robert 30–1, 32, 218
Gansfort, Wessel 10
Gardiner, Stephen, Bishop of Winchester 75, 179, 198, 203–4, 205, 208, 211, 216, 275–6, 278
Garret, Thomas 201
Garrod, H. W. 144
Gasquet, Francis N. 207
Gattinara, Mercurino 121, 122, 138, 141, 226–7, 228, 229, 231, 246, 283

Gebwiler, Hieronymus 251
Geldenhauer (Geldenhouwer), Gerard 86, 163–4, 165, 166, 246, 325 n. 64
General Councils 72, 98, 235, 280
Geneva 181, 186, 223, 242
George, Duke of Saxony 127, 131, 138, 140, 141, 246, 253, 255, 278
Gerbel, Nikolaus 251–2
Germany 8, 80, 118, 122, 129, 138, 140, 141, 172, 186–7, 188, 216, 231, 236, 238, 243, 246–57, 258, 261, 263, 282, 287, 289–90
Gerrish, Brian A. 133
Gerson, Jean 30
Giberti, Gian Matteo, Bishop of Verona 237, 241
Glapion, Jean 123, 127
Glareanus, Henricus 155
Gleason, John B. 35–7
Goclenius, Conradus 165, 264, 266
Gois, Damião (Goes, Damien à) 188
Goletta 188
'Gospellers' 159, 165, 166, 178, 199, 201
Gospels 91, 98, 101, 118, 133, 142, 290, 297
——, John 51, 160, 177, 204, 243
——, Matthew 15, 103, 104, 174
——, Luke 15–16, 204, 274
Gouda 21, 22, 29
Grace, Divine 6, 8, 38, 56, 103, 109, 116, 117, 132–3, 134, 136, 137, 145, 152, 156, 160–1, 219, 224, 236, 257, 281, 282, 285, 291, 293, 299
Granada 283
Granvella, Nicolas 293
Gravius, Tielmann 187, 188
Grebel, Conrad 173–4, 175, 177–8, 179–80, 183
Greek studies 12, 14–16, 34, 42, 58, 59
Grendler, Paul and Marcella 241
Grindal, Edmund, Archbishop of Canterbury 212
Grocyn, William 12, 34, 195–6
Groningen 187, 188, 265
Groote, Gerard 9, 10
'Grunnius', Letter to 20, 22
Habsburg Dynasty 243, 244, 245, 246, 260, 294
Halle 255
Halsteren 26–7
Harbison, E. H. 37
Hedio, Caspar 131
Hegius, Alexander 22
Heidelberg 249
Henckel, John 258
Henry IV, King of France 288
Henry VII, King of England 43, 45
Henry VIII, King of England, 12, 34, 39, 44–5, 46, 47, 50, 68, 105, 124, 128, 129, 131, 138, 163, 195, 198, 203, 204, 207, 208, 215, 235, 282, 287
Herborn, Nicolaus 144–5, 284
Heresbach, Conrad (Konrad) 188, 256, 257
Hermans, William (Willem) 27
Himelick, Raymond 340 n. 63
Hoen, Cornelisz 157, 160, 173, 265
Hoffman, Manfred 316 n. 38
Hoffman, Melchior 162, 187, 188
see also Melchiorites
Holbein, Hans, the Younger 43, 214, 250
Holland 106, 186–8, 254, 264, 265
see also Netherlands
Holy Roman Empire 48, 247, 249, 289
Hoogstraten, Jakob von (Hochstrat, Jacob) 18, 272
Hooper, John, Bishop of Gloucester 91, 201, 202, 211, 213
Horace 58
Hubmaier, Balthasar 157, 162, 173–4, 175–6, 183, 184
Huizinga, Johan 38, 134
Humanism, Classical 3, 13–14
——, Christian 14–15, 63, 90, 115, 135, 147, 160, 205, 207, 217, 219, 220, 236, 252, 280
Humanists, Protestant 93, 122, Chapter Seven passim, 216, 250–3, 254–5
Hungary 242, 243, 244–5, 258, 260, 266, 289
Hus, John 182

Hussites 61, 122, 255, 268, 274, 289
Hutten, Ulrich von 120, 123, 127, 128, 157, 162, 248, 253, 278
Hutterian Brethren 181
Hyma, Albert 9, 38, 305 n. 26

Index, 109, 240, 294, 295
  Pauline 241, 295
Indulgences 51, 103, 104, 117, 128, 136–7, 256, 290, 299–300
Inquisition, Holy 225, 226, 228, 229, 240, 241, 277, 294, 295
Interest (Usury) 72, 88–9
Investiture Contest 289
Italy 12, 14, 34, 35, 47, 62, 155, 193, 229, 233–42, 244, 248, 249, 264, 274, 287, 288–9, 290, 294, 295

James IV, King of Scotland 44
Jarrott, Catherine A. L. 37
Jedin, Hubert 246
Jerome, St 15, 26, 38, 48, 49, 98, 116, 123, 261, 271
Jesuits 9, 294
  see also Loyola
Jesus Christ 6, 7, 15, 26, 27, 33, 38, 39, 50, 51, 52, 55, 56, 57, 60–1, 62, 65, 66, 67, 69, 70, 72, 73, 75, 84, 91, 93, 94, 96, 98, 100, 101, 102, 104, 106, 107, 108, 109, 116, 117, 118, 121, 122, 124, 125, 128, 129, 133, 134, 143, 144, 145, 151, 155, 160–1, 166, 167, 173, 174, 175, 178, 179, 182, 183, 190, 201, 202, 207, 212, 218, 222, 262, 263, 269, 271, 273, 274, 275, 276, 277, 280, 281, 282, 285, 290, 291, 296, 297
Jiménez, Francisco Jiménez de Cisneros: *see* Ximénes
Joanna, Queen of Castile, wife to Philip of Burgundy (son of Maximilian) 28
John, Apostle 51
Jonas, Justus 122–3, 149, 150, 254, 255
Jud, Leo 160, 163, 174, 250, 275
Julius II, Pope 43, 57, 65, 71–2, 87
Justification, Concept of 101, 116, 132, 134, 135, 143, 146, 150, 156, 167, 176, 178, 179, 281, 293, 296, 300

Kappel, Battle of 148, 166
Kaufman, Peter I. 38–9, 320 n. 107
Ket's Rebellion 214
Knappen, M. M. 213
Knights' Revolt 247, 248
Knox, John 229
Kohls, Ernst-W. 52, 95, 101
Konarski, John, Bishop of Cracow 258
Krzycki, Andrea (Cricius, Andrew), Bishop of Plock 108, 258, 259, 261, 262

Lang, Johann 124, 254
Lasco, John à (Laski, Jan), Senior 260
Lasco, John à (Laski, Jan), Junior 209–10, 258, 259, 260
Last Supper 106, 108, 109, 159, 167, 174, 202, 204, 265, 300
  see also: Communion, Eucharist, Mass
Latimer, Hugh, Bishop of Worcester 91, 211
Latimer, William 34
Latomus, Bartholomew 188
Latomus, Jacobus (Jacques Masson) 272, 274
Laud, William, Archbishop of Canterbury 213
Laurinus, Marcus 123, 127, 263
Le Sauvage, Jean, Chancellor of Burgundy 262–3
Lecler, Joseph 255
Lee, Edward 101–2, 104, 202–3, 207, 221, 227, 230, 238, 254, 272, 273–4
Lee, Sidney 37
Lefèvre d'Étaples, Jacques 31, 58, 206, 217, 218–19, 221, 224, 225, 260, 273, 274, 276
Leipzig 255, 283
——, Court of 255
——, Religious Colloquy of, 1534 246, 256

Leo X, Pope 18, 21, 22, 44, 49, 54, 58, 73, 96, 126, 234, 235, 238
Lerma, Pedro de 229
Levi, A. H. T. 320 n. 106 and n. 109
Leyden, Jan of 186, 187
Linacre, Thomas 12, 34, 195, 231
Lips, Martin, 182
Locher, Gottfried 156
Lollards, English 73, 226, 233
London 33–4, 39, 46, 47, 68, 210, 306 n. 50
Longland, John, Bishop of Lincoln 46
Lord's Supper:
 see Last Supper *see also*: Communion, Eucharist, Mass
Lorraine, Cardinal of, Charles of Guise 294, 295
Louis II, King of Hungary and Bohemia 69, 244
Louis XI, King of France 28
Louis XII, King of France 50
Louis XIV, King of France 248
Louvain 48, 121, 122, 128, 138, 193, 195, 203, 227, 229, 234, 237, 249, 251, 260, 262, 264, 265, 272, 273
——, University of 58, 118, 121, 193, 264, 272
——, Trilingual College of, 48–9, 58
Low Countries: *see* Netherlands
Loyola, St Ignatius 31, 225, 226, 233, 294
Lucian 42, 54, 137
Lupset, Thomas 196, 200, 233
Luther, Martin 3, 5, 9, 10, 14, 17, 18, 49, 62, 64, 87, 88, 90, 93, 102, 107, 110, Chapter Six passim, 148, 149, 150, 151, 152, 153, 156, 157, 158, 159, 161, 162, 163, 166, 167, 168, 174, 184, 190, 194, 201, 202, 203, 206, 219, 223, 224, 226, 227, 229, 234, 238, 240, 247, 248, 249, 250, 251, 252, 253, 254, 255, 256, 268, 272, 274, 278, 279, 280, 284, 289, 290, 291, 292
Lutheranism, Lutherans 73, Chapter Six passim, 150, 152, 153, 157, 158, 159, 167, 176, 182, 184, 206–7, 217, 220, 221, 225, 226, 227, 232, 234, 236, 237, 238, 239, 246, 249, 250, 251, 252, 253, 254, 255, 256, 264, 272, 283, 288, 290, 296, 297

Maastricht, 188
McConica, James K. 91, 200, 329 n. 11
McGrath, Alister E. 336–7 n. 22
Machiavelli, Niccolò 64, 66, 67, 70, 91
Magisterial Reformation 61, 146, 170, 176, 178, 189, 190, 268, 272
Mainz 48, 248, 249, 252
——, Archbishop of: *see* Albert of Brandenburg
Maldonado, Juan 184, 231, 232
Manichaeans 51, 132, 134
Manrique, Alonso, Archbishop of Seville and Inquisitor General 141, 227, 228, 231, 232
Mansfield, Bruce xiv, 296, 340 n. 51, 341 n. 5
Manz, Felix 175
Marbeck, Pilgram 174
Marburg 255
Marck, Erard de la, Prince Bishop of Liège 263
Marguerite d'Angoulême 217, 218, 219, 222
Marius, Richard 90, 203
Marliano, Luigi 121, 122
Marshall, William 198, 200, 211
Marsilius of Padua 65, 198
Martyr, Peter 229
Mary of Austria, Queen of Hungary and Bohemia 244–5, 258, 263, 266
Mary Tudor, Queen of England 204, 210, 211, 214, 215
Mary, daughter of Charles the Bold, wife to Maximilian I 28
Mass 9, 106, 107, 108, 109, 129, 164, 165, 174, 202, 282, 293, 296, 300
Maximilian I, Holy Roman Emperor 28, 68, 79, 245
Meaux 219
——, Bishop of: *see* Briçonnet

Mechelen (Malines) 50
Melanchthon, Philip 106, 107, 123, 131, 135, 137, 138, 140, 141, 144, 148–54, 157, 162, 164, 165, 168, 177, 199, 225, 228, 229, 236, 238, 253, 254, 255, 259, 260, 280, 284, 293, 297
Melchiorites 145, 187–8, 189
Melton, William, Chancellor of York 39
Menchi, Sylvana Seidel 240–1, 335 n. 75
Mennonite Encyclopedia 173, 175
Mercklin, Balthasar, Bishop of Constance 107–8
Mirandola, Pico della 12, 35
Mohacs, Battle of 244
Mombaer, Jan 31
Montaigne, Michel de 224
Montaigu, Collège de, Paris 29, 217, 220, 224
Moravia 181, 182, 240
More, Thomas 34, 35, 38, 42, 45, 46, 49 54, 58, 64, 66, 84, 85, 90–1, 105, 140, 146, 168, 184, 195, 198, 200, 203, 207, 214, 262
Morillon, Guy 187
Morison, Richard 91
Morone, Giovanni, Cardinal 295
Mosellanus, Petrus 254
Mountjoy: *see* Blount, William
Münster 172, 178, 180, 181, 186–7, 188, 189, 256, 264, 272
Müntzer, Thomas 181, 189
Mutianus, Conrad 247, 254
Myconius, Osvaldus 179

Nachtigall, Ottmar 251
Naples 233, 239
Nationalism 67, 69, 247, 289, 290, 292
Nausea, Fridericus, Bishop of Vienna 240, 245, 246, 256
Neoplatonism 3, 6, 11, 12, 13, 35, 38, 42, 51, 247
Netherlands 8, 61, 76, 88, 187–8, 189, 195, 238, 243, 245, 262–6, 278, 287
see also Brabant, Flanders, Holland
New Testament 5, 7, 14–16
Nominalism 7
Noonan, J. T. 88
Nuremberg 50, 123, 253

Occam (Ockham), William of 5, 137
Ochino, Bernardino 171, 229, 240, 260, 294
Oecolampadius, Johannes (Hussgen, Johann) 60, 107, 108, 145, 149, 151, 157, 158, 159, 160, 161, 162, 164, 165, 166, 168, 177, 184, 185, 201, 236, 245, 253, 260, 284
Olah, Nicholas (Olahus, Nicolaus) 159, 244–5, 266
Olde, John 205
Olivar, Pedro Juan 229, 231
Olmedo 230, 231
Origen 11, 42, 52, 57, 98, 123, 137, 204
Original Sin, Concept of 150, 158, 293, 300
Osiander, Andreas 158
Oxford 12, 34, 35
——, University of 45, 201, 204

Pace, Richard 34, 306 n. 54
Padua 13, 34, 43, 44, 237, 239, 240
Paget, William 208
Papacy 10, 119, 152, 233–5, 240, 247, 248, 283, 289, 293, 294
Papal Curia 233, 237, 240, 278
Parc, Abbey of 16
Paris 29–33, 109, 121, 128, 188, 193, 195, 219, 253, 258, 259, 260, 262, 276, 288
——, Parlement of 221, 222
Parker, Matthew, Archbishop of Canterbury 214
Parr, Catherine, Queen of England 204, 205
Paul, Apostle 6, 12, 13, 14, 15, 16, 37, 38, 51, 55, 56, 57, 58, 59, 85, 116, 132, 133, 178, 291
Paul III, Pope 100, 235, 262, 281, 294–5
Paul IV, Pope (Caraffa, Gian Pietro) 53, 225, 236, 295
Pavia, Battle of 221
Payne, John B. 97

Paynell, Thomas 199
Peasants' Revolt 189, 247
Pelagius, Pelagianism 5, 6, 116, 132, 134, 136–7, 150, 296, 300
Pellican, Conrad 107, 149, 157–8, 162, 163, 165, 168, 212, 260
Penance, Sacrament of 15, 104, 202, 213, 275
Peter, Apostle 55, 56, 70, 72
Petit, Guillaume 217
Petrarch 13, 30
Pfefferkorn, Johann 18
Pflug, Julius, Bishop of Naumburg 142, 246, 255, 256, 283–4, 285, 293
Philip 'the Good': *see* Burgundy
Philips, Dirk 190
Phillips, Margaret Mann 69, 89, 143, 332 n. 19
Philosophes, Eighteenth-century 266, 296, 341 n. 11
Pighius, Albert 138
Pio, Alberto, Prince of Carpi 142, 144, 233, 239, 240, 273, 275, 276, 278
Pirckheimer, Willibald 99, 107, 122, 123, 125, 127, 128, 131, 134, 139, 184, 222, 253, 254
Pisan, Christine de 211
Piso, Jacobus 244
Pistoris, Simon 255
Plato 4, 6, 11–13, 42, 51, 57, 76, 87, 223
Platonism 11–13, 33, 51, 247
see also Neo-Platonism
Plethon, Gemistos 11–12, 14
Plotinus 11
Poland 154, 186, 242, 243, 244, 258–62, 289
Pole, Reginald, Cardinal 76, 200, 233, 295, 296
Politiques 288
Poncher, Étienne, Bishop of Paris 217, 220
Poppenruyter, Johann 50
Porter, H. C. 309 n. 21
Portugal 188
Post, R. R. 8–9, 302 n. 9 and n. 13
Predestination, Concept of 101, 123–4, 130–7, 139, 145, 146, 150, 152, 156, 158, 160–1, 176, 190, 207, 212, 218, 224, 241, 242, 277, 291, 297, 300
Price, Sir John 215
Printing 3, 30, 45, 249, 250, 258
Protestantism 8, 63–4, 73, 90, 115, 116, 135, 243, 250–55, 265, 278, 283, 285, 291
Puritans, Puritanism 212, 213, 240

Rabelais, François 218, 223–4, 239
Rabil, Albert 99, 313 n. 86, 321 n. 120
Radical Reformation 93, 110, 115, 142, 145, 146, 147, 167, Chapter Eight passim, 275
see also Anabaptists, Socinians, 'Spiritualists'
Radice, Betty 79
Ratramnus, of Corbie 160, 202
Real Presence, Doctrine of 105–10, 160, 183, 265, 282, 300
Reformed Churches 159, 160, 161, 292
Regensburg (Ratisbon), Colloquy of 246, 293, 340 n. 51
Reimann, Swiss Anabaptist martyr 178
Renaudet, Augustin 240, 283, 285
Reuchlin, Johann 17–18, 120, 128, 149, 248, 249, 252, 254
Rhine, Rhineland 8, 10, 172, 248–9, 253, 287
Ridley, Nicholas, Bishop of Rochester and London 91, 160, 204
Rinck, John 145, 187
Rome 43, 44, 72, 115, 122, 215, 234, 235, 237, 238, 244, 290
——, Sack of 235, 237, 290
——, Church of 42, 72, 126, 135, 176, 193, 199, 200, 255, 268, 277, 283, 284, 291
Roper, Margaret 197
Rosemondt, Godschalk 121
Rothman, Bernard 190
Rotterdam 21
Roy, William 197
Rummel, Erika 315 n. 11, 339 n. 12 and n. 20
Rupp, E. Gordon 116
Ruysbroeck, John van 9

Sacerdotalism 173, 178, 300
Sacraments, the Seven 38, 295–6, 300
Sacramentarians 144, 159, 160, 164, 171, 173, 265, 292
Sadoleto, Jacopo, Cardinal 126, 134, 138, 154, 233, 235–7, 238
St Gallen 179
St Omer 52
Salesbury, William 215
Sapidus, Johannes (Johann Witz) 252–3
Sattler, Michael 162
Savonarola, Girolamo 249
Saxony 289, 290
Scaliger, Julius Caesar 239, 273
Schets, Erasmus 142, 159, 187, 263
Schlettstadt (Sélestat) 161, 248, 249, 251, 252, 253
Scholasticism 3–7, 30, 35, 37–8, 136–7, 247, 254, 258, 274
Screech, Michael A. 57, 223
Scribner, Robert W. xiv, 337 n. 26
Scriptures 4, 6, 37, 75, 156, 175, 177, 212, 213, 219, 223, 235, 239, 256, 291, 293
Scrivener, F. H. 60
Selwyn, David G. xiv
Sepulveda, Juan Ginés de 239, 273
Servatius 25
Servetus, Michael 171, 176, 177, 185–6, 244, 268
Seymour, Edward, Duke of Somerset, Protector 75, 179, 205
Seymour, Anne, wife to Edward 205
S'Hertogenbosch 22, 23
Sickingen, Franz von 248
Sigismund I, King of Poland 106, 142, 244, 259, 260, 261
Simons, Menno 176, 178–9, 180, 189–90, 287
Sinapius, John 186
Sion 24
Slechta, Jan 100, 182
Smith, Preserved xiv, 99, 280, 308 n. 1, 322 n. 162, 338 n. 60, 340 n. 62
Socinianism, Socinians 242, 300
Sozzini brothers 260, 300
Sorbonne 223, 227
——, Theological Faculty of 32, 217–18, 220, 221, 222, 275
Sowards, J. K. 304 n. 1 and n. 5
Spain 140–1, 193, 194, 203, 225–33, 234, 240, 241, 247, 257, 260, 262, 283, 287, 288
Spalatin, Georg 116, 118, 119, 125, 136, 151, 152
'Spiritualists' 171, 185, 189, 250
Standish, Henry 202–3, 275
Standonck, Jean 29, 31
Starkey, Thomas 76, 91, 200, 211, 233
Steucho (Steuchus), Agostino 97
Steyn, Augustinian Monastery of 24–5, 49
Strassburg 48, 86, 110, 142, 149, 154, 159, 161, 162, 163, 164, 165, 166, 167, 168, 172, 174, 175, 178, 185, 186, 187, 246, 248, 249, 250, 251, 252
Stromer, Heinrich 254, 256
Stuart, Alexander 44
Stumpf, Jacob 177–8
Stupperich, R. 52
Sturm, Jacob 251
Surtz, Edward 76, 84
Switzerland 154, 174, 249, 261, 280, 289, 290
Sylvester, John 258
Synergism 133, 135, 152, 154, 223, 297

Taverner, Richard 197, 199–200
Tetzel, Johann 256
Theodoric, Vincentius 272
Thomas, George 105
Thomas à Kempis 6, 9–10, 52, 100, 101, 110, 215
Thompson, Craig R. 32, 33, 130
Thurzo, John, Bishop of Breslau 244
Titelmans, Frans 272
Todd, Margo 213, 314 n. 102
Toleration, Religious 181–2, 267–8
Tomiczki, Piotr (Peter), Bishop of Cracow 187, 188, 259, 261–2
Topley, Thomas 201, 202, 203
Toronto, University of xiv, 230
Tovar, Bernardino 229, 230
Tracy, James D. 66, 71, 251, 320–1 n. 109

Transubstantiation 7, 56, 105–10, 157, 204, 293, 296, 300
Trent 246
——, Council of 137, 233, 241, 246, 282, 285, 292, 294–6
Trilingual College: *see* Louvain
Trinity, Holy 143, 176–7, 185–6, 242, 274, 277, 300
see also Anti-Trinitarianism, Arius
Troeltsch, Ernst 213, 267
Tunstall, Cuthbert, Bishop of London and of Durham 34, 46, 79, 128, 131, 174, 195, 201
Turin, University of 43
Turks 243, 244
Turner, William 209, 213, 240
Tyndale, William 197–8, 203, 211

Udall, Nicholas 198, 204–5
Utenhove, Charles 222, 263, 264
Utraquism 182–3, 223, 245, 295, 300

Valdés, Alfonso de 228–9, 231, 232
——, Juan de 171, 226, 228, 229, 230, 233, 239, 240, 295
Valdesiani 239
Valla, Lorenzo 14–17, 39, 42, 49, 53, 58, 198, 224, 248, 262
Valladolid, Conference and Articles of 104, 141, 227, 228, 229, 231, 232, 273–7
Velius, Caspar Ursinus 244
Venice 43–4, 128, 237, 241, 293
Vergara, Francisco de 229, 231, 232
——, Juan de 228, 229–30, 231, 232, 238, 274
Verona 237, 241
Via Moderna 5
Vienna 240, 243, 245, 246
Villey, Pierre 224
Villon, François 30
Virgin Mary 15–16, 55, 144, 247, 265, 273, 274
Virgin Birth 143
Virués, Alonso Ruiz de 230–1
Viterbo, Egidio da 239
Vitrier, Jean, of St Omer 52, 255
Vives, Juan Luis 64, 87, 134, 138, 141, 153, 179, 226, 228, 230, 238
Vlatten, Johann von 256–7
Voltaire, François Marie Arouet de 341 n. 11
Volz, Paul 82, 117, 138, 252, 253
Vulgate Bible 14–16, 42, 49, 53, 58, 59

Waldenses 171, 268
Waldshut 184
Wales 214–16
Warham, William, Archbishop of Canterbury 34, 42, 46–7, 124, 127, 131, 195, 197, 209, 261
Wars of Religion 288, 292
Wesel 187
Westphalia 186, 187, 188
Whitford, Richard 199, 213, 214–15
Whitgift, John, Archbishop of Canterbury 212
Williams, G. H. 170
Wimpfeling, Jacob 249, 251, 253
Winckel, Pieter 21, 22, 23
Windesheim 8, 9, 22, 31
Wittenberg 148, 149, 150, 151, 161, 168, 176, 254
Witzel, Georg 87, 143, 144, 255, 257, 284
Wolsey, Thomas, Archbishop of York, Cardinal, Legate 79, 120, 195
Worms, Diet of 121, 122, 127, 150, 285
Wyclif, John 123, 132
Wycliffites 122, 126, 274

Ximénes de Cisneros, Francisco, Cardinal Archbishop of Toledo 17, 59, 225, 229, 234, 311 n. 52

York 212

Zasius, Ulrich 134, 251, 252, 276
Zealand 265
Zebrzydowski, Andrzej 258, 259, 261
Zins, Henryk xiv, 258, 259
Zuichemus, Viglius 186, 187, 263–4
Zúñiga, Diego López (Stunica) 104, 122, 129, 230, 234, 236, 238,

273, 274, 278, 311 n. 52
Zurich 87, 155, 156, 157, 158, 159, 161, 167, 173, 175, 179
Zwingli, Huldrych 68, 70, 87, 106, 107, 110, 128, 142, 145, 147, 148, 151–2, 154–61, 163, 164, 166, 167, 168, 171–2, 174, 177, 184, 190, 194, 202, 245, 250, 260, 265, 268, 284, 290, 292
Zwinglians 182, 208, 210, 249, 250, 254, 289